KU-613-040

Introduction to the Team Software Process^{SM}

TSPi Glossary

Term	Definition or Formula	Reference
Defect profile	A graph of the defect-removal history of a program by phase. It is typically given in defects/KLOC.	100
Defect-prone modules	Those modules in a system that, based on their defect-removal history, are judged likely to have defects remaining.	171
Defect ratio	The ratio of the numbers of defects found in a review phase and a compile or test phase. Low ratios typically indicate low-quality reviews.	101
Defects/KLOC	The number of defects in a program, normalized by the number of KLOC in the program. Defects/KLOC = 1000*(defects found)/(LOC)	100
Development cycle	That development activity that builds one product increment in a cyclic development process.	6, 9
Earned value (EV)	The percent the estimated task hours are of the total project hours. EV is earned only when the task is fully completed.	67
Estimated defects remaining	Using the capture-recapture method, the estimated remaining defects are T = A*B/C, where A is the number of major defects found by one engineer, B the number found by another engineer, and C the number found by both.	345
Facilitator	A person who helps teams hold efficient and effective team meetings. The principal responsibilities are to keep the meeting focused on the agenda and ensure that everyone participates.	204, 212
Failure time	The time spent finding and fixing defects. In PSP and TSP, it is the total time an engineer spends compiling and unit-testing a program.	102
Inspection	A process in which several engineers review a product produced by another engineer to help find defects.	335
Integration test	The test that verifies that the system is properly built, that all the parts are present, and that they function together.	181
Issue	A known problem or concern that must be addressed.	53
KLOC	Thousands of lines of code, or LOC.	85
LOC	Lines of code, as defined in the team's lines-of-code standard.	144
Major defects	These are the problems that, when fixed, would change the executable program.	100
Minor defects	All defects that are not major.	100
Module	Modules are typically composed of multiple objects or functions, and they are the smallest testable program element.	70
Notebook	See *project notebook*.	213
Owner	See *product owner*.	324
Part	Any part of a system. It could be an object, module, component, product, or subsystem. Parts may also be assemblies of lower level parts.	70
PDF	See *percent defect-free*.	98

(continued inside back cover)

Introduction to the Team Software Process^{SM}

Watts S. Humphrey
with Support Tool by
James W. Over

 **ADDISON-WESLEY**

An imprint of Addison Wesley Longman, Inc.

Reading, Massachusetts • Harlow, England • Menlo Park, California
Berkeley, California • Don Mills, Ontario • Sydney
Bonn • Amsterdam • Tokyo • Mexico City

 **Software Engineering Institute**

The SEI Series in Software Engineering

Many of the designations used by manufacturers and sellers to distinguish their products are claimed as trademarks. Where those designations appear in this book, and Addison Wesley Longman, Inc. was aware of a trademark claim, the designations have been printed in initial capital letters or all capital letters.

The author and publisher have taken care in preparation of this book, but make no expressed or implied warranty of any kind and assume no responsibility for errors or omissions. No liability is assumed for incidental or consequential damages in connection with or arising out of the use of the information or programs contained herein.

The publisher offers discounts of this book when ordered in quantity for special sales. For more information, please contact:

Computer and Engineering Publishing Group
Addison Wesley Longman, Inc.
One Jacob Way
Reading, Massachusetts 01867
(781) 944-3700

Copyright © 2000 by Addison Wesley Longman, Inc.

All rights reserved. No part of this publication may be reproduced, stored in a retrieval system, or transmitted, in any form or by any means, electronic, mechanical, photocopying, recording, or otherwise, without the prior written permission of the publisher. Printed in the United States of America. Published simultaneously in Canada.

Text printed on recycled and acid-free paper.

ISBN 020147719X

3 4 5 6 7 8 CRW 06 05 04 03

3rd Printing September 2003

Trademark acknowledgments and credits appear on page 463, which is a continuation of this copyright page.

IN MEMORY OF MY FATHER, WATTS S. HUMPHREY (1896–1968)

He provided critical support at a difficult time in my life.

FACULTY FOREWORD

The increasing complexity of software development and the demand by industry for better-qualified and better-prepared software engineers means software development curricula must provide students with knowledge and experience related to the practice of software engineering. The Embry-Riddle Aeronautical University Industrial Advisory Board[1] has identified the following issues as critical for the preparation of entry-level software engineers:

communication (both oral and written)

ability to work as part of a team

front-end part of software development (requirements and high-level design)

professional attitude toward work

knowledge and skills in using software processes

computing fundamentals

breadth of knowledge (ability to learn new technologies)

In my eight years of teaching an introductory software engineering course, I have tried to provide to students an overview of the full "life-cycle" development of software and to have them work as part of a team. I have tried real projects, toy projects, small-team development, large-team development, extensive tool use, almost no tool use, emphasis on product issues, and emphasis on process issues. Until recently, I have had only limited success. Most of the time, I have tried to do

---

[1]The Advisory Board members come from several organizations, including Boeing, Harris, Lockheed-Martin, Motorola, and the Software Engineering Institute.

too much, with the result that both the students and the teacher ended up frustrated and disappointed.

This past year, I used a draft of *Introduction to the Team Software Process*[SM] (TSPi) and had the best success in my experience. Although the TSPi is no silver bullet, it has had a dramatic effect in improving our delivery of software engineering education. The TSPi shows both teachers and students what to do, how to do it, and when to do it. This book includes all the required TSPi materials: the scripts, forms, and instructions for almost all aspects of student-team software development. It does an excellent job of explaining and motivating the TSPi activities, and it provides a complete description of each team role. It offers common-sense advice on how to handle team management problems, and it specifies quantitative techniques for planning, tracking, and assessing performance and quality.

Although the book includes an initial statement of requirements for two projects, the TSPi is flexible enough to handle a variety of projects of modest size. The TSPi could be adjusted for a maintenance project, used in a requirements/design course, or adapted to just about any team software activity. For example, we are now using the TSPi in our senior design course to develop a product for a real customer. The TSPi incorporates an incremental development methodology that provides a sound software development strategy and an excellent pedagogy. In the first increment (using a simple set of requirements), students learn the TSPi process and get comfortable working with a team. In the subsequent one or two increments, the teams can use their previous experience to improve their performance.

Although there is much to be gained by using the TSPi in a software engineering project course, students must have prior experience with the Personal Software Process (PSP)[SM], either through a previous course or by self-study. At Embry-Riddle, we introduce our students to the PSP in their freshman programming courses; this provides sufficient preparation for study and use of the TSPi. The TSPi course requires a great deal of time on the part of both teacher and students. In several attitudinal surveys (one at the end of each increment), students overwhelmingly endorsed the TSPi. A common complaint concerned the collection and recording of data—although most admitted they understood its importance.

In summary, if you have struggled with how to deliver a quality software engineering project course, I strongly encourage you to look at the TSPi. It provides the guidance, direction, and support for teaching students the practice of software engineering and preparing them for the workplace.

Thomas B. Hilburn,
Embry-Riddle Aeronautical University

STUDENT FOREWORD

To help in preparing this student foreword, Professor Tom Hilburn selected three students from his first TSPi course at Embry-Riddle. Two of these students had worked as coops in industry, and all three were team leaders for their teams. Tom asked these students what they would say to their classmates when asked about this course; the following paragraphs are excerpts from what they wrote.

Why learn TSPi? Why use it when it takes more time to fill out all the forms than to do the project itself? These questions have very good answers. When you learn something new, you do not want to try something so big that you cannot handle it. You need to start small to get the hang of what is going on. That is how you learn TSPi. You start with a small project that could probably be done without the process. Once you have mastered the TSPi, you realize that it is a necessity. Although the TSPi is not needed for most school assignments, it will be needed for larger industrial projects. This is where a process like TSPi will help everyone understand how to do the project. So remember that you are just learning the process, and the benefits of this knowledge will not show up until you are faced with a project that cannot be cranked out at a terminal.

Most computer science students learn how to develop programs individually. In their team projects, they would love to have a structured process to help them in their next team experience. Team interaction is a whole new aspect of the software process. Many issues, such as communication, trust, motivation, problem-solving, commitment, dedication to quality, balancing workloads, allocating roles, feelings of camaraderie, authority issues, and learning about your teammates and how they work, are new issues that are factored into this team process. The TSPi provides advice for handling many of these common issues. Students need to adapt the process to their particular team situation and to learn how to handle other issues that are not addressed.

Some key things we learned were the necessity of good communication and trust among team members and how to work with people we do not know. Most of the team wanted to complete the tasks early, to provide plenty of time for quality reviews. Team members either volunteered to take on additional tasks when the work suited their skills or helped someone who was overloaded. This type of teamwork motivated us not to let the team down and to help out when and where we could. Especially in the first stage of the project, our team was more motivated to produce the product than to follow the process. In the second stage, the engineers could see the value of the forms and planning. This provided more motivation to follow the process.

We had few motivation or commitment problems, but when we did, we had to only briefly discuss them. The hardest thing was to be objective in decisions and dealings with other team members. If we had not communicated as well or as often as we did, the project would have been half as effective, if that. We learned the responsibilities of teamwork, how the roles interrelate, and the importance of helping each other. Also, we learned that if you put forth the effort, the team will be willing to help you. The TSPi gives students a great head start for what they will be dealing with in industry. Ideally, curricula will be better structured in the future to provide such courses.

A word on project management: TSPi requires a good deal of management skill and competence. A wide variety of tools are available to the team through the TSPi, but it is up to the team leader to set the stage for the project. As team leader, I tried several approaches to project management; most worked, and at least one did not. As leader, you must be willing to put in as much time as your teammates and to "get down in the dirt" and help when needed. A leader must be a motivator—by word, by deed, or by both. Give your team the room to work and be creative in their designs, but guide them through the process and foster the teamwork that will prove so valuable in the last days, when problems and failures are most likely. In the short time available, be sure to involve the team in creating the plan, to get everyone's input for each step, and to watch the team's schedule and determine a plan of action if it begins to slip.

The team leader needs to plan for some situations before they occur. Maybe a team member does not contribute or is lost due to injury or illness. Both these situations have happened on my projects. Such problems can tear a team apart and ruin its effectiveness, or they can pull a team closer together and increase its productivity. It all depends on how the situation is handled. That is when you must be willing to lead. Enjoy the team experience, get to know your team, and try to help them motivate themselves and the rest of the team. Work hard and plan. Learn how to use a spreadsheet to save time in number crunching. Keep the lines of communications open, and meet often. Remember that when everything seems to hit you at once, there is a way through it. "Never quit, never die!"

Celeste Berry, Ryan Hoppes, Marc Lovelace
Embry-Riddle Aeronautical University

PREFACE

This book is for students and engineers who have already learned and, preferably, applied the Personal Software Process (PSP)[SM]. You may have learned the PSP in a graduate or senior-level course[1] or in an earlier introductory course.[2] Alternatively, you may be a practicing engineer who seeks guidance on how to use the PSP in an industrial team environment. In any case, when you have learned the PSP, you have the background to use the methods and practices in this book.

After you have learned the PSP, you may need guidance on applying it to the many tasks of the software process. This is the principal role of the Team Software Process (TSP)[SM]: to provide a framework for using sound engineering methods while developing software.

There is a great deal to say about teamwork, and this book covers the basic elements. TSPi (the introductory Team Software Process) introduces team concepts and walks you through the steps of building teams and working on a team. Note, however, that this text is designed for an introductory course and does not cover all the material that you will need to use the TSP for larger-scale industrial projects.

[SM]Personal Software Process and PSP are service marks of Carnegie Mellon University.

[1]The advanced PSP course is taught from my text, *A Discipline for Software Engineering,* Addison-Wesley (1995).

[2]The beginning PSP course uses my book *Introduction to the Personal Software Process,* also from Addison-Wesley (1997).

[SM]Team Software Process and TSP are service marks of Carnegie Mellon University.

How TSPi Helps Engineers

This book teaches engineers about software development teamwork. TSPi provides a structured set of steps, shows engineers what to do at each step, and demonstrates how to connect these steps to produce a completed product. TSPi also provides two interesting and reasonably challenging project exercises. Each is at the same time small enough to be completed in a few weeks and large enough to simulate a typical small project. When capable engineers follow the guidance provided in this book, they will invariably produce a finished working product.

In the suggested TSPi strategy, teams develop a product in two or three cycles. In the first cycle, teams build a small working product kernel. With each succeeding cycle function is added to this base. This strategy demonstrates the benefits of using data from a prior project to plan a new project. Also, by taking new roles for each cycle, engineers will have two or three quite different experiences in just one project. After several development cycles, engineers will have had a broad exposure to teaming methods, and they are likely to continue using the TSPi methods on their own.

Why TSPi Courses Are Needed

Because project courses have proven to be effective in preparing students for software engineering careers, a growing number of universities now offer them. These courses are often oversubscribed. Students seek material that applies to their future jobs, and they see team courses as meeting this need. After graduation, students and employers report that software project courses are useful preparation for work in industry.

There is now a large body of experience with team project courses.[3] Although many of these courses have been successful, three problems are common. First, the students often attempt projects that are too large. Second, they frequently concentrate on the product and ignore the process. Finally, one or more team members are disruptive. Although TSPi cannot prevent all these problems, it provides guidance on how to avoid or mitigate them.

[3]See, for example, A.T. Berztiss, "Failproof Team Projects in Software Engineering Courses," *Frontiers in Education Conference* (IEEE, 1997); D.H. Hutchens, "Using Iterative Enhancement in Undergraduate Software Engineering Courses," *SIGCSE '96*; T.J. Scott, "Team Selection Methods For Student Programming Projects," *8th CSEE, '95*; and J.E. Tomayko, "Carnegie Mellon Software Development Studio: A Five-Year Retrospective," *Proceedings of the Ninth Conference on Software Engineering Education* (IEEE Computer Society Press, 1996).

To make effective use of curriculum time, team software courses should be carefully structured and based on proven project experience. *Without a defined process or a structured team framework, engineers must figure out for themselves how to run their projects.* Without this process and structure, these groups must learn team-building and teamwork basics through an often painful trial-and-error process. This is both expensive and unnecessary because teamwork principles are well known and straightforward.

TSPi guides engineers in effective teamwork methods. It does this by walking them through a team-building process and then using a measured and defined framework for developing products. Assuming that the engineers are PSP-trained, they can follow the TSPi scripts and use the TSPi support tool to plan and manage their work.[4] Following TSPi makes engineers' projects much more efficient and permits them to concentrate on learning about software engineering rather than spend an excessive amount of time on team-building and team management issues.

TSPi provides defined team roles that are allocated among the team members. Each role specifies what is expected and when and how each task is to be done. When all team members know what they and everyone else should do, they are in a better position to work effectively as a team. If a team member does not do his or her job, the other team members will know it, and they can deal with the problem. When teams cannot solve interpersonal problems themselves, they are told to call on their instructor or manager for help. The Instructor's Guide for this book suggests methods for handling many common teamwork issues.

When student team members have explicit roles and the role responsibilities are clearly defined and visible, instructors can provide fairer and more specific grades. Each student can then be rated on individual performance as well as on the overall team's results. Not only does this approach motivate better performance, but it is also a fairer way to grade team courses.

The Organization of This Book

This book is designed to lead teams through the TSPi process. Following the first two introductory chapters (Part I), the chapters in Part II walk teams through a complete development cycle. The text explains the process scripts and gives examples of the completed TSPi forms.

Part III provides detailed descriptions of the TSPi team-member roles: team leader, development manager, planning manager, quality/process manager, and support manager. After reading the chapter on your personal role, you can use these TSPi role scripts for reference while working on the project.

---

[4]The TSPi support tool, the TSPi Instructor's Guide, and other support supplements for this text are described on the Supplements page in the back of this book.

At the start of the TSPi course, each student completes an INFO form (see Appendix F) describing his or her interests and background. The instructor uses this information to divide the class into five-engineer teams and to assign initial roles to the team members. If one or two teams have four or six members, the instructor must make some role adjustments. All the roles must be assigned, and each engineer should have at least one role. For a four-engineer team, the support manager role should be distributed among the team members. For a six-engineer team, the quality/process manager role should be split into two: the quality manager and the process manager.

With the teams selected and roles assigned, the teams start their projects and report on their progress. At the end of each development cycle, the engineers assess the team's overall performance as well as that of each individual role. With this information, the instructor can evaluate the work and better assign team-member roles for the next development cycle. If necessary, the instructor may make some team membership changes, but, unless there are serious problems, teams should be kept together throughout the course.

Using Standard, Predefined Problems

Although TSPi will work for almost any project, this book provides two standard, predefined problems that are designed to meet the needs of a wide variety of courses. Although there could be advantages to using actual customer problems, this practice is not recommended for three reasons. First, courses have firm and unvarying schedules. Although most customers will initially agree to a fixed time scale, few customers know how long it really takes to develop software. Also, because beginning engineers do not generally know how to manage projects on firm schedules, the chances of project failure are high. This problem is compounded by the fact that actual customer requirements are notoriously vague and unstable, leading to frequent changes and extensive delays.

The second reason to use a standard, predefined exercise is that a teamwork course should be designed to teach specific lessons. Although one goal of the project should be to build a working product, the principal course objective should be to demonstrate the benefits of using proven software engineering methods. With an actual customer problem, the first priority must be to satisfy the customer. As the requirements change or the customer takes time to answer questions, the work will slip. As the schedule gets compressed, teams often concentrate on finishing the product and ignore the process. Unfortunately, the principal lesson often learned from such courses is how *not* to develop software.

The third reason to use a standard, predefined problem is that it permits each team to compare its performance with that of other teams. With several implementations of the same problem, all the teams can participate in the class evaluations. Each team can describe its approach and answer questions about its design, implementation, and test choices. This process graphically shows the effectiveness of various development approaches and provides a body of reference data for evaluating future teams.

Although there are advantages to using standard predefined exercises, they do not expose students to some important issues. For example, without actual experience, it is hard to appreciate the confusion and imprecision of customer need statements. Struggling with vague and changing requirements is an important experience, but it can be taught best in a course that concentrates on the requirements process. The approach recommended here is to first teach effective teamwork and process methods and then, in later courses, focus on the complex issues of larger-scale development projects.

Suggestions for Instructors

This book can be used in several ways. The principal use is in a full one- or two-semester team course. In this configuration, TSPi is used to develop a single product such as either of the two described in Appendix A. A one-semester course would take two or three cycles, whereas a two-semester course would use three or more cycles to build a larger product or a full-function version of the Appendix A products. Depending on the scale of the job, the various process steps could be expanded or reduced. Three course options are shown in Figures P.1, P.2, and P.3.

For each development cycle in Figure P.1, the team plans and tracks its work and completes a full miniproject, including requirements, design, code, and test. At the end of each development cycle, the team assesses team and role performance, and the instructor reassigns the team roles. In a three-cycle project, the engineers gain experience with three essentially complete projects and three different team roles. They also have data from each cycle and can see how their experience from one cycle can be used for the next one.

This book can also be used for teamwork exercises in other courses. Small projects could be done in a single cycle of three to seven weeks. A short requirements cycle could take three or four weeks, whereas a design cycle would take four or five weeks. The shortest initial full development project would take six or seven weeks. Figure P.2 shows a several-week team project to develop a set of requirements in a requirements course. Similarly, a design project might be configured as in Figure P.3. The text can also be used for courses that run on a quarter system. Whereas the full three-cycle course takes 15 weeks, a two-cycle course can be done in 11 weeks, and a one-cycle development project would take 7 weeks.

Cycle Week	Cycle 1	Cycle 2	Cycle 3
1	Course introduction, review		
2	Launch, strategy		
3	Plan		
4	Requirements		
5	Design		
6	Implementation		
7	Test		
8	Postmortem	Launch, strategy, plan	
9		Requirements, design	
10		Implementation, test	
11		Postmortem	Launch, strategy, plan
12			Requirements, design
13			Implementation, test
14			Test, documentation
15			Postmortem and evaluation

FIGURE P.1 THE THREE-CYCLE TSPi COURSE

Cycle Week	Cycle 1
1	Launch, plan
2	Requirements
3	Requirements
4	Postmortem

FIGURE P.2 A SHORT TSPi REQUIREMENTS PROJECT

Cycle Week	Cycle 1
1	Launch, plan
2	Requirements
3	Design
4	Design
5	Postmortem

FIGURE P.3 A SHORT TSPi DESIGN PROJECT

In any of these course configurations, the standard TSPi scripts guide the students through forming their teams and planning and implementing their projects. Unless a team has already had experience with a full TSPi course, they will probably not complete any project cycle in less than three or four full weeks. The reason is that it takes time for new team members to learn the process and to figure out how to work together as a team. This is why the first TSPi cycle is planned for seven weeks even though the same work would take only four weeks in a subsequent cycle.

Preparation for This Course

The principal prerequisite for this course is completion of a full PSP course. This PSP course can be either a graduate or an introductory course. If the students took the PSP several semesters ago, they should have used the PSP in their intervening courses. If they have not, they will need a brief refresher lecture or two about PSP planning, data gathering, and quality management. Also, students who have little or no experience using the PSP will almost certainly need careful monitoring and support throughout the team course.

Before attempting a team project, students should have a background in software design and software requirements. Exposure to configuration management, project management, and software testing is also helpful. The students must also be fluent in the programming language and the tools they will use.

Acknowledgments

In writing a book, I often become so immersed in the material that I find it hard to see many of the problems that could trouble first-time readers. This is the principal reason that I seek informed reviewers. I have been particularly fortunate with this book, both because many people were willing to help and because their broad range of backgrounds enabled them to make many helpful suggestions. I particularly appreciate the help and support of Susan Brilliant, Dan Burton, Bob Cannon, Audrey Dorofee, Pat Ferguson, Marsha Pomeroy Huff, Mark Klein, Susan Lisack, Rick Long, Steve Masters, Mark Paulk, Bill Peterson, Bill Pollack, Dan Roy, Jeff Schwalb, Girish Seshagiri, Steve Shook, Laurie Williams, Ralph Young, Dave Zacharias, and Sami Zahran. Julia Mullaney was a great help in combing through the manuscript to find problems and inconsistencies in the manuscript and text. I also wish to thank my brother Philip Humphrey for his continued support and informed comments on much of the teamwork material.

I am also particularly indebted to Tom Hilburn and Iraj Hirmanpour at Embry Riddle Aeronautical University. Both of them have been long-term supporters of my PSP and TSP work. Tom has also taught team courses using the manuscript for this book. The data from his first course provided much of the material for the examples in the text.

As we at the Software Engineering Institute (SEI) have gained experience with the PSP and TSP, the importance of tool support has become increasingly clear. Jim Over has developed a marvelous tool to support TSPi teams, and he has adapted it specifically to support this book. He has also provided many helpful comments on both the process and the text. For that I am deeply grateful.

Again, I am indebted to Peter Gordon and Helen Goldstein and the professional staff at Addison-Wesley. Their help and guidance were invaluable in making the book a reality. Finally, I must again thank Barbara, my wife, for her continued support and good-natured encouragement through yet another book.

I dedicate this book to the memory of my father, Watts S. Humphrey, whose trust, confidence, and enthusiastic support helped and sustained me through my formative years. One of my very earliest memories is of failing first grade. In those days, they did not know about learning disabilities, but my father instinctively knew that I could learn, given proper guidance and instruction. He insisted that I had not flunked, but the school had, so he moved our family to a town where my brothers and I could attend a school that would give me individual instruction. I was extraordinarily fortunate to have had such a father, and I am deeply grateful for his help and support. Although he died many years ago, I still miss him.

Watts S. Humphrey   *Sarasota, Florida*

CONTENTS

PART ONE

Introduction

Part I of this book describes the introductory Team Software Process (TSPi) and explains why it is needed and how it works. Chapter 1 covers the benefits that you can expect from a TSPi course and the principles behind TSPi's design and structure. Chapter 2 describes teams: what they are and what makes them work. The material in Chapter 2 also includes a discussion of teamwork problems and describes how the TSPi can help in handling these problems. Chapter 2 briefly deals with the people-related issues of teams and teamwork. These topics are covered in considerably more detail in the chapters in Part IV.

1

TSPi Overview

Most industrial software is developed by teams. Thus, to be an effective engineer, you need to be able to work on a team. If you have good sense and a willingness to cooperate, you have the basic equipment to be a successful team member. Teamwork, however, is more than just getting along. Teams must plan their projects, track their progress, and coordinate their work. They also must agree on goals, have a common working process, and communicate freely and often.

To meet aggressive schedules and produce high-quality products, practiced teamwork is essential. However, practiced teamwork requires experience and calls for a specific set of skills and methods. This textbook and its accompanying course provide a comprehensive introduction to team software development. The approach is to expose you to realistic teamwork problems and to give you practical teamwork experience. With the experience gained from this course, you will be prepared to participate in a large-scale industrial software project.

This chapter describes the introductory Team Software Process (TSPi), the principles behind the TSPi design, and the overall structure and flow of the TSPi process. It also describes why TSPi is needed and discusses the benefits you can expect from a TSPi course.

1.1   What Is TSPi?

TSPi is a defined framework for a graduate or upper-level undergraduate course in team software engineering. It provides a balanced emphasis on process, product, and teamwork, and it capitalizes on the broad base of industrial experience in planning and managing software projects. TSPi guides you through the steps of a team software project course, and it shows you how to apply known software engineering and process principles in a teamwork environment. Assuming that you have already learned the Personal Software Process (PSP)[SM], TSPi will show you how to plan and manage a team project. It also defines roles for you and your teammates. When everyone on the team has an explicit role with clearly defined responsibilities, you can see what you are supposed to do at each step of the process. By following the TSPi process, you will get practical experience with proven engineering and teamwork methods.

The TSPi design is based on the Team Software Process (TSP)[SM], an industrial process for teams of as many as 20 engineers who develop or enhance large-scale software-intensive systems. Because the TSP is designed for large projects that often take several years to complete, it is a larger and more complex process than you will need. TSPi is thus a reduced-scale version of TSP. It does, however, retain the same basic concepts and methods. After using TSPi, you will find the TSP quite familiar and easy to use.

Why Engineering Teams Need a Process

Merely giving a group of engineers a job does not automatically produce a team. The steps required to build a team are not obvious, and new teams often waste a substantial amount of time handling teamwork mechanics. They must figure out how to work together as a team, how to define the job they need to do, and how to devise a strategy for doing the work. They must allocate the tasks among team members, coordinate each of these tasks, and track and report on their progress. Although these team-building tasks are not trivial, they are not very difficult. There are known methods for doing every one of them, and you and your teammates need not reinvent these methods for yourselves.

Teams don't just happen, and superior team performance is not an accident. Although skilled members and a defined process are essential, teams are more than a collection of talented individuals. To build and maintain effective working relationships, you need common goals, an agreed plan of action, and appropriate leadership. You also need to understand one another's strengths and weaknesses, support your teammates, and be willing to call for help when you need it.

[SM]Personal Software Process and PSP are service marks of Carnegie Mellon University.
[SM]Team Software Process and TSP are service marks of Carnegie Mellon University.

TSPi will also improve your productivity. Although the early planning and team-forming steps may seem to take a great deal of time, they are an essential part of doing a team project. It is a little like the huddle in a football game: experienced teams first agree on the play and each team member's role in it. If football teams didn't huddle, they would do a lot of running around, but they wouldn't win many games.

1.2   TSPi Principles

The TSPi is based on the following four basic principles.

1. Learning is most effective when you follow a defined process and get rapid feedback. The TSPi scripts and forms provide a defined, measured, and repeatable framework for team software engineering. The TSPi provides rapid performance feedback because the team produces the product in several short development cycles and evaluates results after each cycle.

2. Productive teamwork requires a combination of specific goals, a supportive working environment, and capable coaching and leadership. The project goal is to build a working product. The TSPi provides the supportive environment, one of your team members will be the team leader, and the instructor provides the coaching.

3. When you have struggled with actual project problems and have been guided to effective solutions, you will appreciate the benefits of sound development practices. Without the precise guidance of the TSPi, however, you could waste considerable time in defining your own practices, methods, and roles.

4. Instruction is most effective when it builds on the available body of prior knowledge. There has been a great deal of experience with software teams and software team courses. TSPi builds on this foundation.

1.3   The TSPi Design

There are many ways to design a process. In the case of TSPi, there were seven principal design decisions.

1. Provide a simple framework that builds on the foundation of the Personal Software Process (PSP).

2. Develop products in several cycles.

3. Establish standard measures for quality and performance.

4. Provide precise measures for teams and students.

5. Use role and team evaluations.

6. Require process discipline.

7. Provide guidance on teamwork problems.

The following sections discuss each of these topics in turn.

Provide a Simple Framework That Builds on the Foundation of the PSP

The purpose of a process is to help you do a task, such as developing a product or learning how to do a team project. When the process is too complex, you spend so much time figuring out what to do that you can easily lose sight of the objective. On the other hand, if the process is too simplistic, it does not provide enough guidance. You must then invent your own process as you go along. This approach can lead to wasted time, costly mistakes, and even a complete project failure.

Although TSPi has many forms and scripts, most of them are similar to ones you have already used with the PSP. Thus, if you have been PSP-trained, you will need to learn the overall TSPi approach, but you already understand the "language" of the TSPi. If you have not yet been PSP-trained, however, the TSPi process will likely seem overpowering. This is one reason that prior PSP training is a prerequisite for a TSPi course.

Even with PSP training, you must learn a number of new tasks and activities. However, with the role assignments, TSPi permits you to focus on the elements that you personally need to learn. The TSPi roles specify who does each of the team's planning, tracking, quality, support, and leadership tasks. The roles also reduce the amount of material you must understand at the outset. You can concentrate on your specific role tasks and not worry about the other role responsibilities, at least not yet.

During a multicycle TSPi project, try to get experience with several team roles. This experience will provide you the broadest exposure to the TSPi process, and it will give you a deeper understanding of more aspects of team software development. It will also help you to better appreciate your personal interests and abilities.

Develop Products in Several Cycles

In a full TSPi course, you will complete two or three development cycles in one semester. Each of these cycles includes a full requirements, design, implementation, and test development process. In the first cycle, you build a minimum-function subset of the ultimate product. By quickly getting this kernel product running, you can be sure to have a working product at the end of the course. You will also have a solid base for each of the subsequent cycles. This strategy is also more likely to identify design, performance, or usability problems at the beginning of the project when they are easiest to fix.

The second TSPi cycle builds on the results of the first cycle. You might change team roles, adjust the process, or use more disciplined quality methods. At the end of the second cycle, you will have data on two complete projects. Assuming that there is time, you could repeat these cycles for a third and even a fourth time. After two or more cycles, you will feel like an old hand at the development business. You will have clear and convincing evidence of what works best for your team, and you will have the confidence to continue using these methods in practice.

Establish Standard Measures for Quality and Performance

Measurements are an essential part of doing consistently high-quality work. The PSP provides the basic measures and measurement skills you need to measure and evaluate the quality of your work. Until you have lived through a project that uses these measures, however, it is hard to appreciate their value. TSPi shows you how to interpret the PSP measures and how to apply them to a project.

TSPi requires that you and your teammates set personal as well as team goals. Although this task may not seem important, a key part of an engineering education is learning to establish ambitious but attainable goals. The TSPi emphasis on goals and measures helps you to see the benefits of quality measurements and the value of project planning and tracking. Sound planning and tracking also help you to manage your work on a daily basis.

Provide Precise Measures for Teams and Students

With the TSPi measures, your performance and that of your teammates will be obvious. Although it is important for everyone to try hard and to do good work, a common team problem is that some members contribute much less than their fair share of the work.

Although the principal purpose of the TSPi measures is to help you do better work, these measures also make your personal performance visible to your teammates. This, however, is the nature of teamwork: Everyone knows what everyone else is doing. Therefore, if you do not make a reasonable effort, you can expect comments from your teammates.

Use Role and Team Evaluations

Some groups like to use peer evaluations, and others do not. The TSPi provides a peer evaluation capability that can be used if the instructor so desires. The advantage of peer evaluations is that the students are best informed about the team's and one another's performance. If they can be persuaded to make an honest evaluation, the instructor will be best informed and best able to give fair and equitable grades.

Because students are naturally reluctant to evaluate their peers, the TSPi calls for team and role evaluations. The idea is to evaluate how each role was performed and not how the people behaved. Although a role evaluation could be read as a judgment of the person who performed that role, the TSPi emphasis is on evaluating how the process worked and not on how the people performed.

Require Process Discipline

It is hard for software engineers to consistently do disciplined personal work. There are three reasons for this.

1. Software engineering has no tradition of disciplined personal performance. Thus, neither students nor working engineers have role models to emulate.

2. The software process does not impose a natural discipline on engineers. Software development differs from hardware engineering, in which engineers release designs to a factory for volume production. Hardware production engineers must review and accept a released design before they commit to manufacture a product on a schedule, for a cost, and at a scheduled production rate. With software, we have no factory and no production engineers. Therefore, software engineers must discipline themselves.

3. Consistently disciplined work in any field requires high standards and competent support. That is why professionals in the sports and performing arts have coaches, trainers, conductors, and directors. In industry, some accomplished managers have learned to fulfill this coaching role; in academic courses, the instructor acts as the team coach. Unfortunately, however, few people know how to be effective coaches, and coaching is not widely practiced in the software field.

With TSPi, the instructor will require you to follow the process and to gather the data. You must complete the forms and analyze and use the data. If you do not do this, you will not reap the full benefits of the TSPi course.

Provide Guidance on Teamwork Problems

Even in the best-run projects it is common to have teamwork problems. You and your teammates have different roles, and each of these roles has its own objectives. When these objectives conflict, disagreements are likely. In fact, it would be surprising if you did not have some disagreements with your teammates. Don't assume that these are personality problems, however, unless the conflicts become unresolvable. Initially, the best assumption is that your teamwork issues are caused by process problems.

Occasionally, students have problems working on a team. This is not only because they are inexperienced but also because they have backgrounds or personalities that make teamwork difficult. However, with guidance and support, most engineers can be effective team members. The most powerful force for resolving team problems is peer pressure. Most people are concerned about their peers' opinions and are eager to be respected and to fit into the group. Given time and proper coaching, most bright and motivated engineers can learn how to be fully effective team members.

If your team members cannot work together effectively, ask the instructor for help. The instructor, in cooperation with your team, can often help you to overcome the problems. If even this does not work, it may be necessary to remove some member from the team. Although this is a sensitive step, it is usually not a problem if the rest of the team asks the instructor to remove the problem member. For more guidance on these topics, consult Chapters 11, 16, and 17.

1.4 TSPi Structure and Flow

Figure 1.1 shows how the TSPi uses multiple development cycles to build a final product. Cycle 1 starts with a launch, in which the instructor describes the overall product objectives. The team then follows TSPi through its seven process steps: strategy, planning, requirements, design, implementation, test, and postmortem. In cycle 2, the engineers repeat the same steps, this time enhancing the base product produced in cycle 1. If there is time, they can add further enhancements in subsequent cycles.

The Cyclic Development Strategy

When you start a cyclic development strategy, the best plan is to begin with the smallest viable product version. In deciding the size and content of each cycle, you should consider the following constraints.

1. Each cycle should produce a testable version that is a proper subset of the ultimate product.

2. Each cycle should be small enough to be readily developed and tested in the available time.

3. When combined, the cycle products should produce the desired final product.

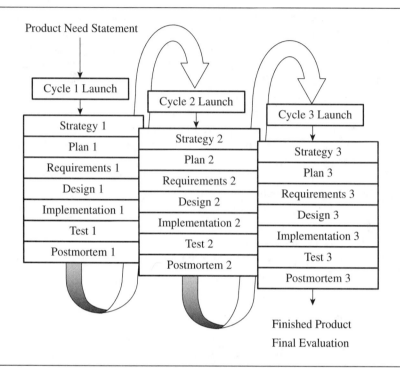

FIGURE 1.1 TSPi STRUCTURE AND FLOW

The TSPi starts by having teams produce a development strategy. Start by picking the smallest reasonable base to develop during the first cycle. Then estimate the sizes of the functions you plan to add in each subsequent cycle. This approach almost guarantees that you will complete a working initial subset of the product. With the data from this initial cycle, you can accurately plan what to add in each subsequent cycle. Don't defer too much function to cycles 2 and 3, however, because the course schedule provides less time for these later cycles.

1.5   The TSPi Process

The development script (DEV) in Table 1.1 shows the overall TSPi flow. Each script step is supported by one or more detailed scripts. Each of these scripts is described in a chapter devoted to that process step. All the TSPi scripts are also included in Appendix D. Table 1.1 also shows a typical TSPi script structure. Here,

TABLE 1.1 TSPi DEVELOPMENT: SCRIPT DEV

Purpose		To guide a team through developing a software product
Entry Criteria		• An instructor guides and supports one or more five-student teams. • The students are all PSP-trained (*Discipline for Software Engineering* or *Introduction to the Personal Software Process*). • The instructor has the needed materials, facilities, and resources to support the teams. • The instructor has described the overall product objectives.
General		The TSPi process is designed to support three team modes. 1. Develop a small- to medium-sized software product in two or three development cycles. 2. Develop a smaller product in a single cycle. 3. Produce a product element, such as a requirements document, a design specification, a test plan, and so on, in part of one cycle. Follow the scripts that apply to your project and mode of operation.
Week	**Step**	**Activities**
1	Review	• Course introduction and PSP review. • Read textbook Chapters 1, 2, and Appendix A.
2	LAU1	• Review course objectives and assign student teams and roles. • Read textbook Chapter 3, Appendix B, and one of Chapters 11–15.
	STRAT1	• Produce the conceptual design, establish the development strategy, make size estimates, and assess risk. • Read textbook Chapter 4.
3	PLAN1	• Produce the cycle 1 team and engineer plans. • Read textbook Chapter 5 and Appendix C.
4	REQ1	• Define and inspect the cycle 1 requirements. • Produce the system test plan and support materials. • Read textbook Chapter 6 and the test sections of Chapter 9.
5	DES1	• Produce and inspect the cycle 1 high-level design. • Produce the integration test plan and support materials. • Read textbook Chapter 7.
6	IMP1	• Implement and inspect cycle 1. • Produce the unit test plan and support materials. • Read textbook Chapter 8.
7	TEST1	• Build, integrate, and system test cycle 1. • Produce user documentation for cycle 1. • Read textbook Chapter 9.

TABLE 1.1 (continued)

Week	Step	Activities
8	PM1	• Conduct a postmortem and write the cycle 1 final report. • Produce role and team evaluations for cycle 1. • Read textbook Chapters 10, 16, 17, and 18.
	LAU2	• Re-form teams and roles for cycle 2. • Read the rest of textbook Chapters 11–15.
	STRAT2, PLAN2	• Produce the strategy and plan for cycle 2. • Assess risks.
9	REQ2	• Update the requirements and system test plan for cycle 2.
	DES2	• Produce and inspect the cycle 2 high-level design. • Update the integration plan for cycle 2.
10	IMP2	• Implement and inspect cycle 2, produce unit test plan.
	TEST2	• Build, integrate, and system test cycle 2. • Produce user documentation for cycle 2.
11	PM2	• Conduct a postmortem and write the cycle 2 final report. • Produce role and team evaluations for cycle 2.
	LAU3	• Re-form teams and roles for cycle 3.
	STRAT3, PLAN3	• Produce the strategy and plans for cycle 3. • Assess risks.
12	REQ3	• Update the requirements and system test plan for cycle 3.
	DES3	• Produce and inspect the high-level design for cycle 3. • Update the integration plan for cycle 3.
13	IMP3	• Implement and inspect cycle 3, produce unit test plans.
	TEST3	• Build, integrate, and system test cycle 3.
14	TEST3	• Produce and review the user manual for the finished product. • Review and update the user manual for usability and accuracy.
15	PM3	• Conduct a postmortem and write the cycle 3 final report. • Produce role and team evaluations for cycle 3. • Review the products produced and the processes used. • Identify the lessons learned and propose process improvements.
Exit Criteria		• Completed product or product element and user documentation. • Completed and updated project notebook. • Documented team evaluations and cycle reports.

the left column contains a sequence number indicating the order of the script steps, or, in this case, the week when that script is scheduled. The second column briefly names the topic of that script section, and the third column contains the descriptive text for each script step.

Every script starts with a brief statement of the overall purpose of the activity. This activity could be, for example, to develop a requirements document, produce a design, or conduct a test. Every script also has entry and exit criteria. These specify what you need to have done before you start the script and what you should have accomplished by the time you finish. Following the entry criteria, there is a "General" section that provides general information about the script. Finally, the numbered script rows are the activities that you are to follow in enacting the script.

1.6 The Textbook Structure and Flow

This textbook has a preface, four main parts, several appendixes, and an index. The Preface discusses where and how this textbook should be used. Part I provides an introduction to the TSPi process and explains what it is and why it is structured the way it is. Part II walks you through the TSPi process, one major step at a time. In Part III you will find a chapter on each of the five standard TSPi roles. Part IV offers guidance on dealing with some of the issues you will likely face in working on a software engineering team.

The seven textbook appendixes contain basic reference materials: the exercise need statements, descriptions of the configuration management and inspection processes, the process and role scripts, the TSPi forms, and the TSPi standards and specifications. Inside the front and back covers you will also find a glossary of the special terms used in the text. Finally, at the back of the book is a complete subject index.

It is most important that you read the textbook chapters on each of the process steps before you attempt that step. The suggested order for reading the textbook chapters and appendixes is given in the DEV script (Table 1.1).

1.7 Summary

The four basic TSPi principles are as follows.

1. Learning is most effective when students follow defined and repeatable steps and get rapid feedback on their work.

2. Productive teamwork requires a defined team goal, an effective working environment, and capable coaching and leadership.

3. When students are exposed to the problems of realistic development projects and then guided to effective solutions, they gain a better appreciation of the value of sound engineering.

4. Instruction is most effective when it builds on the available body of prior engineering, scientific, and pedagogical experience.

Starting from these four principles, the TSPi design involves seven choices.

1. Provide a simple framework that builds on the foundation of the PSP.

2. Develop products in several cycles.

3. Establish standard measures for quality and performance.

4. Provide precise measures for teams and students.

5. Use role and team evaluations.

6. Require process discipline.

7. Provide guidance on teamwork problems.

The TSPi process follows a cyclic development strategy. By starting with a small set of initial functions, the team can quickly complete a working first version of the product. When members have produced this initial version, they can better plan and develop the second cycle product. If there is time for a third cycle, this learning process is further reinforced. The cyclic development strategy is much like the processes followed by successful large-scale software development groups.

2

The Logic of the
Team Software Process

This chapter discusses the introductory Team Software Process and explains how
and why it works. It also defines teams, explains how they work, and discusses some
common teamwork problems.

  • Much has been written about teamwork, and there are many examples of
good and bad teams. This chapter cannot possibly cover all this material, but it hits
the highlights. For further information about teamwork issues, see Chapters 16 and
17. This chapter is only an introduction. As you use the TSPi, you should read
each of the book chapters as you encounter the topics it covers. The contents of
this chapter are as follows.

  □ Why projects fail. A principal problem for software teams is learning how to
     handle pressure. A poor or ineffective response to pressure is often the cause
     of project failure. We open the chapter with a discussion of pressure and how
     TSPi can help teams to handle the normal pressures of software work.

  □ Common team problems. A number of studies of student teams have identi-
     fied their most common problems. We also describe some of the problems
     that the TSPi process is designed to address.

  □ What is a team? Before discussing teams, we must agree on what a team is.

  □ Effective teams. Some teams are more effective than others. This chapter sec-
     tion discusses the conditions and characteristics that differentiate successful
     teams from all the others.

□ How teams develop. Effective teams don't just appear; they usually develop. This chapter section summarizes the process through which effective software teams develop, either by chance or through a deliberate team-building process.

□ How TSPi builds teams. The next topic is a brief review of the steps TSPi uses to build effective teams.

2.1 Why Projects Fail

When software projects fail, it is generally because of teamwork problems and not technical issues. DeMarco [DeMarco 88, page 2] says that

> The success or failure of a project is seldom due to technical issues. You almost never find yourself asking 'has the state of the art advanced far enough so that this program can be written?' Of course it has. If the project does go down the tubes, it will be non-technical, human interaction problems that do it in. The team will fail to bind, or the developers will fail to gain rapport with the users, or people will fight interminably over meaningless methodological issues.

One significant "people" problem is the inability of software teams to handle pressure, especially the pressure to meet an aggressive development schedule. Often, teams respond to this pressure by taking shortcuts, using poor methods, or gambling on a new (to them) language, tool, or technique.

Excessive pressure can be destructive. It causes people to worry and to imagine problems and difficulties that may not be real. Rather than help you to cope in an orderly and constructive way, pressure causes worry about many unknown (and often phantom) issues. And sometimes pressure can cause you to act as if the phantom issues were real. This behavior can have untold consequences for your project, your organization, and even your self-esteem.

When your team knows how to handle the pressure of a tight schedule, you can feel the difference. Before starting a job, you generally don't know precisely what is involved. But after you make a plan and get started, you feel relieved. This is true even if the job is larger than you thought. The reason you feel relieved is that you are now dealing with a known problem rather than an unknown worry.

Handling Pressure

Pressure is something that you feel. For example, you may need to do a task whether or not you think you can do it. The greater the need and the more doubt you have about your ability to do the task, the greater the pressure. Because pressure is internally generated, you have the power to manage it yourself, but first you must find the source of the pressure and then figure out how to deal with it. The apparent source of pressure in software projects is the need to meet a tight schedule. This schedule could come from management, your instructor, or your peers.

The real source of pressure, however, is ourselves. It comes from our natural desire to accomplish what our managers, instructors, or peers want. When this pressure is coupled with normal self-doubts about our ability to perform, it can become destructive. This is particularly true for new software teams that have not yet learned how to handle the normal challenges of their projects. Teams need to know how to work efficiently and to produce quality products, especially when they are under intense schedule pressure.

By guiding teams through a strategy and planning process, the TSPi shows teams how to handle pressure. They analyze the job, devise a strategy for doing the work, estimate the sizes of the products they will build, and then make a plan. Because unrealistic schedules are the principal cause of software project problems, the TSPi helps teams manage their projects more effectively. When they are able to manage their work, teams are much more likely to do a quality job.

2.2 Common Team Problems

Although working on teams can have tremendous advantages, there can also be problems. Studies have found that the most common problems for student teams concern leadership, cooperation, participation, procrastination, quality, function creep, and evaluation [Pournaghshbanb].

Ineffective Leadership

Without effective leadership, teams generally have trouble sticking to their plans and maintaining personal discipline. Although effective leadership is essential, few people are natural leaders. Most of us need to develop our leadership skills and to get practice using them. Until engineers have seen effective leadership in action, however, they often don't know what skills to practice.

Failure to Compromise or Cooperate

Occasionally one or more team members may not be willing or able to work cooperatively with the team. Although this does not happen often, teams need to deal with this problem when it arises. Peer pressure can often resolve such problems, but if a person continues to be intractable you should discuss the problem with your instructor.

Lack of Participation

Team members have different skills and abilities as well as different motivations, energy, and levels of commitment. This means that every member makes a different level of contribution to the team's performance. In fact, the variation among the members' contributions generally increases with increasing group size [Shaw, page 202].

Although some degree of variation in participation is normal, it is important that all team members strive to meet the team's goals. If it becomes clear that someone is not making a serious effort, team spirit generally suffers. Nothing can be more disruptive than to have some people in a group openly getting away with something. Lee Iacocca calls this the equality of sacrifice: "If everybody is suffering equally, you can move a mountain. But the first time you find someone goofing off or not carrying his share of the load, the whole thing can come unraveled" [Iacocca, page 230].

Procrastination and Lack of Confidence

Some teams do not set deadlines or establish goals and milestones. Others set deadlines they never meet. Such teams generally don't track performance and often fail to make decisions in a timely or logical way. They take excessive time to get started, and they drift through their projects rather than attacking them. These problems generally stem from one or more of the following three things: inexperienced leadership, a lack of clear goals, or the lack of a defined process and plan.

Poor Quality

Quality problems can come from many sources. Examples are a superficial requirements inspection, a poorly documented design, or sloppy implementation practices. When teams do not use personal reviews or team inspections, they usually have quality problems, resulting in extensive testing, delayed schedules, long hours, and an unsatisfactory final product.

Function Creep

During product design and implementation, engineers often see ways to improve their products. These well-intentioned modifications are hard to control because they originate from a legitimate desire to produce a better result [Robillard, page 89]. This problem is particularly difficult because there is no clear dividing line between the functions that stem from interpretations of the requirements and those that are true additions to the requirements.

Ineffective Peer Evaluation

Experience has shown that peer evaluation can be invaluable for student teams [Scott, page 302]. However, students are often reluctant to grade their teammates and rarely do so with complete candor. As a result, students often feel that the grading in team courses is not entirely fair, particularly to the highly motivated students. This perception can cause competition among team members and can reduce the willingness of team members to fully cooperate.

2.3 What Is a Team?

There are many definitions of teams. The one I like best is by Dyer [Dyer, page 286]:

A team consists of

(a) at least two people, who

(b) are working toward a common goal/objective/mission, where

(c) each person has been assigned specific roles or functions to perform, and where

(d) completion of the mission requires some form of dependency among the group members.

Team Size

Teams can be of almost any size from two to dozens or even hundreds of people. In practical situations, however, teams are most effective when they develop close relationships among all the members. This is most likely when the teams are small and when the members develop a network of interdependencies. In industry, team size is generally limited by management span of control. Although some projects can be very large, generally there are smaller subgroups of 20 or fewer people, each of them working under the direction of a supervisor or manager. These subgroups form the close-knit teams that the TSP and TSPi are designed to support.

Student teams typically range from about four to 12 students, depending on class size and faculty preferences. Although there have been few studies of the effects of software team size, my experience has been that teams of four to eight engineers are likely to be the most effective. With fewer than four members, there are not enough people to properly handle all the team role assignments. With teams of more than eight members, it is harder for the team to develop the close relationships needed for teams to jell. TSPi is designed for teams of five students, although it can be used with modest changes for teams of four or six students. For teams of other sizes, more role adjustments are required but the other scripts and forms apply.

The Jelled Team

When design and development groups work together smoothly and efficiently, we call them *jelled* teams. DeMarco and Lister, in their marvelous book *Peopleware,* talk about the jelled team [DeMarco 87, page 123]:

> A jelled team is a group of people so strongly knit that the whole is greater than the sum of the parts. The production of such a team is greater than that of the same people working in unjelled form. Just as important, the enjoyment that people derive from their work is greater than what you'd expect given the nature of the work itself.

Basic Teamwork Conditions

Not all groups are teams. There are three basic conditions that must be met for a group to operate successfully as a team [Cummings, page 627; Dyer, page 286; Mohrman, page 279].

1. The tasks to be done are clear and distinct; that is, the job for the team is explicitly defined, the work is meaningful to the team, and the group knows what it must do.
2. The team is clearly identified; the members know the scope of the group, who is in it, and who is not. Everyone on the team is known to the others, everyone's work is visible, and everyone knows everyone else's team role.
3. The team has control over its tasks; members know what to do, how to do it, when to do it, and when they are finished. The members know that they are responsible for the work, and they control the processes they use. They also have the capability to do the job, and they know that no one else is charged with doing it.

2.4   Building Effective Teams

To build effective teams, you need more than just the right kinds of tasks and working conditions. The team must have an important job to do and must be in an environment that supports teamwork. The team must face an aggressive challenge and must be encouraged to plan and manage its own tasks. These needs are met by providing the team with four additional kinds of support: cohesion, goals, feedback, and a common working framework.

Team Cohesion

Cohesion refers to the tight knitting of the team members into a unified working group that physically and emotionally acts as a unit. Members of highly cohesive groups communicate freely and often. Although they need not be good friends, they work closely together and respect and support one another. In less-cohesive groups, members tend to function as individuals. They have trouble compromising and do not have common values and goals. Cohesive teams, however, share a common physical space, spend a lot of time together, and supportively cooperate and interact during these times together.

Challenging Goals

Goals are also a critical element of the jelled team. First, these goals must be specific and measurable. Studies show that teams that have measurable goals are consistently more effective than those that do not [Mohrman, page 176]. Examples of such goals are detailed plans, performance targets, quality objectives, schedule milestones, and so on. And each of the team members must accept these goals as his or her own.

Second, the team's goals must represent a significant challenge [Katzenbach, page 3]. No team jells without a performance challenge that is meaningful to those involved. Although good personal chemistry and the desire to become a team can foster teamwork values, these characteristics alone will not automatically produce a jelled team.

Finally, the goals must be tracked and progress visibly displayed so that the team members can see how they are progressing toward their goals.

Feedback

Goal tracking and feedback are critically important. Effective teams are aware of their performance and can see the progress they are making toward their goals [Stevens, page 515]. In a study of air defense crews, those with frequent and precise feedback on goal performance improved on almost every criterion. This compares with the stable, unimproving performance of crews that did not get feedback [Dyer, page 309].

The team members must also be able to distinguish their personal performance from that of the team as a whole. When they cannot do this, team performance generally suffers. Called *shirking,* this results from people expending less personal effort when the results of their work are not apparent to the rest of the team. The basic cause of shirking is the lack of a team member's personal commitment to the team's common goals. The presence of one or more shirkers generally prevents a team from jelling. Shirking is not primarily a measurement problem, but precise measures generally reveal such problems so that the team can deal with them.

Common Working Framework

Whereas the team's goals must be challenging and clear, the path to achieving them must also be clear: "Team members need to see how to achieve the goal and know what is expected of them" [Shaw, page 388]. This means that all the team members must feel that the tasks are achievable, must understand their roles and responsibilities, and must agree on how to accomplish them. They must know

> What tasks must be done?
>
> When?
>
> In what order?
>
> By whom?

In summary, to jell, teams must be cohesive, have challenging goals, get frequent performance feedback, and have an agreed-upon process or framework for doing the work.

2.5   How Teams Develop

Teams don't just happen; they generally develop over time. This development can happen by luck, or it can result from a conscious team-building process. At the outset, most teams start with individuals who have diverse goals. As teams jell, the members come to accept a common set of team goals. When they do, these goals take on a special significance. Even though the goals may be arbitrary, the team members will pursue them with enormous energy. They do this not because of the nature of the goals but rather because the goals are important to the team.

How Teams Jell

The first step in creating a jelled team is for the team members to converge on a common understanding of the product that they intend to build. This forms a starting point for the team to develop its goals and to make a plan. After the team defines its goals, the members agree on a strategy and a plan for developing the product.

Studies have found that knowledge work can be viewed as an iterative process that begins with several engineers, each of whom has a different understanding of what he or she is to do. Then, through a series of steps, they converge on a common viewpoint and result [Mohrman, page 52]. As the team members increase their common understanding of the product to be built, they also converge on a common approach for doing the work. Throughout this convergence process, the team is gradually becoming a more cohesive unit.

In the beginning, the engineers are not sure what the product will look like or how they should build it. Although they cannot yet agree on the product or the full development process, they can usually agree on the current unknowns and on how to clarify them. Then they proceed in iterative steps: identifying the confusions and disagreements, agreeing on how to resolve them, and resolving them. They then move to a more detailed level, identify additional confusions and disagreements, and resolve them. As they converge on a common understanding, they simultaneously converge on the details of the intended product and the processes for producing it.

What many engineers find surprising is that conflict, confusion, and disagreement are natural parts of this convergence process. It is how the team identifies the issues to work on, and it is what generates the creative process that we call design.

The TSPi supports this jelling process by walking teams through a launch procedure that addresses the conditions required for jelled teams.

2.6   How TSPi Builds Teams

Most small groups can become effective teams by focusing on the basic techniques of team development. These techniques help teams to build the understandings and relationships they need to work together and to support one another. The TSPi guides teams through the team-building steps to set goals, select roles, establish plans, and maintain communication among the team members.

Goals

As teams begin to jell, they first define and accept a set of common goals. The TSPi helps the members accept the team goals by having all team members participate in defining them. Because goal setting is difficult, particularly for new teams, the TSPi defines an initial set of team and team-member goals (see Chapters 11–15 for the role specifications). For the second and subsequent TSPi cycles, teams should review and adjust these goals based on their experience with the first development cycle.

Roles

Immediately after goals, the next issue is responsibilities. How can teams get all members to assume responsibility for their parts of the job? The TSPi addresses this issue by establishing team member roles. The TSPi roles are team leader, development manager, planning manager, quality/process manager, and support manager. These roles cover a broad spectrum of the team's activities, and they provide each member with specific responsibilities.

Without clearly identified responsibilities, it could take some time for a team to understand everything that it must do, to decide who should do each task, and to determine when and how to do it. This is not so much because the engineers don't want to take responsibility but rather because they don't know what all the actions are or they are not sure whether anyone else is already doing them. They may also be reluctant to take on tasks that the team or team leader might plan to give to someone else.

When you explicitly define and assign team member roles, these responsibility concerns are largely resolved. The TSPi defines a standard set of team-member roles (see Part III for more details). These TSPi roles and responsibilities must, however, be distributed among all the engineers and not handled by only one or two of them. Only then will all the team members feel comfortable about acting on problems and issues without being told. Chapters 16 and 17 also have comprehensive discussions of taking responsibility and fostering teamwork.

Plans

After the team agrees on its goals and roles, it next agrees on a strategy for achieving these goals. With the TSPi, the first decision is how to divide the total job into parts for the various development cycles. The team then defines the functional content of each cycle, its expected size, and ways to integrate and test these pieces to produce the finished product.

The team members next decide on and document the process they will use to do the work. With a defined process, the team then estimates the sizes of the products of each cycle, the time to produce each product, the order of this work, and the people who will do each step. When they are finished, they have the development plan.

Communication

The most common team problem is poor communication among the members [Pournaghshbanb]. When team members do not know the status of one another's work, they cannot coordinate their work. Because all the team members are busy, they have little time to meet. Not meeting, however, destroys a key element of teamwork [Scott, page 302]. The TSPi addresses this problem by calling for regular weekly team meetings. If the members hold these meetings every week, it usually solves the communication problem.

The TSPi also aids team communication by providing a foundation for rapid and precise understanding. With their defined roles, processes, plans, and measurements, team members can communicate crisply and concisely. This makes communication more efficient and provides a solid foundation for agreement. This topic is discussed in greater detail in Chapter 17.

External Communication

An important form of team communication occurs between the team and other parties, such as management or the instructor. Often, teams communicate with management only when they are in trouble. Instead of reporting steady and orderly progress, the team appears to be floundering. This means that managers and instructors see only problems and not successes, and that puts the team in a poor light. The second problem is that the team cannot take advantage of the instructor's or manager's knowledge and experience. Most software problems have been encountered many times, and there are known and effective solutions. Without a clear understanding of where the teams stand, it is hard for anyone to help them.

TSPi calls for the team leader to make weekly summary reports to the instructor. Based on the team members' weekly assessments of their status, these reports show what the team has accomplished and what the members plan for the next week. These reports can help the instructor see when the team is having trouble and suggest when help is needed. The reports also provide useful material for the team final reports.

2.7 Summary

This chapter presents an overview and the logic of the TSPi. It covers what teams are, what makes teams work, and how to resolve teamwork problems. The TSPi is designed to capitalize on the natural strengths of teams and to minimize the likelihood or impact of the teams' inherent weaknesses. The process uses defined roles, process scripts, and established standards.

When software projects fail, it is generally because of teamwork problems and not technical problems. One significant people problem concerns engineers' ability to handle the pressures of an aggressive schedule. The TSPi helps teams handle such pressures by developing detailed plans and providing a structured development process.

The criteria for successful teams are that the team is clearly identified, its tasks are clear and distinct, the team members have control of their tasks, and there is a real need for the team. The environment must also support teamwork, encourage the members to plan their work, and expect them to maintain personal discipline.

When teams jell, the team members' skills and abilities combine to provide extraordinary results. They work collaboratively to set team and personal goals, they define their processes, and they establish and work to a common plan. Such teams establish a rapport that provides a meaningful and rewarding working environment. Their enjoyment of the work sustains the team's energy and enthusiasm. It also produces truly exceptional products.

2.8   References

[Cummings] Thomas G. Cummings. 1978. "Self-Regulating Work Groups: A Socio-Technical Synthesis." *Academy of Management* 3, no. 3 (July 1978): 627.

[DeMarco 87] Tom DeMarco and Timothy Lister. 1987. *Peopleware, Productive Projects and Teams*. New York: Dorset House Publishing, 123.

[DeMarco 88] Tom DeMarco. 1988. "Looking for Lost Keys." *Software Magazine,* April 1988.

[Dyer] Jean L. Dyer. 1984. "Team Research and Team Training: a state-of-the-art review." *Human Factors Review,* The Human Factors Society, Inc., 286, 309.

[Iacocca] Lee Iacocca and William Novak. 1984. *Iacocca: An Autobiography.* New York: Bantam Books, Inc., 230.

[Katzenbach] Jon R. Katzenbach and Douglas K. Smith. 1993. *The Wisdom of Teams.* Boston: Harvard Business School Press, 3.

[Mohrman] Susan Albers Mohrman. 1995. *Designing Team-Based Organizations, New Forms for Knowledge Work*. San Francisco: Jossey-Bass Publishers, 52, 176, 279.

[Pournaghshbanb] Hassan Pournaghshbanb. 1990. "The Students' Problems in Courses with Team Projects." Twenty-First SIGCSE Technical Symposium on Computer Science Education. *SIGCSE Bulletin* 22, no. 1 (February 1990): 44–47.

[Robillard] Pierre N. Robillard. 1977. "Teaching Software Engineering through a Project-Oriented Course." *Proceedings of the 10th CSEE,* Virginia Beach.

[Scott] Thomas J. Scott. 1995. "Team Selection Methods for Student Programming Projects." *Proceedings of the 8th CSEE Conference,* New Orleans.

[Shaw] Marvin E. Shaw. 1981. *Group Dynamics, The Psychology of Small Group Behavior.* New York: McGraw-Hill.

[Stevens] Michael J. Stevens and Michael A. Campion. 1994. "The Knowledge, Skill, and Ability Requirements for Teamwork: Implications for Human Resource Management." *Journal of Management* 20, no 2: 503–530.

PART TWO

The TSPi Process

The eight chapters of Part II describe each of the eight major TSPi process scripts. Chapter 3 covers the launch process, in which the instructor reviews the TSPi and this course and assigns students to teams and team roles. Also covered are the product objectives and team and individual goals. The final launch step is a team meeting, when each TSPi team reviews its roles and establishes working practices.

Chapter 4 covers the development strategy and explains why a strategy is needed. The team produces a strategy for doing its work and estimates the sizes of the products and the time needed to do the work. The engineers document the strategy.

Chapter 5 covers the development plan and describes what plans are and what they contain. It then describes why planning is needed and how plans help software development teams do better work. Chapter 6 reviews the TSPi requirements process: what requirements are, why requirements are needed, and how to deal with key requirements issues.

Chapter 7 covers the design process, including design principles, designing with teams, design standards, designing for reuse, designing for usability, designing for testability, and design reviews and inspections. Chapter 8 describes the implementation process, starting with design completion criteria, implementation standards, implementation strategies, and reviews and inspections.

Chapter 9 covers the test plan, the build process, integration testing, and system testing. It also describes defect-prone modules and discusses the implications of defect-prone analysis on testing.

Chapter 10 reviews why a postmortem is needed, how the postmortem process can help engineers learn from their work, and how to follow the steps of the TSPi postmortem process. In the postmortem, the team reviews its work, reexamines what the engineers did in the cycle, and determines how to do the job better the next time.

3

Launching a Team Project

TSPi projects start with a launch step, in which the instructor describes the team launch process. This chapter begins with a brief discussion of why you need a team launch, followed by a review of team goals and how to set them. The chapter concludes with a description of the steps in the launch process and the launch scripts. Following the team launch, the teams hold their first weekly meeting and agree on how and when they will provide their weekly data to the planning manager. Then they follow the TSPi to plan, track, and run their projects.

3.1   Why Conduct a Team Launch?

There are several reasons to start projects with a launch. The process of forming and building a team does not happen by accident, and it takes time. Teams need to establish their working relationships, determine member roles, and agree on goals. The launch is the first step. An hour or so spent on team-building issues at the beginning of the project saves time later.

Defining the roles and agreeing on who will handle each role is an essential first step in team formation. The instructor makes the initial role assignments, but in subsequent development cycles you may be asked for a role preference. The instructor will assign the roles for every cycle, but if your team agrees in advance on who should handle each role the instructor will probably follow your suggestions. The standard TSPi roles and their basic responsibilities are shown in Figure 3.1. These roles are described in Chapters 11–15. If you know which role you have been assigned, read that chapter as soon as you finish reading Chapter 3.

3.2   Team Goals

Goal setting is an essential step in team formation and should usually be done at the start of every project. Establishing goals is simple in concept but often difficult in practice. The reason is that goals should be precisely measured, and few of us are in the habit of being precise about our work. Although the lack of specific goals may not be a problem in most situations, it can be a problem for software teams. The goals establish the framework for the strategy and the plan. These, in turn, provide the foundation for everything that the team will subsequently do. With agreed-on goals, you have the basis for evaluating strategies and settling issues. Without defined goals, there is no orderly way to settle arguments, negotiate strategies, or plan the work.

Goal-setting Considerations

The primary objective of most projects is to attain superior performance, something that is most likely when people strive to meet challenging goals. If the goal is too easy, there will likely be little motivation to strive. On the other hand, a goal that is clearly unachievable also provides little or no motivation. When you set goals, make them aggressive but realistic, and then strive to meet them. It is more important to have aggressive goals that you occasionally miss than safe goals that you always make.

Teams should not be measured on whether or not they actually meet their goals. Instead, they should be evaluated on their willingness to set measurable and aggressive goals and on their efforts to meet them. Too much emphasis on meeting goals is counterproductive because it motivates teams to set goals that they are sure they can meet.

The only way to learn how to establish goals is to set specific and measured goals and then work to meet them. Your initial goals may aim at the wrong items or may be wildly unrealistic. With a little goal-setting experience, you will begin to see how to set aggressive but realistic goals. After two or three development cycles, you will see which goals are meaningful and helpful for you.

Setting Team Goals

It is not easy to establish goals, particularly if you have no historical basis for doing so. Because effective teamwork requires that you have goals to guide your work, TSPi starts by defining standard team goals. You may wish to modify these goals, but don't spend a lot of time worrying about specific goal values until you have some data to guide you. When you have data and want to modify the goals, you should follow five goal-setting steps.

1. Write down the goals you wish to use instead.
2. Specify how to measure these goals.
3. Describe why you have selected these goals instead of the ones provided by the TSPi.
4. Give a copy of your revised goals to the team and to the instructor.
5. Have the team leader put a copy of your goals in the project notebook.

Goal Setting for TSPi

The general guideline for setting goals is to first consider what would be a superior result in the eyes of your customer. In this case, the instructor is your customer. For TSPi, there are three basic goals.

☐ Team goal 1: Produce a quality product.

☐ Team goal 2: Run a productive and well-managed project.

☐ Team goal 3: Finish on time.

These goals may seem obvious, and they are very general. The principal challenge of goal setting is to make the goals measurable. So the second goal-setting step is to define measurements for the goals. The best way to do this is to measure your performance and set goals to improve. To do this, however, you need data on your prior work.

Because few teams will have historical data before the first development cycle, I suggest that you consider the following measures.

Team Goal 1	Produce a quality product.
Measure 1.1	Percent of defects found before the first compile: 80%
Measure 1.2	Number of defects found in system test: 0
Measure 1.3	Requirements functions included at project completion: 100%
Team Goal 2	Run a productive and well-managed project.
Measure 2.1	Error in estimated product size: <20%
Measure 2.2	Error in estimated development hours: <20%
Measure 2.3	Percent of data recorded and entered in project notebook: 100%
Team Goal 3	Finish on time.
Measure 3.1	Days early or late in completing the development cycle: <4

FIGURE 3.1 THE TEAM ROLE RESPONSIBILITIES

Responsibility	Team Leader	Development Manager	Planning Manager	Quality/Process Manager	Support Manager
Build and maintain an effective team	X				
Resolve issues among team members	X				
Track and report team progress	X				
Act as meeting facilitator	X				
Interface with the instructor	X				
Maintain the project notebook	X				
Help the team allocate tasks	X				
Lead all development work		X			
Lead team planning and progress tracking			X		
Lead quality planning and tracking				X	
Provide team process support				X	
Act as inspection moderator				X	

Goal				
Maintain team standards and glossary		X		
Handle meeting reporting		X		
Alert the team to quality problems		X		
Obtain needed tools and support	X			
Handle configuration management	X			
Lead the Change Control Board	X			
Act as team reuse advocate	X			
Manage issue and risk tracking	X			
Maintain the system glossary	X			
Develop the product	X	X	X	X
Make personal plans	X	X	X	X
Track personal work	X	X	X	X
Produce quality products	X	X	X	X
Follow disciplined personal practices	X	X	X	X

After each cycle, examine your performance and set goals for improving in the next cycle. After cycle 1, you will have data for setting new goals for cycles 2 and 3. As you strive to improve performance for these later cycles, however, you will have to work differently than before. Merely setting improvement goals and then working in the same way will not produce consistently better results. Thus, with each goal, consider what you will have to do differently to achieve it. Then figure out how to change your process so that you are likely to meet your new objectives. Then make the needed changes in your process scripts, personal practices, or team standards.

3.3   Team Member Goals

All team members need specific and measurable goals. The TSPi defines goals for the team and for each team member. Although they are only suggestions, you will probably not know how to establish goals for yourself, at least not yet. After the first development cycle, you will have the data and experience to establish goals of your own. For the first cycle, use the standard TSPi team member and role goals. They are listed in the following paragraphs and described in more detail in Chapters 11–15. For the second and subsequent cycles, you can change these goals if you wish. In changing the goals, use the following ground rules.

- □ If you did not meet the prior-cycle goals and if they still appear reasonable, use them again.
- □ If the goals now look unrealistic, set some new and somewhat less challenging goals, but make sure they call for significant improvement over your prior performance.
- □ If you met the prior-cycle goals, set aggressive improvement goals for the next cycle.

Setting Team Member Goals

Team Member Goal 1	Be a cooperative and effective team member.
Measure 1.1	Average PEER evaluation of role for helpfulness and support: >3
Measure 1.2	Average PEER evaluation of role for overall contribution: >3

The first goal for every team member is to work cooperatively with the entire team. Above all else, the team's success depends on all team members contributing their personal best efforts, supporting other team members, and working cooperatively to resolve issues and disagreements.

Team Member Goal 2	Do consistently disciplined personal work.
Measure 2.1	Percentage of personal data recorded and in project notebook: 100%
Measure 2.2	Percentage of weeks a personal form WEEK was completed: 100%

Against these goals, you should track the time, size, and defect data for your personal work and ensure that these data are properly recorded on the TSPi forms. Using form WEEK, you must also report your progress against this plan in the weekly meeting.

Team Member Goal 3	Plan and track all your personal work.
Measure 3.1	Percent of personal project data recorded in SUMP and SUMQ forms: 100%
Measure 3.2	Percent of project tasks with completed plan and actual data on TASK form: 100%

To meet these goals, you must establish personal plans for all your work and must track progress against these plans. This requires that you complete a personal TASK and SCHEDULE form for each development cycle and track your earned value progress against the plan every week.

Team Member Goal 4	Produce quality products.
Measure 4.1	Average percent of defects found before the first compile: >70%
Measure 4.2	Defect density found during compile: <10/KLOC
Measure 4.3	Defect density found during unit test: <5/KLOC
Measure 4.4	Defect density found after unit test: 0

To meet this goal, you must personally review each of your products and call for team inspections when required by the TSPi process. Also, you must record the results of every team inspection on the INS form, produce comprehensive test plans, and report test results on the LOGTEST form.

3.4   The Role Goals

In addition to the team member goals, you will have goals for the role you are assigned. The following paragraphs discuss these goals.

Although the goals of each individual role are important, it is also important to remember that each role represents a single facet of the overall team's activities. Thus, role objectives may occasionally appear to conflict. This is because each role considers the team's activities from only one perspective. To meet the team's over-

all goals, however, the team needs to integrate these role goals into a smoothly functioning whole. You can best do this by giving highest priority to the team's overall
goals and then working cooperatively with the entire team to meet your personal
and role goals.

Team Leader Goals

The team leader's principal goal is to run an effective team. The team should complete all of its planned work, everyone should participate in the team meetings,
and all team members should work hard to finish the project on time. Another way
to measure the team leader's effectiveness is through the team peer evaluations.
The specific team leader goals are the following.

☐ Team leader goal 1: Build and maintain an effective team.

☐ Team leader goal 2: Motivate all team members to work aggressively on the
project.

☐ Team leader goal 3: Resolve all the issues team members bring to you.

☐ Team leader goal 4: Keep the instructor fully informed about the team's
progress.

☐ Team leader goal 5: Perform effectively as the team's meeting facilitator.

The team leader's goals and measures are discussed in more detail in Chapter 11.

Development Manager Goals

The development manager is principally concerned with producing a functioning and high-quality product. The specific development manager goals are the
following.

☐ Development manager goal 1: Produce a superior product.

☐ Development manager goal 2: Fully use the team members' skills and abilities.

The development manager's goals and measures are discussed in greater detail in Chapter 12.

Planning Manager Goals

The planning manager's principal goals are to guide the team in producing a detailed plan and to precisely track progress against that plan. The specific planning
manager goals are the following.

- ☐ Planning manager's goal 1: Produce a complete, precise, and accurate plan for the team and every team member.
- ☐ Planning manager's goal 2: Accurately report team status every week.

The planning manager's goals and measures are discussed further in Chapter 13.

Quality/Process Manager Goals

The quality/process manager's principal goal is to ensure that the team properly uses the TSPi to produce a defect-free product. The specific quality/process manager goals are the following.

- ☐ Quality/process manager's goal 1: All team members accurately report and properly use TSPi process data.
- ☐ Quality/process manager's goal 2: The team faithfully follows the TSPi and produces a quality product.
- ☐ Quality/process manager's goal 3: All team inspections are properly moderated and reported.
- ☐ Quality/process manager's goal 4: All team meetings are accurately reported, and the reports are put in the project notebook.

These quality/process manager goals are discussed in more detail in Chapter 14.

Support Manager Goals

The support manager's principal goal is to ensure that the project is properly supported and controlled. The specific support manager's goals are the following.

- ☐ Support manager goal 1: The team has suitable tools and methods to support its work.
- ☐ Support manager goal 2: No unauthorized changes are made to baselined products.
- ☐ Support manager goal 3: All the team's risks and issues are recorded in the issue-tracking system and reported each week.
- ☐ Support manager goal 4: The team meets its reuse goals for the development cycle.

The support manager's goals and measures are discussed further in Chapter 15.

3.5   The TSPi Launch Scripts

During the initial project launch, the instructor leads your team through the steps in the LAU1 script shown in Table 3.1. LAUn, shown in Table 3.2, gives the steps the instructor will follow in launching the second and third development cycles. Because your team will then understand the TSPi and be familiar with the product need statement, the LAUn script is simpler than LAU1 and the steps do not take quite as long.

In the course overview, the instructor reviews the TSPi course objectives and discusses what you are expected to accomplish. This is the time to ask about how your work will be evaluated and to discuss team versus individual grading.

The overall course objective is to have all the members of each team work co-operatively to produce an effective overall result. Although most students will strive to do good work, some of them might try to get by with a minimum effort. If this were to affect team performance, it would be unfair to give everyone a low grade just because of the poor work of one or two team members. Conversely, it would not be fair to give high grades to everyone if one or two members did not make a reasonable effort. To address this problem, the TSPi grading system is based on both team and individual performance. The TSPi peer evaluations and detailed process data provide the information the instructor needs to determine the quality of each student's work.

Student Information

To be most effective, teams need a mix of talents and abilities. Team members also need to spend time together and have complementary interests and abilities. To provide the necessary information, you will complete the INFO form shown in Table 3.3. Its instructions are shown in Table 3.4. The instructor uses this information to make the team and role assignments. The INFO form shows the students who have compatible schedules, those who are most interested in each role, and each student's background and experience. Before deciding which role you would like, look at the two-page role scripts in Appendix E and the textbook chapters on the roles.

Product Objectives

In the next process step, the instructor describes the product to be built and answers any questions about the course, the product, or the process. Appendix A in this textbook gives two sample projects. Although TSPi will work with almost any product, this text provides two sample *product need* statements. After you have reviewed the product need statement, you will have a chance to ask additional questions.

TABLE 3.1 TSPi CYCLE 1 TEAM LAUNCH: SCRIPT LAU1

Purpose		To start the teams on the first development cycle
Entry Criteria		• All the students have satisfactorily completed a PSP course. • The students have read textbook Chapters 1, 2, 3, and Appendix A.
General		This launch script starts the team projects. The principal objectives are to describe the course. • Form the teams and assign team roles. • Explain the objectives for the product to be developed. • Establish team meeting and reporting times. Steps 1, 2, and 3 are completed during the first class session. Steps 4 through 8 are completed during the second class session.
Step	**Activities**	**Description**
1	Course Overview	The instructor describes the TSPi team course objectives. • What the students are expected to accomplish • How their work will be evaluated and graded • The basic principles of teamwork • The TSPi process
2	Student Information	The instructor explains the criteria for making team assignments. • The information needed to make proper assignments • The team roles, responsibilities, and qualifications The instructor also asks the students to • Complete and return the INFO form before the end of the class • Read textbook Chapter 4 and Appendix B • Read the textbook chapters on the roles that interest them
3	Product Objectives	The instructor describes the product objectives. • The critical product objectives that must be satisfied • The optional and desirable objectives • The criteria for evaluating the finished product
4	Team Assignments	The instructor gives the students their team and role assignments.
5	Team Goals	The instructor describes goal setting. • Why goals are needed and typical team and role goals
6	Team Meetings	The instructor explains the team meeting, its purpose, and conduct. • The meeting purpose, scheduling, and reporting • Weekly data requirements
7	The First Team Meeting	The team leader holds the first meeting of his or her team. • Discusses team members' roles • Discusses and agrees on cycle 1 goals • Establishes a standard time for the weekly team meeting • Agrees on a specific time each week when all team members will provide their weekly data to the planning manager
8	Data Requirements	The planning manager reviews for the team the • Data required from every team member every week • Reports to be generated and provided the team from these data
9	Project Start	The team starts work on the project using the STRAT1 script.
Exit Criteria		• Each student has completed and submitted an INFO form. • The development teams are formed and roles assigned. • The instructor has described the overall product objectives. • The instructor has reviewed and discussed the TSPi and the team's and role goals. • The team has agreed on cycle 1 goals, weekly meeting times, and the weekly data to report.

TABLE 3.2 TSPi CYCLE n TEAM LAUNCH: SCRIPT LAUn

Purpose	To start the teams on the second or subsequent development cycle	
Entry Criteria	The student teams have completed a prior TSPi development cycle.	
General	This launch script starts the second or subsequent project cycle. The principal objectives are to • Review lessons from the prior cycle. • Re-form the teams if necessary and assign new team roles. • Establish team meeting and reporting times. Steps 1 and 2 are completed during one class session. Steps 3 through 8 are completed during the next class session.	
Step	**Activities**	**Description**
1	Lessons Learned	The instructor reviews the results of the prior cycle and • Discusses any process problems and their likely causes • Suggests steps the teams should take to minimize the problems with this cycle • Reviews any teamwork concepts that were problems during the prior cycle and explains how to handle them
2	Student Information	The instructor reviews • The reasons for making role changes • The lessons learned about the roles from the prior cycles • Any role performance problems and how to better handle them in the next project cycle The instructor also asks the students to • Complete and return a new INFO form • Include any changes in their personal schedules • Give their current preferences for team membership and roles
3	Team Assignments	The instructor gives the students their team and role assignments. The students read the chapters on their role assignments.
4	Goal Setting	The instructor discusses goal performance and the need to strive for improved performance with each development cycle.
5	Team Meetings	The instructor discusses the team meetings. • Meeting scheduling • Weekly reporting • Weekly data requirements
6	The First Team Meeting	The team leader holds the first meeting of his or her new team. • Discusses the team member roles. • Reviews and updates the team goals. • Establishes a standard time for the weekly team meeting. • Agrees on a specific time each week when all team members will provide weekly data to the planning manager.
7	Data Requirements	The planning manager reviews for the team the • Data required from every team member every week • Reports to be generated and provided the team from these data
8	Project Start	The team starts work on the project using the STRATn script.
Exit Criteria	• Each student has completed and submitted an updated INFO form. • The development teams are formed and roles assigned. • The team has agreed on an updated set of cycle goals, weekly meeting times, and the weekly data to report.	

TABLE 3.3 TSPi STUDENT INFORMATION SHEET: FORM INFO

Name _____   Instructor _____
Date _____   Number of College Credits _____
Major _____   Expected Graduation Date _____

Briefly describe your relevant experience and interests:
_____
_____
_____

Briefly describe your work on other team projects:
_____
_____
_____

Briefly describe any leadership or management positions you have held (at work or in clubs/organizations):
_____
_____
_____

State your team preferences, if any:
_____
_____

List your class schedule and other times when you have scheduled activities such as work, ROTC, clubs, sports teams, etc.							
Time	Mon.	Tue.	Wed.	Thu.	Fri.	Sat.	Sun.
800–900							
915–1015							
1030–1130							
1145–1245							
1300–1400							
1415–1515							
1530–1630							
1645–1745							

Rank from 1 (least) to 5 (most) your preferences for serving in the following team roles:					
Team Leader	1	2	3	4	5
Development Manager	1	2	3	4	5
Planning Manager	1	2	3	4	5
Quality/Process Manager	1	2	3	4	5
Support Manager	1	2	3	4	5

TABLE 3.4 TSPi STUDENT INFORMATION SHEET INSTRUCTIONS: FORM INFO

Purpose	Use this form to describe your interests and experiences.
General	• Complete this form and give it to the instructor during the first laboratory period of the TSPi course. • The instructor will use it to make team and role assignments. • The schedule information is needed so that teams can be formed that are able to meet during selected times of the week. • For questions about the roles, see the role descriptions in Appendix E and in Part III. • Use additional pages if necessary.
Header	Enter • Your name, the instructor's name, and the date • The number of credits you expect from this course • Your major field of study • Your expected graduation date
Relevant Experience and Interests	• List any experience and interests you feel would be helpful to the instructor in making team and role assignments. • Examples would be language fluency, PSP experience, database design and development, and so on.
Other Team Projects	• List any team experience you feel would be helpful to the instructor in making team and role assignments. • Examples would include the type of project, roles performed, the tools or methods used, and so on.
Leadership or Management	• List any leadership or management experiences you feel would be helpful to the instructor in making team and role assignments. • Examples would include a club business manager, work as a teaching assistant, time spent in office work, and so on.
Team Preferences	• If you have preferences regarding working with particular groups, state them. • You need not make any statement.
Schedule	• List the times you have commitments for classes or other activities. • If the times do not precisely line up with those given, mark the rough periods and note below the precise times.
Role Preferences	• Rank your team role preferences from 1 (least desired) to 5 (most desired). • Note that you can list several as 1s or 5s if you feel they are all equally desirable or undesirable.

Team Assignments

At the second class meeting, the instructor makes the team and role assignments. Although ideally these assignments should be consistent with your interests, it will not always be possible. To the extent practical, every student should be exposed to several roles. Even if someone has been an effective team leader, for example, the others should have a shot at that role if they would like to try it. In three development cycles, each student should get experience with three different roles. This policy will provide useful experience and help you to better understand your personal interests and aspirations.

When possible, the instructor should keep teams together for the entire course. As teams develop effective working relationships, they get more efficient and the work is more fun. If at all possible, such teams should not be disrupted. If a team is not working properly, however, changes should be made. Generally, when teamwork problems become serious, changes should be made immediately, even in the middle of a cycle.

Team Goals

The instructor reviews the goal-setting process and the TSPi goals.

Team Meetings and the First Team Meeting

After the team has been established and the roles assigned, it is time to hold the first team meeting. This meeting is held in the launch step to provide the team an opportunity to discuss and agree on the goals for the development cycle. This first meeting also helps you understand the purpose of the weekly meetings and shows you how to make these meetings brief and effective.

The team meeting is the basic mechanism for team communication, planning, and decision making. Your team should establish a standard time and place for the weekly meeting and hold such a meeting of the entire team every week. To run the meeting, follow the WEEK script given in Table 3.5. Before future meetings, you will need to update your personal TASK and SCHEDULE forms and summarize their contents in the WEEK form shown in Table 3.6. Its instructions are shown in Table 3.7. The planning manager combines the data from all these WEEK forms into a composite team weekly report.

The most important single function of the weekly team meeting is to gather and analyze the team's data for the prior week and for the development cycle to date. To provide these data, all team members must give the planning manager their data at the agreed time. He or she then produces the team's composite WEEK form and the overall team TASK and SCHEDULE forms. By reviewing the team

TABLE 3.5 TSPi WEEKLY MEETING: SCRIPT WEEK

Purpose	To guide the team in conducting the weekly status meeting
Entry Criteria	• All team members are present. • All the team members have provided updated TASK, SCHEDULE, and WEEK forms to the planning manager. • The planning manager has produced the composite weekly team status report from the team members' data (form WEEK). • The team leader has issued a meeting agenda.
General	In advance of the meeting, the team leader has • Asked team members for meeting agenda topics • Prepared and distributed the meeting agenda The team leader leads the weekly meeting. • The quality/process manager records the meeting topics. • Each team member generally reports his or her role work and development work at the same time. After the meeting, the team leader • Issues and distributes the meeting report • Puts a report copy in the project notebook

Step	Activities	Description
1	Agenda Review	The team leader opens the meeting and • Reviews the agenda and asks for additions or changes • Checks that all team members are fully prepared and defers the meeting if any are not
2	Role Reports	Starting with the development manager, the engineers report • Any overall role issues or concerns • Status on any role-related tasks or activities • Status on any issue or risk items that the engineer is tracking The development manager reports on development status. • Items designed, reviewed, inspected, implemented, and tested The planning manager reports on planning status. • Team hours and earned-value status against the plan The quality/process manager reviews data on • Each inspection and every integration and system test defect • The percentage of engineers following the process • Any suspected quality problems The support manager reports the status of the SCM and ITL systems. • Items submitted this week, changes made, system inventory
3	Engineer Reports	Each engineer reports his or her development status. • The hours worked this week and cycle compared to the plan • The earned value gained this week and cycle versus the plan • Times for the tasks accomplished this week and the plan times • The tasks to be accomplished in the next week • The hours to be worked in the next week • Any problem areas or topics of general team interest
4	Meeting Close	The team leader leads the discussion of any remaining topics and • Checks that all committed tasks have been reported • Verifies that all risks and issues have been reviewed • Ensures that next week's tasks have been identified and assigned • Discusses the items to include in the team's weekly report

Exit Criteria	• The meeting report completed and filed in the project notebook • Updated team and engineer TASK, SCHEDULE, WEEK, and CSR (Configuration Status Report) forms in the project notebook • Updated copy of the ITL log in the project notebook

TABLE 3.6 TSPi WEEKLY STATUS REPORT: FORM WEEK

Name _____   Team _____   Instructor _____
Date _____   Cycle No. _____   Week No. _____

Weekly Data			Planned	Actual
Project hours for this week			_____	_____
Project hours this cycle to date			_____	_____
Earned value for this week			_____	_____
Earned value this cycle to date			_____	_____
Total hours for the tasks completed this phase to date			_____	_____

Team Member Weekly Data	Hours Planned	Hours Actual	Planned Value	Earned Value
Team Leader	_____	_____	_____	_____
Development Manager	_____	_____	_____	_____
Planning Manager	_____	_____	_____	_____
Quality/Process Manager	_____	_____	_____	_____
Support Manager	_____	_____	_____	_____
	_____	_____	_____	_____
Totals	_____	_____	_____	

Development Tasks Completed	Hours Planned	Hours Actual	Earned Value	Planned Week
_____	_____	_____	_____	_____
_____	_____	_____	_____	_____
_____	_____	_____	_____	_____
_____	_____	_____	_____	_____
_____	_____	_____	_____	_____
Totals	_____	_____	_____	

Issue/Risk Tracking
Issue/Risk Name   Status
_____   _____
_____   _____
_____   _____
_____   _____

Other Significant Items
_____
_____
_____
_____
_____

TABLE 3.7 TSPi WEEKLY STATUS REPORT INSTRUCTIONS: FORM WEEK

Purpose	• Use this form to prepare the weekly status reports.
General	• Each team member completes this form every week showing work accomplished last week and plans for the next week. • Every week, the planning manager prepares a copy of form WEEK with a composite summary of the team's status and week's accomplishments. • Attach additional sheets if needed.
Header	• Enter your name and the instructor's name. • Enter the team name, cycle number, date, and week number.
Weekly Data	• Enter the total hours actually spent on the project this week and the hours planned for the week. • Also enter the actual and planned cumulative hours spent during this development cycle. • Enter the planned value and the actual earned value for the week. • Enter the cumulative planned value and cumulative earned value for the development cycle to date. • Enter the total planned and actual hours for the tasks completed on this development cycle to date.
Team Member Weekly Data	For each team member report • Enter the total actual and planned time for each engineer. • Enter the engineer's planned and earned value for the week. • Enter the engineer's total planned and actual hours worked.
Team Weekly Data	For the composite team report • Enter the total actual and planned time for the team. • Enter the team's planned and earned value for the week. • Enter the team's total planned and actual hours worked.
Development Tasks Completed	For the tasks completed this week • Enter the name of each task. • Enter the total actual and planned time for that task. • Enter the week number when it was planned. • Enter the earned value for the task.
Issue/Risk Tracking	• For the risks and issues tracked, summarize the status and any important changes this week.
Other Significant Items	• List any significant accomplishments or events during the week. • Role examples include coding standard completed, change control procedure approved, and so forth. • Development examples include designing, coding, inspecting, or testing the various product elements.

and individual data, the team members can see where they stand against their plans and where they need to rebalance or adjust their personal plans.

Data Requirements

An important part of the first weekly meeting is having the team members agree on the data they will provide to the planning manager and the deadline for providing these data. Pick a day and stick with it. The planning manager needs the data to generate the weekly status update. Without these data, neither you nor the instructor can understand where you are against your plan. The team leader also needs these data for the weekly report to the instructor.

Project Start

At this point, the launch process has been completed and the team is ready to start on the project, following the STRAT script. Before the team starts, however, you need to be familiar with the project notebook and the TSPi support tool, which are described in the following paragraphs.

The Project Notebook   TSPi calls for teams to establish and maintain a project notebook. Its purpose is to provide a standard way to save all the key project information. The project notebook specification is contained in Appendix G. The team leader is responsible for establishing and maintaining the project notebook, and all team members are responsible for providing the needed materials for the notebook.

The TSPi Support Tool   The TSPi has a support tool to assist your planning, data entry, and tracking work. If you use this tool to record the data on all your activities, it will automatically complete the project summary forms for you. This tool can save you a substantial amount of time while ensuring that your reports are accurate and complete. To do this, however, you must be sure to enter all the (plan and actual) time, size, and defect data for everything you do.

3.6 **Summary**

This chapter describes the steps in the TSPi launch process. During the launch, the instructor leads the students through the course overview, student information gathering, product objectives, team assignments, team goal setting, and the team meeting. The teams then hold their first weekly meeting and agree on how and when they will provide weekly data to the planning manager. Following the team launch, the teams follow the TSPi process to start their projects.

The launch process is used to form and build the teams, determine team member roles, establish team goals, and help the teams decide on their working practices. Defining and agreeing on who will handle each role is an essential first step in team formation. The instructor makes the initial role assignments, but in subsequent development cycles you may be asked to state your role preferences.

Goal setting is done at the start of every TSPi project cycle. The team's goals establish the framework for the strategy and plan. These, in turn, provide the foundation for everything that the team will subsequently do. Teams should not be measured on whether or not they actually meet their goals but rather on their willingness to set aggressive goals and on their efforts to meet these goals. The only way to learn how to establish useful goals is to actually set goals and then work to meet them.

For TSPi, the three basic goals are to produce a quality product, to run a productive and well-managed project, and to finish on time. The measures of success are that each team produced a quality product with the intended functions according to the planned schedule.

4

The Development Strategy

This chapter describes the development strategy and how to produce it. In the launch step, your team agreed on what a successful project would look like and established measurable role and team goals. In the strategy step, you devise a strategy for doing the work, create a conceptual product design, and make a preliminary estimate of the product's size and development time. If this estimate indicates that the work will take longer than the time you have available, you then revise the strategy until the work fits the available time. Finally, you document the strategy.

The development strategy is produced before you start on project planning. In producing the strategy, you will also produce materials needed in planning. Because the strategy and planning activities are closely related, this chapter starts with a brief discussion of planning, and it explains why you need to plan before you start a project. Next, we discuss risk management and the importance of reuse. After these points, we describe the TSPi strategy scripts and the configuration management plan.

4.1   Planning First

TSPi requires that you make a plan before you produce the requirements. You might wonder how you can do this. Until you have analyzed the requirements and produced a high-level design, for example, you can make only a rough estimate of the product's size and development time. In fact, before you have analyzed and documented the requirements, you don't really know what the product is supposed to do. So how can you be expected to make a plan?

The answer to this is another question: Will you be committed to developing this product? Somehow, engineers feel comfortable committing to do a job they know nothing about. At the same time, however, they object to planning the same work. Clearly, if you do not need to commit to the job, you don't need a plan to do the work. On the other hand, if you will commit to develop a product before you know the requirements, you can certainly make a plan at the same time. Another way to say this is that, if you can't make a plan, you have no business making a commitment.

Planning Before Committing

There are three reasons for planning before starting a project.

1. In the process of developing a plan, teams gain a common appreciation of the work they must do.

2. The plan provides the basis for tracking the work. This information helps teams to estimate when they will finish, and it provides early warning of likely problems.

3. If they don't start by making a plan and reviewing it with their managers (or instructors), teams end up committed to the managers' date whether or not they believe they can meet it.

The first two points are discussed in more detail in Chapter 5, The Development Plan. We discuss the third point now: getting committed to someone else's date.

In industry, most development work is started because of a business need. A new product is wanted, and management has obtained funds to pay for the work. They pick you and some other engineers and give you the job of producing this product on a schedule they think you can meet.

You and your teammates have now been asked to produce an as yet ill-defined product by a management-selected date. What do you think? If you simply start to do the work, management can properly assume that you have accepted the assignment and will try to meet their date. As a result, you become committed to management's date, regardless of how this date was developed. Worse, from this point on you will have to defend yourself whenever it appears that you cannot meet the date.

Planning for This Course

This course is no different. You have been given a product definition and a fixed course schedule on which to build it. What do you think? Is this a job you can do or not? Although you probably don't know at this point, developing a strategy is the first step in finding out.

Instead of meekly accepting an arbitrary date, start by making a plan. You will then be in a much stronger negotiating position. You will have examined the job and can tell the instructor what you can do and how long you think it will take. You will then have a plan you are willing to commit to. If it differs from the original date, you can explain why and negotiate changes in the schedule, resources, or product functions.

Although the product you will build with TSPi is a modest one, this course exposes you to the methods you will need for larger projects. The strategy and planning steps will take a larger proportion of this project than normal, but you will get valuable experience with the kind of schedule-resource-requirements negotiations you will face in the future.

4.2 What Is a Strategy?

One of the principal problems in software development is to figure out how to build big systems. Some years ago it was common to build big modules and components, but no one advocates this approach any more. Big systems are now built as collections of small parts, or modules. In developing a system, however, you still need to decide how to assemble the parts. Although there are many ways to do this, the principal choices are to build the whole system in one giant single release or to assemble the system in a cyclic series of incremental versions.

In the TSPi, we have already made a basic strategic decision: you will develop the product with a cyclic process. The number of development cycles was decided by the instructor when the course was scheduled, but the content of the cycles is up to you. Thus, your development process starts with a first cycle, in which you design, implement, and test a basic product version. Then, in a second cycle, you enhance this product to produce a second version. Finally, if there is time, you produce a third product version.

4.3   The Conceptual Design

The *conceptual design* is the starting point for project planning. The reason you need a conceptual design is that you must make a plan for building a product. You can't use the requirements document for this purpose because it describes what the user or customer wants and not what you will deliver. Because normally there are many alternative ways to build a product, you must start with an agreed approach for building this product.

To make a conceptual design, ask yourself four questions.

1. Based on what I now know, how would I build this product?
2. What are the principal components I will need to build this product?
3. What functions must these components provide?
4. How big do I think these components will be?

In a sense, you are playing magician. You postulate some components that, if you had them, would constitute all the pieces needed to assemble the finished product. Although you may not yet know how to design all these components, you can at least postulate what they must do. For a line of code (LOC) counter, for example, you would probably want a line counter, a component that reads files, some kind of report generator, a display manager, and a main control loop.

The principal problem many engineers have with both PSP and TSP planning is that they spend far too much time on the conceptual design. They are so concerned about making a good plan that they actually produce much of the product design during planning. This is not necessary. You should produce the design concept and general product structure, but leave any real design work until you have analyzed and inspected the requirements.

After you have the conceptual design, you can estimate the size of this hypothetical product and the time required to develop it. It is important to remember, however, that the conceptual design is only a planning tool. When you get into the actual design phase, you will want to consider various alternative approaches and may end up with an entirely different product structure.

4.4   Risk Management

In establishing a strategy, you must

- ☐ Define the strategy criteria.
- ☐ Determine the possible alternative strategies.

☐ Identify the risks and benefits of each alternative strategy.

☐ Make a comparative evaluation of these alternatives.

☐ Make the strategic decision.

☐ Document the selected strategy.

When you address these topics, the principal objective is to minimize the risk of running into trouble. In a course, the most likely problem is an attempt to build too large a product, causing you to run out of time. Some other risks you might consider in selecting your strategy are the following.

☐ You may encounter one or more functions that you don't know how to design.

☐ You may run into support system problems that delay your work.

☐ The product may be so defective that testing takes too long.

☐ You might lose control of the product or product changes and waste time reconstructing programs you have already developed.

☐ Your team may not be able to work together effectively.

Managing Risk

Something that is certain to happen is an *issue,* and you must allow time in your plan to handle all the known issues. If something may or may not happen, it is a *risk.* The reason to think about risks early in the project is that most risks can be avoided or controlled if you think about them in advance and take adequate mitigation steps.

For the risks mentioned earlier, effective mitigation actions might include the following.

☐ Too large a product. Start with a small kernel product and then add functions in later development cycles.

☐ Difficult or complex functions. Prototype these functions at the beginning of the project, when you have time to consider alternatives.

☐ Support system problems. Build an early prototype or small product version to make sure that you know how the support system works.

☐ Testing time. If you consistently follow the TSPi and use disciplined PSP methods, your product will have few defects and testing will not be a problem.

☐ Product control. It is easy for teams to lose control of their products. This is why TSPi addresses configuration management at the beginning of the project.

☐ Teamwork problems. If your team is having trouble working together, discuss the problems openly to see whether you can resolve them. If the problems persist, get help from the instructor. Also, look at Chapters 16 and 17 for further guidance.

4.5   A Reuse Strategy

One of the key risks for any software project is code growth, in which functions require substantially more code than expected. One way to reduce this risk is to adopt a reuse strategy. If you can develop code that meets multiple needs, you can add functions with little or no additional code. This strategy can reduce the required development effort, sometimes substantially.

Although you will not likely have much opportunity for reuse in the first development cycle, you should think about it at the beginning of the project. With proper design, the code for the first cycle will provide the base for the second and subsequent cycles. Although this is a form of reuse, it is not the kind of reuse we are talking about here. To save development time, you want to look at the ultimate product and identify any cases where a single reusable component or function could satisfy several functional needs. Examples might be string handling, error messages, screen management, and so forth. The earlier you identify such reuse opportunities, the more development time you are likely to save.

The reuse strategy I have found most helpful is to start every design by identifying all the likely reusable parts. Then, before developing the product, I specify and design these reusable parts, put them into a reuse library, and use them when developing the product. In TSPi, the support manager is the reuse advocate. This responsibility is described further in Chapter 15.

4.6   The Strategy Scripts

The TSPi strategy process is described in the STRAT1 and STRATn scripts shown in Tables 4.1 and 4.2. STRAT1 is for development cycle 1, and STRATn is for any subsequent cycles. STRATn differs from STRAT1 because the second and subsequent cycles start from the STRAT1 base. Thus, in STRATn you evaluate and enhance the earlier strategy rather than create a new one. Also, in STRAT1 the instructor explains the various strategy activities. These explanations are not required for STRATn.

Entry Criteria

First, check that you have met the entry criteria. If you have not, stop and address the missing items before proceeding. After you have completed all the steps given in the LAU1 process script, you should have met the STRAT1 entry criteria. This assumes that you have also read this chapter.

TABLE 4.1 TSPi CYCLE 1 DEVELOPMENT STRATEGY: SCRIPT STRAT1

Purpose		To guide a team through producing a TSPi development strategy and preliminary size and time estimates
Entry Criteria		• The students have read textbook Chapter 4. • The instructor has reviewed and discussed the TSPi process. • The instructor has described the overall product objectives. • Development teams have been formed and roles assigned. • The teams have agreed on goals for their work.
General		The development strategy specifies the order in which product functions are defined, designed, implemented, and tested. • The way the product will be enhanced in future cycles • How to divide the development work among the team members The development strategy is produced at the beginning of the process to guide size estimating and resource planning. • If the development strategy changes during planning, requirements, or development, it must be updated. The preliminary size and time estimates • Cover the planned work for each development cycle • Provide the basis for allocating work among team members
Step	**Activities**	**Description**
1	Strategy Overview	The instructor describes the development strategy. • What the strategy is, how it is produced, and how it is used • Criteria for an effective strategy • The need for and ways to produce the size and time estimates
2	Establish Strategy Criteria	• The development manager leads discussion of strategy criteria. • The meeting reporter (quality/process manager) documents these criteria and provides copies to the team members and instructor.
3	Produce the Conceptual Design	The development manager leads the team in producing the conceptual design for the overall product.
4	Select the Development Strategy	The development manager leads the team through producing the development strategy. This involves • Proposing and evaluating alternative strategies • Allocating product functions to each development cycle • Defining how to subdivide and later integrate the product
5	Produce the Preliminary Estimate	The planning manager leads the team through producing the preliminary size and time estimates, which must include • Size and time estimates for all the current-cycle products • Rough estimates for the products of subsequent cycles
6	Assess Risks	Identify and assess project risks and enter them in ITL.
7	Document the Strategy	The meeting reporter documents the selected strategy (STRAT).
8	Produce the Configuration Management Plan	The support manager produces the configuration management plan. • Identifies the configuration control board and its procedures • Specifies any needed support tools and facilities • Reviews the procedures with the team for their agreement
Exit Criteria		• A completed and documented development strategy • Completed and documented size and time estimates for all product elements to be produced during the next cycle • Completed and documented estimates for the products to be produced in subsequent development cycles • Documented configuration management procedure • Risks and issues entered in the ITL log • Conceptual design and completed STRAT form • Updated project notebook

TABLE 4.2 TSPi CYCLE n DEVELOPMENT STRATEGY: SCRIPT STRATn

Purpose	To guide a team through updating the strategy, size estimates, and time estimates for a second or subsequent development cycle
Entry Criteria	• The prior development cycles have been completed and evaluated. • Team membership is adjusted if needed and roles reassigned. • The engineers have read the textbook chapters on their roles.
General	The degree to which the development strategy should be changed depends on the results of the prior cycles. • If the strategy was followed and it worked, don't change it. • If the team did not follow the strategy, adjust it. Note: if the strategy worked, the team should avoid changing it. • Every job is a learning experience. • It is usually a mistake to change course in the middle of a project unless you discover major errors or mistakes. The estimate should be updated to reflect the prior-cycle results. • Measure the first cycle products and use the data in the update.

Step	Activities	Description
1	Strategy Review	The instructor describes why the strategy should be updated. • When changes are appropriate and why to avoid them • The technical and business symptoms of strategy problems • The logic for determining the next-cycle size and size range The instructor also describes any problems with the prior strategy process that should be corrected for this development cycle.
2	Update the Development Strategy	The development manager leads the team through updating the development strategy. • Review results of prior cycles and make needed changes. • Define how to subdivide and later integrate the cycle products. If no strategy changes are needed, the team should skip STRATn steps 3 and 5.
3	Produce the Updated Size and Time Estimates	The planning manager leads the team through producing the updated size and time estimates. These cover • Size and time estimates for all the next-cycle products • Rough sizes for the products of any subsequent cycles Note that these estimates should generally be updated while the development strategy is being revised.
4	Assess Risks	Review, update, and assess project risks and enter in ITL.
5	Document the Strategy	The meeting reporter documents the selected strategy (STRAT).
6	Review and Update the Configuration Management Plan	The support manager leads the team in reviewing the configuration management plan and identifying needed modifications to • The configuration control board or change control procedures • The support tools and facilities
Exit Criteria		• A documented update to the development strategy • Updated and documented size and time estimates for all product elements to be produced during the next development cycle • Completed and documented estimates for the products to be produced in any subsequent development cycles • Updated configuration management procedure • Updated risks and issues entered in the ITL log • Updated conceptual design and STRAT form • Updated project notebook

Establish Strategy Criteria

Although there can be many viable strategies for even simple products, it is important to first establish the criteria for evaluating the strategies and then use these criteria to review the proposals. It is usually easier to agree on criteria in advance and then use them to help you objectively review the alternative strategies. As mentioned before, the principal objective of the strategy is to minimize the risk that you will exceed the available development schedule. The suggested criteria for accomplishing this objective are as follows.

1. The cycle-1 product provides a minimum-function working subset of the final product.
2. The cycle-1 product provides a base that can be easily enhanced.
3. The cycle products are all of high quality and can be easily tested.
4. The product design has a modular structure that permits the team members to work independently.

Although you can add or delete some items from this list, these sample criteria provide a starting point for team discussion.

Produce the Conceptual Design

The development manager leads the team in producing the conceptual design. In the first development cycle, this design should include all the functions you intend to develop in all three development cycles. As part of the strategy process, you will decide which functions to develop in each cycle.

Select the Development Strategy

With the criteria established, the next step is to produce a proposed development strategy. One way to do this is to examine the desired functions for the total product and then select a minimum working subset. The sample strategy shown in Table 4.3 is one hypothetical way to approach the design of the change counter product defined in Appendix A. This example starts by building a small initial product with a main control loop and several functions. Then it adds enhancements to this foundation. The overall objective is to have several functional elements under development in each cycle. This approach provides each engineer with an opportunity to contribute to the product design and implementation.

In developing a strategy, you should recognize that some product elements are likely to be much larger than planned. Thus, if you attempt to include too much function in the first cycle, the work could take much longer than planned and you might not have enough time to complete the subsequent development cycles. The

TABLE 4.3 A SAMPLE CHANGE COUNTER DEVELOPMENT STRATEGY

Name _____ Date _____

Team   _Example Team B Data_____ Instructor _____

Part/Level _Change Counter/System_____ Cycle   _1_____

Reference	Functions	Cycle LOC			Cycle Hours		
		1	2	3	1	2	3
1.1	Compare modified program with prior version		X				
1.2	Identify added and deleted LOC		180			18	
1.3	Count added and deleted LOC			100			10
1.4	Count total LOC in modified program			X			
1.5	Attach line labels		50			5	
1.6	Provide change label header	50			5		
1.7	Maintain change record history in header		100			10	
1.8	Retain prior change history			X			
1.9	New program source file with change info.	120			12		
1.10	Write for one programming language	X					
1.11	Enhance to three languages						
1.12	Print program listing with change labels	50			5		
1.13	Print line numbers on listing		50	150		5	15
1.14	Print program change report			75			7.5
2.1	Count text lines with coding standard			X			
2.2	Count LOC with syntax counter						
2.3	Compare for added and deleted LOC		X				
2.4	Count changed lines as added and deleted		X				
2.5	Analyze added-deleted pairs for change LOC						
3.1	Comment header section	X					
3.2	List prior program modifications in order		X				
3.3	Count new programs as version 0		100			10	
3.4	Provide change information in label	50			5		
3.5	Provide change data in label	50			5		
3.6	For defect fixes, note fix number in label	X					
3.7	For enhancements, note project data in label	X					
4.1	Label each changed line with change number		150			15	
4.2	Retain deleted line in comment			150			15
4.3	Note previously deleted and added lines			50			5
4.4	Insert line numbers before listing lines						
4.5s1	Where lines too long, roll to next line		50			5	
4.5s2	Retain LOC count when rolling lines			150			15
4.6	Retain original program indenting						
4.7	Indent rolled lines to middle of listing		X				
	System control and overhead	185	50	100	18.5	5	10
Totals		505	730	775	50.5	73	77.5

key is to produce a minimum workable product that you can test and demonstrate even if it does not have the full function defined in Appendix A. Only then should you worry about adding functions to achieve the capabilities given in Appendix A.

Although your team can select any method for developing the strategy, it is usually a good idea to have the development manager propose an initial strategy and conceptual design. Then have the team review it. If other team members also wish to make proposals, they should do so. Then evaluate the proposed strategies and either select one or combine and adjust them to produce one that is acceptable to the team.

Produce the Preliminary Size Estimate

In producing the strategy, you must estimate how many LOC each proposed function in the conceptual design will likely require. These estimates are necessarily hypothetical because you have not yet decided how to build the product. However, they give you a base for judging which functions you can implement in the available time.

After postulating the likely functions and components, consider each program element and judge how many new and changed LOC will likely be needed. Then record the estimates on the STRAT form as shown in the example in Table 4.3. With each subsequent development cycle, reassess this strategy and the size and time estimates. You will learn a great deal from cycle 1, so the cycle 2 and cycle 3 estimates can then be more accurate. For every cycle, however, consider all the functions for the full product. Then you will know what is coming and can make provisions in your initial designs for these subsequent enhancements.

Produce the Preliminary Time Estimate

Next, using the estimated program size and an LOC-per-hour rate, estimate how long it is likely to take to develop each function. Until you have better data, you should use your PSP course experience. When working on components for large products, however, we have found that engineers should use somewhat lower LOC/hour rates than the rates they achieved with the PSP course exercises. Typical experience has been around 50% of the course rate (or a little higher). Lower rates generally apply when the new and changed LOC are small parts of larger programs. The smaller the new code is relative to the existing base program, the lower your productivity is likely to be.

The second and third cycles add functional enhancements. In developing each component, consider the enhancements that you will add later. For example, when designing the control logic, consider but don't implement the entire logic flow of the ultimate product. Then small additions will likely suffice for the later cycles.

Similarly, the file-management routines must ultimately handle multiple files, must rewrite files, must produce new files, and so forth. Also, when you design the LOC counter remember that its future use will be to count both entire programs and small program fragments.

Assess Risks

The team leader next guides the team in identifying and assessing the principal project risks. After you and your teammates suggest the risks you think could be significant, judge which ones are most likely and which ones could have the greatest schedule impact. Do this by rating each risk according to its likelihood of occurrence and impact. The ratings are H (high), M (medium), or L (low). Assign any risks that are not LL (for low likelihood and low impact) to a team member to track. Discuss these risks in the weekly team meeting and consider how to mitigate any significant risks before they occur. Enter the data on each risk in the ITL form.

Document the Strategy

At the end of each strategy-development step, use the STRAT form (as in Table 4.3) to document the strategy. Following the STRAT form instructions in Table 4.4, list each need statement function in Appendix A down the side of the form. Next, enter the development cycle in which you intend to incorporate this function. Note that at the bottom of this list, the main control function is included even though it does not show up in the need statement. This is because this function manages program operation but does not directly supply user function. Depending on your strategy, you may wish to include other system-related functions that are not covered by the need statement.

Update the Development Strategy

For subsequent development cycles, update the strategy using script STRATn. Enter the names and sizes of the components already developed and the functions they cover. Then define the functions to be added for the next development cycle, describe how these functions are to be allocated among the existing modules, and define any new modules that are needed and their functions. Next, estimate the sizes of these additions and check that they are not too large to develop in the time available. Also, seek a balanced workload in which every team member has a roughly equal opportunity to contribute to the overall project.

TABLE 4.4 TSPi STRATEGY FORM INSTRUCTIONS: FORM STRAT

Purpose	• This form is used to record strategic decisions. • It is used during strategy development to allocate product functions to cycles. • It is also used during high-level design to allocate SRS functions to components.
General	• This form suggests a way to record strategic decisions. • Use it or any other format that contains the same data.
Header	• Enter your name, date, team name, and instructor's name. • Name the part or assembly and its level. • Enter the cycle number.
Reference	• Use this column to list the need statement or SRS paragraph or sentence number for every function.
Functions	• In this column, list all the functions to be included in the product in all cycles.
Cycle LOC	• Use these columns for the estimated LOC for each function. • Enter the LOC estimated for each function under the number of the cycle that will include that function. • If you plan to implement a function partially in two or even three of the cycles, enter the estimated new and changed LOC for each cycle. • If one function is included in another function's LOC, mark it with an X.
Cycle Hours	• Use these columns for the estimated time required to develop each function. • Enter the time estimated for each function under the number of the cycle in which you plan to include that function. • If you plan to implement a function partially in two or even three of the cycles, enter the estimated development time for each cycle. • If one function is included in another function's hours, mark it with an X.

Produce the Configuration Management Plan

When teams do not use adequate configuration management procedures, they often don't know which modules have been fixed, enhanced, or tested. They build products with the wrong or missing functions, and they do not know which tests have been run or which defects have been fixed. The time lost because of these problems is truly wasted because you must then reconstruct work that you have already completed. These problems are particularly troublesome because, when you have them, you are usually almost finished with development and have little or no time to recover.

The configuration management process has several key functions. It must record the following.

1. Copies of each version of each product element
2. A record of all changes made to every baseline
3. Who made the change
4. When they made the change
5. What the change was
6. Why they made the change

Although this may sound like a lot of detail, with a simple procedure you can complete these steps in a few moments. Then the team members will always know how to find the official version of any program or program element. You will also know what changes have been made, when, and why. With complete backups and change records, you can always back any troublesome change out of the product if necessary.

The support manager produces the configuration management plan and reviews it with the team. This plan can be relatively simple as long as all the engineers agree to follow it. If there is any chance that one or more engineers will not rigorously follow these procedures, you must make the procedures more elaborate. TSPi assumes that all engineers will follow the configuration management procedures and that automated protections are not needed.

After the support manager drafts the configuration management plan, the entire team should review it and agree that it is appropriate and will be used. While doing this, resolve any identified problems and update the configuration management plan as needed. Then put the configuration management plan itself under configuration control. Appendix B includes a more comprehensive discussion of the configuration management process.

Exit Criteria

At the end of strategy development, the team should ensure that all the specified products have been produced, that the strategy is complete, and that it is documented. Also document, review, and baseline the configuration management process. As a final step, check that all the data are recorded in the time logs and on the STRAT form. Then have the support manager put copies of all these materials in the project notebook.

4.7 Summary

This chapter describes what a strategy is and how to develop one. The STRAT1 and STRATn scripts describe the steps of the TSPi strategy process.

Following the STRAT1 or STRATn script, teams agree on strategy criteria and then produce or update their strategies. The strategy objective is to produce a quality product with the required functions in the available time. It is also important to have a modular design with separable elements that each engineer can develop. Teams should start by first producing a small running product of high quality. Then they should enhance this product to produce the desired final functions. When developing the strategy, you should start with a conceptual design and then make size and development time estimates. If the total time is more than you have available, reassess the strategy and consider reducing the product's functional content.

Whenever several people cooperate in developing a single program, there are always coordination problems. The larger the team and the more complex the product, the more likely you are to have problems. This is why TSPi requires that you develop and use a configuration management process.

5

The Development Plan

This chapter describes what plans are, why plans are needed, what a balanced plan is, and how a balanced plan will help your team. It also discusses the TSPi support tool and explains how to use it to plan and track your work. After describing the rationale for planning and the overall planning approach, the chapter walks you through the steps of the PLAN1 script. This is followed by a discussion of how to track progress against your plan. The final section describes quality planning and quality measures and discusses how they can help you to do consistently high-quality work.

5.1   The Need for Planning

Depending on the context, plans can be simple or complex. The complexity of a plan is governed largely by the complexity of the work you are planning to do. Not surprisingly, large and complex projects often require large and complex plans. It should also be no surprise that planning such large projects can take a lot of time. For TSPi, your plans can be quite simple, but they follow the same methods used with industrial TSP projects. Although you need only a few hours to produce a TSPi plan, planning still involves considerable work.

Why Make Plans?

There are several reasons to make plans. First, when you have a detailed plan, you can work more efficiently. After you have thought through the work, you know what to do and when to do it. Think of the planning process as designing the way you will do the job. Just as in programming, the plan (or design) provides the framework and context for doing the work.

When people don't plan, they often do things in an unproductive order, waste time replanning at every step, or overlook important tasks. Much like a shopping list, the plan doesn't contain anything you don't already know, but it helps you do the work in a rational order. It also reminds you to do tasks you might otherwise forget.

When you plan, you are more likely to meet your commitments. Because you must finish this course by a specific date, planning is particularly important for you. With a firm schedule and fixed resources, your only flexibility is to increase or reduce the amount of work you plan to do. This means that you will have to adjust the amount of function you will put into the product. Because you will make these decisions during planning, the quality of your plan will have a major impact on the success of your project.

The essence of teamwork is support and cooperation, and meeting commitments to your teammates is an important part of being cooperative. With a sound plan, you will know what you can do and when you are likely to finish. Your commitments will be realistic, and your teammates will be able to rely on you to do what you say.

With a plan, you also do better work. Under schedule pressure, engineers are likely to skip a review or rush through an inspection. Because the defects missed in these superficial reviews and inspections must be found in testing, it generally delays the project and results in poor-quality products. With a realistic plan, you will do better work.

Balanced Plans

One of the principal causes of scheduling problems is an unbalanced workload, in which some engineers have much more work to do than others. In this situation, the few overcommitted engineers often delay the entire team. A plan is balanced when all the engineers complete their planned tasks in the proper order and at roughly the same time. With a balanced plan, no one needs to wait for anyone else, and everyone is fully utilized. Because it produces the shortest possible schedule, you obviously want a balanced plan. The engineers who do the work must balance the plan, however, because they are the only ones who can plan in enough detail.

Tracking Progress Against the Plan

A detailed plan helps you track and manage your work. In developing software, there are many different kinds of tasks. In addition to designing and coding, you analyze requirements, review and inspect products, and write documents. You also develop test plans, run tests, and report on your work. These and many other tasks are needed, and all of them contribute to producing the final product.

Because you are likely to finish at least some of these tasks in a different order than planned, you need a way to tell whether you are ahead of or behind schedule, and by how much. With TSPi, the principal project-tracking measures are planned value (PV) and earned value (EV). These measures provide a way to determine the schedule contribution of each task. Then you can give yourself credit for all the tasks you have completed, regardless of their order.

Table 5.1 shows the planned-value calculations for cycle 1 of a project to develop the change counter described in Appendix A. The team expected the strategy phase to take 29.5 hours, and the estimate for planning was 27.5 hours. The overall first-cycle workload was estimated at 220.5 hours, so these tasks contributed 13.38% and 12.47% to the total job and, when done, accumulated an earned value (EV) of 25.85. These tasks thus had planned values of 13.38 and 12.47, respectively. Therefore, according to this plan, when the engineers had completed the strategy and planning phases, they would have completed (13.38% + 12.47% =) 25.85% of the total cycle 1 job. During planning, we call this the planned value because this is the plan, and the value for a task is earned only when that task is completely finished. There is no partial credit for half-done tasks.

By tracking earned value against planned value, you can see where you are on a project. This knowledge helps you to manage your work precisely and also helps you to meet the schedule. As you can see from Table 5.1, calculating the PV is not hard. PV is the planned percentage of the total job that each task contributes. At any point, EV is the sum of all the PVs for the tasks that have been completed at that point. In TSPi, the planned-value and earned-value numbers are completed for you by the TSPi support tool. You can find a more detailed discussion of the earned-value method in Chapter 6 of *A Discipline for Software Engineering* [Humphrey 95].

Planning in Detail

One reason to make a plan is to track the progress of your work. As an example of why detailed plans are important, suppose you estimated a development job to take 250 hours but did not estimate in any greater detail. Even if the 250-hour estimate was accurate, you would have trouble determining where you were in the job at any point. After working for 150 hours, for example, you might feel you were more

TABLE 5.1 SAMPLE PLANNED-VALUE CALCULATIONS

Task	Plan Hours	Cumulative Hours	Plan Value (PV)	Cumulative PV
Launch and strategy	29.5	29.5	13.38	13.38
Planning	27.5	57.0	12.47	25.85
Requirements	17.0	74.0	7.71	33.56
System test plan	2.5	76.5	1.13	34.69
Requirements inspection	2.0	78.5	.91	35.60
High-level design	43.0	121.5	19.50	55.10
Integration test plan	2.0	123.5	.91	56.01
HLD inspection	5.0	128.5	2.27	58.28
Detailed design	14.0	142.5	6.35	64.63
Detailed design review	3.0	145.5	1.36	65.99
Test development	6.5	152.0	2.94	68.93
Detailed design inspection	2.5	154.5	1.13	70.07
Code	15.0	169.5	6.80	76.87
Code review	6.5	176.0	2.94	79.82
Compile	2.5	178.5	1.13	80.95
Code inspection	2.5	181.0	1.13	82.09
Unit test	1.5	182.5	.68	82.77
Build and integration	5.5	188.0	2.49	85.26
System Test	6.5	194.5	2.94	88.21
Documentation	9.0	203.5	4.08	92.29
Postmortem	17.0	220.5	7.71	100.00
Total	220.5		100.00	

than half finished but could not tell precisely. The problem is that the smallest planning increment is 250 hours. If, as with TSPi, you planned in 10-hour or smaller chunks, your uncertainty about job status would be at most 10 hours. Thus, by estimating precisely, you could accurately know the job's status.

This is why the TSPi process requires that teams estimate tasks to a granularity of about 10 or fewer hours. This level of granularity, however, is needed only at the engineer level. For the requirements and high-level design work, for example, even though many of the tasks take longer than 10 hours, they are performed by several engineers. Thus, if five engineers plan to spend four hours in a planning meeting, the total would be 20 task hours. Because each engineer would be spending only four hours, however, this task need not be broken into smaller increments. If, however, the team planned to spend 80 hours on this work, it would average to 16 hours per engineer. Tasks of this size should be broken into two or more pieces.

For tasks such as writing small programs, the TSPi uses the same project plan summary form (SUMP) that is used for planning the overall team project. In the planning phase, you make a preliminary plan for each of the program modules. Then, during implementation planning, you can make more accurate plans, again using the SUMP form. At the same time, you can also remake the quality plan using the SUMQ form, which is discussed later in this chapter.

For nonprogramming tasks that are estimated to take more than about 10 hours, TSPi provides the SUMTASK form. This form is much like the PSP project plan summary, but it is designed for general tasks such as writing documents, defining processes, or making test plans. Copies of this form and its instructions are in Appendix F.

Handling Unplanned Tasks

Unless you are doing a job that is similar to one you have done before, you will probably run into tasks you did not anticipate. If these are major tasks that affect the overall schedule, you should make a new plan. When you have a well-defined process, however, most of these unanticipated tasks will be quite small, and re-planning the project would take more time than the tasks themselves. Without a plan, however, you would have to spend at least some time on unplanned tasks, and these tasks would not generate any EV.

Until you have completed one or more development cycles, therefore, you should allow a small amount of time each week for unplanned work. This is the reason that the TSPi provides a phase when you can record time spent on "management and miscellaneous" (M&M) tasks. In planning the first cycle, I suggest that you allow 5 to 10 percent of your total project time for tasks that you cannot anticipate. One way to do this is to insert occasional two-hour M&M tasks into your task plan. Then, whenever you encounter an unplanned task you can earn value for the M&M tasks. After the first cycle, you should understand the process well enough so that you can identify many of the M&M tasks and won't need to make an allowance for them.

Estimating Level

With the PSP, engineers estimate programs by first identifying the objects or functions they contain and then estimating the sizes of these objects or functions. Then, using the PSP estimating methods, they estimate the program's new and changed

LOC. From that point, they make the time and defect estimates for the total program and not for its objects or functions. With TSPi, you do the same thing: estimate size at a low level of detail and then estimate time and defects at the next higher level. Thus, when planning at the system level, you estimate the sizes of the system's parts and then add the part LOC to get system LOC, which you then use for estimating overall development time and defects.

For the programs developed for this course, there are typically only three levels: the system, the modules or system components, and the module's objects or functions. In the more general case, however, TSPi refers to *parts* and *assemblies*. Thus, a module-sized program is considered a part as well as an assembly of its lower-level parts, or objects. When a program has several parts, it is called an assembly. Similarly, as shown in Figure 5.1, assemblies can also be parts. For example, a system might be an assembly of components, with each component an assembly of modules. We use this assembly/part terminology so that the same

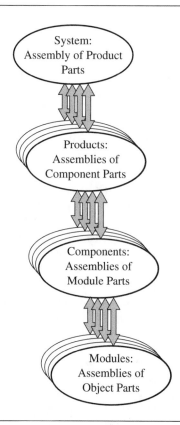

FIGURE 5.1 PARTS AND ASSEMBLIES

TSPi process and tool can be used for any program, whether it is a system, a product, a component, or a module.

Because projects developed with the TSPi typically have only two assembly levels, you should make the system plan by estimating the sizes of the module-level parts. However, because you will make this plan before completing the high-level design, you will not yet know which modules the system will contain. This is the reason for starting with a conceptual design.

Implementation Planning

At the beginning of a project, you know rather little about the intended product. Because you need a plan, however, start by postulating the product you will build. This is the conceptual design that you produced during the strategy phase. At that time, you also decided which parts of this conceptual design to develop in each cycle and recorded that information on the STRAT form. Until you know more about the product, you should continue to base your planning on this conceptual design.

As development progresses, you will learn a great deal about the intended product. After completing the high-level design, for example, you will know what program parts or modules will be needed and their intended functions. You will also have a better idea of how big these modules will be. Then, in the planning step of the implementation phase, you will use PSP and TSPi planning methods to estimate the size, development time, and defects for each program module. You will then have SUMP and SUMQ plans for all the module-level assemblies. For now, however, use average data to produce the system-level SUMP and SUMQ plans.

5.2   The TSPi Planning Process

Figure 5.2 shows the steps in producing a TSPi plan. The numbered ovals represent what you do, and the rectangles show the products you produce. The following paragraphs briefly discuss these steps. There is a more detailed description of the planning process in the discussion of the development plan script later in this chapter.

Although the TSPi planning process has several steps and can seem complicated at first, each step is simple. The numbered steps in Figure 5.2 are as follows.

1. In the strategy phase, as described in Chapter 4, you produced the conceptual design. You will use this conceptual design throughout the planning process.

2. During the strategy phase, you estimated the sizes of the various parts of the conceptual design, decided which parts to develop in each cycle, and entered the information on the STRAT form.

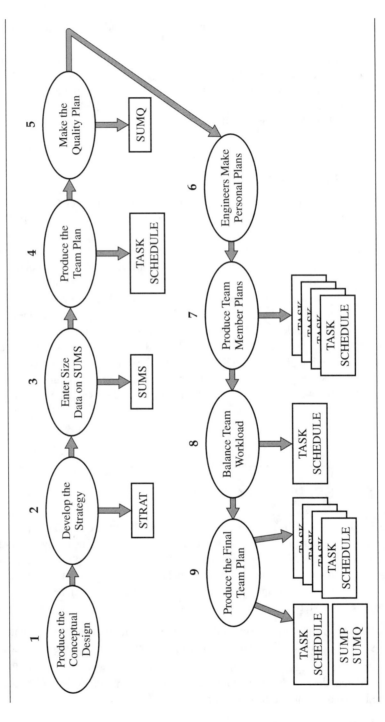

FIGURE 5.2 TSPi PLANNING OVERVIEW

3. Now, during the planning phase, you enter on the SUMS form the names and estimated sizes of the components you will develop in cycle 1. You also identify any other products you will need to develop for cycle 1, such as test plans or requirements specifications, and enter these items and their estimated sizes on the SUMS form.

4. List the tasks required to build the products identified in step 3, estimate how long each task will take, and enter this information on the TASK form. Where you can, also enter the time each engineer will spend on each task. Also, estimate how much time the full team will spend on the project each week and enter this information on the SCHEDULE form. When you are finished, use the TSPi tool to produce the TASK and SCHEDULE forms for the team. The tool will calculate the PV and expected completion date for each task.

5. Make the quality plan, SUMQ. Again, you use the TSPi support tool to do this, as explained a little later in this chapter.

6. Make copies of the team TASK and SCHEDULE forms for each engineer and have each engineer produce personal TASK and SCHEDULE forms. If you noted how many hours each engineer expected to spend on each task in step 4, this step will consist merely of each team member deleting the tasks the other engineers will do and adjusting the SCHEDULE form to reflect his or her weekly times.

7. Use the TSPi tool to generate individual TASK and SCHEDULE forms that show the PV and completion times for each of your personal tasks. Every team member should do this.

8. With the TASK and SCHEDULE forms for every engineer, you have the data to balance the team workload. Do this by identifying those engineers who will complete tasks later than desired and reassigning some of their work to other team members. Then generate new TASK and SCHEDULE forms for every engineer whose tasks were changed.

9. Use the TSPi tool to roll up the individual engineer plans to produce the final team plan. Also generate final copies of the team and engineer TASK and SCHEDULE forms as well as copies of the SUMP and SUMQ forms for the total project. Give copies of these forms to each engineer and to the instructor.

5.3 The TSPi Support Tool

The TSPi tool provided with this textbook and described on the Supplements page at the back of the book contains all the logs, forms, and templates needed for planning and tracking TSPi projects. If your team uses this tool for planning, it will automatically generate all the plan forms you need. If you use the tool to record all the actual time, size, and defect data, the tool can also generate complete project status and tracking information.

Although the TSPi tool can handle most of the mechanics of planning and tracking, it does not fully automate this work. In theory, one could develop a tool that could start with a size estimate, quality criteria, and historical data and generate a complete set of plans. Such a planning process would save time, but the team would not then understand the plan or be committed to its dates. We reject this approach because a principal reason to make a plan is to build a common team understanding of the work and a shared team commitment to the plan.

5.4   The Development Plan Scripts

The PLAN1 and PLANn scripts are shown in Tables 5.2 and 5.3. Use PLAN1 for planning the project during cycle 1, and PLANn for subsequent cycles. Although the planning process is similar in both scripts, the following paragraphs describe the PLAN1 scripts. Most of the comments also apply to the PLANn script. Figure 5.3 shows how the planning steps relate to the steps in the PLAN1 script and to the TSPi forms. The numbers in the figure relate to the step numbers in the PLAN1 script. For example, script step 2 relates to steps 2.1 and 2.2 in the figure. For a more detailed explanation of the various items in the quality plan, consult the final section of this chapter.

Entry Criteria

Before starting on the PLAN1 script, make sure that you have completed the development strategy and the conceptual design. If you have not met the PLAN1 entry criteria, stop now and correct the deficiency before proceeding. Also, if you have not finished reading this chapter, do so now.

Project Planning Step 2.1

List the products to be produced in this development cycle and estimate their sizes.   During the strategy phase described in Chapter 4, you produced the conceptual design. Now you name the system parts and estimate how big each one will likely be. You also identify any other products to be produced and estimate their sizes. Examples of these other-than-code products are requirements documents, high-level design pages, user documentation, test materials, and so forth.

TABLE 5.2 TSPi CYCLE 1 DEVELOPMENT PLAN: SCRIPT PLAN1

Purpose	**To guide a team through producing individual and team task, schedule, and quality plans for development cycle 1**
Entry Criteria	• The team has a development strategy and conceptual design. • The students have read textbook Chapter 5.
General	The task plan defines the • Time required to perform each process task • Rough order in which the tasks will be performed • Planned value of each task The schedule plan gives • Each engineer's planned time for each project week • The total planned team hours by week • The anticipated completion week for each task • The planned value for each week If the task and schedule plans indicate the project will not be completed on time, readjust the strategy and replan.

Step	Activities	Description
1	Planning Overview	The instructor describes the planning process. • The task and schedule plans and how they are produced • The quality plan and how it is produced
2	Enter the Size Estimates in Form STRAT	Starting with the conceptual design and STRAT form produced in the strategy phase, the planning manager leads the team in • Identifying any other products to be produced and their sizes • Recording the STRAT form and other size data in SUMS
3	Produce the Task Plan	The planning manager leads the team through • Producing a task list with team and engineer time estimates • Entering these data in the TASK form
4	Produce the Schedule Plan	The planning manager obtains the estimated number of hours each team member plans to spend on the project each week and • Enters the weekly hours in the SCHEDULE form • Produces the team TASK and SCHEDULE forms • Reworks the plan if the hours are inadequate
5	Produce the Quality Plan	The quality/process manager leads the team through • Reviewing the team's quality objectives • Estimating the defects injected and defect-removal yields • Generating and assessing trial SUMP and SUMQ plans • Making needed process adjustments to get a satisfactory plan
6	Produce the Individual Engineer Plans	The planning manager helps the engineers make personal plans. • Allocating the tasks among team members • Estimating the time to perform each task • Entering the data in the TASK and SCHEDULE forms • Producing the planned-value schedule and task completion dates
7	Balance Team Workload	The planning manager leads the team through • Identifying workload imbalances • Reallocating tasks to minimize the schedule • Producing balanced engineer plans • Producing the consolidation team plan (TASK, SCHEDULE, SUMP, and SUMQ forms)
Exit Criteria		• Completed team and engineer TASK and SCHEDULE forms • Completed SUMP, SUMQ, and SUMS forms • Updated project notebook

TABLE 5.3 TSPi CYCLE n DEVELOPMENT PLAN: SCRIPT PLANn

Purpose	To guide a team through producing individual and team task, schedule, and quality plans for a second or subsequent cycle
Entry Criteria	• Completed plan and actual data for the prior cycles
General	The subsequent-cycle task plans are based on • The actual tasks and times from prior cycles The schedule plan is based on • The actual hours the team members have spent on prior cycles The quality plan is based on • The team's quality criteria • The original team quality goals If the task and schedule plans indicate the cycle will not be completed on time, adjust the strategy and replan.

Step	Activities	Description
1	Planning Overview	The instructor briefly describes any problems with the prior plans and suggests how to improve the plans for this cycle.
2	Update the Size Estimates	Starting with the updated STRAT form, the planning manager leads the team through updating the product list and the size estimates. • Recording these data in the SUMS form
3	Produce the Updated Task Plan	The planning manager leads the team through • Producing a next-cycle task list with time estimates • Allocating these tasks among team members • Estimating each member's time for these tasks • Entering the data in the TASK form
4	Produce the Updated Schedule Plan	The planning manager obtains the estimated number of hours each team member plans to spend on the project each week and • Enters the weekly hours in the SCHEDULE form • Produces the overall team TASK and SCHEDULE forms • Produces a composite team planned-value schedule • Reworks the plan if the hours are inadequate
5	Produce the Updated Quality Plan	The quality/process manager leads the team through • Comparing the team's quality performance with objectives • Establishing improvement goals for the next development cycle • Estimating the defects injected and defect-removal yields • Generating and assessing trial SUMP and SUMQ plans • Making needed adjustments to get a satisfactory plan
6	Produce the Individual Engineer Plans	The planning manager helps the engineers make personal plans. • Allocating the tasks among team members • Estimating the time to perform each task • Entering the data in the TASK and SCHEDULE forms • Producing the planned-value schedule and task plans
7	Balance Team Workload	The planning manager leads the team through • Reviewing the team and individual plans • Identifying workload imbalances • Reallocating tasks to minimize the schedule • Producing balanced engineer plans • Producing the consolidated team plan (TASK, SCHEDULE, SUMP, and SUMQ forms)
Exit Criteria		• Completed team and engineers' TASK and SCHEDULE forms • Completed SUMP, SUMQ, and SUMS forms • Updated project notebook

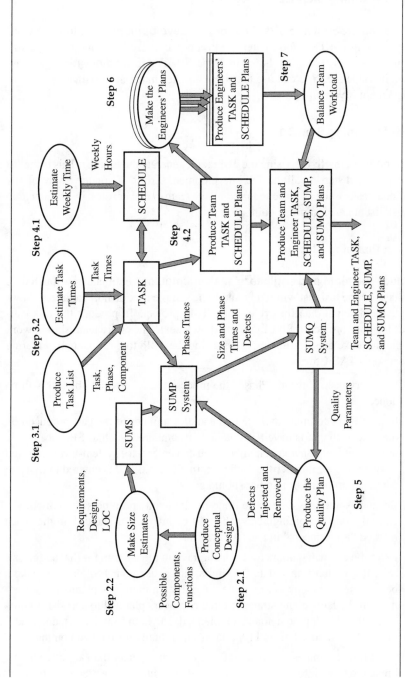

FIGURE 5.3 TSPi SYSTEM-LEVEL PLANNING

Project Planning Step 2.2

Record the product and size data for this development cycle in the SUMS form.   Using the TSPi tool, enter the product and size information in the size summary (SUMS) form, as shown in Table 5.4. The instructions for SUMS are shown in Table 5.5. You can use the size estimates made in the strategy phase or change them if you wish.

Project Planning Step 3.1

Produce the task list.   Using the TSPi tool, generate the task list. This is the list of the principal steps in all the TSPi development scripts. If you are aware of any additional tasks, such as those required by the team-member roles, insert them into the task list at an appropriate point.

Project Planning Step 3.2

Produce the team and engineers' task estimates.   Estimate how much time each task on the task list will likely take. The sample task plan in Table 5.6 shows the plan and actual data for cycle 1 of a TSPi project. To produce the task estimates for your project, follow the steps shown next. The entire team should work together to make these estimates, either using the TSPi tool or manually entering the data on a TASK form.

1. For every task, enter in "Phase" the process phase in which the task will be done.

2. In the "Part" column enter the name and/or number of the part produced by the task. If the parts have been named or numbered, such as SRS or module number, enter the name or number. You can enter **S** for system-level parts and enter a name or number for each part. In Table 5.6, a **P** is entered to indicate where a part name or number should go.

3. Because some tasks are to be done by the team and others by individuals, enter the number of engineers who will be involved in the task in the space marked "# Engineers" in the TASK form.

4. Enter the estimated hours for each engineer in the column for that engineer's role. If you don't have data for similar tasks, use your PSP data or make a best guess. For example, in Table 5.6, all team members planned to participate in the launch and strategy: three engineers planned to spend 1.3 hours each, the development manager planned 5.0 hours, and the team leader planned 2.9 hours. This is 11.8 total planned hours for the team on that task.

5. If the time estimates for some of these tasks are greater than about 10 hours, break the tasks into smaller subtasks and estimate the time required for each

TABLE 5.4 TSPi SIZE SUMMARY: FORM SUMS

Plan _____ **Assembly** _____ **Actual** __X__

Name	Example Team B Data	Date _____
Team	Change Counter/System	Instructor _1_
Part/Level		Cycle _____

Product or Part Names and/or Numbers	Size Measure	Base	Deleted	Modified	Added	Reused	New and Changed	Total	Total New Reuse
SRS	Text Pages				11		11	11	
HLD	HLD Pages				18		18	18	
Main	DLD Lines				31		31	31	
	LOC				160		160	160	
LOC	DLD Lines				16		16	16	
	LOC				12		12	12	
Compare	DLD Lines				116		116	116	
	LOC				480		480	480	
Indent	DLD Lines				102		102	102	
	LOC				182		182	182	
Output	DLD Lines				52		52	52	
	LOC				127		127	127	
Totals	Text Pages				11		11	11	
	HLD Pages				18		18	18	
	DLD Lines				317		317	317	
	LOC				961		961	961	

TABLE 5.5 TSPi SIZE SUMMARY INSTRUCTIONS: FORM SUMS

Purpose	• This form summarizes the data for product size. • At the lowest level, it summarizes all the part size data. • At higher levels, it summarizes the size data for an assembly and its parts.
General	• Use this form to hold size data for the parts of an assembly. • If you are using the TSPi tool, these data are automatically rolled up to the next-level SUMP form. • If you are not using the TSPi tool, enter the totals from this form in the appropriate places in the assembly-level SUMP form. • Note: the number of rows in this form is variable, depending on the number of products and parts.
Header	• Enter your name, date, team name, and instructor's name. • Name the part or assembly and its level. • Enter the cycle number.
Plan/Assembly/ Actual	Check whether this form is for plan, assembly, or actual data. • Plan: In system-level planning, use SUMS to hold the estimated sizes of the system and all its parts. • Assembly: Use a separate SUMS form for the estimated size data for the parts of each assembly. • Actual: Use a SUMS form for the actual size data for the parts of each assembly.
Product and Part Names	• List the name or other identification of each product or part. • It is also a good idea to number the product components, particularly if there will be very many of them. • Include system-level products such as SRS and HLD.
Size Measure	• Enter the size measures used for each product item listed.
Program Size	• For each product, enter the actual or estimated program base, deleted, added, modified, reused, and new and changed LOC.
Totals	• Enter the totals for each size category and column.

subtask. Again, look at the script for that process phase for ideas on how to do this. Note that the 10-hour guideline applies to tasks that are done by an individual engineer. For example, even though the 11.8-hour task described in step 5 was planned to take more than 10 hours, this is a shared task and need not be subdivided.

6. Enter the total time in hours for each task.

Project Planning Step 4.1

Enter the weekly hours in the SCHEDULE form.   Estimate how many hours you and your teammates will spend on the project each week. While planning in cycle 1, include hours for eight or more weeks, at least until after the first trial plan. In that way, the TSPi tool can complete the initial plan even if it takes longer than you expect.

Project Planning Step 4.2

Produce the overall team TASK and SCHEDULE forms.   After entering the weekly hours in the SCHEDULE form for the team, use the TSPi tool to calculate the planned value and anticipated completion date for each task. Without the tool, you will have to make these calculations yourself. Then generate the completed TASK and SCHEDULE forms. The SCHEDULE form for the team B example is shown in Table 5.7. As you can see in the example, the TASK and SCHEDULE forms list the weekly hours, the weekly PV, all the tasks, the task hours, the number of the week when each task is to be completed, and the PV for each task.

As a final step in completing the team's plan, check that the plan includes enough hours to produce the product in the available time. Follow these steps.

1. Total the hours that all team members plan to spend on the project during this project cycle.

2. Compare the total time from step 1 with the total time required to do all the tasks for this cycle.

3. If the task times exceed the total planned work time, there is no point in going to the next step. The job is too big for the time available.

4. If the job is too big, the choices are to work more hours or to reduce the planned work. If you decide to put in more hours, enter the new hours in the schedule template and see whether the schedule then fits the available time.

5. If you decide to reduce the amount of work, return to the strategy step and revise the functions to be implemented in this cycle. Then redo the plan.

One thing you should not do is to reduce the estimates to make them fit the available time. Initial team estimates are generally low. Although the aggregate of your initial task estimates is probably pretty accurate, you have likely overlooked some tasks. Thus, if you reduce the estimates, you can expect either to finish the project late or to work a great many more hours than planned.

After you have completed the TASK and SCHEDULE forms for the team's work for this cycle, complete the size and time portions of the SUMP form. You will need these data in the next planning step, which is to make the quality plan.

Project Planning Step 5

Produce the quality plan.   This section describes the steps involved in making the TSPi quality plan. Quality planning and the various parts of the TSPi quality

TABLE 5.6 SAMPLE TASK PLANNING TEMPLATE: FORM TASK

Name _____ Date _____

Team _____ Example Team B Data Instructor _____

Part/Level _____ Change Counter/System Cycle 1

	Task			Plan Hours							Plan Size/Value					Actual		
Phase	Part	Task Name	# Engineers	Team Leader	Development Manager	Planning Manager	Quality/Process Manager	Support Manager	Total Team Hours	Cumulative Hours	Size Units	Size	Week No.	Planned Value	Cumulative PV	Hours	Cumulative Hours	Week No.
St	S	Launch and strategy	5	2.9	5	1.3	1.3	1.3	11.8	11.8	Pages	2	1	3.4	3.4	12.3	12.3	1
Mg	S	Mgt. and misc.	5	3.0	3.0	3.0	3.0	3.0	15.0	26.8			1	4.3	7.7	10.0	22.3	1
Pl	S	Plan - task and schedule	5	4.5	4.5	9.0	4.5	4.5	27.0	53.8			2	7.7	15.4	13.3	35.6	2
Pl	S	Generate Q&T plans	5	3.5	3.5	3.5	5.0	3.5	19.0	72.8			2	5.4	20.8	9.9	45.5	2
Mg	S	Mgt. and misc.	5	3.0	3.0	3.0	3.0	3.0	15.0	87.8			3	4.3	25.1	3.4	48.9	2
Rq	S	Review need statement	5	4.0	6.5	2.0	2.0	2.0	16.5	104.3	Pages	3	3	4.7	29.9	17	65.9	2
Rq	S	Produce SRS	5	4.0	5.5		2.0	2.0	15.5	119.8	Pages	54	3	4.4	34.3	15.6	81.4	3
Rq	S	System test plan	0						0.0	119.8			3	0.0	34.3	0.0	81.4	3
Rq	S	Req. inspection	4	2.0		2.0	2.0	2.0	8.0	127.8	Pages	5	3	2.3	36.6	2.8	84.2	3
Mg	S	Mgt. and misc.	5	2.0	2.0	2.0	2.0	2.0	10.0	137.8			4	2.9	39.5	5.9	90.1	3
Hd	S	High-level design	5	2.0	3.5	1.0	2.0	1.0	9.5	147.3	Pages	10	4	2.7	42.2	16.5	106.6	4
Hd	S	SDS	5	4.0	2.0	4.0	4.0	4.0	18.0	165.3	Pages	20	4	5.2	47.3	9.5	116.1	4

		Phase															
Hd	S	Integration plan	2		2.5	2.0	2.0	4.0	169.3	Pages	10	4	1.1	48.5	4.0	120.1	4
Hd	S	HLD inspection	2.5	0.3	2.0	2.0	2.5	10.3	179.5	Lines	137	5	2.9	51.4	0.0	120.1	5
Mg	S	Mgt. and misc.	2.0	2.0	3.0	2.0	2.0	10.0	189.5			5	2.9	54.3	21.5	141.6	5
Dd	P	Detailed design	3.0	3.0	2.0		3.0	12.0	201.5	Lines	137	5	3.4	57.7	40.2	181.9	5
Dr	P	DLD review	2.0	2.0			2.0	8.0	209.5	Lines	137	5	2.3	60.0	10.5	192.4	5
Td	S	Test development			3.0	3.0	1.5	1.5	211.0			5	0.4	60.5	0.0	192.4	5
Di	P	DLD inspection	3.0	3.0	3.6	3.6	3.0	15.0	226.0	Lines	137	5	4.3	64.8	8.9	201.3	5
Cd	P	Code	3.6	3.6	3.0	3.0	3.6	18.0	244.0	LOC	410	5	5.2	69.9	8.1	209.4	5
Cr	P	Code review	3.0	3.0	3.0	3.0	3.0	15.0	259.0	LOC	410	5	4.3	74.2	7.3	216.7	5
Cp	P	Compile	0.4	0.4	0.4	0.4	0.4	2.0	261.0	LOC	410	5	0.6	74.8	1.0	217.7	5
Ci	P	Code inspection	1.0	1.0	1.0	1.0	1.0	5.0	266.0	LOC	410	5	1.4	76.2	2.7	220.4	5
UT	P	Unit test	1.5	1.5	1.5	1.5	1.5	7.5	273.5	LOC	410	5	2.1	78.4	18.7	239.1	5
Mg	S	Mgt. and misc.	4.0	4.0	4.0	4.0	4.0	20.0	293.5			6	5.7	84.1	11.2	250.3	6
St	S	Build and integration		2.0		2.0	2.0	6.0	299.5			6	1.7	85.8	1.6	251.8	6
St	S	System test	4.0	4.0		4.0	4.0	12.0	311.5	LOC	410	6	3.4	89.3	15.0	266.9	6
Dc	S	Documentation	5.0		5.0			10.0	321.5	Pages	15	6	2.9	92.1	1.6	268.4	6
Pm	S	Postmortem	2.0	2.0	2.0	2.0	2.0	10.0	331.5			6	2.9	95.0	2.0	270.4	6
Mg	S	Mgt. and misc.	5.5	3.0	3.0	3.0	3.0	17.5	349.0			6	5.0	100	9.5	280.0	6
		Totals	73.4	73.3	68.6	64.8	68.8	349					100		280		

TABLE 5.7 SAMPLE SCHEDULE PLANNING TEMPLATE: FORM SCHEDULE

Name _____   Date _____

Team   _Example Team B Data_____   Instructor _____

Part/Level   _Change Counter/System_____   Cycle ___1___

		Plan			Actual			
Week No.	Date	Direct Hours	Cumulative Hours	Cumulative Planned Value	Team Hours	Cumulative Hours	Week Earned Value	Cumulative Earned Value
1	9/14	26.8	26.8	7.7	27.0	27.0	7.7	7.7
2	9/21	56.5	83.3	20.9	44.4	71.4	22.2	29.9
3	9/28	47.0	130.3	36.6	35.8	107.2	9.6	39.5
4	10/5	47.8	178.1	48.5	64.0	171.2	9.0	48.5
5	10/12	107.0	285.1	78.4	75.4	246.6	29.9	78.4
6	10/19	63.9	349.0	100.0	33.4	280.0	21.6	100.0

plan are described in more detail later in this chapter. To make the quality plan, you should start by estimating the defects to be injected by phase. Do this for the complete product to be produced in this cycle, using the quality criteria in Table 5.8. Next, enter the yield goal for each defect-removal phase. Finally, generate a trial quality plan and see whether it meets the criteria. If it does not, make adjustments and run another trial plan. Follow these steps.

1. Estimate how many defects your team will likely inject in each phase. Base this estimate on the time spent by phase multiplied by the defect-injection rate (see Table 5.8).

2. Estimate the yield the team will achieve for each defect-removal phase. Base this number on the yield criteria in Table 5.8. For example, in the sample plan in Table 5.9, the team planned to achieve 70% yields in every review and inspection phase. When you enter the yield, the TSPi tool calculates the defects in the product at that phase and deducts the yield percentage.

3. In estimating yield for the test phases, note that test yield depends on the defect density entering the test phases. For example, with five or fewer defect/KLOC at unit test entry, unit test yield can be as high as 90%. However, when the defects/KLOC are 20 or more, unit test yields are generally less than 50%. Similarly, in build, integration, and system test, with fewer than 1.0 defects/KLOC at test entry, yields can approach 80%. With 10.0 or more defects/KLOC at integration or system test entry, however, yields can be as low as 30%. Start with the yield goals for these test phases and see whether the defects/KLOC values come out within the specified ranges. If too many defects are found, reduce the test-phase yields until the yields and defects/KLOC match the criteria.

4. Use the TSPi tool to generate a trial quality plan.

5. Compare the values in this trial quality plan with those shown in Table 5.8. If the total defects/KLOC are not within the suggested range for PSP-trained engineers, increase or decrease the development times for the design and code phases or adjust the defects injected in one or more of the phases. Continue adjusting the phase times or defect-injection rates until the total defects/KLOC is within the criteria. Note that, if you are using the TSPi tool, you must change the phase times by updating the TASK form.

6. If the defect-removal rates and review and inspection rates are not reasonably close to the criteria, adjust the time spent in the defect-removal phases or change the defect-removal yields until these values are closer to the criteria. Again, if you are using the TSPi tool, only change the phase times by adjusting the task times on the TASK form and updating the task plan.

7. If the defect ratios are low, reexamine the data to ensure that all the other criteria are met. If they are, the defect ratios should meet the criteria.

8. If the defects/KLOC numbers are too high in compile or test, check again that the total defects/KLOC value is within range. If it is, check the yields for the reviews and inspections. If they are too low, increase the yields for these phases until the defects/KLOC are proper. You may also have to increase the review or inspection times to keep the defect-removal rates within range. If the total defects/KLOC are not in range, check the other data to make sure they are correct. If they are, the defect/KLOC numbers should be close to or within range.

9. Repeat steps 4 through 8 until the quality plan meets the team objectives.

10. Use the TSPi tool to generate the final quality plan on form SUMQ.

If you are not using the TSPi support tool, you should follow the same procedure but must make all the calculations yourself. Because the time, size, and defect data for all the phases are interrelated, you should carefully check all the quality calculations to make sure that nothing was omitted or done incorrectly. For

TABLE 5.8 TSPi QUALITY CRITERIA: STANDARD QUAL

Measure	Goal	Comments
Percent Defect Free (PDF)		
Compile	> 10%	
Unit Test	> 50%	
Integration Test	> 70%	
System Test	> 90%	
Defects/KLOC		
Total defects injected	75–150	If not PSP trained, use 100–200.
Compile	< 10	All defects flagged by compiler
Unit Test	< 5	Only major defects
Build and integration	< 0.5	Only major defects
System Test	< 0.2	Only major defects
Defect Ratios		
DLD review defects/unit test defects	> 2.0	Only major defects
Code review defects/compile defects	> 2.0	Only major defects
Development Time Ratios		
Requirements inspection/requirements time	> 0.25	Include elicitation time
HLD inspection/HLD time	> 0.5	Design work only, not studies
DLD/coding time	> 1.00	
DLD review/DLD time	> 0.5	
Code review/code time	> 0.5	
Review and Inspection Rates		
Requirements pages/hour	< 2	Single-spaced text pages
HLD pages/hour	< 5	Formatted design logic
DLD text lines/hour	< 100	Pseudocode lines equal about 3 LOC each
Code LOC/hour	< 200	Logical LOC

Defect Injection Rates		
Requirements defects/hour	0.25	Only major defects
HLD defects/hour	0.25	Only major defects
DLD defects/hour	2.0	Only design defects
Code defects/hour	4.0	Only major defects
Compile defects/hour	0.3	All defects flagged by the compiler
Unit test defects/hour	0.2	Only major defects
Defect Removal Rates		
Requirements inspection defects/hour	0.5	Only major defects
HLD inspection defects/hour	0.5	Only major defects
DLD review defects/hour	2.0	Only design defects
DLD inspection defects/hour	0.5	Only design defects
Code review defects/hour	6.0	Only major defects
Code inspection defects/hour	1.0	Only major defects
Phase Yields		
Requirements inspections	~ 70%	Not counting editorial comments
Design reviews and inspections	~ 70%	Using state analysis, trace tables
Code reviews and inspections	~ 70%	Using personal checklists
Compile	~ 50%	90+ % of syntax defects
Unit test at 5 or fewer defects/KLOC	~ 90%	For high defects/KLOC: 50–75%
Build, integration, system test – at < 1.0 defects/KLOC	~ 80%	For high defects/KLOC: 30–65%
Process Yields		
Before compile	> 75%	Assuming sound design methods
Before unit test	> 85%	Assuming logic checks in reviews
Before build and integration	> 97.5%	For small products, 1 defect max.
Before system test	> 99%	For small products, 1 defect max.

TABLE 5.9 A QUALITY PLAN EXAMPLE: FORM SUMQ

Name _____ Date _____

Team ___Example Team B Data_____ Instructor _____

Part/Level ___Change Counter/System_____ Cycle ___1___

Summary Rates	Plan	Actual
LOC/hour	1.17	3.43
% Reuse (% of total LOC)	0	0
% New Reuse (% of N&C LOC)	0	0
Percent Defect-Free (PDF)		
In compile	80	20
In unit test	90	20
In build and integration	95	60
In system test	99	40
Defect/page		
Requirements inspection	1.2	0
HLD inspection	0.7	0
Defects/KLOC		
DLD review	20.2	55.2
DLD inspection	6.1	15.6
Code review	65.0	27.1
Compile	15.1	28.1
Code inspection	10.6	0
Unit test	4.1	16.6
Build and integration	0.4	6.2
System test	0.1	6.2
Total development	151.2	170.7
Defect Ratios		
Code review/Compile	4.3	0.96
DLD review/Unit test	4.9	3.31
Development time ratios (%)		
Requirements inspection/Requirements	25	9
HLD inspection/HLD	37	0
DLD/code	67	497
DLD review/DLD	67	26
Code review/code	83	91
A/FR	2.23	0.89
Review rates		
DLD lines/hour	17.1	30.0
Code LOC/hour	27.3	131.1
Inspection rates		
Requirement pages/hour	0.63	3.93
HLD pages/hour	0.98	Inf.
DLD lines/hour	9.13	35.71
Code LOC/hour	82.00	362.64

TABLE 5.9 (continued)

Name	_____	Date	_____
Team	*Example Team B Data*	Instructor	_____
Part/Level	*Change Counter/System*	Cycle	1

	Plan	Actual
Defect-injection Rates (Defects/Hr.)		
Requirements	0.25	0.00
HLD	0.25	0.00
DLD	0.75	2.11
Code	2.06	5.69
Compile	0.50	9.80
Unit test	0.00	0.32
Build and integration	0.00	0.00
System test	0.00	0.07
Defect-removal Rates (Defects/Hr.)		
Requirements inspection	0.70	0.00
HLD inspection	0.64	Inf.
DLD review	1.03	5.03
DLD inspection	0.17	1.69
Code review	1.78	3.55
Compile	3.10	26.47
Code inspection	0.87	0.00
Unit test	0.22	0.85
Build and integration	0.02	3.87
System test	0.00	0.40
Phase Yields		
Requirements inspection	70	Inf.
HLD inspection	70	Inf.
DLD review	70	58.9
Test development		
DLD inspection	70	40.5
Code review	70	40.6
Compile	50	56.3
Code inspection	70	0.0
Unit test	90	59.3
Build and integration	80	54.5
System test	80	100.0
Process Yields		
% before compile	81.3	74.1
% before unit test	97.0	86.6
% before build and integration	99.7	93.3
% before system test	99.9	96.9
% before system delivery		

further information on these calculations, see the SUMQ form instructions as well as the final section of this chapter.

Project Planning Step 6

Make individual engineer plans.   At this point, you are ready to make the detailed plans for each engineer. One approach that many teams have found to be quick and efficient is to work together to do steps 6 and 7. In essence, you start with the estimated hours for every task and the weekly hours each engineer will have available and then assign tasks to each engineer for each week, starting at the beginning of the development cycle. While assigning tasks, keep track of the hours for each engineer and, when one engineer is fully committed, assign tasks to the other engineers until they too are fully committed for that week. Then move to the next week. If you assign the tasks in this way, the engineers' personal plans will be balanced when first produced. The procedure for doing this is explained more fully in Chapter 13.

After you have assigned tasks to all the engineers, give them copies of the team TASK and SCHEDULE forms and have them eliminate all the hours for tasks the other engineers will do. Then they should add any times for role activities that are not already covered, using the M&M process phase if no other phase is appropriate. Also, have each engineer adjust the schedule template times to reflect the weekly hours he or she plans to spend on the project. Finally, use the TSPi tool to generate a TASK and SCHEDULE form for each engineer.

Project Planning Step 7

Balance team workload.   When you and your teammates have completed personal TASK and SCHEDULE forms, check to see whether the workload is balanced. The first step is to see whether any engineer's tasks run beyond the desired schedule. If they do, find other engineers whose plans finish early. To balance the workload, reassign tasks from the engineers who plan to finish late to those who plan to finish early. This reassignment might involve splitting some tasks into multiple parts so that two or more engineers can share the work. If you need to adjust any tasks, return to step 3.1 and redefine them. Also, remember that if you are using the TSPi tool and change the task times, you must update these times on the TASK form. These changes will then also change the SUMP and SUMQ forms.

Final Planning Step

Produce and distribute the plans.   When the engineers' plans are balanced, the final planning step is to produce the consolidated team plan: the team-level plan summary (SUMP), the team-level quality plan (SUMQ), and TASK and

SCHEDULE forms for the team and for each engineer. These plans show the product plan data for time, size, and defects; the team's weekly planned value; the weekly task hours; the planned time for each task; and the time when each task is to be completed. A copy of a student team's SUMP plan is shown in Table 5.10. The SUMP instructions are in Table 5.11.

Note that in SUMP, the planned values for defects removed are fractional because, in calculating defect values, the TSPi tool uses yield to calculate the numbers of defects removed by phase. Because this is a plan, however, it calculates fractional defect values and uses these fractions in the defects/KLOC calculations. Although the actual defect numbers will always be integers, fractional values are useful because they indicate the likelihood of finding defects in a given process phase. This indication is particularly useful for small products such as those produced with TSPi.

Exit Criteria

The exit criteria for the PLAN1 and PLANn scripts require completed TASK and SCHEDULE forms for the team and for each engineer. These plans must be balanced and must show that the work can be completed in the available schedule. You also need the size summary (SUMS), a summary plan (SUMP), and a quality plan (SUMQ) for the total cycle product. You must also put copies of all these materials in the project notebook (described in Chapter 3 and in the notebook specification in Appendix G).

5.5 Tracking the Work

The reason to track a project is to determine the status and quality of the work. On industrial projects, engineers must periodically report to management on whether they are on schedule and when they expect to finish. With TSPi, you also need to track the work. This practice helps you manage your personal work and allows the team leader to report weekly status to the instructor.

Figure 5.4 shows the TSPi project tracking process. Although the figure looks complex, most of the steps are handled automatically by the TSPi tool. All you need to do is to enter the data indicated in the ovals. By comparing Figures 5.3 and 5.4, you can see that project planning and project tracking are quite different processes. As before, the ovals represent things you do and the rectangles are for steps the TSPi tool can do for you. Note that if you do not use the TSPi tool, you will follow exactly the same steps but make all the calculations and complete all the forms by hand. The steps in the project tracking process are as follows.

TABLE 5.10 SAMPLE TSPi PLAN SUMMARY: FORM SUMP

Name		Date	
Team	Example Team B Data	Instructor	
Part/Level	Change Counter/System	Cycle	1

Product Size	Plan	Actual
Requirements pages (SRS)	5	11
Other text pages		
High-level design pages (SDS)	10	18
Detailed design lines	137	316
Base LOC (B) (measured)		
Deleted LOC (D)	(Estimated)	(Counted)
Modified LOC (M)	(Estimated)	(Counted)
Added LOC (A)	410	961
Reused LOC (R)	(N–M)	(T–B+D–R)
Total New and Changed LOC (N)	(Estimated)	(Counted)
	410	961
Total LOC (T)	(Estimated)	(A+M)
	410	961
Total New Reuse LOC	(N+B–M–D+R)	(Measured)
Estimated Object LOC (E)		
Upper Prediction Interval (70%)		
Lower Prediction Interval (70%)		

Time in Phase (hours)	Plan	Actual	Actual %
Management and miscellaneous	87.5	61.5	21.95
Launch	11.8	12.3	4.39
Strategy and planning	46.0	23.2	8.29
Requirements	32.0	32.6	11.64
System test plan			
Requirements inspection	8.0	2.8	1.00
High-level design	27.5	26.0	9.29
Integration test plan	4.0	4.0	1.43
High-level design inspection	10.2		
Implementation planning			
Detailed design	12.0	40.3	14.39
Detailed design review	8.0	10.6	3.79
Test development	1.5		
Detailed design inspection	15.0	8.9	3.18
Code	18.0	8.0	2.86
Code review	15.0	7.3	2.61
Compile	2.0	1.0	0.36
Code inspection	5.0	2.7	0.96
Unit test	7.5	18.7	6.68
Build and integration	6.0	1.5	0.54
System test	12.0	15.0	5.36
Documentation	10.0	1.6	0.57

TABLE 5.10 (continued)

Name _____ Date _____

Team _____Example Team B Data_____ Instructor _____

Part/Level ___Change Counter/System___ Cycle ____1____

Time in Phase (hours)	Plan	Actual	Actual %
Postmortem	10.0	2.0	0.71
Total	349.0	280.0	
Total Time UPI (70%)			
Total Time LPI (70%)			
Defects Injected	**Plan**	**Actual**	**Actual %**
Strategy and planning			
Requirements	8		
System test plan			
Requirements inspection			
High-level design	7		
Integration test plan			
High-level design inspection			
Detailed design	9	85	51.81
Detailed design review		9	5.49
Test development			
Detailed design inspection			
Code	37	46	28.04
Code review		7	4.29
Compile	1	10	6.10
Code inspection			
Unit test		6	3.66
Build and integration			
System test		1	0.61
Total Development	62	164	
Defects Removed	**Plan**	**Actual**	**Actual %**
Strategy and planning			
Requirements			
System test plan			
Requirements inspection	5.60		
High-level design			
Integration test plan			
High-level design inspection	6.58		
Detailed design		4	2.44
Detailed design review	8.27	53	32.31
Test development			
Detailed design inspection	2.48	15	9.15
Code		11	6.71
Code review	26.65	26	15.85
Compile	6.21	27	16.46
Code inspection	4.35		
Unit test	1.68	16	9.76
Build and integration	0.15	6	3.66
System test	0.03	6	3.66
Total Development	62.00	164	

TABLE 5.11 TSPi PLAN SUMMARY INSTRUCTIONS: FORM SUMP

Purpose	• This form holds plan and actual data for program assemblies.
General	• An assembly could be a system with multiple products, a product with multiple components, or a component with multiple modules. • A part could be an object, module, component, or product. • Note: the lowest-level assemblies or modules typically have no system-level data, such as requirements, high-level design, or system test.
Using the TSPi Tool	When using the TSPi tool, the plan values are automatically generated. • The time and size data are computed from the TASK and SUMS forms. • The defect values are automatically generated during the quality planning process (SUMQ). The actual values are also automatically generated by the TSPi tool. • Time and size values come from the LOGT, TASK, and SUMS forms. • Defect data come from the LOGD forms. When not using the TSPi tool, follow the instructions below.
Header	• Enter your name, date, team name, and instructor's name. • Name the assembly and its level. • Enter the cycle number.
Columns	• Plan: This column holds the part or assembly plan data. • Actual: For assemblies, this column holds the sum of the actual data for the parts of the assembly (at the lowest level, the modules).
Product Size	• For text and designs, enter only the new and changed size data. • For program parts or assemblies, enter all the indicated LOC data. • Obtain the data from the SUMS form.
Time in Phase	• Enter estimated and actual time by phase. • At the lowest level, obtain these data from the TASK forms. • For higher-level assemblies, obtain the part-level time data from the totals on the SUMT form and the assembly-level data from the assembly-level TASK form. • For example, HLD time would come from the assembly TASK form and total module unit test time would come from the SUMT form. • Actual %: Enter the percent of the actual development time by phase.
Defects Injected	• Enter estimated and actual defects injected by phase. • Enter the defect estimates while producing the quality plan. • For modules, obtain actual data from the LOGD forms for those modules. • For assemblies, get module-level defect data from the totals of the SUMDI form and assembly-level data from the assembly LOGD form. • For example, HLD defects would come from the assembly LODG form and the total module coding defects would come from the SUMDI form. • Actual %: Enter the percent of the actual defects injected by phase.
Defects Removed	• Enter estimated and actual defects removed by phase. • Enter the defect estimates while producing the quality plan. • For modules, obtain actual data from the LOGD forms for those modules. • For assemblies, obtain module-level defect data from the totals of the SUMDR form and assembly-level data from the assembly LOGD form. • For example, HLD review defects would come from the assembly LOGD form and the total module code review defects would come from the SUMDR form. • Actual %: Enter the percent of the actual defects removed by phase.

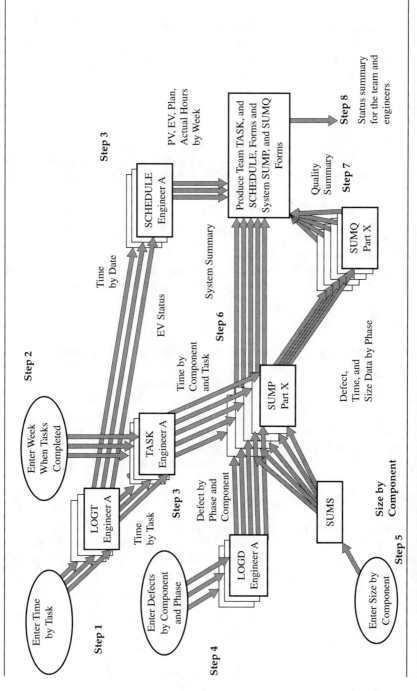

FIGURE 5.4 THE TSPi PROJECT TRACKING PROCESS

Project Tracking Step 1

Record time in the time recording log (LOGT).   As you track time in the time recording log, the data are used to automatically update the actual task times in your personal TASK form and the actual weekly times in your personal SCHEDULE form.

Project Tracking Step 2

Enter the week when tasks are completed.   Whenever you complete a task, enter the week number in the TASK form. The TSPi tool then automatically includes this task in the earned-value total for that week.

Project Tracking Step 3

Generate the TASK and SCHEDULE data.   You can now use the TSPi tool to generate the updated TASK and SCHEDULE templates showing the actual task times, weekly hours, and EV status of your work. Then enter these and any other needed data on the WEEK form and give a copy to the planning manager.

Project Tracking Step 4

Enter defects in the defect recording log (LOGD).   As you record defects in the defect recording log, the TSPi tool automatically enters these data in the SUMP form for the phases and parts in which the defects were injected and removed. These data are also totaled and included in the SUMP forms for the higher-level assemblies. The TSPi tool also retains the defect type and fix time data for later analysis. Note, however, that the inspection defect data in form INS are not automatically picked up by the TSPi tool. The product owner must enter each of these defects in the TSPi tool (form LOGD) during the inspection meeting.

Project Tracking Step 5

Enter size by component.   After you have developed a product element, enter its size in the SUMS form for that part. This includes, for example, the requirements and high-level design pages, the detailed design text lines, and the source code LOC. Whenever you change the size of a product or part, be sure to update its size data in form SUMS. The TSPi tool then uses these data to complete the SUMP and SUMQ entries.

Project Tracking Step 6

Update the SUMP form.   As the work progresses, the TSPi tool automatically updates the SUMP forms with the engineers' time, size, and defect data. The tool maintains a separate SUMP form for each assembly and totals the times for all engineers for each phase and assembly.

Project Tracking Step 7

Generate the SUMQ form.   With the time, size, and defect data, the TSPi tool can automatically generate a copy of SUMQ for each assembly.

Project Tracking Step 8

Produce the consolidated team status summary.   Every week, after preparing your personal weekly report, provide a current electronic copy of your entire TSPi workbook to the planning manager. After all these workbooks are turned in, the planning manager can consolidate them automatically to produce the updated team TASK and SCHEDULE forms. Then the planning manager can complete the WEEK form for the team.

   The team's status summary consists of updated TASK and SCHEDULE templates and SUMP and SUMQ forms with plan and actual data. SUMP and SUMQ forms are generated for every assembly, and TASK and SCHEDULE templates are generated for the team and for each engineer. The assembly-level SUMP form contains the data for generating the assembly-level SUMQ form.

   If you are not using the TSPi tool, additional forms are provided for generating the assembly SUMP from all their part SUMP forms. These forms are a time summary form (SUMT), a defects injected summary form (SUMDI), and a defects removed summary form (SUMDR). These forms hold the consolidated time, size, and defect data for all the parts in the assembly. The totals on these forms are used to complete the assembly-level SUMP form. Copies of the SUMDI, SUMDR, and SUMT forms are given in Appendix F.

   TSPi also includes a weekly reporting script (WEEK) and a weekly reporting form (also WEEK) that each engineer uses to report to the team and the team uses to report to the instructor every week. This reporting process is discussed in Chapters 3 and 11 and described in the WEEK script and WEEK form instructions in Appendixes D and F.

5.6   The Quality Plan

The quality plan (SUMQ), an example of which is shown in Table 5.9, gives the quality performance for every assembly in the system. The quality plan has the following sections:

☐ Summary rates

☐ Percent defect-free (PDF)

- ☐ Defects per page
- ☐ Defects per KLOC
- ☐ Defect ratios
- ☐ Development time ratios
- ☐ A/FR
- ☐ Review rates
- ☐ Inspection rates
- ☐ Defect injection rates
- ☐ Defect removal rates
- ☐ Phase yields
- ☐ Process yields

The earlier discussion of the PLAN1 script describes how to produce the quality plan. Here we discuss the quality plan contents and the criteria for a good quality plan. The sample SUMQ form in Table 5.9 shows the plan and actual quality data for a student team. This is the same project that was used for the sample SUMP, TASK, and SCHEDULE forms in Tables 5.6, 5.7, and 5.10.

Summary Rates

The three summary measures provide an overall perspective on process quality. *LOC/hour* measures the team's overall productivity; a higher number indicates higher productivity and lower costs. The *% reuse* measures the percent of the total LOC of this product that were reused from previously developed products. For a program with 350 total LOC, 10% reuse would mean that 35 LOC were reused. Similarly, *% new reuse* measures the contribution of this cycle to the productivity improvement of future cycles or projects. For example, a figure of 25% new reuse would mean that 25% of the new and changed LOC developed for this project have been added to the reuse library and can be used by other projects or in later development cycles.

Percent Defect-Free

PDF measures the percent of a product's components that had no defects in any given phase. For example, if an assembly had five parts and four of them had compile defects in cycle 1, the assembly would be 20% defect-free in compile. This is true regardless of the number of compile defects in each part. Similarly, if only two of the five parts had defects in integration test, the assembly would be 60% defect-free in integration test.

Clearly, the larger the assembly and the smaller its parts, the more parts there will be. Also, the larger the number of parts, the more accurately PDF will measure the quality of the assembly. With 100 parts, for example, a single defect in one part in one phase would give a 99% PDF value for that phase. Conversely, with a one-part product, any single defect in a phase would result in a zero PDF for that phase.

PDF data provide an early indication of quality problems. For example, if PDF is not steadily increasing, look for the parts that continue to have large numbers of defects. These parts will likely have the most defects in future phases. Although the PDF measure can indicate the presence of a quality problem, it cannot identify the parts that are the source of the problem. For that, you must look more deeply at the part data.

With PDF data on all defect-removal phases, you can see how quality improves throughout the development process. High-quality products should have steadily improving PDF numbers that look like those shown for the A product in Figure 5.5. This TSP team produced a high-quality product that has subsequently had no defects in several months of customer use. Conversely, the B product shown in Figure 5.5 did not show a continuously increasing PDF value and did not reach a high final value. To produce high-quality products, strive for a PDF curve that looks more like the A product in Figure 5.5. PDF should steadily increase and should reach or exceed 90% in system test.

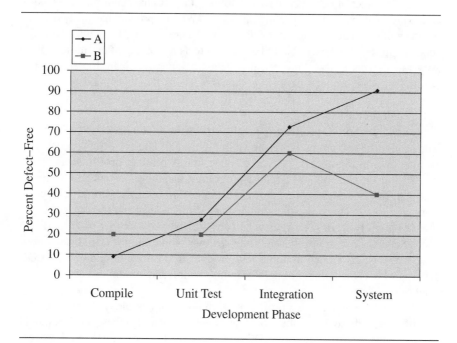

FIGURE 5.5 PERCENT DEFECT-FREE

Defects Per Page

The defects per page measure shows the average number of defects removed from each page of the requirements and HLD (high-level design) documents. Although these data vary widely among teams, most groups are surprised by how many defects they can find and fix in these early development stages.

Defects/KLOC

In any discussion of defects, there is often confusion about precisely what is meant. First, a *defect* is any requirements, design, or implementation element that, if not changed, could cause improper design, implementation, test, use, or maintenance of the product. Also, as in the PSP, in the TSPi we are principally concerned with major defects. A *major* defect is any problem that, when fixed, would change the executable program. Thus, defects in comments or formatting generally should be considered *minor.* Some other defect categories could also be classed as minor, such as questions of programming style or standards, but if the changes to fix these problems modify the executable code in any way they are major defects. Even if the program would run properly without the change, if the executable code is changed, the defect must be classed as major.

The number of defects per KLOC found in a test phase indicates the quality of the product entering and leaving that phase. When a product has many defects, testing will find many of them but will also miss a great many. Thus, with many defects in unit test, there will likely be many defects remaining after unit test. With very few defects in test, however, products are generally clean. Experience has shown that when products have fewer than 0.5 defects/KLOC in build and integration test and fewer than 0.2 defects/KLOC in system test, they generally have no defects left for the users to find.

A defects/KLOC profile graphically shows the defect history of a program. The profiles of two products are shown in Figure 5.6. These are the products that were shown in Figure 5.5. As you can see, the A product profile steadily declined after the code review. Because program A had more defects/KLOC in unit test than in the design review, however, the design reviews were probably not done very well. The B product defects/KLOC declined from the outset but increased slightly from code review to compile. This shows that product B had more defects in compile than in code reviews, something that indicates poor code reviews. As shown in Table 5.9, product B's overall high defects/KLOC level as well as the number of defects in integration and system test also indicate quality problems.

By looking at the defect profiles of each program module, you can generally identify the likely source of the problems. Note, however, that these profiles should use the same size measure in KLOC as the divisor for the defects in all process phases.

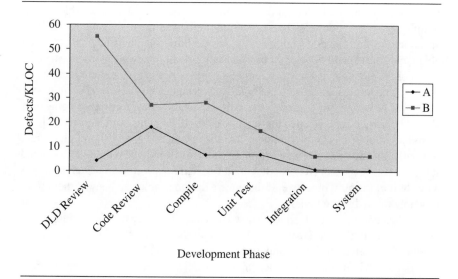

FIGURE 5.6 THE DEFECT PROFILE

Defect Ratios

Defect ratios provide insight into the quality of the design and code reviews. For example, experience shows that when engineers find twice as many defects in a code review as they find in compiling, they have generally done a good code review. This would give a code review/compile defect ratio of 2.0. As you can see in Table 5.9, team B planned to find 4.3 times as many defects in code review as in compile, but the actual ratio was only 0.96. Thus, for the next cycle, they should concentrate on improving their code reviews.

Another ratio compares the number of defects found in design review to the number found in unit test. Again, experience indicates that the ratio should be more than 2.0. In Table 5.9, team B set aggressive goals for this ratio and came quite close to meeting them. Thus, their design reviews were probably good.

Development Time Ratios

Another way to evaluate a process is to look at the time spent in each development phase. When engineers spend more time in detailed design than in coding, for example, experience shows that they generally produce a quality design. This outcome is not guaranteed, but it is likely. Similarly, when they spend more than 50% of detailed-design time in a detailed-design review, experience shows that the design review was reasonably thorough. Again, this is not guaranteed, but it is likely.

For requirements, the historical data are much less clear, but a reasonable rule of thumb is to spend about 25% or more of requirements time in the requirements inspection. For high-level design, the data are similarly inconclusive, but a reasonable target is to spend 50% or more of design time in reviews and inspections.

For the example in Table 5.9, team B spent very little time in requirements inspection and none in inspecting the high-level design. This indicates potential system-level problems. In addition, the ratio of detailed-design time to code time should be more than 100% and this team reached 497%. This implies either that the team had a lot of design problems or that they produced a very thorough design. Similarly, the ratio of code review time to code time should be more than 50%, and this team reached 91%. At 26%, the ratio of design review time to design time was a bit short of the 50% objective. If there were design problems, many of them were probably missed in the reviews.

When engineers are learning a new language, the process ratio guidelines are not as useful. In this case, for example, some of the team's ratios look reasonably good but the defects/KLOC numbers are still very high. Because this team found 55.2 defects/KLOC in detailed-design review, 15.6 in detailed-design inspection, and 16.6 in unit test, it appears that they had design problems. When engineers are not reasonably fluent in a programming language, they are likely to make so many mistakes that almost any process ratios would be misleading. Under these conditions, it is better to use the compile and unit test defects/KLOC numbers as the principal quality guide.

A/FR

Another useful development time ratio is A/FR, which stands for appraisal to failure ratio. This is the ratio of the time spent in appraisal-type activities (such as reviews and inspections) to the time spent in failure-type activities (such as compile and test). The A/FR should generally be greater than 2.0 for small stand-alone programs. For somewhat larger products such as those produced with TSPi, A/FR ratios of 1.0 should be adequate. This is because larger and more complex products usually take a substantial amount of test time even when the products have few or no defects.

For the team B example in Table 5.9, the A/FR plan was aggressive and the actual number was a little low. This suggests that one or more of the program modules was inadequately reviewed and had problems in compile or test or both.

Review and Inspection Rates

To achieve high quality, plan to spend enough time in reviews and inspections. One way to measure the adequacy of inspection and review times is to use review rates. It is best, however, to gather data on a number of projects and use these data to establish your own rate targets. In cycle 1, I suggest you use the following review rates as guidelines.

  □ Requirements reviews and inspections: < 2.0 single-spaced text pages/hour
  □ High-level design reviews and inspections: < 5 design pages/hour
  □ Detailed-design reviews and inspections: < 100 pseudocode lines/hour
  □ Source code reviews and inspections: < 200 LOC/hour

Here, total inspection time equals the sum of all the inspection preparation times plus the meeting time multiplied by the number of engineers at the meeting. Use these rates for the first cycle and then examine your team data to see how these criteria worked. If your data indicate that different rate criteria would produce better results for your team, consider modifying the criteria.

The actual review and inspection rates in Table 5.9 show that the requirements inspection rate at 3.93 pages per hour was significantly higher than the target of 2.0 and that HLD inspections were not done. The detailed-design review and inspection rates look reasonable, and the code review rate was good. Code inspections, however, were a bit fast. The lack of an HLD inspection and the high code inspection rates suggest that the product would likely have an excessive number of defects in test, and it did.

Although low review rates are important, merely spending time in a review does not guarantee that you will find defects. It is necessary to use effective review methods. For code reviews and inspections, use a personal checklist and update it frequently from the compile and test defects found in the programs you have reviewed and inspected. For more information on how to do this, see *A Discipline for Software Engineering,* Chapter 8 [Humphrey 95].

To conduct effective design reviews, you need a well-documented design, and you must do more than just look at the design. Without analyzing a program's logic, you will not find the sophisticated problems. For this, you must use analysis methods such as execution tables, trace tables, or state machine analyses. For further information on how to properly document a design and how to do good design reviews, see Chapters 10 and 12 in *A Discipline for Software Engineering* [Humphrey 95].

Defect-Injection Rates

One of the common characteristics of programmers is that they inject a lot of defects. Most of them, in fact, are surprised to discover how many defects they inject. Figures 5.7 and 5.8 are based on data from several hundred programs written by students and experienced engineers when they took the PSP course [Humphrey 95]. These data, which are for the final four programs in the course, show that

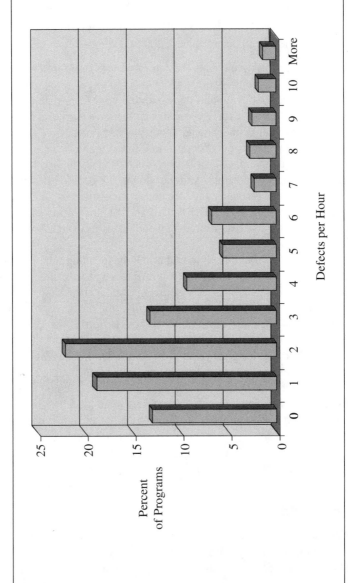

FIGURE 5.7 DEFECTS INJECTED PER HOUR IN DETAILED DESIGN (429 PROGRAMS)

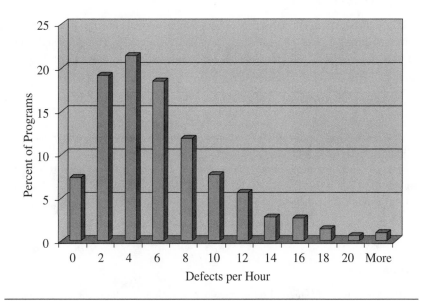

FIGURE 5.8 DEFECTS INJECTED PER HOUR IN CODING (642 PROGRAMS)

injection rates of two defects/hour are common during detailed design and six defects/hour are normal during coding. Although most of these data were for experienced engineers, the rates for PSP-trained engineers do not vary significantly with experience.

When you have data on defect-injection rates, you have a basis for estimating how many defects you will inject during each phase of a programming job. Then you need only multiply the expected defect injection rate by the estimated time to be spent in that phase. This calculation will give you a reasonably good estimate of the defects you can expect to inject. Of course, as you can see from Figures 5.7 and 5.8, defect injection rates vary considerably among engineers and even among programs written by the same engineer.

Defect-Removal Rates

It is also possible to calculate defect-removal rates for programming work. Here, however, the data are much more varied. We have found that removal rates in code review run from zero to more than 20 per hour. The most likely rate is about six defects/hour, with 61.5% of the PSP-trained engineers removing six or more defects per hour in their final four programs. For design reviews, the typical results were equally varied, with 57.9% of the engineers removing two or more defects per hour in their final programs.

Phase Yield

In TSPi, phase yield refers to the percentage of the defects in a program that were removed during a given phase. Thus, if you had 19 defects in a program at code review entry, injected one defect during the code review, and found 15 of these defects in the review, you would have a 75% code review yield. That is,

yield = 100*(defects found)/(defects in the product) = 100*15/(19+1) = 75%

This same yield formula can be applied to any process phase.

Because there could still be undiscovered defects in the program, you cannot calculate the actual yield of any phase until after the program has been completed, tested, and used for some period. Therefore, as these undetected defects are later found, the yield numbers will decline. Experience has shown, however, that with a high-quality development process, the early yield estimates will not change a great deal.

Process Yield

TSPi also uses a measure called process yield, which measures the percentage of the defects removed before a given phase. Thus, the process yield up to compile, or yield before compile, measures the percentage of the defects injected before compile that were removed before compile.

Reasonable process yield goals with TSPi are to remove 97.5% or more of all defects before build and integration entry and to remove more than 99% before system test entry. With such high yields, the process will generally produce very high quality products. To achieve these yields, however, you must strive for process yields of 75% before the first compile and 85% before the first unit test. If all team members update their review checklists and do thorough personal reviews and if you completely inspect the requirements, high-level design, detailed design, and code, you should be able to reach these yield goals.

In the sample quality plan in Table 5.9, Team B did not reach its plan but the members did a creditable job. The only serious concern is that most of the phase yields were quite low. This indicates that a number of defects made it through to build and integration, to system test, and probably into the final product. A reasonable goal is to achieve 70% or greater yields for all the review and inspection phases.

Handling Poor-quality Parts

When the quality data indicate problems, look at the part data to find the cause. The key is to look for parts that have high numbers of defects in several phases. To find the source of the problems, look first at the data for the modules and see which of them have poor values for defects, rates, ratios, and yields. Then look at both the program's design and its source code to understand why the program was troublesome. Often, the source of the problem is a poorly documented design. If the design looks good, the problem probably stems from poor coding practices, ineffective code reviews, or poorly done inspections.

Fixing the problems you find might then involve retests, reinspections, rereviews, rework, or even complete replacement of the part. When you know what the problems are, fix them before going on to build, integration, and system test. Trying to clean up poor-quality parts in integration and system test invariably takes longer than it would have taken to fix the problems properly in the first place.

Quality Criteria

The criteria discussed in this section are summarized in Table 5.8. Use these criteria when you first use the TSPi process. After you have completed the first project cycle, you will have some experience and may wish to adjust some of the values. Until you have data on two or more cycles, however, it is not a good idea to make more than modest criteria adjustments. If you make criteria changes, be sure to document them in the project notebook and the cycle report. Regardless of the source of the criteria, however, strive to improve process and product quality with each successive development cycle.

5.7 Summary

The complexity of a development plan is governed largely by the complexity of the work you plan to do. A completed TSPi plan has several forms that contain size and time estimates, the schedule, and a quality plan. Because TSPi projects are small, the plans you make can be simple, and you should need only a few hours to produce them.

There are several reasons to plan. First, when you have a detailed plan, you can work more efficiently. When people don't plan, they often do things in an unproductive order, waste time replanning each step, or overlook important tasks. With a plan, you can make commitments you are likely to meet, and you are more likely to do quality work.

This chapter introduces the TASK and SCHEDULE forms, the project plan (SUMP), and the quality plan (SUMQ), together with examples of how to complete them. The earned-value method is described, together with an explanation of how this method can help in project tracking. Completed examples of the various TSPi plan forms are also given.

The steps in making a quality plan are also reviewed, with guidance on how to make defect-injection and yield estimates. By entering the defect and yield data and producing a trial quality plan, you can see whether the plan meets your team's quality objectives. If it does not, you should adjust the defect, yield, and time data and generate a new trial quality plan. Again, examine this plan and, if it does not meet the criteria, adjust it again. Keep doing this until the plan meets the criteria. A sample quality plan is also given, together with a discussion of its strong and weak points and suggestions for how to improve them.

5.8   Reference

[Humphrey 95] Watts S. Humphrey. 1995. *A Discipline for Software Engineering.* Reading, MA: Addison-Wesley Publishing Co.

6

Defining the Requirements

This chapter describes the TSPi requirements process. It explains what requirements are and why they are needed, and it discusses key requirements issues. We also step through the REQ1 script and describe the steps of the requirements process. Because defining requirements involves a great many issues, you should read the entire chapter before starting on the requirements phase.

6.1 What Are Requirements?

In the requirements phase, your team produces the software requirements specification (SRS). The SRS should provide a clear and unambiguous description of what the product is to be, and it should include precise criteria for evaluating the finished product to ensure that it does what it is supposed to do. The SRS also provides feedback to the customer on what you intend to build. For the TSPi course, you provide this feedback to the instructor, who acts as your customer.

Most *needs statements* are vague and imprecise, but you must know exactly what the product is supposed to do before you can build it. Thus, starting with a typical customer need statement, you must determine where the need statement is unclear or incomplete and then fill all the gaps. You do this by asking questions and clarifying uncertainties. To have any hope of producing a quality product, you must get answers to all your questions, and these answers must represent what the user really wants the product to do. If you make assumptions or guesses about the requirements, you will almost certainly end up with an unsatisfactory product.

Thus, the requirements process consists principally of asking and answering questions. After you understand what is wanted and how it will be used, you can rewrite the requirements in your words and check back with the users to verify that this is what they want. To do an effective job of developing requirements, you need the following.

☐ An initial statement of the customer's needs. For the standard TSPi exercises, this could be one of the need statements in Appendix A.

☐ Someone who can explain why the product is wanted. For the products defined in Appendix A, the users are people much like you. Thus, you can generally tell what functions they would want. In any event, the instructor is the final authority on requirements questions.

In an actual project, you would need access to an end user or end-user representative. Without such access, you have no way to get reliable answers to many requirements questions. And without reliable requirements information, you cannot produce a quality product. In fact, with poor requirements information, you will almost inevitably produce an unusable and often an unwanted product.

The TSPi requirements process is simpler than most of the ones used for industrial projects. Although the mechanics of producing and inspecting an SRS are much the same, most industrial requirements phases involve a great deal of uncertainty and debate and usually take a substantial amount of time. In TSPi, the requirements phase takes one week for cycle 1 and half a week each for cycles 2 and 3.

6.2 Why We Need Requirements

Although the SRS document is useful, the requirements development process is more important. The reason is that during requirements development, you review the customer's needs and formulate questions about how the product is to work. Then you discuss these questions with your teammates and decide which ones you understand and where you need additional information. As you gain additional information, you again check on any further questions. Through this process, your team gains a common understanding of what you plan to build. Although the SRS document is a necessary part of this process, your goal is to reach a common team agreement on what to build. That is why a well-structured requirements process is important and why it is essential that everyone participate in defining the requirements.

Many inexperienced engineers think that requirements work is a waste of time. To them, coding and testing seem like the real development work. The planning, requirements, and design work, however, are what make the difference between successful projects and failures. Think of the requirements as a map. If you were in a hurry to go someplace and you were not sure how to get there, you would probably take a few minutes to consult a map. Otherwise, you could end up driving at high speed in the wrong direction.

6.3   Requirements Changes

Changes in requirements are often a problem because users generally cannot know precisely what they need until they try to use the finished product. They often think that they know, but this knowledge is based on how they do their tasks today. Introducing a new system, however, usually changes the way they work. Thus, as the development work progresses, they begin to appreciate how the product will affect their environment. The better they understand, the more likely they are to think of new functions and features. Thus, the requirements almost always change, and they keep on changing until they are frozen in a product.

The difficult part of the software requirements process is to learn what the users believe they need and to help them define their needs in terms of useful product functions. You should do this as quickly as you can and make this understanding as specific as possible. The next step is to agree with the users on an SRS that represents your common best understanding of what they need. But because these requirements will start to change as soon as you agree to them, you must manage all the requirements changes. If you don't, you may never get anything built, and if you do, it won't be right.

There is no such thing as a free requirements change. All changes cost time and money. This raises one key question: how do you distinguish between requirements clarifications and significant functional additions? The only way to do this is to start with a precise agreement on what is to be in the product so that you have a mechanism for settling requirements disagreements. You can best reach this agreement by producing a clear and precise SRS document. The SRS helps you to manage changes, and it is your only protection against a customer insisting on a new interpretation of a function you have already designed. With an SRS, your words describe how you interpreted the need statement. After the customers have read the SRS and agreed with its contents, you can argue that any changes will cost time and/or money. That is why the SRS is important.

Requirements Elicitation

On industrial software projects, the requirements process typically starts with an elicitation step. It is here that you interrogate the customers, users, or other important stakeholders to discover what they really need. Assuming that you are starting with one of the need statements in Appendix A, you will not need an elicitation process step for the TSPi. The ideas behind the elicitation process are important, however, and you should consider them as you review the need statement and produce the SRS. The principal steps of requirements elicitation are as follows.

1. Assess system feasibility.
2. Understand the organizational issues.
3. Identify the system stakeholders.
4. Record the requirements sources.
5. Define the system's operating environment.
6. Assess the business issues.
7. Define the domain constraints.
8. Record the requirements rationale.
9. Prototype poorly understood requirements.
10. Define the usage scenarios.
11. Define the operational processes.

This is a big list of topics, and only a few of the points apply directly to TSPi projects. Still, these are all key topics that any qualified software engineer should understand and apply. To find out more, consult Sommerville's text on requirements engineering [Sommerville, page 63].

6.4   The Software Requirements Specification

The software requirements specification describes, in your words, what you plan to develop and how you intend the product to perform. The requirements should not describe or even imply how to build the product. That is a design decision, and all design issues should be left for the design phase. Your objective is to produce requirements that leave you as free as possible to make design choices. Focus the SRS on what the product is to do and avoid specifying how it will be designed and built.

There are many standards for SRS documents [Davis, page 202; Somerville, page 42; Pressman]. For the TSPi, however, you will concentrate on the functional and operational requirements. Here, the principal topics to address are

☐ Functional requirements: inputs, outputs, calculations, and use cases

☐ External interface requirements: user, hardware, software, communications

☐ Design constraints: file formats, languages, standards, compatibility, and so on

☐ Attributes: availability, security, maintainability, conversion, and so on

☐ Other requirements: database, installation, and so on

For TSPi, your principal objective is to document the team's agreements on the functions and external interfaces. To the extent that any other requirements seem important, also describe them. Remember, the SRS should not be a big document. Your objective is to reach agreement among the team members and with the user or instructor on precisely what you intend to build. The outline of one team's SRS is shown in Table 6.1. Although this document has only nine pages, it describes in the team's words what they intended to build.

Requirements Traceability

To ensure functional traceability, number the paragraphs and sections of the SRS so that you can later identify every requirements item. You started to establish requirements traceability in the strategy phase, and now you must maintain traceability

TABLE 6.1 SAMPLE SRS CONTENTS

1. Table of contents
2. Introduction
     Purpose of the SRS
     Problem statement
     Team project information
3. Statement of functional requirements
     Description of the system function requirements
     Cycle 1 requirements
     Cycle 2 requirements
     Top-down structure
4. Definition of rules used in the requirements
5. External interface requirements
     User interface
     Screen layouts
6. Design/implementation constraints
     Standards compliance
     Development constraints
7. Special system requirements
     Documentation
     Compatibility
8. References and sources of information

through the SRS and into the design. For an example of how to do this labeling, look at how the need statements are numbered in Appendix A.

The suggested approach is to label every SRS statement with the Appendix A reference in parentheses immediately after the statement. Where Appendix A has several requirements statements in a single paragraph, give the paragraph number and sentence number—for example, 4.5s2. This label refers to the function described in the second sentence of paragraph 4.5. When possible, keep functional statements in separate sentences.

Balancing Workload

Because an SRS produced for a TSPi project is usually only a few pages long, it should not take very long to develop. More generally, however, SRS documents can be quite large and take a great deal of work. Although it is usually possible to divide the writing among the team members, often a few engineers end up doing most of the work. If any engineers have time for other activities during this period, this would be a good time to work on such role-related tasks as defining standards or arranging for support facilities. It is also an opportunity to prototype the product's high-risk functions or to start thinking about the high-level design.

6.5   The TSPi Requirements Scripts

TSPi has two requirements development scripts: REQ1 and REQn. They are shown in Tables 6.2 and 6.3. Although the two scripts are similar, REQ1 produces the SRS for the first development cycle and REQn updates this SRS for the next and subsequent cycles. Because the activities are essentially the same, however, the following sections concentrate on the REQ1 script. We note only the major areas where the REQ1 and REQn actions differ.

With REQ1, detail only the functions defined by the development strategy for cycle 1. It is a good idea also to include definitions for any other functions you might need to add during the design of the first product version.

Entry Criteria

The entry criteria for the requirements phase are as follows.

- ☐ You have a development strategy and plan.
- ☐ You have the conceptual design, which was produced during strategy development.

TABLE 6.2 TSPi CYCLE 1 REQUIREMENTS DEVELOPMENT: SCRIPT REQ1

Purpose	**To guide a team through developing and inspecting the requirements for cycle 1 of a team development project**	
Entry Criteria	• The team has a development strategy and plan. • The students have read Chapter 6, the test sections of Chapter 9, and the need statement.	
General	The requirements development process produces the Software Requirements Specification (SRS), which defines • the functions the product is to perform • use-case descriptions for each normal and abnormal function The team should be cautious about expanding the requirements. • Without experience with similar applications, seemingly simple functions can take substantially more work than expected. • It is generally wise to add functions in small increments. • If more time remains, add further increments.	

Step	Activities	Description
1	Requirements Process Overview	The instructor describes the requirements process and its products. • How the requirements process is performed • How the requirements inspection is conducted and reported
2	Need Statement Review	The development manager leads the team in reviewing the product need statement and formulating questions for the instructor about • The functions to be performed by the various product versions • How these functions are to be used
3	Need Statement Clarification	The development manager provides consolidated questions to the instructor, who discusses the answers with the team.
4	Requirements Tasks	The development manager leads the team through • Outlining the SRS document and the work to produce it
5	Task Allocation	The team leader helps allocate the tasks among the team members and • Obtains commitments for when they will complete these tasks
6	Requirements Documentation	Each team member • Produces and reviews his or her portions of the SRS document • Provides these to the development manager The development manager produces the SRS draft.
7	System Test Plan	The development manager leads the team in producing and reviewing the system test plan (see Chapter 9 on system test).
8	Requirements and System Test Plan Inspection	The quality/process manager leads the team through • Inspecting the SRS draft and system test plan (see script INS) • Identifying questions and problems • Defining who will resolve each question and problem and when • Documenting the inspection in form INS
9	Requirements Update	The development manager obtains the updated SRS sections and • Combines them into a final SRS • Verifies traceability to the need statement or other sources
10	User SRS Review	• The development manager provides a copy of the final SRS to the instructor (user) for approval. • After approval, the team fixes any identified problems.
11	Requirements Baseline	• The support manager baselines the SRS.

| Exit Criteria | • A completed and inspected SRS document and system test plan
• A completed INS form for the requirements inspection
• Time, defect, and size data entered in the TSPi support system
• Updated project notebook | |

TABLE 6.3 TSPi CYCLE n REQUIREMENTS DEVELOPMENT: SCRIPT REQn

Purpose	To guide a team through updating and inspecting the requirements for a second or subsequent development cycle
Entry Criteria	• The team has an updated development strategy and plan.
General	Update the software requirements specification to reflect • Requirements problems with the prior cycles • Previously specified SRS functions that were not developed • Previously unspecified SRS functions that are now required The team should be cautious about expanding the requirements. • Without experience with similar applications, seemingly simple functions can take substantially more work than expected. • It is generally wise to add functions in small increments. • If more time remains, add further increments. The updated SRS defines the new product functions, including added use-case descriptions for each normal and abnormal user action.

Step	Activities	Description
1	Requirements Update Considerations	The instructor describes any problems with the prior requirements process that should be corrected for this cycle.
2	Need Statement Review	The development manager leads the team in reexamining the product need statement and formulating any new questions about • The functions to be performed by this product version • How these functions are to be used
3	Need Statement Clarification	The development manager provides consolidated questions to the instructor, who discusses the answers with the team.
4	Update Tasks	The development manager leads the team through • Identifying the requirements changes to be made • Updating the component functional allocations
5	Task Allocation	The team leader helps allocate the tasks among the team members and • Obtains commitments for when they will complete these tasks
6	Update Documentation	• Each team member updates and reviews his or her SRS sections and provides them to the development manager. • The development manager produces the updated SRS.
7	System Test Plan	The development manager leads the team in updating and reviewing the system test plan.
8	Update Inspection	The quality/process manager leads the team through • Inspecting the SRS draft and system test plan (see script INS) • Identifying questions and problems • Defining who will resolve each question and problem and when • Documenting the inspection in form INS
9	Requirements Update	The development manager • Combines these sections into the final updated SRS • Verifies traceability to the need statement or other sources
10	User SRS Review	• The development manager provides a copy of the final SRS to the instructor for approval. • After approval, the team fixes any identified problems.
11	Update Baseline	• The support manager baselines the updated SRS.
Exit Criteria		• An updated and inspected SRS document and system test plan • A completed INS form for the requirements inspection • Time, defect, and size data entered in the TSPi support system • Updated project notebook

☐ All team members have read this chapter and the product need statement. For TSPi, the product need statement is contained in Appendix A.

If your team does not meet these conditions, stop and complete the criteria before proceeding.

Need Statement Review

At this point, the team has read the need statement, created a conceptual design for the product, devised a strategy for developing the product, and produced a plan for the work. The next step is to define the product requirements. In industry, one or more marketing or user representatives typically meet with the team at this point to discuss the product and to answer questions. Although the ostensible purpose of this meeting is to convey information, the real objective is to get the engineers excited about the product. When engineers are excited about building an important product for a significant need, they are most likely to do a superior job.

In the TSPi course, the first step is to review the need statement and to identify questions or uncertainties. The development manager leads you through this review and ensures that all questions are clarified among the team members or noted for discussion with the instructor. Assuming that you and your teammates have read the need statement and noted questions or uncertainties, this review should not take very long.

In this review, concentrate on those functions that you expect to include in development cycle 1. Until you have completed the design, however, you cannot be absolutely certain what these functions are. Thus, plan to define any functions that you think might be needed in this cycle. This work will probably not be wasted because you will have these functions defined if you need them for a subsequent cycle.

Need Statement Clarification

After reviewing the need statement, the development manager reviews the list of questions and the team's clarification notes with the instructor. Depending on the issues, the desires of the team members, and the instructor's availability, the development manager can have a private meeting with the instructor or hold the review in a team meeting. In either case, the development manager should document the answers and give copies to every team member and to the instructor.

Requirements Task Allocation

Next, the development manager leads the team in laying out the SRS document design and identifying the work needed to produce the SRS. After dividing the work into sections, the team leader helps the team allocate these sections to the team members and get their commitments for when they will complete each section.

Requirements Documentation

In documenting the SRS, produce a brief (but clear) statement of what you intend to build. If everyone agrees on what a particular need statement means, there is no need to expand on it. Although you must ensure that everyone really agrees, the key is to be as brief and specific as you can. For example, for the use cases, list the steps in a simple PSP-like script. Use lots of tables and bulleted lists and try to avoid long paragraphs of text. Text takes time to write, is hard to read, and often confuses the reader.

One way to ensure that you have reached agreement is to define a use case for how each function will be used. These use cases can then serve as system test scenarios to verify the product's functions. When the work is finished, provide the SRS sections to the development manager, who combines them into the SRS draft and gives copies to each engineer for review.

During this work, be sure to track and record the source of every requirements statement. This record will be useful later if there is confusion on what is meant by a need, and it provides the only way to verify that the product actually implements the desired functions. It is also the only way to ensure that every function in the product addresses a true user need.

System Test Plan

The requirements phase is also the time to plan for system testing. The reason is that system testing is aimed at ensuring that the system does what you and the users agree it is supposed to do. As noted earlier, the use cases should provide a substantial amount of the required system test plan material. In addition, however, you should consider limits testing and stress testing. You should also test under various error conditions as well as consider usability and recovery issues. Although the TSPi system tests need not be extensive, you should mention these issues in your plan and explain which ones you will test, which ones you will not test, and why. See Chapter 9 for a more complete discussion of the system test strategy and test planning.

Requirements and System Test Plan Inspection

Next, hold a team inspection of the entire SRS draft together with the system test plan. Make sure to take enough time to prepare thoroughly for the inspection. When engineers take less than an hour to review five or six SRS pages, they do not find very many problems. Expect to spend about half an hour per single-spaced text page. In this time, try to analyze the requirements from various points of view and look for inconsistencies and omissions. The time spent finding these problems now will save a great deal of rework and redesign time later.

In the SRS inspection, identify questions or disagreements and then get together with the team for an inspection meeting. Have the quality/process manager lead the inspection and follow the inspection script (INS). Record all the defects you find and the time you spend and report these data on the INS form. For more information on the inspection process, see Appendix C.

The objective of the inspection is to find any SRS problems and inconsistencies before you start the design work. The inspection is not intended to fix problems. During the inspection, the team decides who will correct the identified problems; the corrections are made after the inspection.

Requirements Update

Following requirements inspection and approval, update the SRS and system test plan to correct any problems found in the inspection. Also, ensure that all SRS statements are traceable to the need statement and are labeled for reference during design. Then provide the corrected SRS sections to the development manager, who combines them into a final SRS document and distributes it to all the engineers and to the instructor.

User SRS Review

After you have produced, inspected, and corrected the SRS and the system test plan, have the end users read the SRS and agree that it describes what they want. This practice gives you a sound foundation for producing a quality product, and it also gives you a baseline against which to negotiate requirements changes. If your team is using one of the Appendix A need statements, the instructor will act as your user. After the review, make any needed changes and distribute the approved SRS.

Requirements Baseline

The support manager baselines an official SRS copy, which the team can now change only by using the change control procedure (form CCR).

At this point, the SRS documents all the functions you plan to implement in this cycle. Your team also agrees on precisely what each function is supposed to do. Because you also have user agreement with the SRS, you now have a firm baseline against which to negotiate the cost of changes.

Exit Criteria

At the conclusion of the requirements phase, you must have

☐ The completed, inspected, and updated SRS and system test plan under configuration control

- ☐ All personal time, defect, and size data entered in the TSPi forms and support system
- ☐ The completed inspection form from the requirements inspection
- ☐ Copies of all the forms, the SRS, and the system test plan in the project note-book

6.6   Summary

In the requirements phase, you produce the software requirements specification. Its purpose is to describe, in your words, those functions you intend the product to perform. The SRS should also provide clear and unambiguous criteria for evaluating the finished product as well as guidance on verifying that it does what it is supposed to do. Although the SRS document is useful, the requirements development process is more important. What you really want is a common team agreement on what to build. That is why a well-structured requirements process is important.

As the users learn more about the product, they will want to change the requirements. Because late requirements changes are often a serious problem, you should recognize that there is no such thing as a free requirements change. All changes cost time and money.

To ensure functional traceability, number the paragraphs and sections of the SRS so that you can identify the source of every statement. You need traceability from the code to the design and from the design to the SRS and the need statement. Label every SRS requirements statement with the Appendix A reference in parentheses immediately after the statement. When possible, keep functional statements in separate sentences, and keep them brief and precise.

6.7   References

[Davis] Alan M. Davis. 1993. *Software Requirements, Objects, Functions, and States.* Englewood Cliffs, NJ: Prentice Hall.

[Pressman] Roger S. Pressman. 1997. *Software Engineering: A Practitioner's Approach.* 4th ed. New York: McGraw-Hill Companies, Inc.

[Sommerville] Ian Sommerville and Pete Sawyer. 1997. *Requirements Engineering: A Good Practice Guide.* New York: John Wiley & Sons.

7

Designing with Teams

This chapter deals with design, an enormous subject that is continually changing. Ideas that seemed firm and immutable just a few years ago have been supplanted by new and even more powerful methods, and this dynamic state seems likely to persist for some time. Because anything I say about specific design methods will almost certainly be supplanted by something better in the future, this chapter does not address specific design methods. Instead, it focuses on design principles and on a process for doing design. You can use this process with whatever design methods seem most appropriate at the time.

In TSPi, the design phase focuses on the system's overall structure. This phase produces the software design specification (SDS), which documents the high-level design. The next design level, or the detailed design, is addressed in the implementation phase. This chapter starts with a discussion of the following topics:

- ☐ Design principles
- ☐ Designing in teams
- ☐ Design standards
- ☐ Designing for reuse
- ☐ Designing for usability
- ☐ Designing for testability
- ☐ Design reviews and inspections

The chapter concludes with a step-by-step review of the DES1 and DESn scripts. I suggest that you read the entire chapter before starting to design your product.

The principal objective of the design process is to produce a precise, complete, high-quality foundation for product implementation. When one person produces a design, he or she does the entire job. With a team, you can work faster by dividing the product into component parts and having each of the team members design and implement one or more of these parts. This approach, however, requires some kind of high-level design that defines the parts well enough that they will fit together to form the desired system. If this high-level design is not clear, precise, and well conceived, the system's parts will not work together. This is often the reason that the integration and the system-testing phases of many projects take a long time. This time is devoted largely to finding and fixing the high-level design problems that should have been resolved during the design phase.

7.1   Design Principles

Design is the creative process of deciding how to build a product. It must produce more than just general ideas; it must produce a complete and precise specification of how the product is to be built. A complete design defines the principal parts of a product, describes how these parts interact, and specifies how they are put together to produce the finished result.

After the requirements have been defined, the entire software process concerns various levels of design. High-level design differs from detailed design and implementation only in scope and detail. For example, at the highest design level, you break the product into parts that can be separately designed and implemented. The high-level design must therefore produce a specification that several engineers can use as they work independently to design the parts.

When the design is vague or imprecise, the engineers waste time during detailed design filling the gaps in the high-level specifications. Each engineer must individually resolve these questions as they arise, and there is no easy way to ensure that all their separate decisions are consistent. This situation often produces component incompatibilities that cannot be detected until integration and system test. It not only wastes time in implementing the wrong design, but it also causes a serious schedule overrun.

When the high-level design is complete and precise, engineers can quickly produce the detailed designs of the components. To do this, they need to know the complete functional specifications of each component, its interfaces, and its state behavior. Then, to produce the final product, the implementing engineers need a detailed design that defines the logical structure, all the loop initialization and stepping conditions, the detailed state structure, and the state transitions for every program.

The implementation engineers then produce the code that implements the design. Their objective is source code that correctly performs all the specified functions, that properly uses all system facilities, that incorporates available reuse functions, and that follows all coding and system standards and conventions. The final implemented product should be a source program that compiles and runs without any errors or problems.

Although all these design steps concern various levels of design, each is unique in form and has unique objectives. In TSPi, the first design activity occurs during the strategy phase when you produce the conceptual design. This is not a full design, but it is needed as a basis for defining the development strategy and producing the plan. After the strategy, planning, and requirements phases comes the design phase, where the DES1 and DESn scripts walk you through the high-level design process. The detailed-design process is described in the IMP1 and IMPn scripts. They are used in the implementation phase, which is described in Chapter 8.

7.2 Designing in Teams

When you design a product by yourself, your principal questions concern how to produce the design and the order in which to design the product's various parts. When you work with a team, however, you face these questions as well as three others: Who should design each part? In what order should they do the work? How do the parts fit together?

Using the Entire Team

A common problem in designing large software systems is the need to define the overall system structure before you can specify anything else. Until this structure is settled, it is difficult to divide the work. One way to attack this problem is to have the entire team work together on the overall structural design. Another approach is to identify other tasks that the rest of the team can do while one or two of the engineers define this structure and specify the system's components in enough detail that their design can be completely specified.

Having the entire team work together on the overall design might seem like an attractive alternative, but it can waste a lot of time. The reason is that unless you are developing a very large system, only a few people can productively work on this design job at one time. Generally, one or two of the engineers will do the bulk of the design work and the others will ask questions and offer opinions. Although this is a useful way to define the initial design concepts, thereafter such debates do not generally help the designers and are likely to slow them down. Thus, although the entire team can usefully brainstorm the initial design ideas, after the team has picked a general approach only one or two engineers are usually needed to document the highest level design, specify the interfaces, allocate system functions among the components, and define the overall program structure and logic.

For small systems such as those typically developed with TSPi, this highest level design work probably won't take very long. For larger products, however, in general everyone will be forced to wait until this work is completed. An alternative is to identify other team tasks the engineers could do. Three categories of such work are design studies, standards development, and reuse. The following paragraphs discuss design studies. We cover standards and reuse in later sections of this chapter.

Design Studies

To conduct a useful design study, you must start with some preliminary ideas about the likely product components and their functions. These ideas are generally defined during the team's initial brainstorming design session. Then, while the system designers are producing the external component specifications, other engineers could think about alternative ways to design the components. They might even build prototypes.

The user interface is another function for which prototyping is often worthwhile. One or two engineers could build a simple user interface and possibly even test it with typical users. Although the choice of what to prototype should depend on the design questions faced by each project, building early interface prototypes is almost always a good idea.

Using All the Team's Talents

Another issue in team design concerns the effective use of all the members' ideas. A principal benefit of teams is their potentially powerful range of skills and knowledge. The most critical problem in teamwork, however, is to get all the members to fully contribute. When people work in groups, they are occasionally reluctant to speak up or to offer suggestions and ideas. This problem is particularly important in software teams because the major design decisions must be made early in the project, perhaps shortly after the team has been formed, when the engineers know the least about one another. This is also when team members are most reluctant to speak up.

All team members should be aware of this problem and should recognize that the team has a wide variety of experience and knowledge. Everyone should contribute, whether or not they think they have special knowledge and experience. Whoever leads any team meeting or discussion should make a frequent practice of stopping to ask if anyone has further ideas or relevant knowledge on the topics being discussed. Then take advantage of these contributions. Teams that do this are generally much more effective than those that do not. These issues are covered in more detail in Chapters 16 and 17.

7.3   Design Standards

There are many types of design standards. Following are some important ones.

- ☐ Naming conventions. Perhaps the first standard you should establish is naming. Specify the naming structure and have the support manager establish a system glossary. Define the hierarchical program type names (such as system, product, component, module, object), the conventions used in program, file, variable, and parameter names, and the procedures for setting, controlling, and changing names.

- ☐ Interface formats. Define the format and content of the component interfaces. This includes defining which parameters are for variables, error codes, or other conditions. When all interfaces are consistently specified, you will make fewer mistakes and will quickly spot oversights and errors during reviews and inspections.

- ☐ System and error messages. Establish standard formats and procedures for system and error messages. A usable system must have consistent-looking, understandable messages. By establishing standard and reusable messages and message facilities, you can save development time.

- ☐ Defect standards. I suggest you use the PSP defect type standard. The PSP defect types are shown in Table 7.1 [Chillarege].

- ☐ LOC counting. Size standards are typically defined in the implementation phase, but if you are developing either the difference counter or the program analyzer described in Appendix A you will need an agreed-on LOC counting standard before you start the design.

- ☐ Design representation standards. The design representation standard defines the product of the design work. It is particularly important that you define

TABLE 7.1 THE PSP DEFECT TYPE STANDARD

Type Number	Type Name	Description
10	Documentation	Comments, messages
20	Syntax	Spelling, punctuation, typos, instruction formats
30	Build, package	Change management, library, version control
40	Assignment	Declaration, duplicate names, scope, limits
50	Interface	Procedure calls and references, I/O, user formats
60	Checking	Error messages, inadequate checks
70	Data	Structure, content
80	Function	Logic, pointers, loops, recursion, computation, function defects
90	System	Configuration, timing, memory
100	Environment	Design, compile, test, or other support system problems

and use such standards because an imprecise or ambiguous design representation can lead to serious implementation and test problems.

Design Representation Standards

Design representation is important because the team must frequently determine whether or not it has a complete design—for example, at the start of every design review or inspection. To know whether you have a complete design, you need a specification for what a complete design contains.

Without a clearly understood and agreed-on design standard, engineers often cut corners. For this course, you need to precisely document every design. One way to do this is to use the four PSP design templates: the operational scenario template, the functional specification template, the state specification template, and the logic specification template. They are described in detail in Chapter 10 of the text *A Discipline for Software Engineering* [Humphrey 1995]. Whether you use the PSP design templates or some other representation, it is most important that your design be complete and precise. This not only saves implementation time but also produces a reviewable design that can be verified before implementation.

Use-cases or PSP Operational Scenarios

A *scenario* describes the program's externally visible dynamic behavior by describing a sequence of input actions and the system responses that result from each of these actions. Examples are menu selection behavior or the correct program actions with erroneous inputs. Scenarios help you to think about how a program will be used. While producing the scenarios, you often uncover subtle design questions or usability problems.

Scenarios can also be used to define test conditions. During high-level design, produce scenarios that specify the test sequence for every one of the program's key functions. Use these scenarios later when you produce the integration and system test plans. Component-level test scenarios can also expose interface, functional, or usability problems.

State Machine Analysis

Regardless of the design method you use, a state machine analysis can help to uncover complex and hard-to-detect logical issues and problems. Although most programs have rather simple state characteristics, occasionally one will be much more complex than you expected. You cannot always tell which programs will have complex state behavior and which ones will not, so it is a good idea to do a state machine analysis whenever you are in any doubt about a program's behavior. Often, a state analysis is the only way to truly understand how such programs work.

State machine analysis is particularly important when programs are being enhanced in several development cycles. Occasionally, the state behavior of a program that seemed simple in the first development cycle will become complex after one or two enhancements. To ensure that none of these enhancements introduces impossible or contradictory conditions, it is a good idea to define and analyze the program's state machine behavior.

Producing Precise Designs

Although it can take a fair amount of time to produce a precise design, such designs will save more implementation and testing time than they take to produce. When you build a product of any size, and particularly when you build products in several development cycles, it is easy to get confused. It is also easy to forget the logic of some part of the design when you later make an enhancement. With a fully defined design, you can quickly understand even very complex program behavior.

Precise designs are critically important in team projects because superficial designs frequently have basic logical problems that no individual engineer can see. These problems are generally hard to diagnose during tests, and sometimes they cannot be fixed without reworking major portions of the implementation.

7.4   Designing for Reuse

One way to productively use a team member's available time during the high-level design phase is in defining the team's reuse standards. This work could include identifying likely common functions and proposing an initial set of reusable parts. Teams generally achieve higher reuse levels when someone produces an initial reuse standard and specifies a starter set of reusable parts.

Reuse is a potentially powerful way to increase team productivity. By establishing a reuse program, you can often save engineering time in the first development cycle and save even more time in subsequent cycles. It usually helps to start considering reuse at the beginning of a project, but with the small TSPi products we introduce reuse in the design phase. On larger projects, you could profitably start thinking about reuse during requirements and strategy development.

The principal issues in designing for reuse are to define standard interfaces and calling conventions, to establish documentation standards, to produce high-quality products, and to provide application support.

Reuse Interface Standards

One of the key issues in reuse is to make parts convenient to use. The best way to do this is to define reusable functions that are self-contained and cleanly isolated. To do this consistently, you need a way to compare designs. The criterion suggested with TSPi is to see which design has lower coupling and higher cohesion. These terms are defined in the second sample need statement in Appendix A.

One of the most important reuse standards is that of the call-return interfaces. When possible, make these standards similar to those used in the product you are building. This practice saves standards-definition work, eliminates a source of confusion, and reduces errors. As with the product's interface standards, specify which parameters are used as the variables, which ones for returns, and which ones for special messages and error conditions. Also, define standard error messages and conditions and standard ways to react to error conditions. Finally, set naming conventions for the variables and parameters as well as for the reusable parts themselves.

When developing reusable parts for a single project, you also have the advantage of a common architectural framework and a unique set of system standards. This combination of framework and standards makes it easier to share parts among the engineers, and it increases your ability to identify common parts and routines.

Reuse Documentation Standards

Documentation standards can make the difference between usable parts and unusable ones. When a part's functions are not well documented, the potential user must search through the source code to determine how it works. Because this can take time, most engineers limit their reuse to routines that they have personally written and understand. Team reuse is maximized when engineers do not have to look at the source code to understand anything about how to use a reusable program. This requires that the reusable-parts list contain a complete specification of each part's external behavior. It is also a good idea to have a how-to-use comments section at the top of the source program listing for each reusable part.

Reuse Part Quality

High quality is an essential element of any reuse strategy. Users typically give up on a reusable part as soon as they find its first defect. The design and code quality must be obvious when the user looks at the product. It must look clean, with clear and frequent comments and precise and complete design materials.

To achieve high part quality, use a fully defined process and conduct personal reviews and peer inspections of both the design and the code. In PSP, this would generally call for a PSP2.1 or PSP3.0 personal process, with inspections added [Humphrey 95]. Also, run thorough unit tests to ensure that the routine works properly for all variable and parameter values. This includes testing at nominal values, at upper and lower limits, and outside these limits. The parts should also be designed with error messages that clearly identify any erroneous inputs or conditions.

Before deciding to reuse an existing program, you should consider the following questions.

1. Does the program have the correct functions?
2. Is the program interface suitable for the new application?
3. Is the program performance appropriate for the new application?
4. Are all the needed materials available: source code, test cases, test data, and application instructions?
5. Has the program been produced to suitable standards, such as language level, coding standards, naming and file standards, and message and help standards?
6. Is the program of demonstrably high quality?

If the answer to any of these questions is no, expect to spend a considerable amount of time adopting the program for reuse. If the answers to many of the questions are no, reuse will likely cost more than it saves.

Application Support

To maximize reuse, make it easy for engineers to find the available parts and to see how to use them. It also helps to have an index of the parts that includes a clear specification of each part's functions. The PSP functional specification template is one example of how to do this [Humphrey 95]. Then, when you start on the design or implementation of a program, make a practice of reusing available components wherever possible. One team did this by holding a brief daily meeting of all the designers to review the functions that they were developing and to update their list of reusable functions.

For TSPi, the support manager acts as the reuse advocate and is responsible for supporting the reusable parts and for maintaining complete records about them. This provides a central point where the team can go for help. The support manager also maintains the team's focus on reuse in high-level design and during design and code inspections, helping the team to identify likely reusable parts and ensuring that they are more widely used.

7.5   Designing for Usability

Usability is a large subject that warrants an entire book and course of its own [Nielsen, Rubin, Shneiderman]. Whether or not you have studied usability, it is important to think about the subject during design. One way to make products usable is to produce scenarios for every key user function. Then analyze these scenarios and make sure that they reflect the kind of system you believe the users will want. When you are not sure how any function should work, either review the relevant scenarios with an application expert or build and demonstrate a simple prototype. If you can get efficient prototyping tools, it is usually a good idea to prototype and demonstrate all user interfaces.

7.6   Designing for Testability

For a multicycle project, thorough testing is important. Unfortunately, thorough unit testing often requires special test code to provide a suitable test environment. For some products, this special test code can be as much as one-half of the product's total LOC. Because it takes time to develop all this test code, you should try to produce a design that minimizes the amount required.

It is also important to do a thorough job of test planning. When teams properly plan their integration and system tests, they generally find more defects during test planning than they do during the actual testing. Again, a complete design and a comprehensive set of scenarios can accelerate test planning and improve the effectiveness of testing.

Black-box and White-box Testing

There are two general kinds of testing: black box and white box. Black-box tests verify the program's external specifications and do not consider the program's internal structure. White-box tests, on the other hand, consider the program's logical paths and structure. Both kinds of tests are highly useful and should be used.

Black-box testing at the system level requires no special provisions because these tests simulate the way users are supposed to use the product. Black-box testing of individual modules or components, on the other hand, generally requires some kind of interface drivers as well as special support programs to provide a simulated system environment. By developing the components in the proper order, however, you can often minimize the need for such special drivers.

White-box testing also requires some thought during design. Here, the problem is to provide a capability to test every aspect of the program's structure. Often, general-purpose test tools can help to do this, but specially developed test code or unique test facilities are also often needed. Again, think about how your design and development strategy can minimize the need for special test code.

7.7   Design Reviews and Inspections

Design reviews and inspections can be very effective in improving the quality of your designs. For an effective design inspection, the first thing you need is a well-documented design. Next, when you are doing a personal design review or preparing for a design inspection, you must do a thorough design analysis. Just looking at a design will not uncover its problems. Check each design element to ensure that it works properly. For example, check the interfaces; examine loop initiation, stepping, and termination; and analyze state behavior. For further information on how to conduct design inspections, see Appendix C.

Other Inspection Benefits

Inspections are valuable for much more than finding defects. Each additional reviewer adds to the overall background and knowledge of the inspection team. An experienced and capable inspection team often sees requirements and design issues that the author could not have found. On the other hand, the more people who are involved in an inspection, the more engineering time it will take. If you have the time, use more reviewers. Otherwise, be guided by the yields the reviewers have historically achieved. See Appendix C for more information on this topic.

7.8   The TSPi Design Scripts

The TSPi design scripts DES1 and DESn are shown in Tables 7.2 and 7.3. They are similar except that the DES1 script describes the design steps for development cycle 1, whereas DESn describes the subsequent-cycle design steps.

Entry Criteria

Start the design phase by checking the entry criteria. These criteria call for a completed development strategy and plan, documented design standards, and a completed and inspected SRS. For DESn, the criteria call for an updated strategy, plan, and SRS. You cannot do a competent design job unless you have a high-quality SRS that has been inspected. You also need to have a complete and documented strategy and plan. In addition, the team must also have agreed on how to represent the completed design. If you have not completed all this work, stop now and address the shortcomings before proceeding.

High-level Design

In cycle 1, you produce the overall design concept for all cycles and then refine and document the design for the cycle functions. In subsequent cycles, you revise the overall design if needed and document the functions for the next cycle. To do this, produce the high-level design in the following steps: decide on the overall product structure, name the product components, allocate product functions to components, produce the component external specifications, allocate use-case function to these components, and identify the design tasks to be completed. The development manager leads the team through these steps.

Design Standards

The quality/process manager leads the team in producing the design standards and name glossary.

Overall Product Structure

When initially defining the overall product structure in cycle 1, you first produce a high-level conceptual design. This identifies the component parts, names their general functions, and decides how they relate. There are many ways to produce a design. You might use flow charts, use cases, or some other methodology. At the

TABLE 7.2 TSPi CYCLE 1 DESIGN: SCRIPT DES1

Purpose	To guide a team through developing and inspecting the software design specifications for a team development project
Entry Criteria	• A development strategy and plan • A completed and inspected SRS • The students have read textbook Chapter 7.
General	The design process produces the software design specification (SDS), which defines the overall product structure for cycle 1. • Major product components and their interface specifications • The allocation of use cases to components The SDS also specifies • File and message standards, definitions, naming conventions • Design notation and standards

Step	Activities	Description
1	Design Process Review	The instructor describes the design process and its products. • How the design process is performed and a sample SDS • How the design inspection is conducted and reported • Design standards and conventions
2	High-Level Design	The development manager leads the team through • Defining the cycle-1 product structure • Naming the product components • Allocating use cases to these components • Identifying the design tasks to be completed and documented
3	Design Standards	The quality/process manager leads the effort to produce the name glossary and design standards.
4	Design Tasks	The development manager leads the team through • Outlining the SDS document and the work to produce it
5	Task Allocation	The team leader helps allocate the tasks among the team members and • Obtains commitments for when they will complete these tasks
6	The Design Specification	Each team member • Produces and reviews his or her portions of the SDS document • Provides these to the development manager The development manager produces a composite SDS draft.
7	Integration Test Plan	The development manager leads the team in producing and reviewing the integration test plan.
8	Design and Integration Test Plan Inspection	The quality/process manager leads the team through inspecting the SDS draft and integration test plan (see script INS) so that • Every use case is covered and referenced in the design • The design is complete and correct • The integration test plan is adequate • Each problem is recorded and fix responsibility assigned The inspection is documented in form INS, and defects are recorded in LOGD.
9	Design Update	The development manager obtains the updated SDS sections and • Combines them into a final SDS • Verifies traceability to the SRS
10	Update Baseline	The support manager baselines the SDS.

Exit Criteria	• A completed and inspected SDS and integration test plan • The design standards and name glossary • Updated SUMP and SUMQ forms and INS inspection forms • Updated project notebook

TABLE 7.3 TSPi CYCLE n DESIGN: SCRIPT DESn

Purpose	To guide a team through developing and inspecting the software design specifications for a second or subsequent development cycle
Entry Criteria	The team has an updated development strategy, plan, and SRS.
General	The subsequent-cycle design process produces an updated SDS that defines • The overall product structure for the second or subsequent cycle • The new or modified product components • The allocation of new use cases to each component • An updated component interface specification For this cycle, the team also updates • File and message standards, definitions, and naming conventions • Design notation and standards

Step	Activities	Description
1	Design Process Review	The instructor describes the cyclic design process. • Things to consider in enhancing a product • Common enhancement problems and pitfalls • Any problems with the prior cycle design process, methods, or standards to be corrected in this cycle
2	High-Level Design	The development manager leads the team through • Defining the second or subsequent cycle structure • Naming for any new product components • Allocating use cases to the new or modified components • Identifying the design tasks to be completed and documented
3	Design Standards	The quality/process manager leads the team in updating the name glossary and design standards.
4	Design Tasks	The development manager leads the team through • Outlining the SDS document and the work to produce it
5	Task Allocation	The team leader helps allocate the tasks among the team members and • Obtains commitments for when they will complete these tasks
6	The Design Specification	Each team member • Produces and reviews his or her portions of the SDS document • Provides these to the development manager The development manager produces an updated SDS draft.
7	Integration Test Plan	The development manager leads the team in producing and reviewing the integration test plan.
8	Design and Integration Test Plan Inspection	The quality/process manager leads the team through inspecting the updated SDS draft and integration test plan (see script INS) so that • Every new use case is covered and referenced in the design • The design changes are complete and correct • The integration test plan is adequate • Each problem is recorded and fix responsibility assigned The inspection is documented in form INS, and defects are recorded in LOGD.
9	Design Update	The development manager obtains the updated SDS sections and • Combines these into a final updated SDS • Updates the product element to use case cross reference • Submits the SDS for change control
10	Update Baseline	The support manager baselines the updated SDS.

Exit Criteria	• A completed and inspected SDS document for this cycle • Updated SUMP and SUMQ forms and INS inspection forms • Updated name glossary and project notebook

end, however, your team should agree on the high-level structure, the component names, and the allocation of product functions among these components.

To allocate the product functions to the various components, use a traceability table like the one used to define your strategy. Also consider when and where you will add the enhancements planned for each development cycle. Although you already made a first pass at this allocation during the conceptual design phase, you now need to consider alternative approaches and make sure your design is sound.

As shown in the example in Table 7.4, use the STRAT form to list each component with its functions. Group the functions by component, together with the SRS paragraph references for each function. Then, with a letter or some other label for each component, note which function is to be developed in each development cycle. You could also list the estimated LOC and development hours for the function, although that is not necessary at this time. When a function is partially satisfied by several components, list that function with each component and note that it is partially satisfied. As shown in Table 7.4, several functions are partially satisifed by components C and D.

The advantage of using this table is that it provides a quick way to see what each component does and to identify omitted or redundant functions. The table can also be used during test planning, program documentation, and product maintenance.

Design Task Allocation

With the overall design specified and the components named, the next step is to produce the design specifications. The development manager leads the team in laying out the design of the SDS document, identifying the work needed to produce this document, and dividing this work into sections. Then, with the team leader's help, the team allocates these sections to the team members and gets their commitments for when they will complete each section. The key allocation issues concern determining who has the requisite design skills, the application knowledge, and the available time to specify each component. To help make these assignments, make sure that the team knows about your special skills or relevant experience.

The Design Specification

While you're producing the SDS, define the external interfaces and functional specifications for every component. As part of the SDS, generate a complete set of scenarios that covers all the components' external functions. Note, however, that each scenario will likely cover several functions.

The final step in high-level design is to produce the various design documents specifying the logic and structure of the main system program. Although this may seem like a detailed design job, it is important to precisely define this logic. It is

TABLE 7.4 SAMPLE STRAT FORM WITH COMPONENT ALLOCATION

Name _____ Date _____

Team _____ Instructor _____

Part/Level _____ Cycle _____

Reference	Functions	Cycle LOC			Cycle Hours		
		1	2	3	1	2	3
	Diff						
1.1	Compare modified program with prior version		A				
1.2	Identify added and deleted LOC		A				
2.3	Compare for added and deleted LOC		A				
4.1	Label each change with change number (P)		A				
	Counter						
1.3	Count added and deleted LOC			B			
1.4	Count total LOC in modified program			B			
2.1	Count text lines with coding standard			B			
2.4	Count changed lines as added and deleted		B				
3.3	Count new programs as version 0		B				
4.5s2	Retain LOC count when rolling lines (P)			B			
	Listing						
1.5	Attach line labels		C				
1.6	Provide change label header	C					
1.7	Maintain change record history in header		C				
1.8	Retain prior change history			C/D			
3.1	Comment header section	D					
3.2	List prior program modifications in order		D				
3.4	Provide change information in label	D					
3.5	Provide change data in label	D					
3.6	For defect fixes, note fix number in label	C/D					
3.7	For enhancements, note project data in label	C/D					
4.1	Label each change with change number (P)		D				
4.2	Retain deleted line in comment			C			
4.3	Note previously deleted and added lines			C			
4.5s1	Where lines too long, roll to next line		C				
4.5s2	Retain LOC count when rolling lines (P)			C/D			
4.6	Retain original program indenting			C/D			
4.7	Indent rolled lines to middle of listing		D				
	File						
1.9	New program source file with change info.	E					
	Report						
1.12	Print program listing with change labels	F					
1.13	Print line numbers on listing		F	F			
1.14	Print program change report			F			
Totals							

the only way to ensure that the component functions and interfaces are completely specified. Until you have precisely defined this logic, there is a good chance that the component interfaces and functional specifications will be incomplete or inaccurate.

After you and your teammates have produced the SDS, review your work and fix any problems that you find. Careful personal reviews are particularly important because simple errors and oversights in unreviewed designs waste time and can cause reviewers to miss more significant design mistakes.

When you have personally reviewed your part of the SDS document, give it to the development manager, who incorporates it into the overall SDS draft and distributes copies to the team.

Integration Test Plan

It is also important to produce the integration test plan while you are producing the design specifications. The reason is that the integration tests are supposed to check and verify all the interfaces among the system components. In making the integration test plan, you must review all these interfaces and devise ways to test them. In defining these tests, you will likely find many design oversights and mistakes that would often be missed in a review or inspection. To ensure that all the interfaces are properly tested, it is also a good idea to inspect the integration test plan when you inspect the SDS.

Design Inspection

Following the INS inspection script, the quality/process manager leads the team in inspecting the SDS draft and the integration test plan. The entire team should participate in this inspection, both to find the maximum number of design defects and to ensure that all team members understand the design. You should also follow the INS script and document the inspection on the INS form. Also, do not forget to enter the inspection defects in the TSPi tool with a LOGD form.

Design Update

After the design inspection, fix the identified errors in your part of the SDS and/or integration test plan and, if needed, have one or two engineers check the corrections. Then provide the corrected SDS and/or test plan sections to the development manager, who produces and distributes the completed documents.

Design Baseline

The support manager baselines an official SDS copy, which the team can now change only by using the change control procedure (form CCR).

Exit Criteria

Check that you have completed all the required design work and, if you have not, stop and correct any deficiencies before proceeding.

The final design products are as follows.

- ☐ The completed, inspected, and corrected SDS, including all needed design materials
- ☐ The completed, inspected, and corrected integration test plan
- ☐ The design standards and name glossary
- ☐ The completed inspection forms (INS)
- ☐ Updated SUMP and SUMQ forms
- ☐ The engineers' time, size, and defect data entered in the TSPi support tool
- ☐ Copies of all the design materials in the project notebook

---

7.9 Summary

The principal objective of the design process is to ensure that engineers produce thorough, high-quality designs. In designing with teams, you first produce the overall design structure and then divide this overall product into its principal components. The team members then separately design these components and provide their designs to the development manager, who combines them into the system design specification. It is also important to produce and inspect the integration test plan at the same time that you produce and inspect the SDS.

Design is the creative process of deciding how to build a product. Its objective is to provide a precise, complete, and high-quality foundation for implementation. A complete design must also define how the product's parts interact and how they will be assembled to produce a finished and working system. When the high-level design is complete and precise, engineers can implement components without further design guidance. This requires that the designers use a precise and unambiguous design notation.

The TSPi process for producing the high-level design consists of the following four steps: deciding on the overall product structure, allocating product functions to components, producing the component external specifications, and deciding which components and functions to develop in each development cycle.

One problem in designing large software products is that the basic structure must be defined before anything else can be specified. Until this structure is settled, it is difficult to divide the work among the team members. This in turn makes it difficult to fully utilize all the team members' energies and abilities. This provides an excellent opportunity to conduct design studies, produce interface prototypes, develop team standards, or develop reuse plans and specifications.

This chapter also covers several important design topics, including standards and reuse. Standards deal with naming conventions, interface formats, system and error messages, and size standards. Perhaps the most important design standard concerns the design representation. Reuse is a potentially powerful way to improve team productivity. The key reuse issues are standard interfaces and calling conventions, documentation standards, product quality, and application support.

7.10 References

[Chillarege] Ram Chillarege, Inderpal S. Bhandari, Jarir K. Chaar, Michael J. Halliday, Diane S. Moebus, Bonnie K. Ray, and Man-Yuen Wong. 1992. "Orthogonal Defect Classification—A Concept for In-Process Measurements." *IEEE Transactions on Software Engineering,* 18 (11): 943–956.

[Humphrey 95] Watts S. Humphrey. 1995. *A Discipline for Software Engineering.* Reading, MA: Addison-Wesley.

[Nielsen] Jakob Nielsen and Robert L. Mack. 1994. *Usability Inspection Methods.* New York: John Wiley & Sons, Inc.

[Rubin] Jeffrey Rubin. 1994. *Handbook of Usability Testing: How to Plan, Design, and Conduct Effective Tests.* New York: John Wiley & Sons, Inc.

[Shneiderman] Ben Shneiderman. 1992. *Designing the User Interface: Strategies for Effective Human-Computer Interaction.* 2nd ed. Reading, MA: Addison-Wesley.

8

Product Implementation

This chapter describes the implementation process. We start by discussing design completion criteria, implementation standards, implementation strategies, and reviews and inspections. Then we follow the steps of the IMP1 and IMPn scripts to describe the TSPi implementation process.

8.1 Design Completion Criteria

Before starting implementation, check to see whether you have truly completed the high-level design. For large systems, high-level design often requires several stages. At the first level, you subdivide the system into subsystems, components, or modules. While doing this, you should follow the DES1 or DESn process steps described in Chapter 7. At the end, you should have the external specifications for each subsystem, component, or module and should also have the detailed design of the highest level logic for the system.

Levels of Design

If these subsystems are reasonably large, repeat the high-level design process, this time for each subsystem or component. Again, you should end up with the external specifications for the subsystem components and the detailed design of the highest level logic of each one. Depending on the size of the system, you might even continue this process through several more iterations. At some point, you will end up with the external specifications for the system's lowest level atomic modules. That is when you move from high-level design to implementation. With truly large systems, the successive system levels might be

- System
- Subsystem
- Product
- Component
- Module

Continue this iterative design process until you have produced the external specifications for the truly basic system elements. These elements are small enough to implement directly, and their sizes should generally be about 150 or fewer LOC. Although these modules may contain even lower level objects or routines, these subordinate routines either are relatively small, have already been developed, are reusable parts, or are available library functions.

It may require a substantial effort to reach this lowest level specification, but until you do you are not ready to start implementation and should continue repeating the DES1 or DESn script. Also, with large systems, you sometimes must implement some product elements before you can finish designing others. This is not generally a problem unless you are required to complete all of the design before starting any of the implementation. Although development contracts occasionally require such lock-step processes, it is usually a mistake. The reason is that design is a highly irregular process, and true understanding often requires more thorough analysis and even implementation of some areas before you can start to design the others.

Parallel Implementation

With a large enough development team, you could start implementing any of the components as soon as you have completed their external specifications. Although it is risky to start implementing any part of the system before you have defined all of the highest level specifications, you can minimize such problems by breaking larger systems into components and then implementing the components when their external specifications are complete and have been inspected. If a short development cycle is important, this approach can save a great deal of time.

8.2 Implementation Standards

A great deal can be said about the importance of standards, but the actual job of developing and using standards should not take a great deal of time. A few minutes spent defining standards early in the project can save a lot of time later. First, agree as a team on the standards you need and then ask one or two team members to develop drafts. Then the team can productively discuss the drafts and agree on the content of the specific standards they will use. The quality/process manager leads the team's standards activities.

The implementation standards add to and extend the standards defined during the design phase. In the following paragraphs we discuss these standards issues:

- □ Standards review
- □ Naming, interface, and message standards
- □ Coding standards
- □ Size standards
- □ Defect standards
- □ Defect prevention

Although defect prevention is not generally considered a standards issue, it is closely related to the defect standards and so is discussed here.

Standards Review

When you're reviewing proposed standards, be pragmatic. If a proposed standard looks as if it will work, use it and then improve it after you have some experience with it. Don't try to produce a perfect standard the first time. You could easily waste a great deal of time debating proposals in the abstract. You will produce better standards in less time if you start with reasonable drafts and then update them after you have tried using them.

Review the name, interface, and message standards developed during the design phase to ensure that they are still appropriate and are being properly used. Also, check that the list of reusable routines is complete and that all the team members are using it.

Next, review the name glossary to ensure that everyone is using the same name for the same item and that all systemwide names are recorded in the glossary. Check the component and subelement names and review the shared variable, parameter, and file names for consistency. Also, check the standard interfaces and messages to ensure that all the internal and external system interfaces and messages have been defined, have been recorded in the glossary, and are known and used by all team members.

Coding Standards

If you plan to use the same language that you used in the PSP course, you can probably use the same coding standard [Humphrey 95]. Make sure, however, that the entire team agrees to use the same standard. A common coding standard ensures that all the team's code looks much the same. This consistency will make code inspections easier, quicker, and more effective.

A well-constructed coding standard also defines the commenting practices. Good commenting practices speed code reviews and make programs easier to enhance in subsequent development cycles. A common coding standard also facilitates code sharing among team members. When a program looks like code you have written and when it uses the same conventions and commenting practices, you are much more likely to consider reusing it in your programs. Such reuse can often save a great deal of design and implementation time.

Size Standards

Presumably, you have a personal LOC counting standard from the PSP. Again, however, you need a common team standard. If you did not agree on this standard during the design phase, do so now.

In addition to LOC, most projects produce several types of products. Examples are documents such as the SRS and SDS. In the TSPi, we suggest that you use page counts to measure document size. Following are some of the product elements that might need size measures.

□ Requirements (SRS)

□ High-level design (SDS)

□ Detailed design

□ Screens and reports

□ Databases

□ Messages

□ Test scripts and test materials

For requirements, you can use counts of either text pages, numbered paragraphs, or *shalls*. Shall statements, used in U.S. government and some industrial procurements, define the actions that the planned products are supposed to perform. One shall statement is generally used for each desired function. For example, "4.2—When the line is deleted, the program shall include the deleted line in a comment at the program location from which it was deleted."

The simplest measures of high-level design are counts of template pages, text lines, or use cases. For detailed design, pseudocode text lines are probably adequate. For small programs, I use LOC estimates. Then, when I have an actual LOC count, I use actual LOC to measure the size of the detailed-design products.

Measuring the Sizes of Other Product Types

Measuring the remaining items is harder. If your team is implementing a relatively small product in a one- or two-semester course, you probably do not need to consider any size measures beyond text pages and LOC. Even if you feel such measures are needed, they will probably not be useful for this project unless you have historical data on these measures. If you want to gather these data for future products, do so, but don't spend a lot of project time doing it. Concentrate on building this product.

If you still want additional measures, consider two questions. First, does the time spent on this product type represent a significant part of the project's work? If it does not, there will be little or no project benefit from measuring it. The project work involved is probably too small to justify a size-based estimate and plan. Because the principal reason you want size measures is to help estimate and track the work, there is no need for size-based estimates when the development effort on any product type is a small part of the total job. Merely estimate the amount of time that you expect this work to take.

Assuming that a product type represents a significant amount of work, you need a size measure that correlates with the time required to develop the product. If you can devise such a measure, it will likely be adequate. If you cannot, your only choice is to use a count of the product elements as a simple size proxy. With screens, for example, you are not likely to find a simple measure that correlates with development time. In this case, use a screen count and historical data on the average time to develop a screen.

With a reasonable amount of data, you could use the same procedure used for object LOC in the PSP. Divide the screen data into categories. Some screens might take an average amount of development time, whereas others might take very small, large, or very large amounts of time. The method used in the PSP is to divide these data into very small (VS), small (S), medium (M), large (L), and very large (VL) categories. Then subdivide your historical data into these categories and produce average development times for each category. With even more data, you could subdivide the product data into types, such as data entry, menu selection, and so on.

In planning, you then estimate how many screens, for example, are required, and you judge how many fall into each of these five categories. You can use the same approach with any other size measure. To see how to estimate size and use size data in this way, refer to *A Discipline for Software Engineering,* Chapters 4 and 5 [Humphrey 1995].

Defect Standards

The standard PSP defect types should be adequate for your needs. The PSP, however, does not discuss defects in test materials. Here, rather than add any new defect types, treat the test materials as one or more components. List all the test-material defects against these components and don't count them against the products.

Before you create any new defect types, consider the following points. First, there is an almost infinite variety of ways to define defect types. Thus, you and your teammates could spend hours debating the types you prefer. Although you might produce a superb standard, it probably would not materially affect your project's performance.

Second, the reason to categorize defects into types is to help analyze and improve the development process. Although the defect types will help you to categorize a large volume of defect data, you must examine reports on specific defects to improve the process. The common way to do this is to first analyze your data to identify the key types.

For an individual defect type (say, function defects of type 80), look in more detail at specific type-80 defect reports to see which types caused the most problems. When you identify a key problem area (say, off-by-one errors), determine how to find such errors in design and code reviews. Although you could possibly break type-80 defects into multiple subtypes, it is exceedingly hard to do. The reason is that you will almost always have an "other" category that invariably contains the most cases. If you ultimately get a fine enough breakdown to avoid this problem, you will have a very large list of defect types that will be impractical to use for anything but research.

Third, defect type standards are useful only if they are small. One graduate student who worked as a PSP course assistant was writing a thesis on defect types. He thought that the 10 PSP defect types were inadequate, so he devised a new six-page standard. The other students found this standard unusable. The more types in a standard, the more errors you will make selecting defect types, and the more time it will take to categorize and record each defect. This suggests that you add to the PSP standard only if you have enough defect data to demonstrate the need for a new type.

Many people make the mistake of confusing defect *causes* with defect *types*. They want types for incomplete requirements, poor application knowledge, design misunderstandings, or language inexperience. These are not defect types; rather, they are defect causes. For example, most requirements errors would, if not corrected early, result in a functional defect in the final product. Such defects are injected in the requirements phase and are generally caused by poorly defined requirements. The defect types, however, are generally data (70), function (80), or system (90).

Defect Prevention

An understanding of defect causes can help in defect prevention. Unfortunately, categorizing defect causes is hard. I once gathered data on more than 3,000 defects and categorized every one in terms of both the defect type and the cause. I did not, however, find the cause categories to be of any value. To devise effective preventive actions, I had to go back and look at specific defect reports to understand the problems and then to figure out how to prevent them. The problem here is one of generality. To limit the number of cause types, they must be very general, but you cannot devise preventions for general causes. If you could, you wouldn't need the defect data.

The four categories I suggest you start with are:

☐ Education: learn more about the language, environment, or application

☐ Communication: fix the process

☐ Transcription: use better tools

☐ Oversight: refine your process and use better methods

Although there are many ways to use defect causal analysis in defect prevention, I have found the following approach most helpful.

1. Pick the defect types that seem to be causing the most trouble. These defects may waste the most test time, be hardest to diagnose and fix, or otherwise be most annoying.

2. Examine a number of defects of this type to identify particular defect causes and decide which ones to address.

3. When you see a defect you think you can prevent, make a process change to prevent it.

4. Assuming this action is effective, start looking for the next defect category and handle it the same way.

In my case, I initially had the most trouble with relatively simple defect types. For example, I often failed to initialize variables. I solved this problem by changing my coding standards to initialize every variable when I first declared it. I also consistently reinitialized every variable at the beginning of every routine unless its prior value was needed. In addition, I updated my code review checklist to ensure that I actually followed this standard. These actions resolved my problems with uninitialized variables.

The key to defect prevention is to look for ways to change what you do in order to prevent the defect. Then incorporate this change in your process. Next, track your performance to see how this change works. If the defect types persist, figure out why the previous change didn't work and adjust the process again.

When you know the cause of a defect, note it in the comment space on the LOGD form. If you mix defect types and defect causes in the same standard, however, your data will be unusable. The reason is that the same defect types could show up in several different places. This would prevent you from ranking defect types by frequency, and that is a principal reason for getting defect data in the first place.

8.3   The Implementation Strategy

The implementation strategy should generally conform to the design strategy; that is, you should implement programs consistently with the way you designed them. To avoid implementation and test problems, I also suggest that you consider the following three topics:

☐ Reviews

☐ Reuse

☐ Testing

Implementation Strategy: Reviews

In design, start with the big picture and work down into detail. With reviews, however, consider starting with the details and working up to the big picture. When reviewing a component, for example, you will encounter called functions or subordinate objects. Unless you know what these functions do, you must examine each one to make sure that it does what your program expects. The strategy I have found most efficient is to review from the bottom up. First, review all the lowest level objects that have no subordinate parts. When you are sure that these atomic objects perform according to their external specifications, move to the next higher level. Then, when you encounter these objects in the next higher-level reviews, you can rely on them and need not review them again.

To follow this bottom-up strategy, also implement the lowest level objects first and then move progressively up to higher levels. This is generally the quickest way to identify problems with the lowest level object specifications. By finding these specification problems early, you can fix them before they are widely implemented. This practice can save a substantial amount of testing and rework time. Because the lowest level atomic objects are easiest to reuse, a bottom-up implementation strategy also facilitates reuse.

Implementation Strategy: Reuse

By following some simple implementation practices, you can make programs much easier to reuse. For example, use standard comment headings for every source program. These headings should provide all the important using information in one place, helping potential users quickly see what the program does. Start with a user section at the top of the source listing immediately below the program name and identification block. In this section, briefly describe (in words or formulas) what the program does, specify the call and return formats, name all the variables and pa-

Design Inspections for Source Programs

It is hard to find sophisticated design defects when doing a review or inspection of a source program. Not only is there more paper, but also you are likely to get tangled in coding details and lose sight of the design. To produce quality programs, you must produce thorough and complete design documents and then review, inspect, and fix them before you start coding. After you have done this, there is no need to reinspect the design during implementation unless, of course, you changed the design. But if the program's design has not been inspected, you must inspect it during implementation. For a more detailed discussion of inspection methods, see Appendix C.

8.5   The IMP Scripts

The IMP1 and IMPn scripts are shown in Tables 8.1 and 8.2. Although these scripts are similar, IMP1 is for initial product implementation and IMPn is for implementing the subsequent enhancement cycles.

Entry Criteria

To meet the entry criteria for IMP1, you must have

- ☐ A completed development strategy and plan
- ☐ Completed, reviewed, and updated SRS and SDS specifications
- ☐ A defined and documented coding standard
- ☐ Available copies of the routine functional specification list, name glossary, and all the other standards the team has adopted

If you don't have all these items, stop now and correct the deficiency. For IMPn, the entry criteria require only that you have the updated strategy and plan, the updated SRS and SDS specifications, and the current versions of the name glossary and team standards.

Implementation Planning

In implementation planning, the first step is to review the work to be done and make sure that all the tasks are assigned to the various team members. The engineer who designed each module or routine is probably the most knowledgeable person to

TABLE 8.1 TSPi CYCLE 1 IMPLEMENTATION: SCRIPT IMP1

Purpose	To guide a team through implementing and inspecting the software for cycle 1 of a team development project

Entry Criteria	• The team has the development strategy and plan.
	  • SRS and SDS specifications and name glossary
	  • Documented coding and other standards
	• The students have read textbook Chapter 8.

General	The implementation process produces a reviewed, inspected, and unit-tested product that must • Completely cover the SDS and SRS functions and use cases • Conform to established coding and design standards • Follow the PSP2.1 or PSP3 process

Step	Activities	Description
1	Implementation Process Overview	The instructor describes the implementation process, including • The importance of a quality implementation • The need for and content of the coding standards • The strategy for handling poor-quality components
2	Implementation Planning	The development manager leads the work to • Define and plan the implementation tasks (SUMP, SUMQ)
3	Task Allocation	The team leader helps allocate the tasks among the team members and • Obtains commitments for when they will complete these tasks
4	Detailed Design	The engineers produce the detailed design. • Do a design review using thorough design review methods. • Complete forms LOGD and LOGT.
5	Unit Test Plan	The engineers produce the unit test plans.
6	Test Development	The engineers follow script UT to develop the unit test cases, test procedures, and test data.
7	Detailed-Design Inspection	The quality/process manager leads the team in a DLD inspection of each component (script INS and forms INS and LOGD).
8	Code	The engineers produce the component source code. • Do a code review using a personal checklist. • Compile and fix the code until it compiles without error. • Complete forms LOGD and LOGT.
9	Code Inspection	The quality/process manager leads the team in a code inspection of each component (script INS and forms INS and LOGD).
10	Unit Test	The engineers, following script UT, • Conduct the unit tests and complete forms LOGD and LOGT
11	Component Quality Review	The quality/process manager reviews each component's data to determine if component quality meets established team criteria. • If so, the component is accepted for integration testing. • If not, the quality/process manager recommends either • That the product be reinspected and reworked • That it be scrapped and redeveloped
12	Component Release	• When the components are satisfactorily implemented and inspected, the engineers release them to the support manager. • The support manager enters the components in the configuration management system.

Exit Criteria	• Completed, inspected, configuration-controlled components • Completed INS forms for the design and code inspections • Unit test plans and support materials • Updated SUMP, SUMQ, SUMS, LOGD, and LOGT forms • Updated project notebook

TABLE 8.2 TSPi CYCLE n IMPLEMENTATION: SCRIPT IMPn

Purpose		**To guide a team through implementing and inspecting the software for a second or subsequent development cycle**
Entry Criteria		The team has updated its development strategy and plan. • SRS and SDS specifications and the name glossary
General		The implementation process produces products that must • Be thoroughly reviewed, inspected, and unit tested • Completely cover the SDS and SRS functions and use cases • Conform to established coding and design standards
Step	**Activities**	**Description**
1	Implementation Process Review	The instructor describes the enhancement implementation process. • Things to consider in enhancing a product • Common enhancement problems and pitfalls • Any problems with the prior-cycle implementation process, methods, or standards to be corrected in this cycle
2	Implementation Planning	The development manager leads the work to • Define and plan the implementation tasks (SUMP and SUMQ)
3	Task Allocation	The team leader helps allocate the tasks among the team members and • Obtains commitments for when they will complete these tasks
4	Detailed Design	The engineers produce the detailed design. • Do a design review using thorough design review methods. • Complete forms LOGD and LOGT.
5	Unit Test Plan	The engineers produce the unit test plans.
6	Test Development	The engineers follow script UT to develop the unit test cases, test procedures, and test data.
7	Detailed-Design Inspection	The quality/process manager leads the team in a DLD inspection of each component (script INS and forms INS and LOGD).
8	Coding	The engineers produce the component source code. • Do a code review using a personal checklist. • Compile and fix the code until it compiles without error. • Complete forms LOGD and LOGT.
9	Code Inspection	The quality/process manager leads the team in a code inspection of each component (script INS and forms INS and LOGD).
10	Unit Test	The engineers follow script UT to • Conduct the unit tests and complete forms LOGD, SUMP, and SUMQ

11	Component Quality Review	The quality/process manager reviews the updated component's data to determine if component quality meets established team criteria.
		• If so, the component is accepted for integration testing.
		• If not, the quality/process manager recommends either
		  • That the product be reinspected and reworked
		  • That it be scrapped and redeveloped

12	Component Release	• When the components are satisfactorily implemented and inspected, the engineers release them to the support manager. • The support manager enters the components in the configuration management system.
Exit Criteria		• Completed, inspected, configuration-controlled components • Completed INS forms for the design and code inspections • Unit test plans and support materials • Updated SUMP, SUMQ, SUMS, LOGD, and LOGT forms • Updated project notebook

implement it. Because some engineers are better implementers than others, however, different assignments could make sense. One approach is to have some engineers concentrate on design and others specialize in implementation. Because some engineers may also be more fluent with certain implementation features, they may be better choices for implementing certain products even if they didn't design them. The key is to consider the interests and abilities of each of the engineers in making these assignments. If necessary, the team leader can help the team make these assignments.

After the tasks have been assigned, each engineer plans his or her implementation work. For those tasks that are expected to take only a few hours, a simple time estimate is usually adequate. For larger jobs, such as implementing a program object or module, you should make a simple PSP-like plan using the SUMP and SUMQ forms. For substantial nonprogramming tasks, make a plan using form SUMTASK.

Assuming that you already have an LOC estimate for each component, module, and object and that you have personal productivity data, the planning work should not take very long. After you have made the plans, update your TASK and SCHEDULE forms to reflect the newer level of planning detail and produce a new earned-value plan. Also have the planning manager update the team plan.

Detailed Design and Design Review

At this point, you are ready to develop the detailed design for the program modules you plan to implement. Although there are several ways to proceed at this point, many engineers find it most efficient to carry one program all the way from detailed design through unit test before starting the detailed design of the next program. In many cases, however, the designs of several programs are so closely related that they should be designed at the same time. In any event, be guided by the specific case and follow the design strategy that makes the most sense for your case.

The next step is to conduct a personal design review of each module or object. In this review, do more than just scan the design with a checklist. Check the loops and all complex logic with trace tables or a state machine analysis.

Test Development

After fixing the problems found in the review, develop any special unit-test code and facilities. Because test development usually finds more design problems than either the design inspection or unit testing, it is important to do this test development before the detailed-design inspection. The test-development work should follow the test plan and should include checks of all the logic decisions, logic paths, and loop stepping and termination conditions. It should check all the variables and parameters at nominal values, at upper and lower limits, and outside these limits. Last, make sure that the program behaves properly under all anticipated error conditions. In particular, wherever a human action is called for, test for every possible type of error.

Detailed-Design Inspection

Following test development, have the quality/process manager lead you and one or two teammates through a detailed-design inspection. As noted in Appendix C, if team yields are consistently more than 70%, you need have only one other engineer inspect the design. Although such simple inspections need not involve the quality/process manager, you should enter the inspection data on an INS form and the major defects in your LOGD. Also give copies of the completed INS form to the quality/process manager and to the team leader for inclusion in the project notebook.

Regardless of how you do this inspection, make sure that at least one engineer completes a trace table, execution table, or state machine analysis for every loop or state machine structure in the program. One way to do this is to meet with the inspection team and decide who will do each kind of analysis for each part of the design. If you decide to do both a state machine and a trace table analysis of the same code segment, have two different engineers do these analyses. This approach maximizes their likelihood of finding problems.

Coding and Code Review

Following the design inspection, code the module. Then before you personally review it, look at your defect history and judge how many defects you are likely to have injected during coding. One approach is to note the number of defects that you typically inject per hour of coding. Also, determine the number of defects you inject per KLOC. When you have a sense for your maximum and minimum historical defect rates, you can arrive at a good estimate of the upper and lower ranges for the number of defects in the program. Then set a target to find this number of defects in the code review.

To guide the code review, it is also a good idea to set a time target. I suggest a minimum of at least 50% (and preferably 75%) of the time that you spent coding the program. Because a single reading of the source program will take much less than this amount of time, keep going back over the program until you have used all this planning time. Instead of looking at the code the same way every time, however, look for different things each time. Check name consistency one time, then initializations, punctuation, equals and equal-equal, and then pointers, calling sequences, and includes.

There are plenty of things to look for. Just make sure to use your checklist as a guide. As long as you are finding defects, keep looking even if you take more time than planned. If you can't find enough defects in the review, ask another engineer to review your code before you compile it. Then compile the program.

Code Inspection

After compilation, compare your design, design review, code, and code review times to the team quality plan. Also check defect levels and defect rates. If your data indicate that you are having problems or if you are not sure what the data mean, review your results with the quality/process manager. One way to tell whether program quality is reasonably good is to use the quality criteria given earlier in Table 5.8.

☐ The time spent in design should be greater than the coding time.

☐ The time spent in design review should be greater than 50% of the design time.

☐ The time spent in code review should be greater than 50% of the coding time, and preferably greater than 75%.

☐ You found at least twice as many defects in the code review as you did in compiling.

☐ You found more than 3 defects per review hour.

☐ Your review rate was less than 200 LOC per hour.

After this quality check, use the quality assessment results to guide the code inspection. If program quality looks good and if your and the reviewer's yields have been consistently around 70%, have only one other engineer review the code. If program quality is poor or if your and the other engineer's personal yields have been much less than 70%, ask the quality/process manager to conduct the code inspection using two or more reviewers. The poorer the program quality and the lower the yields, the more reviewers are needed. Follow the INS script and the inspection guidelines in Appendix C during the code inspection.

If the program appears to have quality problems, have one or more engineers do another review before you fix the known defects. Use engineers who have not already reviewed the program, and don't tell them which defects you and the others have already found. When they are finished, check their review data and reestimate the yield using the method described in Appendix C. Again, if they find many defects that no one previously found, do another review in the same way. Keep doing these reviews until every defect has been found by at least two engineers or until you run out of reviewers.

Unit Test

After the code inspection, the next step is to run the unit tests. Use the test materials that have been developed and follow the test plan prepared during detailed design.

Component Quality Review

Following the code inspection and unit test, have the quality/process manager review the component data to determine whether component quality is good enough for inclusion in the baseline system. Here, the criteria are the ones that the team established in the quality plan. As shown in the sample SUMQ form in Table 8.3, these data cover defect levels, defect ratios, process times, and time ratios. If a component has quality problems in any of these areas, the team should discuss the situation and decide what to do. The choices are to put the component into the system baseline anyway, to do more design or code reviews and inspections, or to have another engineer rework the component before integration.

Although reinspections or rework could take a few hours of engineering time, they generally save the entire team several days (or even weeks) of integration and system test time. The suggested criteria for these decisions are shown in Figure 8.1. In zone II of the figure, inspect the program design again. Have the reviewers carefully check the program design using trace tables or execution tables. Similarly, if the program has multiple states, the reviewers should also do a state machine analysis. Rather than have every engineer check the entire program in this way, have each reviewer pick one or more program segments to check thoroughly.

In zone III, conduct another set of thorough code inspections, again following the procedure described earlier. In zone IV, have an engineer rework the entire program. This involves working through the program from the beginning and rewriting any code that looks questionable or sloppy.

The objective of this component quality review is to make sure that every program logical segment is analyzed at least once with an execution table or trace table. Also, for every program segment that has state behavior, ensure that it is checked at least once with a state machine analysis. When program logic is particularly complex or if the program has many defects, have two (or even three or more) engineers perform the same checks. Also, when doing different analyses of the same routine, use different engineers.

Although Figure 8.1 gives absolute criteria for each of the four zones, remember that these are only suggestions. As programs have increasing numbers of compile or unit test defects, you can expect them to have increasing numbers of undiscovered defects. By looking at the component's code and the process data, you can sense whether or not the program has serious quality problems. In this review, use the regions in Figure 8.1 to guide your judgment.

TABLE 8.3 SAMPLE TSPi QUALITY PLAN: FORM SUMQ

Name _____   Date _____

Team   Example Team B Data   Instructor _____

Part/Level   Change Counter/System   Cycle   1

Summary Rates	Plan	Actual
LOC/hour	1.17	3.43
% Reuse (% of total LOC)	0	0
% New Reuse (% of N&C LOC)	0	0
Percent Defect-free (PDF)		
In compile	80	20
In unit test	90	20
In integration test	95	60
In system test	99	40
Defect/Page		
Requirements inspection	1.2	0
HLD inspection	0.7	0
Defects/KLOC		
DLD review	20.2	55.2
DLD inspection	6.1	15.6
Code review	65.0	27.1
Compile	15.1	28.1
Code inspection	10.6	0
Unit test	4.1	16.6
Build and integration	0.4	6.2
System test	0.1	6.2
Total development	151.2	170.7
Defect Ratios		
Code review/Compile	4.3	0.96
DLD review/Unit test	4.9	3.31
Development Time Ratios (%)		
Requirements inspection/Requirements	25	9
HLD inspection/HLD	37	0
DLD/code	67	497
DLD review/DLD	67	26
Code review/code	83	91
A/FR	2.23	0.89
Review Rates		
DLD lines/hour	17.1	30.0
Code LOC/hour	27.3	131.1
Inspection Rates		
Requirement pages/hour	0.63	3.93
HLD pages/hour	0.98	Inf.
DLD lines/hour	9.13	35.71
Code LOC/hour	82.00	362.64

TABLE 8.3 (continued)

Name _____   Date _____

Team   *Example Team B Data*   Instructor _____

Part/Level *Change Counter/System*   Cycle   1

	Plan	Actual
Defect-injection Rates (Defects/Hr.)		
Requirements	0.25	0.00
HLD	0.25	0.00
DLD	0.75	2.11
Code	2.06	5.69
Compile	0.50	9.80
Unit test	0.00	0.32
Build and integration	0.00	0.00
System test	0.00	0.07
Defect-removal Rates (Defects/Hr.)		
Requirements inspection	0.70	0.00
HLD inspection	0.64	Inf.
DLD review	1.03	5.03
DLD inspection	0.17	1.69
Code review	1.78	3.55
Compile	3.10	26.47
Code inspection	0.87	0.00
Unit test	0.22	0.85
Build and integration	0.02	3.87
System test	0.00	0.40
Phase Yields		
Requirements inspection	70	Inf.
HLD inspection	70	Inf.
DLD review	70	58.9
Test development		
DLD inspection	70	40.5
Code review	70	40.6
Compile	50	56.3
Code inspection	70	0.0
Unit test	90	59.3
Build and integration	80	54.5
System test	80	100.0
Process Yields		
% before compile	81.3	74.1
% before unit test	97.0	86.6
% before build and integration	99.7	93.3
% before system test	99.9	96.9
% before system delivery		

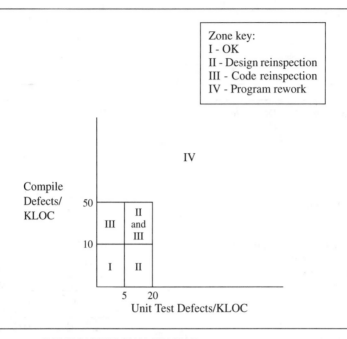

FIGURE 8.1 COMPONENT QUALITY MAP

Component Release

After the completed component has passed the quality review, give it to the support manager to enter into the system baseline.

Exit Criteria

To complete the implementation phase, you must have the following.

- ☐ Completed, reviewed, and inspected components
- ☐ The components entered into the configuration-management system
- ☐ Completed INS and LOGD forms for the design inspections, code inspections, and reinspections
- ☐ Updated SUMP, SUMQ, and SUMS forms for the system and all its component parts
- ☐ Unit test plans and support materials

□ Size, time, and defect data

□ An updated project notebook

8.6 Summary

The principal steps in the implementation process are implementation planning, detailed design, detailed-design inspection, coding, code inspection, unit testing, component quality review, and component release. Implementation standards are also developed to add to and extend the standards defined in the design phase.

The implementation strategy should be consistent with the design strategy; that is, you should implement in roughly the same order that you design. In doing so, however, consider testing, reuse, reviews, and reinspections.

One of the principal criteria used in producing the development strategy is testability. This strategy must now be extended to implementation. To make the reviews and inspections most efficient, implementation should start with the details and work up to the big picture. This means that when you implement components, you should start implementing the lowest level modules or objects and work up to the higher-level structures. In both design and implementation, also consider reuse. Make a practice of discussing implementation plans in a brief daily team meeting to see whether anyone has reusable routines that other engineers could use.

In the implementation step, the team leader first guides the team in allocating the implementation tasks. Next, the engineers produce the detailed design for each module and conduct a personal design review. They also develop any required unit test materials. Then the quality/process manager leads the engineers through detailed-design inspections. In these inspections, at least one engineer should complete a trace table, execution table, or state machine analysis of every loop or state machine structure in the program. Following the design inspection, the engineers code the modules and personally review them.

After compiling their modules, the engineers review the quality data with the quality/process manager and then use this quality assessment to guide the code inspection. The poorer the program quality, the more reviewers are needed. Follow the INS script for this code inspection.

In these inspections, some defects will be found by several engineers, and other defects by only one engineer. If many defects are found by only one engineer, it generally means that the program has quite a few remaining defects. Following the directions with the INS form, the team estimates the likely number of remaining defects and the inspection yield. When the estimated inspection yield is less than about 90%, one or more additional engineers should do another inspection. After the code inspection, the final implementation step is unit test.

Following the code inspection and unit test, the quality/process manager reviews the component data to determine whether component quality is good enough for inclusion in the baseline system. Here, the criteria are those that the team established in making the quality plan. If the component has quality problems, the choices are to put the component into the system baseline anyway, conduct more design or code inspections, or have another engineer rework the component before integration.

After passing the quality review, the completed components are given to the support manager to enter into the baselined system. At the end of the implementation phase, the team must have completed, reviewed, and inspected components that are under configuration management. They should also have completed INS and LOGD forms for the design inspections, code inspections, and reinspections. They also need updated SUMP and SUMQ forms for the system and all its components, all the process data entered in the TSPi support tool, and an updated project notebook.

8.7   Reference

[Humphrey 95] Watts S. Humphrey. 1995. *A Discipline for Software Engineering.* Reading, MA: Addison-Wesley.

9

Integration and
System Testing

This chapter covers both testing and documentation. The chapter starts with testing principles, test strategies, and test planning. Then we review test measurement and tracking, defect-prone modules, and the implications of defect-prone analysis on testing. Next, we discuss the things to consider when you produce the user documentation. Finally, using the TEST1 and TESTn scripts, we review the TSPi test process.

9.1 Testing Principles

In TSPi, the purpose of testing is to assess the product and not to fix it. Although you should certainly fix any defects you find in testing, you should have found and fixed almost all the defects *before* the testing phase. When poor-quality products are put into test, testing time is greatly extended, and you probably won't find most of the remaining defects.

Figure 9.1 shows how long it can take to test software systems. The software for the Magellan spacecraft was developed by a capable and experienced software

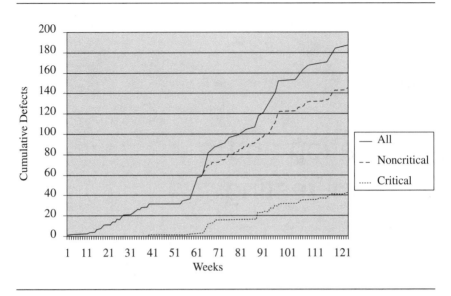

FIGURE 9.1 MAGELLAN SYSTEM TEST DEFECTS

group that used traditional software development and testing methods [Nikora]. The defect data show that even after two and a half years of system testing, the product still had critical defects. Even with all this testing, the Magellan mission had operational problems. Although it fulfilled its mission, it had a number of software-related emergencies.

The key point to take from Figure 9.1 is that with a test-based quality strategy, it can take a great deal of time to get even small systems to work reasonably reliably. The Magellan system had only 22 KLOC of software. It had a total of 186 defects in system test, 42 of them critical. What is more, only one critical defect was found in the first year of system testing. With the Galileo spacecraft in Figure 9.2, testing took six years. The final 10 critical defects were found after 288 weeks of testing. That is more than five years.

The quality of a product is determined when it is developed. There is now irrefutable evidence that competent engineers who use standard software development methods consistently produce poor-quality programs. Then, when they put these programs into test, testing takes a very long time and does not find all the problems. When you put a poor-quality product into test, you generally get a poor-quality product out of test.

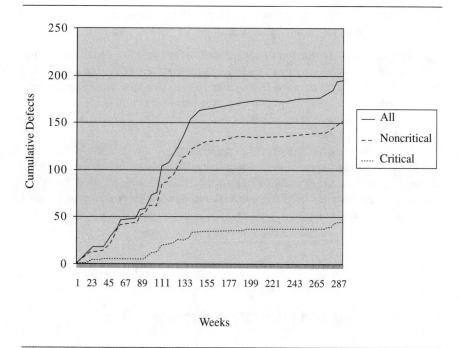

Weeks

FIGURE 9.2 GALILEO SYSTEM TEST DEFECTS

9.2 The TSPi Testing Strategy

With TSPi, the objective is to put quality programs into test. Then, in testing, you verify that the products are of high quality. The principal TSPi testing activities are as follows.

1. Using the developed and unit-tested parts, build the system.
2. Integration-test the system to verify that it is properly built, that all the parts are present, and that they function together.
3. System-test the product to validate that it does what the system requirements call for.

While doing this, you should also do the following.

1. Identify poor-quality modules or components and return them to the quality/ process manager for assessment and cleanup.

2. Identify poor-quality components that are still troublesome after cleanup and return them to the quality/process manager for rework or replacement.

The overall testing steps are build, integration test, and system test. The build step assembles the various system parts into a complete system ready for test. This is called a *system build.* Integration testing then ensures that all the proper parts have been included in the system and that their interfaces are compatible and work together. Finally, system testing validates the system's functions and performance against the requirements.

In subsequent development cycles, regression tests are also needed to ensure that the development work for this cycle has not unintentionally changed the functionality or performance produced in prior cycles. Although all these functions generally have been tested before, if you don't rerun the earlier tests in what is called a *regression bucket,* you often do not know whether a later change caused regression problems.

9.3   The Build and Integration Strategy

The purpose of the build process is to ensure that all needed parts are present, to assemble a working system, and to provide this system to integration and system test.

The integration strategy defines the approach to integration testing. Basically, integration testing should merely check that all the components are present and that all their calls and other interactions work. You should not test the components' functions. That is done in system testing. The integration strategy depends largely on the development strategy, but it also depends on the work you have done so far. For example, you can integrate only available components. That is why the implementation plan is important: to make sure that you implement the system parts in an order that makes sense for integration. This was also a principal objective of the development strategy.

The Big-Bang Strategy

With the parts that are available, you have various choices on how to proceed. The most obvious approach is to put all the parts together and see whether they work. This so-called *big-bang* strategy is an attractive alternative because it requires the least amount of test development. It is rarely successful, however, particularly with poor-quality systems. In one large system, for example, integration testing found 30,000 defects. Although this was for a system of several million LOC, it is not unusual to find 10 or more defects per KLOC during integration testing. This is why development quality is important: to fix each defect found in integration test can take an average of 5 to 10 or more hours. Generally, the bigger and more complex the system, the longer it will take to diagnose and fix each defect. Unless you have very high-quality parts, the big-bang strategy is not a good idea.

The One-at-a-time Strategy

A second strategy is to add the available parts one at a time. Because you will have a simpler system with fewer problems, this strategy is generally more effective. First, you get two parts working together, and then you add a third and get it to run. Then you can add a fourth part, a fifth part, and so on. With each addition, you look for problems with the newly added parts. This will usually lead you fairly quickly to the problem causes. This strategy has the disadvantage of possibly requiring more test development work.

The Cluster Strategy

A third strategy is to add parts in clusters. You can't, however, simply take whatever parts happen to be implemented. Instead, you examine the available parts and pick those of a particular type; that is, you identify a class of related components and integrate them. An example might be all those parts concerned with file handling, printing, or some other systems area. This approach could be helpful, for example, if a certain function were needed to test the rest of the system. This strategy could also reduce the need for special test drivers or facilities.

The Flat-system Strategy

The fourth strategy is to build a flat system. Here, the idea is to integrate all the highest level parts first and then delve down into successive system layers in parallel. Again, you can test all the new parts at once or add one component at a time. The advantage of this strategy is that you can detect systemwide issues early. It also provides the greatest flexibility by quickly building a total skeleton of the system. The principal problem with the flat-system strategy is that it usually requires large numbers of stubs or special scaffolding to provide dummy returns for all the functions that are not yet available.

Unfortunately, no integration strategy will be best for all systems. The best approach is to consider all the options and pick the one that seems best for your particular project. Unless you have a poor-quality system, almost any logical integration strategy will work, so don't spend a lot of time agonizing over the one best choice. In general, however, try to add new code in reasonably small increments.

9.4   The System Test Strategy

In system testing, you seek to answer four questions:

1. Does the system properly perform the functions that it is supposed to perform?
2. Does the system meet its quality goals?
3. Will the system operate properly under normal conditions?
4. Will the system operate properly under adverse conditions?

In answering these questions, check a number of key areas. For example, can the system be installed? Does it start up properly? Will it perform all the functions given in the requirements? Will it recover from hardware or power failures? Is its performance adequate? For performance, evaluate response time, throughput, and capacity. You also need to know whether the system is usable. Will users find it convenient, or will they have trouble running the tasks and answering normal operating questions?

Thus, system testing has many objectives. Because you will rarely have enough time to perform all the tests you can visualize, you need a test plan to cover those tests that are most important for your project. The first step is to identify the principal objectives of the system and then to devise a strategy to ensure that all these objectives are met.

Alternative System-testing Strategies

You can address these objectives in various ways. For example, you could test each objective in series. You first test each of the system's intended functions. Then you check operation under stress conditions, evaluate usability, and finally measure performance.

This is the most common system-testing strategy because, with poor-quality products, most of the available system test time is spent just getting the system to work. Unfortunately, this approach leaves little or no time to do any real system testing. With TSPi, you should have a high-quality system and should be able to run more-comprehensive system tests. For comprehensive testing, however, the function-first strategy is probably not efficient. With a carefully designed test plan, you can probably assess several product characteristics with each test.

A second strategy focuses on selected functional areas, covering all aspects of each area before moving to the next functional area. For example, you might start by testing the numerical calculations for normal and adverse operation, usability, performance, and quality. This strategy largely eliminates test duplication, but it does not address overall system behavior. By testing at a microscopic level, you may not adequately check the system's overall performance and "feel."

This suggests a third strategy that combines the preceding two. Start by testing lower level functions for normal, abnormal, and stress behavior. Next, move to the next higher level and test functional aggregates to ensure that they work together. Again, check them under various normal and stress conditions. Then continue testing at progressively higher levels until you have covered the full system. This strategy is essential with poor-quality systems because many systemwide functions do not initially work at all. The disadvantage of this strategy is that it can take a long time to progressively test all the important functional combinations for a large system.

The fourth strategy takes the reverse approach. Here, you start with the highest level functions and work down, again doing normal and stress tests. Depending on system size and the principal system concerns, you may then wish to do extensive testing of various functional combinations. Here, you are essentially testing the system against a series of operational profiles, use cases, or test scripts. Although this strategy covers the system issues most quickly, it works only with a high-quality product. You can generally determine the product's quality from your component data as well as from the build and integration test data. In general, after integration you should move to testing at the system level as quickly as you can. If you encounter quality problems, return the offending components to the quality manager for repair or replacement.

9.5   Test Planning

Test planning is done in several places in the TSPi process. Just as with the PSP, start by producing a conceptual test design, estimating the sizes of the test materials to be developed and how long the test development and testing work will take. You need test plans for the build, integration testing, and system testing activities. Although the build and integration plans should be simple, it is still important to plan the testing before you do it.

When completed, the testing plan describes what tests you plan to run, the order to run them, and the test materials needed for each test. With a complete plan, you should be able to show how each requirement is tested and how the test scripts or scenarios cover the requirements areas. You should also know which requirements areas are thoroughly tested and which ones have sparse coverage.

In addition, you should name each anticipated test, define the results it should produce, and predict how long it will probably run. Also, estimate the defects to be found in each test phase, the total defect repair time, and the total test time. Next, estimate the sizes of the test materials required. In addition to LOC size estimates, you will probably need test scripts for interactive tests as well as test data. For some systems, test data preparation can be a larger job than test case development.

At the end of test planning, you should have

☐ A list of all the testing steps to be performed

☐ The supporting materials required for each test

☐ The results that the tests are to produce

☐ An estimate of the defect-free run time, the defects to be found, and total time for each test

☐ An estimate of the work required to develop each item in the test plan

You will also need a listing of

☐ All the test support materials required and which tests they support

☐ The objectives for every test

☐ How large these materials are expected to be

☐ How long their development is likely to take

☐ Who will develop each test support item

☐ When these development tasks are to be completed

Finally, develop the test materials. If you plan a substantial test program, you may also want self-checking test cases. They automatically check actual test results against those planned and provide an output indicating whether the result was correct. With such test cases, you can run a large batch of tests and check only at the end to see which tests found defects. In general, if you lack a complete set of test tools it is not practical to develop self-checking tests.

9.6   Tracking and Measuring Testing

If you anticipate running many tests, you will want data on test effectiveness—that is, how many defects each test uncovers as a function of its running time. Then you can use these defects/hour data as a figure of merit in selecting tests to include in a regression test bucket. A rule of thumb is to include in the regression bucket all the tests that have previously found defects as well as all the tests that verify previously tested systems areas that were modified in the most recent development cycle.

Because you will be running a full set of tests for every TSPi development cycle, some test measurements would be helpful. In addition to the data you record in LOGD and LOGT, you need to answer the following questions.

☐ How long did it take to run this test?

☐ How many defects did it find?

☐ Does it require manual intervention, or can it be batched with other tests?

☐ Is it self-checking?

To answer all these questions, you should record data on test run time, the number of defects found, and the test conditions. A convenient way to keep these data is in a test log.

The Test Log

Following are the kinds of information to record in the test log.

☐ The date the test was run

☐ The name of the person running the test

☐ The tests run, name and/or number

☐ The product and configuration being tested

☐ The time each test was started

☐ The time each test was completed

☐ The number of defects found, with the LOGD references and numbers

☐ The test results

In addition, you may want to include the following.

☐ The system configuration being tested

☐ Any special tools or facilities used

☐ Whether operator intervention was required and how much

The simplest way to record the basic information is in a chronological log that is much like the time recording log. An example is shown in Table 9.1. Then include all the added information in a test report that you file in the project notebook along with a copy of the test log.

Defect-prone Modules

Sample quality data for a large IBM product are shown in Figure 9.3 [Kaplan]. Here, the x axis shows the defects per component found in development test, and the y axis shows the defects reported by the customers. The correlation between these two is 0.9644, with a high significance of more than 0.001. This means that when components have a lot of defects in test, they are also likely to have a lot of defects left after test. In other words, the more defects you find in test, the more you do not find.

This suggests that one could use test data to assess the risk that the system would have one or more defect-prone parts. To do this, sort the module defect data to find which modules had the most defects found in each test. Typically, those modules with the most defects are likely to have the most defects remaining after test. If

TABLE 9.1 SAMPLE TEST LOG (FORM LOGTEST)

Name _____   Date _____

Team _____   Instructor _____

Part/Level _____   Cycle _____

Date	Test/ Phase	Product	Start	Stop	Interruption Time	Delta Time	Problems	Comments

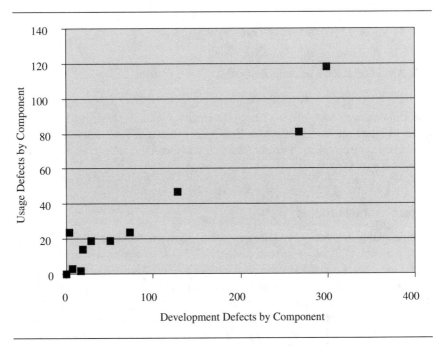

FIGURE 9.3 DEVELOPMENT VERSUS USAGE DEFECTS IBM RELEASE 1
($R = 0.9644$)

a few modules look particularly poor, you can often save a great deal of testing time and produce higher quality products by temporarily suspending testing. Then reinspect and fix these defect-prone components before continuing with testing.

Module Defect Data

The TSPi tool provides two ways to examine module defect data. The SUMP form for a module gives the numbers of defects removed in each phase. You can also generate a SUMQ form that gives all the quality measures for an individual module. With these data for every module, you should be able to quickly identify any defect-prone modules. Note, however, that in making this check, you should look at every defect-removal phase of every product development cycle. Then you can determine the phase in which a module's problems started.

Tracking Defect Data

To track and analyze defect-prone modules, you need data on each defect for each test. Also, in the weekly meeting, review every defect found in build, integration, or system testing with the entire team. These defects escaped the entire development process, and their data can provide important clues for finding or preventing similar defects in the future. Following are some of the questions you can answer with these data.

□ What process steps did the defects escape?

□ How can you change these steps so that this doesn't happen again?

□ How can you modify the development process to prevent these defects in the future?

□ Where in the system could similar undiscovered defects remain?

□ How can you find and fix these defects now?

After testing, the quality/process manager should lead a review of all the build, integration test, and system test defects with the entire team. Then have someone look for and fix the undiscovered defects that you suspect remain in the system. Also, update the process with the changes you have identified.

9.7   Documentation

As is the case with many other parts of the software process, documentation is a large subject that is worth an entire course of its own. This chapter covers a few of the key points about software documentation and provides references to a few texts on the subject. If you have had a course on technical writing, now is a good time to practice what you have learned. If you have not had such a course, now is a good time to start thinking about this important topic.

In the TSPi test phase, part of the team drafts and reviews the user documentation while the rest of the team conducts the tests. Although commercial systems generally need a broad range of documents to cover installation, maintenance, training, and marketing needs, with TSPi we address only the basic user documentation.

The ratio of team members to assign to testing or to documentation varies depending on the quality and functional content of the product. During the first development cycle, it is a good idea to assign more engineers to testing and then, in subsequent cycles, to increase the number assigned to documentation. The need for test development should decline in later cycles, and the documentation workload will likely increase with each increment of added product functionality.

The Importance of Documentation

Documentation is an essential part of every software product. In many ways, the documentation is more important than the program code. In one company, for example, the engineers followed the common practice of deferring documentation work until after they finished testing. They often even deferred working on some documents until after the products had been shipped to customers. The customers became so upset by this that they finally refused to pay for the programs. They told the company that they did not want the programs shipped at all until they came with all the required documentation. As far as they were concerned, a program without the documentation was useless.

The best time to document a function is right after you have designed it. If you produce the documents before completing the design, you will probably have to make a lot of changes. On the other hand, if you defer the documentation work too long, this work will take longer than if you did it when the design was fresh in your mind. The TSPi thus includes the document development work in the test phase. With larger systems, this work should generally start much earlier and continue all the way through testing. In fact, it is a good idea to test the user documents as part of system testing.

Documentation Design

Writing useful and helpful user manuals is a challenging problem for software engineers. After you design and build a product, it is natural to want to describe what you built. Unfortunately, this natural desire—to describe your wonderful creation—generally leads to a terrible document. The reason is that you are writing about what you did and not what the reader needs.

A useful guideline for determining the quality of a manual is to look at the table of contents. If the manual is organized around the product's design, it is probably a poor document. A well-designed manual should be organized around the reader's needs and not the product's structure. Generally, the first section should address what the user needs to know first: how to get started. Next, you might explain what the user can do with the product. Finally, make it easy for people to find what they want to know. Here are some suggestions.

- ☐ Use a glossary to define any terms that aren't in a standard dictionary.
- ☐ Include a section on error messages, troubleshooting procedures, and recovery procedures.
- ☐ Have an index of key topics.
- ☐ Provide a detailed table of contents.

Documentation Outline

The first step in documentation is to produce a detailed outline. Start with a high-level outline and then go into detail. Before starting to write the text, check the outline to make sure it covers all the key user scenarios for this build. The only exceptions are those scenarios that will be changed in subsequent development cycles. Describing them now would probably be a waste of time.

When you finish the outline, review it with the engineers who are making the test plan to make sure that you both understand the same functions in the same way and that neither of you has omitted anything important. This simple check often uncovers system defects that neither group by itself can see. Documentation and test planning provide different perspectives from those used in the design. In fact, teams often find more defects in documentation and test planning than during testing.

Writing Style

In general, write short sentences, use simple words and phrases, and use lots of lists and bulleted items. For example, when explaining a procedure such as test development in the TEST1 script, write it as follows.

Test Development	The development manager or alternate leads test development.
	The test team members perform their test development tasks.
	☐ Allocate the test-development tasks to the test team.
	☐ Define any required build processes and procedures.
	☐ Develop the integration test procedures and facilities.
	☐ Develop the system test procedures and facilities.
	☐ Measure the size and running time for each test.
	☐ Review the test materials and correct errors.

Often, people write such a listing in paragraph form, as follows:

> The development manager or alternate leads test development. The test team members perform their test development tasks. They allocate the test development tasks to the test team members, define any required build processes and procedures, develop the integration test procedures and facilities, develop the system test procedures and facilities, measure the size and running time for each test, review the test materials, and correct errors.

Although the words are almost identical, the reader must struggle through the paragraph to figure out what to do. When you organize the same words in list form, it is easier to understand the job and see how to do it. This structure also makes it far easier for the user to brush up on a procedure after not using it for a while.

One final comment concerns document quality. Most experienced writers will spend 5 to 10 times as long rewriting a document as it takes to write the first draft. After many rewrites, however, it is easy to end up with prose that is technically correct but hard to read. One way to solve this problem is to read each paragraph out loud. If it is hard to say, it is probably hard to read. Rewrite it until you can easily say what you wrote. Then you probably have a readable document. For more information on technical writing, I suggest you consult some books on the subject [Chicago, Dupre, Strunk, Tichy, Williams, Zinsser].

Document Review

After drafting and rewriting the user documentation, have one or more of your peers review it. If this is a product for customers or users, run user tests to ensure that the writing is clear, accurate, complete, and understandable. Some items to check in this review are the following.

- ☐ Document organization. Is the document organized around what the user will be doing or around the product's contents? User documents should address the user's needs and not the product's structure or content.

- ☐ Document terminology. Does the document presume knowledge that the user might not have? Software experts often use special terminology even when writing for people who might not understand it. Any words that are not in the dictionary should be defined.

- ☐ Document content. Does the document cover all the required material?

- ☐ Accuracy. Do the methods and procedures actually work as described?

- ☐ Readability. Is the document easy to read? Read it out loud and see whether you feel comfortable saying what is written.

- ☐ Understandability. Can lay people understand what is written? This question is generally the most difficult one to answer. The best test is to recruit someone who has not previously been exposed to the system and ask him or her to follow the manual in using the system. Then observe your subject's reactions, record any problems, and rework the document to address these problems.

9.8   The TSPi TEST Scripts

The TEST1 and TESTn scripts are shown in Tables 9.2 and 9.3. They are almost identical except that in TESTn you will have data from the previous test cycles. You also do regression testing with the TESTn script, something that is unnecessary with TEST1.

Entry Criteria

The entry criteria for the TEST scripts require that

- ☐ You have the completed and inspected SRS and SDS specifications
- ☐ You have the implemented, inspected, and unit-tested components under configuration control
- ☐ For TESTn, you have a configuration-controlled prior version of the product

Test Development

Following are some of the items to produce during test development.

1. A build-completeness test. This first step in integration testing checks that the system has been built and that all the planned components are included. Think of this test as a roll-call check that verifies that each component is present. Make this as simple a test package as you can. For small systems, it could even be a manual procedure.

2. The integration procedures for testing all interfaces under normal and error conditions. These tests verify that the build has produced a system that is ready for system test. From the build-completeness test, you know that all the components are present. Now you make sure that the built system can be started and run, that all components can call the other components, and that all system interfaces are properly matched and function. This is not a comprehensive test; it demonstrates only that the interfaces match and function properly.

TABLE 9.2 TSPi CYCLE-1 INTEGRATION AND SYSTEM TEST: SCRIPT TEST1

Purpose	To guide a team through integrating and testing the product components into a working cycle-1 system
Entry Criteria	The team has a development strategy and plan. • Completed and inspected SRS and SDS specifications • Implemented, inspected, and unit-tested components under configuration control The students have read textbook Chapter 9.
General	When defects are found in build, integration, or system test, the quality/process manager determines whether testing should continue. Every defect found in integration or system testing is recorded in the defect log (LOGD) and reviewed by the entire team to determine • Where similar defects might remain in the product • How and when to find and fix these defects • The process changes to prevent similar defects in the future

Step	Activities	Description
1	Test Process Overview	The instructor describes the integration and system test process. • The need for quality components before testing • The need for and content of the testing standards • The strategy for handling poor-quality components
2	Test Development	The development manager or alternate leads test development. The team leader helps allocate the test development and testing tasks among the team members. The test team members perform their test development tasks. • Define any required build processes and procedures. • Develop the integration test procedures and facilities. • Develop the system test procedures and facilities. • Measure the size and running time for each test. • Review the test materials and correct errors.
3	Build	The team builds the product and checks it for completeness. • Verify that all needed parts are on hand. • Build the product and provide it to integration test. • Product owner (developer) records all defects in the defect log (LOGD).
4	Integration	The development manager or alternate leads the integration tasks. • Check completeness and integration-test the product. • Record all test activities in the test log (LOGTEST). • Product owner (developer) records all defects in the defect log (LOGD).
5	System Test	The development manager or alternate leads the system test tasks. • Test the product for normal and stress conditions. • Test the product for installation, conversion, and recovery. • Record all test activities in the test log (form LOGTEST). • Product owner (developer) records all defects in the defect log (LOGD).
6	Documentation	The development manager or alternate leads the team in • Producing the user-documentation outline and tasks • Allocating these tasks to the documentation team • Reviewing the outline with the test team for completeness • Drafting the first-cycle user documentation • Reviewing, correcting, and producing the user documentation
Exit Criteria		• An integrated and tested cycle-1 product • Completed LOGD and LOGTEST forms for all the tests • Completed and reviewed user documentation • Time, size, and defect data entered in the TSPi support system

TABLE 9.3 TSPi CYCLE n INTEGRATION AND SYSTEM TEST: SCRIPT TESTn

Purpose		To guide a team through integrating and testing the product components into a working cycle-2 or subsequent cycle system
Entry Criteria		The team has a development strategy and plan. • Completed and inspected SRS and SDS specifications • Implemented, inspected, and unit-tested components and prior product versions under configuration control
General		When defects are found in build, integration, or system test, the quality/process manager determines whether testing should continue. Every defect found in integration or system testing is recorded in the defect log (LOGD) and reviewed by the entire team to determine • Where similar defects might remain in the product • How and when to find and fix these defects • The process changes to prevent similar defects in the future
Step	**Activities**	**Description**
1	Test Process Review	The instructor describes problems with the prior-cycle integration and test process to be corrected in this cycle. • The reasons for regression testing • How to do regression testing
2	Test Development	The development manager or alternate leads test development. The team leader helps allocate the test development and testing tasks among the team members. The test team members perform their test development tasks. • Define any required build processes and procedures. • Develop the integration test procedures and facilities. • Develop the system test procedures and facilities. • Measure the size and running time for each test. • Review the test materials and correct errors.
3	Build	The team builds the product and checks it for completeness. • Verify that all needed parts are on hand. • Build the product and provide it to integration test. • Product owner (developer) records all defects in the defect log (LOGD).
4	Integration	The development manager or alternate leads the integration tasks. • Check completeness and integration-test the product. • Record all test activities in the test log (LOGTEST). • Product owner (developer) records all defects in the defect log (LOGD).
5	System Test	The development manager or alternate leads the system test tasks. • Test the product for normal and stress conditions. • Test the product for installation, conversion, and recovery. • Regression-test the system. • Record all test activities in the test log (LOGTEST). • Product owner (developer) records all defects in the defect log (LOGD).
6	Documentation	The development manager or alternate leads the team in • Updating the user-documentation outline and tasks • Allocating these tasks to the documentation team • Reviewing the outline with the test team for completeness • Drafting the subsequent-cycle user documentation • Reviewing, correcting, and producing the user documentation
Exit Criteria		• An integrated and tested cycle-2 or subsequent system • Completed LOGD and LOGTEST forms for all tests • Updated and reviewed user documentation • Time, size, and defect data entered in the TSPi support system

3. The integration-test materials. Even though each of the tests is simple, interface testing requires preparation. Because you may have to test many interfaces under a wide variety of conditions and parameter values, you may want a simple automated procedure to walk through the tests and indicate that they have been successfully completed. For small systems, however, manually driven interface tests are usually adequate.

4. The system-test materials. These materials should test all system functions under normal and stress conditions. They should also check how the system will be used—during installation, conversion, operation, or recovery. System testing should also consider usability, performance, date anomalies, and mathematical correctness and precision. Because this product is being built in several cycles, you should conduct the usability and performance tests with the first cycle if possible. Fixing performance and usability problems is hard after a product has been initially built. If major changes are required, they must get top priority in the next development cycle.

5. A clear statement of the expected results from every test. When possible, make the system-test materials self-checking. As noted before, a self-checking test case is one that lists the actual results and whether or not they are correct. When you run a batch of tests, this capability allows you quickly to check whether there were problems. Making tests self-checking may take extra work, but it is often a good investment, particularly for tests you expect to use in regression-testing subsequent system builds. If you do not have a comprehensive set of testing tools, however, the extra effort to provide self-checking capability is probably not worthwhile.

Build

After planning and test development, the next step in the TEST1 and TESTn scripts is build. The build steps are as follows.

1. Check all the needed components to ensure that they are on hand and meet their dependency requirements. Here, a component dependency is a capability required in the base system to support that component. Examples include a database, an error-handling capability, and device support. Where components need functions that are not available, special test drivers or stubs may be needed; check that they are planned and will be available. There may also be other dependencies, such as for defect repairs. For example, a component may have been dropped in the preceding development cycle because of an interface error. Check that all such defects have been fixed.

2. Review the items supplied for the build and identify any missing pieces. Make sure that the system can be built without these pieces, and make sure that these needs are also addressed during integration planning and test development.

3. Check the proposed build for consistency and completeness. This is a final paper check of everyone's work to ensure that all the required parts are included and that a build of these components will be a complete product suitable for integration testing.

4. Build the product. For small products, this consists of compiling and linking the system components and recording your time in the test log (LOGTEST) and any defects in the product owners' LOGD forms.

If defects are found during build, decide whether to continue with the build or to return one or more components to the developers for repair. Report the defects on the product owner's LOGD forms and ask the quality/process manager to help you decide how to proceed. If the repair can be made quickly, you could rebuild. Otherwise, you may have to reschedule the build.

Integration

The integration tasks are as follows.

1. Check the completeness of the built product. Run a completeness check on the build to verify that all the needed parts are present in the build.

2. Run the integration tests. Run the planned integration tests.

3. For these tests, record the test data in the test log (form LOGTEST). Record your name, the date, the time, the system being tested, the tests run, their run times, and the defects found.

4. If defects are found, the product owner logs every defect. Then have the quality/process manager determine whether testing should continue. If possible, continue integration testing and have the defects fixed in parallel. If the system has seriously defective components, however, abort integration testing and conduct a complete inspection of these defective components.

If there were defects, return the defect data to the appropriate engineers for repair. After the fix, have a team member inspect the fix to make sure that it is correct. The quality/process manager should also review these defects in the next team meeting. For larger systems and projects, you normally need enough information to re-create the problem so that the development engineers can diagnose and repair it. This information typically includes the hardware and software configuration, the jobs being run, any data on files and data required, and so on. For TSPi, however, the simple LOGD and LOGTEST data should be adequate.

System Test

For system testing, follow the test plan to test the system. Again, record all defects in the product owner's defect log and hold a team review. When defects are found, have the quality/process manager determine whether testing should continue or be aborted. As in integration, you generally want to continue system testing if you can and have the defects fixed in parallel. If the system has seriously defective components, however, abort system testing and do a complete reinspection of the defective parts. When the defects have been found and fixed, and when the fixes have been inspected, continue system testing until completed.

Regression Testing

The final step in system testing is to run regression tests from prior development cycles to ensure that the product continues to function as before. Regression testing involves rerunning some system tests from prior development cycles. Usually, the regression test bucket would be a subset of the tests from prior-cycle system testing. After the system and regression tests have been run successfully, the system is ready for delivery or the next development cycle. With TEST1, there is no need for regression testing. Again, complete the LOGD, LOGT, and LOGTEST forms.

Documentation

Complete the user documentation.

Exit Criteria

At completion of the test phase, you should have the following.

- ☐ A completed, integrated, system-tested, and regression-tested product version
- ☐ A complete test record in the test log
- ☐ Completed LOGD entries and a defect analysis for every defect found
- ☐ Completed and reviewed user documentation
- ☐ Updated SUMP and SUMQ forms for the system and all its modules or components
- ☐ A copy of all the test data and forms in the project notebook

9.9   Summary

This chapter covers both testing and documentation. The purpose of testing is to assess the product, not to fix it. With TSPi, however, you have the data to judge which parts of the system are most likely to be defect-prone. Typically, those modules with the most defects in test are likely to have the most defects remaining after test. These modules should then be pulled from test and fixed by the developers. Trying to fix them in test is time-consuming and rarely is effective.

In the build and integration steps, you assemble the parts of the system, make sure that all the necessary parts are included, and ensure that all their interfaces function properly. In system testing, you seek to answer the following questions.

☐ Does the system properly perform the functions it is supposed to perform?

☐ Does the system meet its quality goals?

☐ Will the system operate properly under normal conditions?

☐ Will the system operate properly under adverse conditions?

☐ Does the system start up properly?

☐ Will the system perform all the functions given in the requirements?

☐ Will it recover from hardware or power failures?

☐ Is the system's performance adequate?

☐ Is the system usable?

In test planning, describe the tests you plan to run and in what order and describe the test materials that are needed to run each test. Then name each planned test and specify how long you expect it to run, the anticipated test results, and the sizes of the test materials to be developed. In addition to special test code, you may need interactive test scripts and test data.

In the testing phase of each development cycle, some members of the team draft and review the user documentation while other members do the testing. A well-designed manual is organized around the user's needs and not the product's structure and functions. The first documentation step is to produce a complete outline and then to review it with the test group to make sure that both groups are covering the same topics in the same way. In writing, use short sentences, simple words and phrases, and lots of lists and bulleted items. After you have written and personally reviewed the manual, have others review it. For products that will be delivered to end users, also test the documents with typical users and during system testing.

9.10 References

[Chicago] The University of Chicago Press. 1993. *The Chicago Manual of Style: The Essential Guide for Writers*. 14th ed. Chicago: The University of Chicago Press.

[Dupre] Lyn Dupre. 1995. *Bugs in Writing: A Guide to Debugging Your Prose*. Reading, MA: Addison-Wesley.

[Kaplan] Craig Kaplan, Ralph Clark, and Victor Tang. 1994. *Secrets of Software Quality: 40 Innovations from IBM.* New York: McGraw-Hill, Inc.

[Nikora] Allen P. Nikora. 1991. "Error Discovery Rate by Severity Category and Time to Repair Software Failures for Three JPL Flight Projects." Software Product Assurance Section, Jet Propulsion Laboratory, November 5.

[Strunk] William Strunk, Jr., and E.B. White. 1995. *The Elements of Style.* 3rd ed. New York: Macmillan Publishing Co.

[Tichy] H.J. Tichy. 1988. *Effective Writing for Engineers, Managers, and Scientists.* 2nd ed. New York: John Wiley & Sons.

[Williams] Joseph Williams. 1996. *Style: Ten Lessons in Clarity and Grace.* 5th ed. Glenview, IL: Scott Foresman.

[Zinsser] William Zinsser. 1998. *On Writing Well: An Informal Guide to Writing Nonfiction.* 6th ed. New York: Harper and Row, Publishers.

10

The Postmortem

The postmortem is the final step in the TSPi process. Here, you review the team's work to ensure that you have completed all the needed tasks and recorded all the required data. You also reexamine what you did in this cycle, both to learn what went right and wrong and to see how to do the job better the next time.

Perhaps the best way to describe the principle behind the postmortem is with a definition: "Insanity is doing the same thing over and over and expecting a different result" [Brown]. This definition captures the spirit of the postmortem process. If we do not change the way we work, we continue to perform much as we have in the past. The postmortem provides an orderly way to identify areas that need to be improved and to make the needed changes.

This chapter reviews why a postmortem is needed and how the postmortem process can help you. It also describes the steps in the TSPi postmortem process.

10.1 Why We Need a Postmortem

Continuous improvement is particularly important for software creators because of the kind of work we do. Software now provides the logic for almost all new products and services in almost every industry. In typical development groups, more than half of the engineers do software work. With few exceptions, every new hardware, software, or service offering has software at its core.

Software now is, or soon will be, important to almost every industry. Thus, knowing how to develop software is a critical skill for about every engineer and scientist. An important prerequisite for success in almost all technical fields will soon be software competency and the discipline to use personal skills in the most effective way. To keep up with this technology and to meet the more challenging needs of the future, you should view every project as a chance to improve.

10.2   What a Postmortem Can Do for You

Every TSPi development cycle ends with a postmortem, which provides a structured way to learn and improve. In the postmortem, you examine what you did compared to what you planned to do. You look for improvement opportunities and decide how to change your practices for the next cycle or the next project. Merely trying harder, however, will not produce consistent improvement. You must actually change what you do. You can either change the processes or discover how to better follow the processes that you have.

By using the postmortem process, you will see changes from one cycle to the next. The first TSPi cycle provides a baseline. You assess the products produced, the effort spent to produce them, and the process steps that you followed. You determine the accuracy of your plans and the suitability of your processes. You identify problems, determine their causes, and devise prevention measures. The postmortem phase is the appropriate point to identify specific improvement opportunities and decide where and how to incorporate these changes into your personal and team processes.

10.3   The Process Improvement Proposal

The key to successful improvement is to focus on small changes. You will occasionally see major opportunities, but they will be rare. As you assess your work, however, you will see many small ways to improve things. Each small improvement will help a little, and, over time, by compounding these many small changes you will see a significant overall change. Even more important, however, you will have learned how to continuously improve your personal performance.

The problem with small changes, however, is that they are easy to forget. That is why both the PSP and the TSPi use the process improvement proposal

(PIP). If, as you use a process, you keep a blank PIP form at hand, you can easily note any improvement ideas that occur to you. These ideas might include better personal practices, improved tools, process changes, or almost anything else. When it is time for the postmortem, you will be able to reconstruct these ideas and deal with them in an orderly way.

10.4   The TSPi Postmortem Scripts

The PM1 and PMn scripts are shown in Tables 10.1 and 10.2. The only difference between these two scripts is that PM1 calls for the instructor to describe the PM process. In PMn, this opening discussion time is used to cover any problems or lessons from the prior postmortems and to make suggestions for how to conduct a better postmortem. In PMn, you also evaluate the effectiveness of the process changes made in prior postmortem phases and decide which of them to retain, drop, or modify.

The product of the postmortem is the cycle report. You and your peers write sections describing what you did in this cycle, comparing it with your plans and with any prior development cycles. The TSPi postmortem scripts call for a team discussion of the project data and a review and critique of the roles. In these discussions, concentrate on those topics most relevant to your role responsibilities and note any ideas or relevant facts and data that you could use in your parts of the report.

Entry Criteria

The postmortem entry criteria are as follows.

☐ The team has completed and tested the product.

☐ The engineers have gathered all the data and completed all the required forms.

☐ All the engineers have read this chapter.

Review Process Data

In the review step, the quality/process manager leads the team through a review of the cycle data, including the completed SUMP and SUMQ forms for the product and its components. The objectives of this review are to

☐ Examine the data on what the team and team members did

☐ Identify where the process worked and where it did not

TABLE 10.1 TSPi CYCLE-1 POSTMORTEM: SCRIPT PM1

Purpose	• To gather, analyze, and record project data • To evaluate the team's and each role's performance • To identify ways to improve the cycle-2 process • To produce the cycle-1 report
Entry Criteria	• The engineers have completed and tested the product. • They have gathered all the data and completed all the forms. • The students have read textbook Chapters 10, 16, 17, and 18.
General	The cycle-1 report contains an analysis of the project by each role. • Overall team performance: team leader • Plan versus actual performance: planning manager • Overall product design and standards: development manager • Change management and project support: support manager • Process and product quality: quality/process manager The cycle report should • Use process data to support the engineers' statements • Thoughtfully consider the meaning of the results produced • Be short and concise

Step	Activities	Description
1	Postmortem Process Overview	The instructor describes the postmortem process. • The need for complete and accurate process data • The contents of the cycle report • The peer evaluation process and forms
2	Review Process Data	The quality/process manager leads the team in analyzing project data and identifying problem and improvement areas. • Leadership, planning, process, quality, or support • Suggested team actions and responsibilities • Areas for instructor or facility improvement The engineers prepare and submit PIPs on these improvement suggestions.
3	Evaluate Role Performance	The team leader leads the team in evaluating the effectiveness of the team roles, the instructor's actions, and the support facilities. • Where they were effective • Where there is room for improvement
4	Prepare Cycle-1 Report	The team leader leads the team in outlining the cycle-1 report. • Allocating report work to the team members • Obtaining commitments for report section completion • Assembling, reviewing, and correcting the completed report
5	Prepare Role Evaluations	Each engineer completes an evaluation of the team and of each team role using form PEER. • Each role's difficulty and contribution • Percents must total 100% • The effectiveness of each role on a scale of 1 (inadequate) to 5 (superior).
Exit Criteria		• The development cycle has produced a high-quality product with all required documentation. • The completed product is under configuration control. • All process data have been evaluated and PIPs submitted. • The peer evaluations are done and submitted (PEER). • The cycle-1 report has been completed and submitted. • SUMP and SUMQ forms are completed for the system and all its components. • The project notebook has been updated.

TABLE 10.2 TSPi CYCLE n POSTMORTEM: SCRIPT PMn

Purpose	• To gather, analyze, and record data for the latest cycle • To evaluate the team's and each role's performance • To identify ways to improve the subsequent cycle process • To produce the cycle report
Entry Criteria	• The engineers have completed and tested the product. • They have gathered all the data and completed all the forms.
General	The cycle report contains an analysis of the project by each role. • Overall team performance: team leader • Plan versus actual performance: planning manager • Overall product design and standards: development manager • Change management and project support: support manager • Process and product quality: quality/process manager The cycle report should • Use process data to support the engineers' statements • Thoughtfully consider the meaning of the results produced • Be short and concise

Step	Activities	Description
1	Postmortem Process Review	The instructor describes any problems with the prior-cycle postmortem process that should be corrected for this cycle.
2	Review Process Data	The quality/process manager leads the team in • Analyzing project data and identifying problem areas • Assessing the effectiveness of prior-cycle PIPs and actions Where improvement is needed, identify • Leadership, planning, process, quality, or support items • Suggested team actions and responsibilities • Areas for instructor or facility improvement Prepare and submit PIPs on these improvement suggestions.
3	Evaluate Role Performance	The team leader leads the team in evaluating the effectiveness of team roles, the instructor's actions, and the support facilities. • Where they were effective • Where there is room for improvement
4	Prepare Cycle n Report	The team leader leads the team in outlining the cycle n report. • Allocating report work to the team members • Obtaining commitments for report section completion • Assembling, reviewing, and correcting the completed report
5	Prepare Role Evaluations	Each engineer completes an evaluation of the team and of each team role using form PEER. • Each role's difficulty and contribution • Percents must total 100% • The effectiveness of each role on a scale of 1 (inadequate) to 5 (superior).
Exit Criteria		• The development cycle has produced a high-quality product with all required documentation. • The completed product is under configuration control. • All process data have been evaluated and PIPs submitted. • The peer evaluations are done and submitted (form PEER). • The cycle-n report has been completed and submitted. • SUMP and SUMQ forms are completed for the system and all its components. • The project notebook has been updated.

    □ Compare the team's performance with its goals and plans

    □ Identify problem areas and needs for improvement

    □ Devise process improvements and prepare PIPs

Quality Review

As part of this process review, compare both the team's and each engineer's personal performance with the quality plan. Start with an analysis of the team's defect data and assess the degree to which the team produced a quality product. If the product had more than one or two defects in system test, assess where the process fell short and what could be done to improve it in the future. Specifically, address the following questions.

    □ How did actual performance compare with the plan?

    □ What lessons can you learn from this experience?

    □ Should you use different personal or team criteria in the future?

    □ Where do you see opportunities for improvement, and why?

    □ Where did you have problems that must be corrected next time?

    For PMn, examine the improvements you made in prior postmortems and judge their effectiveness. Address the following questions.

    □ Where did this team do well, and where did it fall short?

    □ How did your performance compare with what other teams have done?

    □ What goals should you set for the next development cycle or for future projects?

    □ Where should you modify the processes you used?

    Then prepare PIPs for all your improvement suggestions. Also, assess your performance and your team's performance against the goals you established at the beginning of the development cycle. Identify the areas that should now have the highest priority for improvement.

Role Evaluations

The team leader leads the team through examining each role. In these evaluations, focus on objective facts. Start with the team leader's role and then review the other roles. In doing this, consider the following questions.

    □ What worked?

    □ Where were there problems?

    □ Where is there room for improvement?

☐ What improvement goals would make sense for the next development cycle
   or project?

Next, evaluate the faculty and facilities. Where could the instructor have been
more helpful, and what specific improvements would you suggest? Were there facilities problems, tools limitations, or supply needs? Concentrate on constructive
suggestions and be as specific as possible.

Prepare the Cycle Report

The cycle report describes what you produced, the processes that you used, and the
roles you performed. It describes what worked and what did not work and how
you can do better the next time. You should also describe the team's performance
with respect to your responsibilities, as well as your personal performance, both as
a developer and in your team role. Keep the report brief and factual and emphasize
lessons learned and how to improve in the future. Whenever you can, justify your
conclusions with actual data. Also, compare performance with prior development
cycles and highlight any trends.

The Cycle Report

The suggested cycle report outline is as follows.

   Table of contents
   Summary
   Role Reports
        Leadership
        Development
        Planning
        Process
        Quality
        Support
   Engineer Reports

The team leader produces the report table of contents and writes a report summary
that briefly describes the report's key findings.

Role Reports

In the role reports, you should write two sections: how you evaluate your role performance and how you think the team performed with respect to that role's perspective. Discuss the way that you handled your assigned role, what worked, what

did not work, and how the role could be handled better the next time. The objective is not self-criticism but rather guidance to the next person on how to better perform that role.

The team leader's report should review the team's performance from a leadership perspective. This review should cover motivational and commitment issues, areas where additional guidance from the instructor would have been helpful, and the key things learned. He or she should also comment on meeting facilitation: the practices that were used, how they worked, and how to handle this role responsibility better in the future.

The development manager compares the product content to the requirements and assesses the effectiveness of the development strategy. Topics should include whether the strategy worked as expected, what other approaches might have been more effective, and how the strategy should be changed in the future.

The development manager also describes the design and implementation steps taken to address usability, performance, compatibility, installability, maintainability, security, or any other important quality topics. He or she also addresses the effectiveness of these measures and how to address these topics more effectively in future development cycles or projects.

The planning manager describes how the team's performance compared with the plan: weekly hour and earned-value trends, the adequacy of the team's earned-value tracking and reporting, and ways to do the job better in the next cycle. When possible, he or she compares the team's performance with that of prior cycles or with other project results.

The quality/process manager uses actual quality data to describe team performance in comparison to the quality goals. He or she shows the overall quality trends for the development cycles completed to date. In the process section, this review should evaluate the team's process discipline: the degree to which the engineers followed the process, measured their work, used the measures to improve, and submitted PIPs on their improvement ideas. This section should include a summary of all the PIPs submitted by the team and a brief analysis of how they were handled. The quality/process manager also reviews the standards work and the team's conduct of inspections. This review should include an evaluation of the team's and each engineer's inspection yield and suggestions for future improvement.

The support manager describes the support facilities and notes any problems or suggested areas for improvement. He or she also comments on the configuration-management and change control procedures, describes how they worked, and makes improvement suggestions for the next cycle. This review should include change activity data, comments on the impact of late changes, and recommendations for how better to handle changes in future development cycles or projects. The support manager also covers issue tracking and the effectiveness of the team's issue tracking in handling risks and issues.

The support manager also addresses reuse. How did the reuse strategy work? What was the percent reuse achieved by the team and by each engineer? He or she also describes opportunities for improving these reuse percentages in future cycles and suggests how to make these improvements.

Engineer Reports

Every engineer should also report on his or her personal performance on the development tasks. In this report, you should consider your personal planning performance and the quality of the work that you did. Focus on how you can do the work better the next time, and include specific data to support your conclusions. Also describe the one or two most important areas for personal improvement on the next cycle or project.

Producing the Report

The team leader leads the team in defining the report contents, allocating the report-writing tasks, and obtaining commitments for when the engineers will complete and submit their sections. The team leader then assembles and distributes the draft report to the team for review. The quality/process manager leads the report review and the engineers then make any indicated corrections to their sections. They provide the completed report sections to the team leader, who incorporates them in the final cycle report for distribution to the instructor and the team members.

Role Evaluations

Each team member prepares a personal copy of form PEER, shown in Table 10.3. Give your views on the team's performance and on how each role was performed. These reviews provide an opportunity to recognize good work and to suggest where roles or tasks could be better handled in the future. The evaluations also help the instructor evaluate the contributions each engineer made to the team's overall performance.

   In the top section of the form, evaluate the relative difficulty of the roles. That is, if one role required twice as much work as all the others, you should enter 32, 17, 17, 17, 17 in the column under required work. These ratings should consider everything that the engineer did in that team role. List these contributions in percentages, and make them total 100. Thus, if you think that everyone contributed equally, list 20% for all roles.

   Use the same rating scheme for the role difficulty; that is, some roles may seem much more difficult, and others may take substantially less ingenuity and dedication. Again, use a percentage evaluation with the numbers totaling 100.

   For the ratings in the remaining four boxes, rate the team and each role against the criteria shown. Here, you could rate all 5's, all 1's, or any mix in any

TABLE 10.3 TSPi TEAM AND PEER EVALUATION: FORM PEER

Name _____ Team _____ Instructor _____

Date _____ Cycle No. _____ Week No. _____

For each role, evaluate the work required and the relative difficulty in % during this cycle.

Role	Work Required	Role Difficulty
Team Leader		
Development Manager		
Planning Manager		
Quality/Process Manager		
Support Manager		
Total Contribution (100%)		

Rate the overall team against each criterion. Circle one number from 1 (inadequate) to 5 (superior).

Team spirit	1	2	3	4	5
Overall effectiveness	1	2	3	4	5
Rewarding experience	1	2	3	4	5
Team productivity	1	2	3	4	5
Process quality	1	2	3	4	5
Product quality	1	2	3	4	5

Rate role for overall contribution. Circle one number from 1 (inadequate) to 5 (superior).

Team Leader	1	2	3	4	5
Development Manager	1	2	3	4	5
Planning Manager	1	2	3	4	5
Quality/Process Manager	1	2	3	4	5
Support Manager	1	2	3	4	5

Rate each role for helpfulness and support. Circle one number from 1 (inadequate) to 5 (superior).

Team Leader	1	2	3	4	5
Development Manager	1	2	3	4	5
Planning Manager	1	2	3	4	5
Quality/Process Manager	1	2	3	4	5
Support Manager	1	2	3	4	5

Rate each role for how well it was performed. Circle one number from 1 (inadequate) to 5 (superior).

Team Leader	1	2	3	4	5
Development Manager	1	2	3	4	5
Planning Manager	1	2	3	4	5
Quality/Process Manager	1	2	3	4	5
Support Manager	1	2	3	4	5

box. If you wish to make additional comments on any topic, do so on the back of the PEER form or on separate sheets. Be sure to put your name on all the sheets that you submit. Turn in the PEER forms to the instructor, who will use them in the class evaluations. The instructor will not make these ratings public.

Role Evaluation Suggestions

To produce constructive peer evaluations, act as if you were giving your comments directly to the person who performed the role being evaluated. Although you may not intend to do this, you are more likely to think of helpful suggestions if you act this way. It is also a good idea to assume that any evaluation you make will eventually become public. In general, it is wise to remember that few documents stay secret forever, and it is a good idea to write the evaluations so that their publication would not embarrass you or anyone else. Be frank and honest, but be objective and constructive.

You can best do this by focusing on improvement opportunities. How can you help the person who handled this role? If you had held that job, what would you like people to tell you? Although you can criticize an action (or lack thereof), try to accompany every criticism with suggestions on how to handle the situation better the next time. Because the roles are usually rotated among team members, use these evaluations as a way to help the next person to handle the role in a more effective way.

Exit Criteria

The postmortem exit criteria are as follows.

- ☐ The team has produced a high-quality product, together with all the required documentation.
- ☐ The completed product is under configuration control.
- ☐ The process data have been evaluated, and PIPs have been completed and submitted.
- ☐ The role evaluations have been completed and submitted.
- ☐ The development cycle report has been completed, and a copy has been provided to each team member and to the instructor.
- ☐ All TSPi forms have been completed for the system and all its component parts.
- ☐ The project notebook is updated with all pertinent project data and the cycle report.

Before you conclude the postmortem phase, check each item to make sure that you have completed it. Also check that the project notebook conforms to the notebook specifications in Appendix G of this text.

10.5   Summary

The postmortem is the final step in the TSPi process. The postmortem provides a structured way to improve your personal and team performance. Every TSPi development cycle ends with a postmortem.

The postmortem starts with the quality/process manager leading the team through a review of the team's data. This review examines what you did, identifies where the process worked and where it did not work, and compares the team's performance with its goals and plans.

Next, the team leader leads the team in evaluating each role. These evaluations focus on what worked, where there were problems, and where there is room for improvement. The team reviews the team leader's role first and then reviews each of the others. Finally, the team evaluates the faculty and facilities. Throughout all the evaluations, concentrate on suggested areas for improvement, being specific wherever possible.

The cycle report describes what you produced, the process that you used, and the roles you performed. It describes what worked and what did not work and suggests how to do better the next time. Keep the report brief and factual. Emphasize the lessons learned and how to use these lessons to do better work. Whenever you can, justify the conclusions with actual team data. Also, compare performance with prior development cycles and highlight any trends.

In the final postmortem step, every team member completes a PEER form. Here, you give your personal views on the team's and each role's performance. You also have the option of making additional comments on any topics on the back of the form or on separate sheets. Write the evaluations in a constructive way and focus on improvement opportunities.

10.6   Reference

[Brown] Rita Mae Brown, 1988. *Starting from Scratch: A Different Kind of Writer's Manual.* New York: Bantam Books.

PART THREE

The Team Roles

The next five chapters describe the various team roles, their principal goals and activities, and several key issues concerning each role. These roles are

- ☐ Chapter 11: The team leader
- ☐ Chapter 12: The development manager
- ☐ Chapter 13: The planning manager
- ☐ Chapter 14: The quality/process manager
- ☐ Chapter 15: The support manager

These chapters are designed to serve as reference material about the role activities and responsibilities. Rather than force you to look in several places, these chapters provide one place where you can find all the relevant material on each role. The chapters also give references to the places where role-related topics are covered in more detail in the other textbook chapters. When you read these chapters for the first time, I suggest that you concentrate first on the chapter that covers your assigned role.

General Role Objectives

The TSPi role assignments have several objectives:

- To provide students an opportunity to learn about various aspects of running a team project
- To define for student teams how to handle project management tasks
- To help teams to complete their projects successfully

In selecting a role, consider three questions.

- Does this role interest you?
- Do you think that you can do this role?
- Have you already done this role?

In general, I suggest that you seek roles that interest you. You are more likely to exert yourself on topics that you find interesting than on ones that bore you. Keep an open mind, however, for many tasks can be more interesting than you might expect, particularly if you use your imagination and try to do them in a superior way. If the only available role is one that you have not yet done, consider it even if you don't think it will be interesting.

Second, if you don't think that you can handle a role, think twice about taking it on. Your intuition is often a good guide. Don't be too quick to discount your own ability, however, for people are generally more capable than they think. None of the TSPi roles are difficult if you are willing to work at them. Start with the attitude that you can handle a role and, if you ask for help when needed, you will probably do a competent job.

Remember, your principal goal in this course is to learn, so be open to suggestions and try as many of the roles as you have time for. If you follow the TSPi process and use common sense, you will most likely succeed. Also, remember that you are bound to make mistakes, so relax and learn from each one. Just try not to make the same mistakes more than once. With this attitude, you should be able to handle any TSPi role that you are willing to try.

As a team member, you also work as a development engineer. In this role, you must work cooperatively with the other team members, do your own work to the best of your ability, and strive to work in accordance with the TSPi process. This means that you should do the following.

- Record your time in the time recording log (LOGT).
- Enter the week number when each task is completed.
- Update the TASK and SCHEDULE templates, either by hand or with the TSPi tool.

□ Record all the development, inspection, and test defects for the products you own (develop) in your defect recording log (LOGD).

□ Enter the size of each product or component

□ Submit updated copies of completed TASK, SCHEDULE, and WEEK forms to the planning manager and the instructor before the first class or laboratory session of each week.

□ When you have completed any system or component tasks, update the SUMP and SUMQ forms for that component.

□ When you update the SUMP or SUMQ form, give copies to the quality/process manager and instructor.

□ Report all needed changes in configuration-controlled products to the support manager.

□ Report all issues to be tracked to the support manager for the issue tracking log (ITL).

□ Above all, look at and think about the data on your personal work and use these data to help you produce quality work.

11

The Team Leader Role

This chapter describes the team leader's role. If you have been assigned this role, the chapter gives you helpful pointers on how to perform it most effectively. The topics covered are

- ☐ The team leader's goals
- ☐ Helpful team leader skills and abilities
- ☐ The team leader's principal activities
- ☐ The team leader's project activities

The first three sections provide discussion and background on various aspects of the team leader's role. The fourth section lists in one table all the activities you will be responsible for doing in a development cycle. It also provides references to places where these activities are discussed more fully in other chapters. With the TSPi, all engineers fill roles as well as act as development engineers. Thus, as team leader, you participate in the development work along with the other engineers.

11.1   The Team Leader's Goals

With the TSPi, all team members have specific and measurable goals defined by the TSPi process. If you want to modify them, you should do the following.

☐ Write down the goals that you wish to use.

☐ Specify how to measure these new goals.

☐ Describe why you have selected these goals instead of the ones provided by the TSPi process.

☐ Give a copy of your revised goals to the team and to the instructor.

☐ Put a copy of your new goals in the project notebook.

With the TSPi, every team member has two kinds of goals: everyone has the same goal of being an effective team member, and every team role has its own unique goals. All these goals are described in the following paragraphs.

Common Team Member Goal

Be a cooperative and effective team member.   As team leader, your first priority is to be a cooperative and effective team member. You and all the other team members have the primary goal of working cooperatively with the entire team to produce a high-quality product on the agreed schedule. Above all else, the team's success depends on all team members contributing their personal best efforts, supporting other team members, and working cooperatively to resolve issues and disagreements.

Although the individual roles are important, it is most important to remember that each role represents a single facet of the overall team's assignment. Thus, individual role objectives may occasionally appear to conflict because each role considers the team's activities from only one perspective. To meet the team's overall goals, however, you need to integrate these individual goals into a smoothly functioning whole. You can best do this by giving highest priority to the overall team goal of working cooperatively with the entire team to produce a quality product on the agreed schedule.

The suggested measures for this goal are the following.

☐ The PEER form evaluations of the overall team are good (3) or better for team spirit.

☐ The PEER form evaluations of the team leader role are good (3) or better for overall contribution and helpfulness and support.

Team Leader Goal 1

Build and maintain an effective team.   As team leader, your principal goal is to weld the team members into an effective and productive team. The broadest measures of success for this goal are as follows.

- ☐ The team meets its cost, schedule, and quality goals.
- ☐ The PEER form evaluations of overall team effectiveness are 3 or better.
- ☐ The team members' PEER form ratings of the team leader's role are good (3) or better for overall contribution.
- ☐ The team members' PEER form ratings of the team leader's role are good (3) or better for how well the role was performed.

Team Leader Goal 2

Motivate all team members to work aggressively on the project.   This goal calls for you to work with all the team members to ensure that they put in the required time, do their planned work, and work hard to produce quality products. The measures against this goal are as follows.

- ☐ All the team members worked the hours that they had committed to work.
- ☐ All the team members met their earned-value commitments.
- ☐ All the team members followed the defined TSPi process, completed their LOGT and LOGD forms, recorded weekly status on form WEEK, submitted the report on time, and reported product results on forms SUMP and SUMQ.

Team Leader Goal 3

Resolve all the issues team members bring to you.   This goal calls for you to quickly and objectively identify and resolve issues and problems among members. The suggested measure for this goal is

- ☐ The team members' PEER form evaluations of the team leader role are good (3) or better for helpfulness and support.

Team Leader Goal 4

Keep the instructor fully informed about the team's progress.   A key part of running an effective project is to keep your management informed of the team's status, progress, and problems. To meet this goal, you must

- ☐ Provide accurate and complete project status reports to the instructor every week.

☐ Ensure that the instructor is promptly informed of any team problems that might require attention.

Team Leader Goal 5

Perform effectively as the team's meeting facilitator. The best measure of your effectiveness as the team facilitator is the degree to which every team member actively participates in and contributes to the team's meetings and other activities. There is no direct measure of this result, but when team members actively participate, they tend to view the team experience as rewarding. Thus, the suggested measure of this goal is the degree to which the team members rate this development cycle as a rewarding experience (3 or better) on their PEER evaluation forms.

11.2 Helpful Team Leader Skills and Abilities

As shown in Table 11.1, the four most helpful characteristics for a team leader are as follows.

1. You enjoy acting as a leader, and, when in a group, you naturally assume a leadership position. Some people are comfortable leading groups, and others cannot visualize themselves taking such positions. If you have never been a leader, however, don't assume that you cannot be one. It is remarkable how often seemingly ordinary people become very effective leaders when they are thrust into leadership positions. If you would like to lead the team, have a commitment to the job, and are willing to work hard to help this team to do a superior job, you should consider being team leader.

2. You are able to identify the key issues and make objective decisions. The biggest block to effective decision making is to become confused by personalities and extraneous issues. Thus, the crucial first step in making effective decisions is to clearly identify the problems or issues to be resolved. After you have stepped back and looked at these problems objectively, the answers are usually fairly obvious. If you focus on the job to be done, ask your teammates for their views, and weigh all pertinent facts, you can handle this aspect of being a leader.

3. You do not mind occasionally taking unpopular positions and are willing to press people to accomplish difficult or demanding tasks. With the software process, there are many temptations to cut corners in an attempt to finish the project quickly. Unfortunately, such process shortcuts often result in more defects and longer testing, and they generally end up taking much more time than was saved by rushing through the job. The TSPi process can

TABLE 11.1 TSPi TEAM LEADER ROLE

Objective	The team leader leads the team and ensures that engineers report their process data and complete their work as planned.
Role Characteristics	The characteristics most helpful to team leaders are the following. 1. You enjoy being leader and naturally assume a leadership role. 2. You are able to identify the key issues and objectively make decisions. 3. You do not mind occasionally taking unpopular actions and are willing to press people to accomplish difficult tasks. 4. You respect your teammates, are willing to listen to their views, and want to help them perform to the best of their abilities.
Goals and Measures	Team member goal: Be a cooperative and effective team member. • Measures: Team PEER ratings for team spirit, overall contribution, and helpfulness and support Goal 1: Build and maintain an effective team. • Measure 1.1: project performance against cost, schedule, quality goals • Measure 1.2: PEER evaluations of overall team effectiveness • Measure 1.3: PEER evaluations of the team leader's overall contribution • Measure 1.4: team members' PEER ratings of how well the team leader's role was performed Goal 2: Motivate all team members to work aggressively on the project. • Measure 2.1: All team members worked their committed hours. • Measure 2.2: The team members met their earned-value commitments. • Measure 2.3: The team members followed the TSPi process, recorded all data, and completed all required forms. Goal 3: Resolve all the issues team members bring to you. • Measure 3: the team members' PEER ratings of the team leader's role for helpfulness and support. Goal 4: Keep the instructor fully informed about the team's progress. • Measure 4.1: accurate and complete weekly status reports • Measure 4.2: the instructor's timely awareness of project status Goal 5: Perform effectively as the team's meeting facilitator. • Measure 5: the team's PEER evaluation of the project as a rewarding experience
Principal Activities	1. Motivate the team members to perform their tasks. 2. Every week, either before or at the start of the first weekly class or laboratory session, run the weekly team meeting to • Track all committed tasks to see that they have been completed • Check that all team members have submitted the required data • Check that all required forms have been completed on the work accomplished to date • Check on the status of project risks and issues • Identify the tasks to be accomplished in the next week and by whom 3. Every week, report team status to the instructor. • Show the project notebook with the team weekly data. • Seek guidance from the instructor on engineers who consistently fail to complete tasks or submit data on time. • Obtain guidance from the instructor to pass along to the team. 4. Help the team in allocating tasks and resolving issues. 5. Act as facilitator and timekeeper for all team meetings. 6. Maintain the project notebook. 7. Lead the team in producing the development cycle report. 8. Act as a development engineer.

be effective, but only if the engineers consistently use it. A major part of your job as team leader is to help the team members consistently follow the process and regularly gather and use their process data.

4. What is most important, you respect the people you are leading. You are willing to listen to your teammates and want to help them perform to the best of their ability. Here, the key is to recognize that everyone's capabilities differ and that everyone has hidden and untapped potential. The instructor or management selected the people for this team, and their job was to provide members with the requisite skills for the job. Your job is to use these skills and abilities to get the work done. If you are willing to help the engineers do their work to the best of their abilities, you should be able to lead the team effectively.

A Leader Has Followers

You cannot be a leader without followers. There are only three prerequisites to having followers.

☐ You have a vision of what you want to do.

☐ The team is motivated to achieve your vision.

☐ You are committed to helping your team accomplish this vision.

Your objective is to help the team members coalesce around the team goals and to strive to achieve these goals. To do this, you must appreciate the capabilities of all the team members and use their skills whenever and however the tasks require. This means that you must listen to the team members and capitalize on their ideas even when they differ from your own.

You have a pragmatic focus on the end objective and a willingness to listen to anyone who will help you to achieve it. You naturally seek the team's views on all significant issues and are willing to consider suggestions from all sources. Although you strive for team consensus, you are not willing to waste time in prolonged debates on minor issues.

Finally, and above all, you are an energetic optimist. You are personally willing to work hard and to push the team members to also work hard. You are enthusiastic about doing this job and believe it is both important and achievable. You are convinced that the team can do a good job and are excited about this opportunity. Your drive and enthusiasm will help the team overcome the inevitable obstacles, and your excitement will help everyone maintain the energy to do a superior job.

A Leader Demands Performance

You are willing to press your teammates to perform at their best. You know what must be done, and you are willing to insist that the team members do their work in the way they know they should. Most of us know how our jobs should be done, but we are apt to cut corners when the schedule is tight. As the leader, your job is to insist that the team do the job the right way. You know that the right way is invariably the fastest way in the long run.

The problem is how to insist on quality work without seeming like a "boss." There is a delicate balance between maintaining high standards and empowering the team members. A new team is like a machine that must be warmed up. It is potentially powerful, but has yet to be run at full speed. Test the team's abilities and give the engineers a chance to see what they can do. Challenge the engineers to do superior work, and you and they will be surprised at what they can accomplish.

A Leader Takes Difficult Stands

When required, you do not mind taking unpopular positions. As team leader, you will probably have to settle occasional disputes. Some team members may have strongly opposing views, and often there is no clearly best answer. You must sense when to take the time to reach consensus and when to make the call and move on.

Occasionally, there will be a lone holdout who refuses to give in even though everyone else agrees. It is important to recognize that all new ideas start as a minority of one, so take the time to find out whether this lone holdout has the germ of an important idea. Your job is to maintain the team's energy and pace but also to take advantage of everyone's creative ideas.

In addition, most project disasters provide early clues, and often one or two of the engineers will have an uncomfortable feeling. Although they will rarely know what is bothering them and often can't explain the problem, their intuition tells them that something is wrong. With a little patience and some thoughtful probing, the rest of the team can usually figure out the source of the problem and take the action needed to prevent the disaster. Your job is to help the team to do this.

A Leader Handles People Problems

It may be that one team member will not cooperate with the team. He or she may fundamentally disagree with the team's strategy or may be unwilling to spend a reasonable amount of time on the project. Do your best to convince this person to work cooperatively with the team, but don't allow the conflict to go on for too long. Consult the team and take enough time to solve the problem if you can, but as soon as you conclude that the problem is intractable, go to the instructor for help.

Although all these skills and abilities can be helpful, they are not essential. The critical needs are that you be interested in supporting the team, be concerned about the quality of the team's finished products, and be willing to work at whatever role assignment you are given.

11.3   The Team Leader's Principal Activities

As team leader, you are responsible for the eight principal activities shown in Table 11.1. These are discussed in the following paragraphs.

Team Leader Principal Activity 1

Motivate the team members to perform their tasks.   Your first principal activity is to motivate the team members to perform to the best of their abilities. The TSPi builds motivation by involving all team members in planning and managing their personal work. Assuming that all the students are suitably qualified and that the team is properly run, motivation should be a natural consequence of doing a challenging and interesting job.

Following are the most common issues you will likely face.

- ☐ Some team members do not follow the process.
- ☐ Some team members do not make a reasonable effort.
- ☐ It is hard to hold to the project schedule.

We discuss these three issues in the following paragraphs.

Not Following the Process

This is a simple matter of discipline. Emphasize that the engineers must follow the process or the project will likely fail. If some engineers still refuse to cooperate, do not gather data, or do not report on their progress, they are not likely to change without strong action. If you do not resolve this problem promptly, the project is likely to degenerate and could easily fail. Don't delay; if you can't get agreement quickly, take the problem to the instructor and ask for help.

Not Making a Reasonable Effort

This is a common problem, particularly for student teams. Some students have heavy workloads, and others may have jobs or family obligations. With few exceptions, overloaded students feel guilty about not carrying their fair share of the work and do their utmost to compensate. As long as these students are truly making their best efforts, the team members will understand and rebalance their tasks.

The more difficult problem is caused by students who don't show up, miss commitments, and don't seem to care. Don't waste time with these students. People who have such problems have never learned a personal discipline of commitment. They are constantly late, make promises they can't keep, and are generally unreliable. You can do them a big favor by helping them to develop such a discipline now.

The first step is to tell the student that his or her behavior is unacceptable. Also, promptly inform the instructor of the problem but explain that you are working on it and haven't given up yet. Next, get a firm date from this student for a next commitment. If this commitment is also missed, go to the instructor for help. Insist that this engineer either start performing immediately or be removed from the team. One shirker will destroy the team's spirit and seriously reduce the team's performance. You will actually get more done without this student than you would with him or her on the team. Although it is important to make a real effort to solve such problems, some people will not change without a major motivating force. If you can't provide such motivation, maybe the instructor can. If you don't see progress reasonably soon, however, you probably never will. As soon as it is clear that things won't improve, get the student off the team.

Overall team performance will be largely determined by your effectiveness in handling the team leader role, but you cannot be held responsible for team members who are unable or unwilling to work cooperatively with the rest of the team. It is, however, your responsibility to inform the instructor of any such issues in time to get help before the team's performance is seriously damaged.

Not Holding to the Schedule

If the team is putting in the time but the work is not getting done, don't give up too soon, particularly in the first development cycle. Frequently, the problem is unfamiliarity with a new process. This is probably a first project for many of the team members, and it is almost certainly the first time they have used TSPi. This is also probably a new team that is just learning to work together. All this learning takes time, so do not get discouraged too quickly. A little time and some guidance from the instructor will generally help you over the rough spots.

As long as you are not trying to do too much, the best way to hold to the schedule is to use the weekly meeting to set goals for the next week. Then, every week, track what was done against the goals for the prior week and get each team member to commit to the time to be spent and the tasks to be completed in the next week.

If the problem persists, reconsider what you are trying to do. Talk to the team about where and how to cut back. Then rebalance the workload to relieve those who are having the most trouble.

Team Leader Principal Activity 2

Run the weekly team meeting.   Your second principal role activity is to lead the weekly team meeting. This meeting follows the script WEEK, shown in Table 11.2. By holding a weekly meeting, you help the team members to act as a team.

TABLE 11.2 TSPi WEEKLY MEETING: SCRIPT WEEK

Purpose	To guide the team in conducting the weekly status meeting
Entry Criteria	• All team members are present. • All the team members have provided updated TASK, SCHEDULE, and WEEK forms to the planning manager. • The planning manager has produced the composite weekly team status report from the team members' data (form WEEK). • The team leader has issued a meeting agenda.
General	In advance of the meeting, the team leader has • Asked team members for meeting agenda topics • Prepared and distributed the meeting agenda The team leader leads the weekly meeting. • The quality/process manager records the meeting topics. • Each team member generally reports his or her role work and development work at the same time. After the meeting, the team leader • Issues and distributes the meeting report • Puts a report copy in the project notebook

Step	Activities	Description
1	Agenda Review	The team leader opens the meeting and • Reviews the agenda and asks for additions or changes • Checks that all team members are fully prepared and defers the meeting if any are not
2	Role Reports	Starting with the development manager, the engineers report • Any overall role issues or concerns • Status on any role-related tasks or activities • Status on any issue or risk items that the engineer is tracking The development manager reports on development status. • Items designed, reviewed, inspected, implemented, and tested The planning manager reports on planning status. • Team hours and earned-value status against the plan The quality/process manager reviews data on • Each inspection and every integration and system test defect • The percentage of engineers following the process • Any suspected quality problems The support manager reports the status of the SCM and ITL systems. • Items submitted this week, changes made, system inventory
3	Engineer Reports	Each engineer reports his or her development status. • The hours worked this week and cycle compared to the plan • The earned value gained this week and cycle versus the plan • Times for the tasks accomplished this week and the plan times • The tasks to be accomplished in the next week • The hours to be worked in the next week • Any problem areas or topics of general team interest
4	Meeting Close	The team leader leads the discussion of any remaining topics and • Checks that all committed tasks have been reported • Verifies that all risks and issues have been reviewed • Ensures that next week's tasks have been identified and assigned • Discusses the items to include in the team's weekly report
Exit Criteria		• The meeting report completed and filed in the project notebook • Updated team and engineer TASK, SCHEDULE, WEEK, and CSR forms in the project notebook • Updated copy of the ITL log in the project notebook

One of your responsibilities is to chair this meeting and set the agenda. Your principal objectives for the meeting are as follows.

☐ Track progress against the tasks for the previous week.

☐ Make sure that everyone is properly submitting the required time, size, and defect data and completing the proper forms.

☐ Set team and engineer goals for the next week. These goals should include weekly hours, earned-value targets, and the specific tasks to be completed.

☐ Discuss previously identified risks and, if any actions are needed, decide who will take these actions and when.

☐ Also see whether the team is aware of any new risks and, if so, decide who should track and address them for the team.

☐ Identify any new problems that need to be addressed.

Do not try to solve major problems in the weekly meeting. If the issues are simple and everyone agrees on what to do, settle the problem at the time. But for more difficult issues, list the problems and decide who will address them, how, and when.

Team Leader Principal Activity 3

Report weekly status.   As team leader, your third principal activity is to report project status to the instructor. Use the weekly meeting to gather the data needed for this report, and try to hold your team's weekly meeting before the first class or laboratory period each week. If the team members give their data to the planning manager at the end of the previous week, it will allow enough time to summarize these data before the weekly meeting. After the meeting, report these data and any other significant items to the instructor at the week's first class or laboratory session.

Again, if you have problems, now is the time to raise them. If the team has tried but cannot resolve a problem, ask the instructor for help. The weekly team report serves two purposes.

☐ It keeps the instructor informed of your status and progress. By reporting your progress clearly and often, you pass on both the good news and the bad. Then the instructor always knows your status and can help you if you need it.

☐ The weekly report also helps to sustain the team's energy and enthusiasm. By clearly defining and reporting on their progress every week, you help the members to see what they have accomplished and what they must do to continue to meet their plan. They are then more likely to strive to make the project a success.

Team Leader Principal Activity 4

Help the team to allocate tasks.   As team leader, your fourth principal activity is to assist the team in allocating tasks among the members. Many team tasks involve several members, and the work must be allocated among them. In helping the team to allocate the work, make sure that each team member agrees to take the assignment before you make it. Usually, the assignments are obvious and everyone will quickly agree. Occasionally, however, some tasks will be left over. Here is one usually successful way to handle these leftover tasks.

1. Make a list of the unassigned tasks.
2. Make another list of the team members who have time available.
3. Ask each team member to write on a piece of paper the two or three tasks that he or she would prefer to do.
4. Draw a matrix on a blackboard or flip chart, with one task on each row at the side of the matrix and the team member names in the columns at the top.
5. Mark on the board those tasks selected by only one engineer.
6. Work down the task list until all the assignments are taken.
7. Stop assigning tasks to any engineer when he or she has accumulated a fair share of the work.

This procedure usually results in most of the engineers doing tasks they volunteered to do. If some tasks are not selected, identify the engineers with the least amount of work and ask them to divide the remaining tasks among themselves. This usually results in a fair and reasonable allocation of the work.

Team Leader Principal Activity 5

Act as facilitator and timekeeper for team meetings.   Your fifth principal activity is to act as facilitator and timekeeper for all team meetings. The timekeeping activity involves tracking and recording the meeting's progress against the agenda. This requires that team meetings have an agenda and that the agenda have times against which to track. For your first team meeting, make an agenda but merely track the actual times against the agenda items. Thereafter, you will have actual data to guide you in setting agenda times for subsequent meetings. For the weekly team meeting, set the agenda based on the script WEEK, shown in Table 11.2.

As facilitator, your job is to help the team to hold efficient and effective meetings. The principal facilitator responsibilities are as follows.

☐ Focus the discussion on the agenda topics. When a point is off the agenda topic, write it on a flip chart or board so that the team members can see it and come back to it later if they wish. Then get back to the subject at hand.

☐ Restrict the meeting to a single discussion. Side conversations often start during agenda digressions. Such digressions generally indicate that the meeting has drifted off the subject. As facilitator, tactfully ask the group to concentrate on one subject. If the other topics are significant and not on the agenda, put them on a list for later attention.

☐ Do not let anyone dominate the meeting. If someone monopolizes the discussion, ask people to take turns and ensure that everyone gets a chance to talk. Sometimes, you may have to ask outspoken members to hold their comments while you hear from the others.

☐ Make sure that everyone is heard and participates. When people sit quietly or try to raise points but are drowned out, wait for an appropriate time and ask them for their views.

☐ Close the discussion. It is often difficult to sense when a subject has been exhausted and further progress cannot be made. When closing a discussion topic, make sure that the recorder (the quality/process manager) records the final conclusions. If there has been a decision, record what was decided and why. If action is to be taken, note what is to be done, by whom, and when. If the topic is deferred, note why, when the discussion will be resumed, and what additional information or data are needed before you can address that topic. Also note who is responsible for providing this information and who will reschedule the meeting.

Facilitation is a skill that is worth learning. By following these simple guidelines, most people can be effective facilitators. The key is to watch, listen, and be sensitive to what is said and not said. Focus on getting everyone to participate and make sure that all the members feel they have been heard and their views were understood and considered.

Team Leader Principal Activity 6

Maintain the project notebook. Your sixth team leader activity is to maintain the project notebook. This is the official record of all of the team's activities. It includes copies of all work products, test reports, plans, inspection reports, meeting reports, weekly team status reports, the final report for each development cycle, and a full set of completed TSPi project forms. For further information on the project notebook, see Table 11.3 or Appendix G.

Team Leader Principal Activity 7

Lead the team in producing the development cycle report. As team leader, your final task is to lead the preparation of the cycle report. In doing this task, you

TABLE 11.3 TSPi PROJECT NOTEBOOK: SPECIFICATION NOTEBOOK

Purpose	To describe the contents of the project notebook
General	• The project notebook holds the complete project record. • It includes copies of all important project documents. • The notebook contains the official project record. • The project notebook is given to the instructor at the end of each development cycle and at the end of the course. • The team leader maintains the project notebook.
Notebook Format	The notebook should be in an appropriate format. • Small project notebooks may be in a three-ring binder. • Larger notebooks may be in file folders and multiple three-ring binders.
Notebook Sections	The standard notebook sections are as follows. • Outline • Summary • Project cycle reports • Task and schedule plans and actuals • Process documents • System and component plan and actual data • Test plans and data • Inspection reports and defect logs • Working notes and documents These sections are further explained elsewhere in this table.
Outline	• An outline of the notebook contents
Summary	• The project name, dates, team members, and role assignments • The SUMP and SUMQ forms with plan and actual system data • Team TASK and SCHEDULE forms with plan and actual data
Project and Cycle Reports	• Final reports for each development cycle • During the project, this file can be used as a repository for documents to include later in the final report.
Task and Schedule Plans and Actuals	Include all plan and actual resource and schedule data. • A summary of task and schedule performance versus plan • Engineer TASK, SCHEDULE, LOGD, and LOGT forms
Process Documents	• If changed, the defined processes used and all PIPs • The change control procedure and any related documents • The configuration management process • The issue and risk tracking process
Component Data	• The SUMP and SUMQ forms for every product component
Test Plans and Data	• The build, integration, and system test plans • Test logs and test data (LOGTEST) • Test defect review records
Inspection Reports	• All inspection reports (INS) and defect logs (LOGD)
Reports	• The engineers' and team's WEEK report forms
Working Documents	• System requirements specification (SRS) • The development strategy • System design specification (SDS) with SRS traceability • All design documents (design templates, etc.) • Other important documents (CCR, CSR, SUMTASK, etc.)

TABLE 11.4 TSPi TEAM LEADER'S PROJECT ACTIVITIES

Phase Week	General	In addition to the engineer's standard tasks, the team leader does the following tasks each week.	References
LAU 2, 8, 11	Project launch	Hold the first team meeting. • Review the required weekly data and reports	Chapter 3
STRAT 2, 8, 11	Development strategy	Participate in developing and reviewing the strategy.	Chapter 4
	Configuration control	Participate in reviewing the configuration control process.	Appendix B
PLAN 3, 8, 11	Development plan	Participate in making the development plan.	Chapter 5
	Quality plan	Participate in making the quality plan.	
REQ 4, 9, 12	Need statement	Participate in analyzing and clarifying the requirements.	Chapter 6
	Produce SRS	Produce the assigned parts of the SRS.	
	System test plan	Participate in producing the system test plan.	Chapter 9
	SRS inspection	Participate in inspecting the SRS and system test plan.	Appendix C
DES 5, 9, 12	Design specification	Participate in developing the SDS.	Chapter 7
	Integration plan	Participate in producing the integration test plan.	Chapter 9
	SDS inspection	Participate in inspecting the SDS and integration test plan.	Appendix C
IMP 6, 10, 13	Planning	Participate in planning the implementation work.	Chapter 8
	Detailed design	Produce and review detailed designs.	
	Unit test plan	Produce and review unit test plans.	Script UT
	DLD inspection	Participate in inspecting detailed designs and unit test plans.	Appendix C
	Test development	Produce unit test materials.	Script UT
	Implementation	Implement and review programs.	Chapter 8
	Compile	Compile programs.	
	Code inspection	Participate in inspecting programs.	Appendix C
	Unit test	Unit test programs.	Script UT
TEST 7, 10, 13	Test development	Participate in the test development tasks.	Chapter 9
	Build	Participate in building the product.	
	Integration	Participate in integrating the product.	
	System test	Participate in system testing the product.	
	User documentation	Participate in producing the user documentation.	
PM 8, 11, 15	Plan cycle report	Lead the team in planning and producing a report on its work in the latest development cycle. • Allocate report work to the team members. • Obtain completion commitments for this work. • Assemble the completed report.	Chapter 10
	Cycle report	Lead the team in reviewing team performance and producing a report on the latest development cycle.	
	Prepare peer reviews	Complete a peer review for the team leader's role and for all other team roles using form PEER.	
Every week	Data reporting	Provide agreed weekly data to the planning manager.	Chapter 5
	Weekly meeting	Lead the team weekly meeting. • Track committed tasks. • Check on completeness of team member data. • Check on completeness of forms. • Check on the status of project risks and issues. • Identify the tasks for the next week and who will do them.	Script WEEK
	Instructor reports	Every week, report team status to the instructor.	Chapter 11
	Tasks and issues	Help the team in allocating tasks and resolving issues.	
	Project notebook	Maintain a complete record of the team activities in the project notebook.	Appendix G

guide the team members in producing, reviewing, and correcting their assigned portions of this report. As part of this report, you provide the outline and the opening report summary as well as a section on overall team performance. Finally, comment on the team leader role, describing what worked well for you and areas where you had problems. Also comment on how you could handle this role better the next time and explain why this would be an improvement.

Team Leader Principal Activity 8

Act as a development engineer.   As previously noted, every team member is also a development engineer.

11.4   The Team Leader's Project Activities

The team leader's project activities for a full development cycle are listed in Table 11.4. This table cross references coverage of these topics in other parts of this book.

11.5   Summary

This chapter describes the team leader's role. With TSPi, all engineers fill team roles as well as act as development engineers. Thus, as team leader, you also participate in the development work along with the other engineers.

The first goal of all team members is to work cooperatively with the entire team and to produce a high-quality product according to the agreed-on schedule. Above all else, the team's success depends on all team members contributing their personal best efforts, supporting other team members, and working cooperatively to resolve issues and disagreements.

As team leader, your principal goals are to build an effective team, to motivate the team members to work to the best of their abilities, to identify and resolve issues, to keep the instructor informed, and to act as the team's meeting facilitator. As part of this role, you report project status to the instructor every week and ensure that he or she is promptly aware of any team problems.

The four most helpful characteristics for a team leader are as follows.

☐ You enjoy acting as a leader.

☐ You can make objective decisions.

☐ You are willing to press your teammates to perform to the best of their abilities.

☐ You respect the people you are leading.

You also know what must be done, and you are willing to insist that the team members do their work as they know they should. As team leader, you must settle disputes, and you do not mind occasionally taking unpopular positions. You also must sense when to take the time to reach consensus and when to move on. Your job is to maintain the team's energy and pace while also taking advantage of everyone's creative ideas and abilities.

In some cases one team member may not cooperate with the team. He or she may fundamentally disagree with the team's strategy or may be unwilling to spend a reasonable amount of time on the project. Do your best to resolve these problems, but don't allow such conflicts to go on for too long. Consult the team, but if you cannot quickly settle these problems, go to the instructor for help.

The eight principal responsibilities of the team leader are as follows.

1. Motivate the team members to perform their tasks.

2. Hold a team meeting every week.

3. Report team status and progress to the instructor every week.

4. Lead the team in allocating tasks among the team members.

5. Act as facilitator and timekeeper in all the team meetings.

6. Maintain the project notebook.

7. Lead the team in producing the development cycle report.

8. Act as a development engineer.

12

The Development
Manager Role

This chapter describes the development manager's role. If you have been assigned
this role, the chapter gives you helpful pointers on how to perform it most effectively. The topics covered are

- □ The development manager's goals
- □ Helpful development manager skills and abilities
- □ The development manager's principal activities
- □ The development manager's project activities

The first three sections provide discussion and background on various aspects of
the development manager's role. The fourth section lists in one table all the activities you will be responsible for doing in a development cycle. It also provides references to places in other chapters where these activities are discussed more fully.
With the TSPi, all engineers fill roles as well as act as development engineers. Thus,
as development manager, you participate in the development work along with the
other engineers.

12.1   The Development Manager's Goals

With the TSPi, all team members have specific and measurable goals defined by the TSPi process. If you want to modify them, you should do the following.

☐ Write down the goals that you wish to use.

☐ Specify how to measure these new goals.

☐ Describe why you have selected these goals instead of the ones provided by the TSPi process.

☐ Give a copy of your revised goals to the team and to the instructor.

☐ Give a copy of your new goals to the team leader to put in the project notebook.

With the TSPi, every team member has two kinds of goals: everyone has the same goal of being an effective team member, and every team role has its own unique goals. All these goals are described in the following paragraphs.

Common Team Member Goal

Be a cooperative and effective team member.   As development manager, your first priority is to be a cooperative and effective team member. You and all the other team members have the primary goal of working cooperatively with the entire team to produce a high-quality product on the agreed schedule. Above all else, the team's success depends on all team members contributing their personal best efforts, supporting other team members, and working cooperatively to resolve issues and disagreements.

Although the individual roles are important, it is most important to remember that each role represents a single facet of the overall team's assignment. Thus, individual role objectives may occasionally appear to conflict because each role considers the team's activities from only one perspective. To meet the team's overall goals, however, you need to integrate these individual goals into a smoothly functioning whole. You can best do this by giving highest priority to the overall team goal of working cooperatively with the entire team to produce a quality product on the agreed schedule.

The suggested measures for this goal are the following.

☐ The PEER form evaluations of the overall team are good (3) or better for team spirit.

☐ The PEER form evaluations of the development manager role are good (3) or better for overall contribution and helpfulness and support.

Development Manager Goal 1

Produce a superior product.   The development manager's principal goal is to guide the team in producing a superior product. The ways to measure success in achieving this goal are as follows.

- ☐ The team has produced a useful and fully documented product that meets the basic requirements of the need statement.
- ☐ The requirements are traceable from the need statement to the SRS, to the SDS, and to the final implementation.
- ☐ The product design is fully documented and meets the team's design standards.
- ☐ The implementation faithfully represents the design.
- ☐ The product met all quality criteria.
- ☐ The product met its functional and operational objectives.

Development Manager Goal 2

Fully utilize the team members' skills and abilities.   The development manager's second goal is to fully use the knowledge and ability of the team members in designing and developing the product. Although there are no direct ways to measure success in achieving this goal, the following are general indicators.

- ☐ On form PEER, the team members rate the development manager role as good (3) or better on how well it was performed.
- ☐ On form PEER, the team members rate the development manager role as good (3) or better on helpfulness and support.
- ☐ On form PEER, the team members rate product quality as good (3) or better.

12.2   Helpful Development Manager Skills and Abilities

As shown in Table 12.1, the five most helpful characteristics for a development manager are the following.

1. Most important, you like to build things. In software development, we literally create new products out of nothing. There is a marvelous sense of achievement when we produce a large, complex structure that actually performs useful functions. It is your creation, and it works just the way you and your teammates intended. When this joy of creation is coupled with the excitement of a team achievement, software development can be truly rewarding.

TABLE 12.1 TSPi DEVELOPMENT MANAGER ROLE

Objective	The development manager leads and guides the team in defining, designing, developing, and testing the product.
Role Characteristics	The characteristics most helpful to development managers are the following. 1. You like to build things. 2. You want to be a software engineer and would like the experience of leading a design and development project. 3. You are a competent designer and feel you could lead a development team. 4. You are generally familiar with design methods. 5. You are willing to listen to other people's design ideas and can objectively and logically compare the qualities of their design ideas with yours.
Goals and Measures	Team member goal: Be a cooperative and effective team member. • Measures: Team peer ratings for team spirit, overall contribution, and helpfulness and support Goal 1: Produce a superior product. • Measure 1.1: The team produced a useful and fully documented product that met the basic requirements of the need statement. • Measure 1.2: The requirements are traceable from the need statement to the SRS, to the SDS, and to the final implementation. • Measure 1.3: The product design is fully documented and meets the team's design standards. • Measure 1.4: The implementation faithfully represents the design. • Measure 1.5: The product met all quality criteria. • Measure 1.6: The product met its functional and operational objectives. Goal 2: Fully utilize the team members' skills and abilities. • Measure 2.1: peer evaluations of how well the development manager role was performed • Measure 2.2: peer evaluations of the development manager's helpfulness and support • Measure 2.3: peer evaluations of product quality
Principal Activities	1. Lead the team in producing the development strategy. 2. Lead the team in producing the preliminary size and time estimates for the products to be produced. 3. Lead the development of the requirements specification (SRS). 4. Lead the team in producing the high-level design. 5. Lead the team in producing the design specification (SDS). 6. Lead the team in implementing the product. 7. Lead the team in developing the build, integration, and system test plans. 8. Lead the team in developing the test materials and running the tests. 9. Lead the team in producing the product's user documentation. 10. Participate in producing the development cycle report. 11. Act as a development engineer.

2. You want to be a software engineer and would like the experience of leading the design and development work for a project. Although you can learn a lot about software development from courses and books, there is no substitute for actually building a product. The experience of being development manager will give you firsthand exposure to the problems of designing and developing large systems.

3. You are a competent designer and feel that you could lead a design team. The essence of design is to visualize an orderly structure within a seemingly complex jumble of concepts and ideas. Design requires abstract thinking: the ability to relate large numbers of seemingly disparate ideas and to logically arrange them so that they fit together into a coherent whole. For most software systems, there is no single clearly best design. You must consider the few known facts, visualize the many unknowns, and intuitively select the one alternative that appears to best fit the need. Although design is not difficult if you have the aptitude, it is a complex activity and not everyone can do it. If you have such skills, you could be a good candidate to be development manager.

4. You are familiar with the leading design methods. Although design is a creative effort, good designs do not start from scratch. Many software products of almost every conceivable type have been developed. A well-run design effort should take advantage of this body of software design knowledge. It is surprising how often experience in one design context will help in other seemingly unrelated areas. For example, in producing a product to analyze program structure, knowledge of compiler design concepts could be helpful. Similarly, in designing a user interface, knowledge of various interface design approaches will help you to produce a better product.

5. You are willing to listen to and take advantage of other people's ideas. This is perhaps the most difficult and demanding of all the skills required of an effective development manager: to recognize the difference between being the "design guru" and being the development manager. Although your personal ideas are important, your objective as development manager is to use the knowledge and creative talents of the entire team.

Although the idea of using everyone's ideas may seem simple in concept, it is often hard to consider suggestions objectively, particularly when they conflict with your own ideas. It is much easier, however, if you have the right attitude. Start by assuming that several team members have ideas that are critical to the project's success. Your job is to get these ideas on the table so that the whole team can consider them. Then take the time to fully understand these ideas and see how to use them on the project.

Teams invariably produce better results than individuals do. Although teams rarely create coherent systems or strategies, they are far better at proposing ideas, evaluating strategies, or reviewing designs than even the most talented individual engineers. For best results, find out which team members would like to contribute design concepts and ask them to do so. Also, contribute some ideas yourself if you want to. Then use the entire team to review all the ideas.

This ability to invite, listen to, and use creative ideas is important not only during design but also during strategy development, requirements, test planning, and almost everywhere else in the development process. Learn to use all the ideas you can get, whatever their source.

If you do not have several of the five skills and abilities in the preceding list, now may not be a good time to lead a development effort. Remember, one of the important objectives of this project is to use all the team's talents to develop a product. If some other team member seems to have better credentials, let him or her do this job this time. You will likely be better qualified by the next development cycle.

Although all these skills and abilities can be helpful, they are not essential. The critical needs are that you be interested in supporting the team, be concerned about the quality of the team's finished products, and be willing to work at whatever role assignment you are given.

12.3   The Development Manager's Principal Activities

As development manager, you are responsible for the 11 principal activities shown in Table 12.1. They are discussed in the following paragraphs.

Development Manager Principal Activity 1

Lead the team in producing the development strategy.   As described in Chapter 4, the development strategy guides the product design and development work. It is produced first to provide a basis for making an estimate and a plan. In producing the development strategy, the key steps are as follows.

1. Establish strategy criteria.
2. Propose and evaluate alternative strategies.
3. Select a strategic approach.
4. Produce the conceptual design.
5. Allocate functions to each cycle.
6. Record this allocation on the STRAT form.
7. Define how to subdivide these functions into product elements.
8. Decide how to integrate the implemented parts into a working product.

The key to producing a sound strategy is to first agree on the criteria that you will use to select a strategy. Then write these criteria down. These criteria are described in Chapter 4, The Development Strategy. The entire team should agree with the strategy criteria and participate in producing the strategy. Remember that, at least for the first cycle, your objective is to define a product that you know you can complete in the available time.

Development Manager Principal Activity 2

Lead the team in producing the preliminary size and time estimates for the products to be produced. As part of the strategy phase, you make a preliminary estimate of the size and development time for each major product function. In doing so, estimate the product's size, judge how long the development of each part will likely take, and note these data on the STRAT form. With this information, you can make an initial decision on which functions to implement in which development cycle.

Remember, however, that size estimating is a highly judgmental process. Even though no one can know how large the product will be until it has been developed, when everyone contributes ideas, teams can make surprisingly good estimates. So entertain all suggestions and remember that the actual result will occasionally be far from the team consensus. Seriously consider everyone's thoughts, whether or not they agree with the team consensus. The meeting reporter (the quality/process manager) documents the size and development time estimates on the STRAT form and gives a copy to the team leader for the project notebook.

Development Manager Principal Activity 3

Lead the development of the software requirements specification. The SRS describes in the team's words the functions to be developed. In some cases, you may have no doubt what the need statement means, but in others, there may be confusion or disagreement. Your objective with the SRS is to resolve these issues so that the entire team agrees on precisely what it is that you intend to build. Therefore, it is important for the entire team to participate in developing and inspecting the SRS.

In producing the SRS, divide the work among all the team members. This approach has several advantages.

☐ You will get the work done more quickly.

☐ You will get a better-quality result.

☐ The entire team will understand the product that you intend to build.

The following steps are typically needed to produce the SRS.

1. Review the need statement to identify any questions or concerns.
2. Get answers to the questions and resolve the concerns.
3. Define the functions required to address the need statement items to be implemented.

4. Decide which of these functions to include in the next development cycle.

5. Produce an outline of the SRS document.

6. Assign these functions to SRS sections.

7. Analyze these functions to identify inconsistencies and key features.

8. Draft the SRS sections that describe these functions.

9. Conduct personal reviews of these drafts to find and correct errors and inconsistencies.

10. Assemble the draft sections and hold a team inspection of the SRS draft.

11. Correct the drafts.

12. Combine these drafts into the finished SRS.

13. Issue the SRS.

Before the team members can start writing draft SRS sections, the team must have completed steps 1 through 7. Then you can guide the team in allocating steps 8 through 11 to the various team members. After the engineers have drafted, reviewed, and corrected their parts, produce the SRS by completing steps 12 and 13.

In step 10, have the quality/process manager lead the SRS inspection. In this inspection, follow the INS script and have every team member participate. This procedure ensures that everyone understands the SRS, that the requirements are complete and coherent, and that the SRS describes the desired functions. It also helps to produce a clear and consistent SRS. In this inspection, identify all defects and assign each one to a team member to correct.

As you assemble the final SRS, have all significant changes reviewed again by one or more team members. Also, read the entire document to make sure that it is complete and consistent and that it is sufficiently precise to guide the design work to follow.

Development Manager Principal Activity 4

Lead the team in producing the high-level design.   Your next task is to lead the team in producing the high-level design for the product. You need this design before you can produce the software design specification (SDS). The team should debate the product structure, consider alternative ways to allocate functions to components, and identify the interconnections among the components. Although there are many ways to judge the quality of a high-level design, one of the best is to use the coupling, strength, and coupling/strength measures described in Appendix A (the program analyzer). For each design alternative, estimate these three values for each component. In comparing designs, you will find that component designs with lower coupling and lower coupling/strength ratios are easier to design, easier to modify, and less prone to error.

This approach provides a logical way to compare alternative designs, and it helps you to discuss and evaluate the alternatives objectively. Such an analysis can take a significant amount of work, but components with high coupling and/or a high coupling/strength ratio generally have more complex designs, take substantially more code, have more defects, and take substantially more development time than would otherwise be the case. A little more time spent now on producing a good high-level design can save a lot of time later.

As part of this design work, also consider the issue of naming. Names imply functions. Thus, choosing a name that is understood by all the team members reduces the likelihood of design or implementation mistakes. If the quality/process manager has not established an initial naming standard, now is a good time to do so.

The final high-level design step is to list on the STRAT form the components, their sizes, their likely development times, and their functional contents. Also, draw a picture of the design, showing the components and their interconnections.

Development Manager Principal Activity 5

Lead the team in producing the software design specifications.   Teams often make the mistake of not starting to write the SDS until they feel they have completed all the design work. When they start to document the design, they discover that much of the work they have done is incomplete and imprecise. Until you start to produce the SDS, you will not really start to produce the design. The discipline of documenting the design forces you to resolve many of the key design issues.

The SDS is the single most important document the team will produce. It specifies the product design, and it must be accurate, complete, and precise. To produce a quality design, the team must use sound design practices and follow appropriate design standards. So before you produce the SDS, make sure the quality/process manager has established the team's design standards. If she or he has not already done so, agree on these standards now before you start writing the SDS. Then make sure that the team uses these standards consistently in the SDS and in all the other design work. Although I suggest that you use the four PSP design templates, if you choose to use some other methodology, make sure it is at least as complete and precise as the PSP templates.

Following are the steps typically required to produce the SDS.

1. Following the selected high-level design approach, identify the SRS functions designated for the next development cycle and assign them to the components.
2. Produce an SDS outline and assign product components to SDS sections.
3. Analyze the functions in each component category to determine an appropriate design approach.
4. Following the design standards, produce the component designs.

5. Have the team members document these designs in draft SDS sections.

6. Have the engineers personally review and fix their own SDS draft sections for errors and inconsistencies.

7. Assemble the SDS draft sections and hold a team inspection.

8. Have the engineers correct the errors in their SDS draft sections.

9. Combine the corrected drafts into the finished SDS.

10. Issue the SDS to the team.

Before asking the team leader to allocate these tasks to the team members, you must have completed steps 1 and 2. Then the team leader helps the team to allocate the work for steps 3 through 6. After the members have completed these tasks and you have assembled the draft SDS, have the quality/process manager lead the SDS inspection. In this inspection, follow the INS inspection script and have every team member participate. This procedure ensures that all of them understand the SDS, that the design is complete and coherent, and that it performs the desired functions. The inspection should also check that the design conforms to the established design standards. Then assign the defects to various team members to correct. After the engineers have made the indicated corrections, assemble and distribute the finished SDS.

As development manager, you should write the sections of the SDS that describe the overall product structure. Generally, each engineer writes the SDS parts that deal with the components that he or she designed. Do not attempt to take on too much of the SDS work yourself, however, because you should leave yourself time to oversee the team's work and to ensure that the overall SDS holds together logically, meets the team's standards, and is essentially defect-free.

Development Manager Principal Activity 6

Lead the team in implementing the product.   Before starting implementation, first check that all required implementation standards have been established and agreed to by the team. If they have not, stop now and establish these standards before starting implementation.

The first implementation step is for you to define the implementation tasks to be done and to have the team leader allocate these tasks among the team members. Then you and your teammates follow the TSPi process to perform your assigned portions of the implementation.

Development Manager Principal Activity 7

Lead the team in developing the build, integration, and system test plans.
For the test phase, split the team into two groups: one to do the test planning and testing and the other to produce the user documentation. If you plan to work on the

documentation, the testing team should pick one member to be the alternate development manager. This person then leads the test planning and testing work. Conversely, if you plan to work on testing, the documentation team members should select an alternate development manager to lead their documentation work.

At this point, discuss the work to be done with the team and decide who will do which activities. The test group reviews the test plans developed during the design and requirements phases and updates them to reflect any changes. The documentation group plans the documentation work. In both cases, have all the team members who will do each part of the work participate in its planning.

From this point on, the documentation and testing work run in parallel. The documentation group, for example, outlines and produces the documentation drafts and then provides these outlines to the test developers. The test developers then check these drafts against their test plans to ensure that the documentation and testing plans cover all the important functions and are consistent. Similarly, the test developers update and refine the test plans and provide them to the documentation group for review.

Most development groups are surprised to find that these documentation and test plan reviews are a good way to find and fix problems before testing even starts. Often, in fact, they find more product defects during test planning and documentation development than they do during integration and system testing.

The test plan, described in Chapter 9, follows the traditional PSP planning strategy.

1. Devise a testing strategy or conceptual approach.

2. Estimate or measure the sizes of the products to be tested.

3. Estimate the numbers and sizes of the test cases and other test support materials to be developed.

4. Estimate how long the testing and test development work will take.

5. Allocate this work among the team members.

As development manager, your job is to make sure that the test plan is complete and that it does not require an excessive amount of test development or test time.

At the end of test planning, assemble the test plan package, give a copy to the instructor and to each of the team members, and have the team leader put a copy in the project notebook. With the completed test plan, you are now ready to start test development and testing.

Development Manager Principal Activity 8

Lead the team in developing the test materials and running the tests.
Following test planning, the team members develop the test scripts, test data, and supporting test programs. For each test, they should estimate the defect-free test run time and the anticipated test results. In doing the test development work, the

engineers should make personal plans for each task, record their time, size, and defect data, and document the final results using the LOGD, LOGT, and SUMS forms. Clearly label all the data on the test materials as for test components and do not include the defect data from the test components in the product quality analyses.

Although you may choose not to do full team inspections of all the test materials, each test engineer should conduct personal design and code reviews and have at least one other engineer conduct a design review and a code review. Poor-quality test materials can often waste a great deal of test time. Diagnosing and fixing test-case defects frequently takes longer than diagnosing and fixing product defects.

The next step is to allocate the testing tasks among the test team members and to do the testing.

Development Manager Principal Activity 9

Lead the team in producing the product's user documentation.   In producing the documentation, again follow the standard PSP/TSP strategy of first producing a conceptual design of the document. Then note the functions that you will complete with this development cycle and those that you will change or augment in later cycles. To minimize documentation changes, it is a good idea to concentrate on documenting the functions that you will complete in this development cycle.

Before starting the work, the documentation group plans the documentation work. All the engineers who will do documentation work should participate in this planning. Then allocate the documentation work among the team members, develop the document, review the team members' work, and make needed corrections. Finally, combine the document sections into the document draft and distribute it to the team for review.

Have the quality/process manager lead the team review of the draft user documentation and have each engineer correct his or her portion. Finally, assemble the corrected parts into the final document and distribute it to the instructor and the team.

Development Manager Principal Activity 10

Participate in producing the development cycle report.   As development manager, your final task is to prepare your sections of the cycle report. In doing this task, you work under the leadership of the team leader to produce, review, correct, and submit your assigned portions of this report. In your sections, discuss the development work and assess how it was performed and how this work compared with the team's objectives and standards. Finally, comment on how you and the team did the development work, how you could do it better the next time, and why this would be an improvement. Following this, participate in the team peer reviews.

TABLE 12.2 TSPi DEVELOPMENT MANAGER PROJECT ACTIVITIES

Phase Week	General	In addition to the engineer's standard tasks, the design manager does the following tasks each week.	References
LAU 2,8,11	Project launch	Participate in the first team meeting.	Chapter 3
STRAT 2,8,11	Strategy criteria	Lead the team in establishing strategy criteria.	Chapter 4
	Development strategy	Lead the team in developing and reviewing the strategy.	
	Preliminary estimates	Lead the work to make preliminary size and time estimates.	
	Risk assessment	Lead the team in identifying and assessing project risks.	
	Configuration control	Participate in reviewing the configuration control process.	Appendix B
PLAN 3,8,11	Development plan	Participate in making the development plan.	Chapter 5
	Quality plan	Participate in making the quality plan.	
REQ 4,9,12	Need statement	Lead the team in clarifying the need statement.	Chapter 6
	Questions	Clarify the need statement with the instructor.	
	Outline SRS	Lead the team through outlining the SRS.	
	Produce SRS	Lead the team in producing the SRS.	
	System test plan	Lead the team in producing the system test plan.	Chapter 9
	SRS inspection	Participate in inspecting the SRS and system test plan.	Appendix C
	Final SRS	Obtain updates and produce the final SRS.	Chapter 6
	SRS approval	Obtain SRS approval from the instructor.	
DES 5,9,12	HLD	Lead the team in producing the high-level design.	Chapter 7
	Produce SDS	Lead the team in producing the SDS.	
	Integration plan	Lead the team in producing the integration test plan.	Chapter 9
	SDS inspection	Participate in inspecting the SDS and integration test plan.	Appendix C
	Final SDS	Obtain updates and produce the final SDS.	Chapter 7
IMP 6,10,13	Planning	Lead the planning for the implementation work.	Chapter 8
	Detailed design	Produce and review detailed designs.	
	Unit test plan	Produce and review unit test plans.	Script UT
	DLD inspection	Participate in inspecting detailed designs and unit test plans.	Appendix C
	Test development	Produce unit test materials.	Script UT
	Implementation	Implement and review programs.	Chapter 8
	Compile	Compile programs.	
	Code inspection	Participate in inspecting programs.	Appendix C
	Unit test	Unit-test programs.	Script UT
TEST 7,10,13	Test development	Lead the test development work.	Chapter 9
	Build	Lead the work to build the product.	
	Integration	Lead the integration testing work.	
	System test	Lead the system testing of the product.	
	User documentation	Lead the development and review of the documentation.	
PM 8,11,15	Cycle report	Participate in reviewing team performance and producing a report on the latest development cycle.	Chapter 10
	Prepare peer reviews	Complete a peer review for the development manager's role and for all the other team roles using form PEER.	
Every Week	Data reporting	Provide agreed weekly data to the planning manager.	Chapter 5
	Weekly meeting	Participate in the weekly team meetings.	Script WEEK
	CCB	Participate as a member of the configuration control board.	Appendix B
	Build control	Ensure that only baselined products are used in build, integration, and system test of the product.	

Development Manager's Principal Activity 11

Act as a development engineer.   As previously noted, every team member is also a development engineer.

12.4   The Development Manager's Project Activities

The development manager's project activities for a full development cycle are listed in Table 12.2. This table shows where these topics are covered in other parts of this book.

12.5   Summary

This chapter describes the development manager's role. With the TSPi, all engineers fill team roles as well as act as development engineers. Thus, as development manager, you also do some of the development work.

The first goal of all team members is to work cooperatively with the entire team to produce a high-quality product on time. Above all else, the team's success depends on all the team members contributing their personal best efforts, supporting the other team members, and working cooperatively to resolve issues and disagreements.

The development manager's specific goal is to guide the team in producing a superior product. The measure of success in achieving this goal is that the team produces a useful and fully documented product that meets the basic requirements of the need statement. In addition to this general objective, the requirements must be traceable from the initial need statement to the SRS, to the SDS, and to the final implementation. The team must also use a defined development strategy, follow sound design concepts, maximize common element reuse, and conform to the team's established standards. In addition, the implementation must faithfully represent the design and meet all quality criteria. Finally, the test program must demonstrate that the product meets its functional, operational, and quality objectives.

The most helpful skills and abilities of a potential development manager are as follows.

1. Most important, you like to build things.

2. You want to be a software engineer and would like the experience of leading the project's design and development work.

3. You are a competent designer and feel that you could lead a development team.

4. You are familiar with the leading design methods.

5. You are willing to listen to and take advantage of other people's ideas.

The 11 principal responsibilities of the development manager are as follows.

1. Lead the team in producing the development strategy.

2. Lead the team in producing the preliminary size and time estimates for the products to be produced.

3. Lead the development of the software requirements specifications.

4. Lead the team in producing the high-level design.

5. Lead the team in producing the software design specification.

6. Lead the team in implementing the product.

7. Lead the development of the build, integration, and system test plans.

8. Lead the team in developing the test materials and running the tests.

9. Lead the team in producing the product's user documentation.

10. Participate in producing the development cycle report.

11. Act as a product developer.

13

The Planning Manager Role

This chapter describes the planning manager's role. If you have been assigned this role, the chapter gives you helpful pointers on how to perform it most effectively. The topics covered are

- The planning manager's goals
- Helpful planning manager skills and abilities
- The planning manager's principal activities
- The planning manager's project activities

The first three sections provide discussion and background on various aspects of the planning manager's role. The fourth section lists in one table all the activities you will be responsible for doing in a development cycle. It also provides references to places where these activities are discussed more fully in other chapters. With the TSPi, all engineers fill roles as well as act as development engineers. Thus, as planning manager, you participate in the development work along with the other engineers.

13.1   The Planning Manager's Goals

With the TSPi, all team members have specific and measurable goals defined by the TSPi process. If you want to modify them, you should do the following.

- ☐ Write down the goals that you wish to use.
- ☐ Specify how to measure these new goals.
- ☐ Describe why you have selected these goals instead of the ones provided by the TSPi process.
- ☐ Give a copy of your revised goals to the team and to the instructor.
- ☐ Give a copy of your new goals to the team leader to put in the project notebook.

With the TSPi, every team member has two kinds of goals: everyone has the same goal of being an effective team member, and every team role has its own unique goals. All these goals are described in the following paragraphs.

Common Team Member Goal

Be a cooperative and effective team member.   As planning manager, your first priority is to be a cooperative and effective team member. You and all the other team members have the primary goal of working cooperatively with the entire team to produce a high-quality product on the agreed schedule. Above all else, the team's success depends on all team members contributing their personal best efforts, supporting other team members, and working cooperatively to resolve issues and disagreements.

Although the individual roles are important, it is most important to remember that each role represents a single facet of the overall team's assignment. Thus, individual role objectives may occasionally appear to conflict because each role considers the team's activities from only one perspective. To meet the team's overall goals, however, you need to integrate these individual goals into a smoothly functioning whole. You can best do this by giving highest priority to the overall team goal of working cooperatively with the entire team to produce a quality product on the agreed schedule.

The suggested measures for this goal are the following.

- ☐ The PEER form evaluations of the overall team are good (3) or better for team spirit.
- ☐ The PEER form evaluations of the planning manager role are good (3) or better for helpfulness and support.

Planning Manager Goal 1

Produce a complete, precise, and accurate plan for the team and for every team member.   The planning manager's first goal is to help the team produce a complete, precise, and accurate plan. The measures for this goal are the following.

- ☐ The plan is complete when it covers all the tasks the team is to perform in the development cycle and it is fully documented in the TASK and SCHEDULE templates.
- ☐ Every team member must have a personal TASK and SCHEDULE template for his or her work.
- ☐ The team's plan is precise when the average number of hours per task is around 5 hours or fewer per task, with no individual's tasks taking more than about 10 hours.
- ☐ Plan accuracy is measured by the error in the total hourly estimate for the development cycle compared to the effort actually required.
- ☐ A second accuracy measure is the error in the weekly team hours planned versus the weekly hours actually expended.

Planning Manager Goal 2

Accurately report team status every week.   The second planning manager goal is to help and support the team in running a well-tracked project. The measures for this goal are as follows.

- ☐ You provide complete and accurate weekly team status reports, giving data on team and individual hours worked and earned value achieved.
- ☐ The team members update their personal TASK, SCHEDULE, and WEEK forms and provide them to you in a timely way.
- ☐ If one or more team members do not report all their data on time, you seek help from the team leader and the instructor.

Note that if one or more team members do not properly report their data and you have not sought help from the team leader and instructor, you have failed to do your job. Generally the instructor, and often even the team leader, does not know if some team members are not properly tracking and reporting data. To enable you to perform your planning job, all engineers must plan and track their personal work and provide their actual data to you in electronic form weekly. Your job is to help them to do this. The next sections describe some of the steps you can take.

13.2   Helpful Planning Manager Skills and Abilities

As shown in Table 13.1, the four most helpful characteristics for a planning manager are the following.

1. Most important, you have a logical and orderly mind and feel most comfortable doing a job when you have a defined plan for the work.

2. Although you may not always be able to produce a plan, you tend to plan your work when you can.

3. You are interested in process data and look forward to entering your results each week so that you can see where you stand. Are you ahead of schedule or behind? Why was the plan in error? How could the plan be better? In my case, I use earned value to track my personal work. While writing this book, for example, I tracked my data every day and reviewed my status on Sunday mornings. This approach affected me in several ways. First, on Saturday I made a big effort to get as many tasks completed as I possibly could. Then on Sunday morning, I always looked forward to the earned-value and hours status reports. They gave me a clear picture of where I stood against my commitments. If you like the feeling of knowing where you are on a job and are willing to take a small amount of time to track your work, you are likely to be an effective planning manager.

4. You think that planning is important and are willing to press your teammates to track and measure their work. Here, an aptitude and interest in helping people is useful.

Although all these skills and abilities can be helpful, they are not essential. The critical needs are that you be interested in supporting the team, be concerned about the quality of the team's finished products, and be willing to work at whatever role assignment you are given.

13.3   The Planning Manager's Principal Activities

As planning manager, you are responsible for the six principal activities shown in Table 13.1. They are discussed in the following paragraphs.

As you develop the plan, remember why you are doing it.

☐ You need a plan to help constrain the job to a scope that the team can complete in the time available.

☐ You need a plan to guide the work.

TABLE 13.1 TSPi PLANNING MANAGER ROLE

Objective	The planning manager supports and guides the team members in planning and tracking their work.
Role Characteristics	The characteristics most helpful to planning managers are the following. 1. You have a logical mind and feel most comfortable when following a plan for doing your work. 2. Although you may not always be able to produce a plan, you tend to plan your work when given the opportunity. 3. You are interested in process data. 4. You are willing to press people to track and measure their work.
Goals and Measures	Team member goal: Be a cooperative and effective team member. • Measures: Team PEER ratings for team spirit, overall contribution, and helpfulness and support Goal 1: Produce a complete, precise, and accurate plan for the team and for every team member. • Measure 1.1: The team's plan covered all the tasks in the development cycle. • Measure 1.2: The plan was fully documented in TASK and SCHEDULE templates. • Measure 1.3: The average task hours were less than 5, and no individual engineer's tasks were more than about 10 hours. • Measure 1.4: The weekly hours and total plan hours accurately represented the actual cycle results. Goal 2: Accurately report team status every week. • Measure 2.1: You provided complete and accurate weekly team status reports. • Measure 2.2: The team members updated their personal TASK, SCHEDULE, and WEEK forms and provided them to you on time. • Measure 2.3: If one or more team members did not report all their data on time, you sought help from the team leader and the instructor.
Principal Activities	1. Lead the team in producing the task plan for the next development cycle. • Define the products to be produced and their estimated sizes. • Specify the tasks and task hours needed to produce the products. • Document the tasks in the TASK form. 2. Lead the team in producing the schedule for the next development cycle. • Determine the weekly hours that each engineer will spend on the project. • Enter the individual and team hours on the SCHEDULE template. • Produce the team SCHEDULE form. 3. Lead the team in producing the balanced team plan. • Obtain detailed plans from each engineer. • Identify workload imbalances among team members. • Lead the team in adjusting workload to achieve balance. • Generate the consolidated team plan. • Obtain detailed personal plans from each engineer. 4. Track the team's progress against the plan. • Get the team members' weekly data. • Produce a weekly team earned-value and time chart of team status. • Generate the weekly status report. • Produce a weekly analysis of the team's actual performance against plan. • Report personal and consolidated team status to the instructor. 5. Participate in producing the development cycle report. 6. Act as a development engineer.

☐ You need a plan to help the team members to work as a team, to agree on what the team is trying to do, and to reach consensus on how to do it.

Remember that the process of producing the plan is actually one of the principal benefits of planning. To get the most benefit from planning, have the entire team participate and make sure that all the team members contribute. A big part of your job as planning manager is to get the team to do this.

Planning Manager Principal Activity 1

Lead the team in producing the task plan for the next development cycle. The first three principal activities are part of producing the development plan. This is your single most important role responsibility. Before the team has produced the product requirements, the TSPi requires that you make a development plan. Many team members will complain that such early plans are mostly guesswork and that they could make a much better plan after they produce the requirements.

Although they certainly could make a better plan if they waited, that is beside the point. The longer you wait, the better your plan should be. But you need a plan now, before you spend significant time on the requirements. The problem is that you must manage your work to fit into the time available. This is precisely the same problem faced by industrial software teams. The only way to manage this problem is to make a plan. That is how to find out what you can accomplish in the time available, and it is the only way to manage the work so that you can meet your commitments. This is why you must produce a development plan at the very beginning of every project.

Many engineers are surprised to discover that these initial plans are often quite accurate. For example, one industrial team was told on the first day of the project that they had to make a plan. They expected the project to take about a year, and only a few of the 14 engineers had a clear idea what the eventual product was supposed to do. They complained that, by planning before they had defined the requirements, they would have to do a lot of guessing. After some discussion, however, they produced a plan that ended up with an 18-month schedule. With this plan, they then convinced management that their schedule was realistic. They followed the plan and completed the project six weeks ahead of the 18-month commitment. Teams must do a lot of guessing when they make an initial plan, but when they guess in detail their guesses are surprisingly accurate.

Although there are many ways to produce the plan, the steps described in Chapter 5 generally work quite well. In essence, they are as follows.

1. Specify the products that you will produce.
2. Estimate the sizes of these products.
3. For each product, estimate the time required for each process step.
4. Enter all these times in the SUMS and TASK forms.

For the first development cycle, this planning will involve a lot of guesswork, but in later cycles you will have prior-cycle data to guide you. For the first cycle, however, use the data that you have from the PSP course (or anywhere else) and make your best estimates. Don't worry if your first estimates are wildly inaccurate; some of them are bound to be. In aggregate, however, your overall estimate will probably be reasonably accurate. With better historical data, you will then make even better plans.

Planning Manager Principal Activity 2

Lead the team in producing the schedule for the next development cycle.
After you have a task list with estimated hours for each task and estimated sizes for each product, your next step is to generate the overall schedule. Ask each member to specify how many hours he or she plans to spend on this project during each week of the current development cycle. Also, get the planned hours for several weeks beyond this cycle in case the plan extends longer than you expect.

Emphasize that you want estimated task hours. This is time that the engineers will record in their time logs. They should not count the time spent in team meetings, in classes, or on homework. Estimate only the direct time to be spent on the tasks listed in the TSPi scripts and in the TASK form.

Generally, each student has a personal schedule and can plan which days he or she will work on the project. One person, for example, might plan to spend two hours every afternoon, Monday through Friday. Others might commit to four hours on Tuesday and Thursday and two hours on Saturday afternoon. If someone knows about a special commitment in some future week that will limit that week's available hours, adjust the totals for that week correspondingly.

After you have the planned hours for every team member, you can generate the overall team plan. This will give you a sound basis for determining whether the plan is in the ballpark or wildly optimistic. It also provides the framework for the engineers' individual plans. In a sense, it is the high-level design for your plan, and it provides the context for all of the engineers' plans.

Planning Manager Principal Activity 3

Lead the team in producing the balanced plan.   When you generate the overall team plan, you will get planned values for each of the next several weeks as well as the week when each task is to be finished. However, this is only a theoretical plan. It assumes that every engineer will work on whatever tasks need to be done each day and that no one will have any unproductive time. Because this is rarely the case, you must balance the team workload.

Producing the balanced plan is one of the most important steps in the planning process. The reason is that when the team workload is not balanced, some engineers have more work to do than others. They take longer to finish their tasks and delay the entire project. On one project, for example, nine engineers produced individual plans for the next project phase. One engineer ended up with 49 weeks of work, and several other engineers each had less than five weeks of work. By readjusting their plans, they were able to produce a balanced plan in which everyone finished in 15 to 18 weeks. Most engineers had 15 weeks of work, with one at 18 weeks. Because this was the design phase, they could work around the 3-week delay for a single product area. If they had not balanced their plans, everyone would have had to wait for the engineer with 49 weeks of work to do, something that would have seriously delayed the project.

Unless every engineer produces a detailed plan and the team balances the overall workload, projects invariably take longer than necessary. Some engineers always end up with an excessive workload, and they end up delaying everyone else. One of the principal objectives in making a plan is to figure out how to use the entire team's resources and to complete the project as expeditiously as possible. You can do this only by balancing the team's plan.

Balancing the Team Workload

Although the process of balancing plans is conceptually simple, the steps are not obvious. The approach that I have found most successful is to have the entire team participate. To start, the team first produces the overall team plan, with estimated hours for every task. In this plan, you also identify tasks that several engineers will do, such as inspections, and the total hours required.

Next, draw on a board or flip chart a matrix layout like the example shown in Table 13.2. List the engineers' names on the left and the weeks for the current development cycle across the top. Then, starting at the left, pick the first task to be done and mark the hours required for the engineer who will do that task. One way to do this is to draw a bar for when the engineer will work on that task. Also, make the length of each bar proportional to the planned time for that task. Continue assigning tasks to engineers in this way and marking the time required.

Table 13.2 shows a hypothetical plan for three engineers to implement three large modules. As you can see from the plan, it takes some care to ensure that all the engineers' times balance and that all of them are simultaneously available for the team inspections. Here, it is assumed that each team member plans to spend 20 hours a week, so each space in the table represents two task hours.

Generally, all team members should participate in workload balancing. This is a complex process both because there is no one best answer and because a great many factors are involved. Examples are personal skills, preferences, availability, knowledge, and roles. However, most teams can balance their workload quickly as long as everyone participates and they start with a detailed team plan.

In workload balancing, you will often find that some tasks must be assigned to people who do not appear most qualified to do them. Often, however, the team

TABLE 13.2 A LOAD-BALANCING EXAMPLE

Task	Week 1	Week 2	Week 3
Engineer 1			
Module 1 design	◆—◆		
Module 1 design review	◆◆		
Module 1 design inspection	◆◆		
Module 2 design inspection	◆◆		
Module 3 design inspection	◆◆		
Module 1 code	◆◆ ◆◆		
Module 1 code review	◆◆		
Module 1 code inspection	◆◆		
Module 2 code inspection		◆◆	
Module 3 code inspection		◆—◆	
Engineer 2			
Module 2 design	◆——◆		
Module 2 design review	◆◆		
Module 1 design inspection	◆◆		
Module 2 design inspection	◆◆		
Module 3 design inspection	◆◆		
Module 2 code	◆◆ ◆◆	◆◆	
Module 2 code review		◆—◆	
Module 1 code inspection	◆◆		
Module 2 code inspection		◆◆	
Module 3 code inspection		◆—◆	
Engineer 3			
Module 3 design	◆—◆ ◆◆		
Module 3 design review	◆◆		
Module 1 design inspection	◆◆		
Module 2 design inspection	◆◆		
Module 3 design inspection	◆◆		
Module 3 code	◆◆ ◆—◆		
Module 3 code review		◆—◆	
Module 1 code inspection	◆◆		
Module 2 code inspection		◆◆ ◆—◆	
Module 3 code inspection			

members who appear to be most qualified for these tasks also have the heaviest workload. When you balance the workload, it is important to recognize that many people are more capable than they think they are. If you challenge them with more difficult tasks, they often rise to the challenge and do a surprisingly good job.

After you have balanced the workload, have the team members enter these data in their task and schedule templates and generate personal plans. Then, with these plans, generate the composite team plan and give copies to all the team members and to the instructor.

Planning Manager Principal Activity 4

Track the team's progress against its plan.   Although making the plan is your first and most important responsibility, after you have produced the plan your number one priority becomes project tracking. Tracking is important because it provides the team members with a sense of progress, a clear picture of where they are, and a precise understanding of what they must do to finish on time. Tracking thus provides the knowledge required to keep the team motivated and striving to succeed.

To consistently get data in a timely way, you must start out properly. Start by getting agreement from the team members on when they will provide their weekly data to you. Make sure that you get this issue settled during the launch phase at the very beginning of the TSPi process. In the first team meeting, have the team leader decide when and where you will hold the weekly team meeting and get the team to agree on when everyone will submit their data to you. After you have this agreement, you can press any late members to give you their data. If they don't quickly shape up, you will have a sound basis for taking the problem to the team leader and to the instructor.

If team members do not start out reporting their data on time, the odds are that they will continue to be late for as long as they can get away with it. To handle this problem, go immediately to these students and ask for the data. Remind them that they agreed to provide these data and they have not. If they agree to provide the data, get a specific time. If they do not meet these commitments, go to the team leader for help and tell the instructor about the problem. If you do not go promptly to the team leader and the instructor, you will become part of the problem.

Every week before the team meeting, obtain the prior week's data from all the team members. Then record these data on the project's TASK and SCHEDULE forms. With the TSPi support systems, engineers can record their time and defect data on their personal support system and turn these data in to you in electronic form. With these data, you can generate the composite team status and forms without entering any new data. Thus, if you have the TSPi support tool and if all the engineers use it properly, you can quickly generate everything that you need for the team's weekly status report.

In tracking project status, there are several important activities to consider.

☐ Generate the team members' SUMP and SUMQ forms.

☐ Produce a weekly team earned-value and time chart showing team status.

☐ Generate the weekly status reports.

☐ Produce a brief analysis of the team's actual performance against plan.

These points are discussed in the following paragraphs.

Getting the Team Members' Weekly Data

The TSPi tool automatically generates most of the TSPi forms from the engineers' raw data. If you do not have the TSPi tool, you must follow up with the engineers to get them to complete the forms. Make sure that whenever they complete work on any component or system task, they enter the time that they spent, when they finished the task, their weekly hours, the defects that they found, and the product size data in the LOGD, LOGT, SUMS, TASK, and SCHEDULE forms. If team members do not produce these data promptly, they will have trouble producing them later. Therefore, you must get data on all completed tasks every week, and you must make sure that these data are recorded on the engineers' TASK forms.

After you have the individual data, generate composite team TASK, SCHED-ULE, SUMP, and SUMQ forms. Then give copies of these forms to all the engineers and to the instructor. These are the data that each engineer needs to track the plan, to evaluate product quality, and to demonstrate personal and team performance to the instructor. Without these data, you cannot get a good grade for this course.

Producing a Weekly Team Earned-value and Time Chart

Once you have entered the team's data, the TSPi tool can generate an earned-value chart that shows where the project stands. This chart will help you to judge when the team will finish. As discussed in Chapter 5, earned value provides a convenient way of measuring the relative contribution of the tasks that you and your teammates complete. Because the task content for most projects varies widely and because these tasks are rarely done in precisely the order planned, it is often hard to tell whether you are ahead of or behind schedule. For example, when some modules are coded and inspected ahead of schedule but the test planning and documentation work are late, how can you tell where you are? Does the early completion of the coding and inspection work compensate for the delay in test planning and documentation? Earned value provides a way to answer such questions.

The team earned-value plan helps you to judge the relative status of the entire team. That is why earned value is important and why the TSPi requires all engineers to keep their personal earned-value data. Every week, the engineers perform different tasks and complete their work at unplanned times. When you as planning manager review the team's earned-value data in the weekly meeting, everyone can see which tasks are early and which tasks are late. Then they can rebalance their plans and decide how to recover any lost time.

In spite of its many benefits, earned value occasionally can be misleading. If, for example, one engineer is far behind schedule and several others are early, the overall earned value for the team could show that the project is on schedule. In theory, this could be true, but only if you readjusted the work. This means that you must plan to rebalance team workload often. If some engineers are not working as hard as the others, the team should discuss this and decide what to do. Even if everyone is working hard, however, some tasks will normally take much longer than planned and others much less. Don't be surprised if you need to rebalance team workload every week.

Generating the Weekly Status Report

Every week, report personal and consolidated team status to the team and to the instructor. The team's data show the project's status and identify where there are problems or exposures. These data can also help the team determine whether the schedule is exposed and whether any special actions are needed to finish on time. If the schedule is seriously off, for example, you might have to reduce the planned product content or extend the current development cycle and delay the next one. To make proper decisions, the team must have precise weekly status reports.

Similarly, the instructor needs to know whether the students are having a worthwhile experience and whether each person is doing good work. The weekly status reports provide the data needed for both purposes. Instructors can see which engineers are making a real effort and which ones are not. They can also see when the team is achieving its plan and when it needs help.

Producing a Weekly Analysis of Performance Against the Plan

The planning manager produces a brief weekly analysis of the team's performance and compares this performance to the plan. The data that you need are in printouts from the team's and engineers' TSPi support tools. These printouts show the planned versus actual times for each task and time period, and they also provide an overall picture of earned-value progress. These brief reports can serve as a major part of your contribution to the development cycle report.

TABLE 13.3 TSPi PLANNING MANAGER PROJECT ACTIVITIES

Phase Week	General	In addition to the engineer's standard tasks, the planning manager does the following tasks each week.	References
LAU 2,8,11	Weekly meeting	Participate in the first team meeting.	Chapter 3
	Weekly data	Obtain agreement on the data to be provided every week.	
STRAT 2,8,11	Development strategy	Participate in developing and reviewing the strategy.	Chapter 4
	Configuration control	Participate in reviewing the configuration control process.	Appendix B
PLAN 3,8,11	Products and sizes	Lead the work to identify the project's products and sizes.	Chapter 5
	Task list	Lead the team effort to produce the task list.	
	Task hours	Lead the team in estimating the task hours.	
	Weekly hours	Obtain engineers' estimates for their weekly hours.	
	Team plan	Produce the preliminary team plan.	
	Quality plan	Participate in making the quality plan.	
	Individual plans	Help each engineer make a personal plan.	
	Balance the plan	Lead the team in balancing team workload.	
	Final plan	Produce final team and individual engineer plans.	
REQ 4,9,12	Need statement	Participate in analyzing and clarifying the requirements.	Chapter 6
	Produce SRS	Produce the assigned parts of the SRS.	
	System test plan	Participate in producing the system test plan.	Chapter 9
	SRS inspection	Participate in inspecting the SRS and system test plan.	Appendix C
DES 5,9,12	Design specification	Participate in developing the SDS.	Chapter 7
	Integration plan	Participate in producing the integration test plan.	Chapter 9
	SDS inspection	Participate in inspecting the SDS and integration test plan.	Appendix C
IMP 6,10,13	Planning	Participate in planning the implementation work.	Chapter 8
	Detailed design	Produce and review detailed designs.	
	Unit test plan	Produce and review unit test plans.	Script UT
	DLD inspection	Participate in inspecting detailed designs and unit test plans.	Appendix C
	Test development	Produce unit test materials.	Script UT
	Implementation	Implement and review programs.	Chapter 8
	Compile	Compile programs.	
	Code inspection	Participate in inspecting programs.	Appendix C
	Unit test	Unit-test programs.	Script UT
TEST 7,10,13	Test development	Participate in the test development tasks.	Chapter 9
	Build	Participate in building the product.	
	Integration	Participate in integrating the product.	
	System test	Participate in system-testing the product.	
	User documentation	Participate in producing the user documentation.	
PM 8,11,15	Cycle report	Participate in reviewing team performance and producing a report on the latest development cycle.	Chapter 10
	Prepare peer reviews	Complete a peer review for the planning manager's role and for all the other team roles using form PEER.	
Every Week	Data	Obtain the engineers' weekly data.	Chapter 5
	Weekly report	Generate the team's WEEK report.	
	Weekly analysis	Generate a brief analysis of team performance versus plan.	
	Weekly meeting	Participate in the weekly team meetings.	Script WEEK

Planning Manager Principal Activity 5

Participate in producing the development cycle report.   As planning manager, your final task is to prepare your sections of the cycle report. In doing this task, you work under the leadership of the team leader to produce, review, correct, and submit your assigned portions of this report. In your sections, discuss project planning and tracking, and assess how the work was performed and how the results compared with the team's goals and plans. Finally, comment on how you and the team did the planning and tracking work, how you could do it better the next time, and why this would be an improvement. Following this, participate in the team peer reviews.

Planning Manager Principal Activity 6

Act as a development engineer.   As previously noted, every team member is also a development engineer.

13.4   The Planning Manager's Project Activities

The planning manager's project activities for a full development cycle are listed in Table 13.3. This table shows where these topics are covered in other parts of this book.

13.5   Summary

This chapter describes the planning manager's role. With the TSPi, all engineers fill roles as well as act as development engineers. Thus, as planning manager, you participate in the development work with the other engineers.

The first goal of all team members is to work cooperatively with the entire team to produce a high-quality product on time. Above all else, the team's success depends on all team members contributing their personal best efforts, supporting other team members, and working cooperatively to resolve issues and disagreements.

The planning manager's principal goal is to help and support the team in producing a complete, precise, and accurate project plan. A second planning manager goal is to accurately track team progress and produce a weekly project status report (form WEEK) that the team leader uses to report status to the instructor. To help you to perform this planning and tracking work, all engineers must plan and track their personal work and provide their actual data to you weekly in electronic form.

To be a planning manager, you should have a logical and orderly mind and feel most comfortable working to a defined plan. You should also be interested in process data and want to see what the data say. Finally, you feel that planning is important and are willing to press your teammates to track and measure their work. Here, an aptitude and interest in helping people is also useful.

The six principal responsibilities of the planning manager are as follows.

1. Lead the team in producing the task plan for the next development cycle.

2. Lead the team in producing the schedule for the next development cycle.

3. Lead the team in producing the balanced team-development plan.

4. Track the team's progress against the plan.

5. Participate in producing the development cycle report.

6. Act as a product developer.

14

The Quality/Process Manager Role

This chapter describes the quality/process manager's role. If you have been assigned this role, the chapter gives you helpful pointers on how to perform it most effectively. The topics covered are

- [ ] The quality/process manager's goals
- [ ] Helpful quality/process manager skills and abilities
- [ ] The quality/process manager's principal activities
- [ ] The quality/process manager's project activities

The first three sections provide discussion and background on various aspects of the quality/process manager's role. The fourth section lists in one table all the activities you will be responsible for doing in a development cycle. It also provides references to places where these activities are discussed more fully in other chapters. With the TSPi, all engineers fill roles as well as act as development engineers. Thus, as quality/process manager, you participate in the development work along with the other engineers.

14.1 The Quality/Process Manager's Goals

With the TSPi, all team members have specific and measurable goals defined by the TSPi process. If you want to modify them, you should do the following.

- ☐ Write down the goals that you wish to use.
- ☐ Specify how to measure these new goals.
- ☐ Describe why you have selected these goals instead of the ones provided by the TSPi process.
- ☐ Give a copy of your revised goals to the team and to the instructor.
- ☐ Give a copy of your new goals to the team leader to put in the project notebook.

With the TSPi, every team member has two kinds of goals: everyone has the same goal of being an effective team member, and every team role has its own unique goals. All these goals are described in the following paragraphs.

Common Team Member Goal

Be a cooperative and effective team member.   As quality/process manager, your first priority is to be a cooperative and effective team member. You and all the other team members have the primary goal of working cooperatively with the entire team to produce a high-quality product on the agreed schedule. Above all else, the team's success depends on all team members contributing their personal best efforts, supporting other team members, and working cooperatively to resolve issues and disagreements.

Although the individual roles are important, it is most important to remember that each role represents a single facet of the overall team's assignment. Thus, individual role objectives may occasionally appear to conflict because each role considers the team's activities from only one perspective. To meet the team's overall goals, however, you need to integrate these individual goals into a smoothly functioning whole. You can best do this by giving highest priority to the overall team goal of working cooperatively with the entire team to produce a quality product on the agreed schedule.

The suggested measures for this goal are the following.

- ☐ The PEER form evaluations of the overall team are good (3) or better for team spirit.
- ☐ The PEER form evaluations of the quality/process manager role are good (3) or better for overall contribution and helpfulness and support.

Quality/Process Manager Goal 1

All team members accurately report and properly use TSPi process data.
As quality/process manager, your principal goal is to help the team do quality work
as defined by the TSPi and by the quality plan. In doing this, you help the team
members record their time, size, and defect data and enter these data in the proper
TSPi tools and forms. Guide them in identifying and addressing process problems
and in documenting their improvement suggestions on process improvement proposal (PIP) forms. When they have questions about the process, provide guidance
if you can. If you are uncertain about the answer, get help from the instructor.

The measures of success for this goal are the degree to which the team members accurately and completely recorded their TSPi data, the extent to which they
documented process improvement ideas on PIPs, and the degree to which they documented the processes and standards that they used. Examples of some processes
and standards that the team should document and use are

- A change management process
- An issue-tracking process
- Design standards
- Coding standards
- Naming standards and glossary
- Reuse standards
- Quality standard (complete form SUMQ)
- LOC counting standard

Quality/Process Manager Goal 2

**The team faithfully follows the TSPi quality plan and produces a quality
product.**   Your second (and equally important) role as quality/process manager
is to guide the team in producing a quality product. To accomplish this objective,
you need the help and support of all team members. Each member must be personally committed to producing a quality product and must measure and track the
quality of his or her personal work.

The principal measure for this goal is the degree to which the team members
faithfully used the TSPi to achieve their quality-plan objectives. Although a quality product is desired, the key quality lesson of this course is that faithfully following a well-defined and properly designed process will consistently produce
quality products. Another measure of success for this goal is the degree to which
the team's quality performance conformed to the quality plan. The principal quality parameters to use in this measurement are the following.

- [ ] Percent defect-free (PDF) in system test
- [ ] Defects/KLOC in compile
- [ ] Defects/KLOC in unit test
- [ ] Defects/KLOC in system test
- [ ] The percent of total defects removed before the first compile (yield before compile)
- [ ] The percent of total defects removed before unit test (yield before unit test)
- [ ] The percent of total defects removed before system test (yield before system test)

Note, however, that meeting the process quality measures is most important; actual quality results should then follow.

To perform this role most effectively, you must both provide support and act as a quality assurance auditor. Your principal focus should be on helping the team members meet their quality goals. If, however, one or more team members are unwilling to follow the team's quality practices, you must alert the team leader and the instructor. Although you probably will not have to do this very often, occasionally team members refuse to follow the agreed-to practices. Generally, they are trying to meet a tight schedule and do not believe that rushing through a process step will cause the team problems later. You should first try to convince these engineers to use quality methods, but if you can't, alert the team leader and the instructor to the problem. The team must then determine whether and how to maintain process discipline.

The measures against this goal are as follows.

- [ ] The degree to which the team met its quality plan
- [ ] The degree to which the engineers consistently conformed to the team's quality standards
- [ ] The degree to which you kept the team leader and the instructor informed of quality problems
- [ ] The degree to which you accomplished this goal without antagonizing the team or any team members

Although you cannot be responsible for engineers who refuse to use the PSP and TSPi quality methods, you can ensure that the team and the instructor are aware of all such cases before they cause quality problems.

Quality/Process Manager Goal 3

All team inspections are properly moderated and reported.   The measures of success for this goal are as follows.

☐ All inspections were conducted in accordance with the INS process.

☐ All the team's inspections conformed to the team's quality plan.

☐ INS reports were completed for all team inspections.

☐ Copies of all INS forms and meeting reports were provided to the team leader for insertion into the project notebook.

Quality/Process Manager Goal 4

All team meetings are accurately reported and the reports put in the project notebook. Here, the measure of success is the percentage of the team's weekly and other meetings that are reported, with the reports filed in the project notebook.

14.2 Helpful Quality/Process Manager Skills and Abilities

As shown in Table 14.1, the four most helpful characteristics for a quality/process manager are the following.

1. Most important, you are interested in and concerned about software quality. The quality strategy is one of the key differences between the TSPi and traditional ways of developing software. Whereas traditional software methods wait to address quality during testing, the TSPi focuses on quality *at the beginning of the process*. The TSPi thus adds tasks and development time to the beginning of the process. Although this added time will be more than recovered by reduced time in compiling and testing, the amount of time saved depends on the degree to which the engineers faithfully follow the TSPi process. When even one engineer produces a poor-quality program, the entire team will be delayed by excessive testing and repair time.

    For the team to meet its cost, schedule, and quality goals, all the engineers must strive to meet the team's quality goals. By examining their data, you can help the team members recognize the importance of quality and see where they need to make process changes. Thus, the first qualification of a quality/process manager is your conviction that the team must strive to meet its quality goals and that this is the only reliable way to consistently meet cost and schedule goals.

2. You are interested in process and process measurements. When you took the PSP course, you saw how a defined process could help you to do better and

TABLE 14.1 TSPi QUALITY/PROCESS MANAGER ROLE

Objective	The Quality/Process Manager supports the team in defining the process needs, in making the quality plan, and in tracking process and product quality.
Role Characteristics	The characteristics most helpful to quality/process managers are the following. 1. You are concerned about software quality. 2. You are interested in process and process measurements. 3. You have some experience with or awareness of inspection and review methods. 4. You are willing and able to constructively review and comment on other people's work without antagonizing them.
Goals and Measures	Team member goal: Be a cooperative and effective team member. • Measures: Team PEER ratings for team spirit, overall contribution, and helpfulness and support Goal 1: All team members accurately report and properly use TSPi data. • Measure 1: The extent to which the team faithfully gathered and used all the required TSPi data Goal 2: The team faithfully follows the TSPi and produces a quality product. • Measure 2.1: How well the team followed the TSPi • Measure 2.2: How well the team's quality performance conformed to the quality plan • Measure 2.3: The degree to which you kept the team leader and instructor informed of quality problems • Measure 2.4: The degree to which you accomplished this goal without antagonizing the team or any team members Goal 3: All team inspections are properly moderated and reported. • Measure 3.1: All inspections were conducted according to the INS script and the team's quality standards. • Measure 3.2: INS forms are completed for all team inspections and all major defects reported on the owners' LOGD forms. Goal 4: All team meetings are accurately reported and the reports put in the project notebook. • Measure 4: The percentage of the team meetings with reports filed in the project notebook
Principal Activities	1. Lead the team in producing and tracking the quality plan. 2. Alert the team, the team leader, and the instructor to quality problems. 3. Lead the team in defining and documenting its processes and in maintaining the process improvement process. 4. Establish and maintain the team's development standards. 5. Review and approve all products before submission to the CCB. 6. Act as the team's inspection moderator. 7. Act as recorder in all the team's meetings. 8. Participate in producing the development cycle report. 9. Act as a development engineer.

more predictable work. This experience has convinced you that defined processes can help teams meet their objectives. To be effective in this role, you should know what process scripts are, understand how to produce them, and be able to use them.

3. You have had experience with and are aware of inspection and review methods. Part of the quality/process manager's role is to lead team inspections. In an inspection, several engineers, or even the entire team, review the SRS, the SDS, the product designs, the program source code, and the test plans. To be fully effective, these inspections should be carefully structured and professionally run. Thus, it would help if you have been trained in, have participated in, or have run such inspections and are familiar with how they work. The inspection process is discussed in detail in Appendix C.

4. The fourth helpful characteristic for a quality/process manager is an ability to conduct constructive reviews. Principally, this is a question of attitude. Reviewing the quality of other people's work is always difficult. Authors are often defensive about their mistakes, and even simple comments can seem highly critical, at least to them. You have found an error that they made, and by implication, you would not have made the same mistake. You could easily be perceived as saying, "How dumb can you be to make a mistake like this? Didn't you look at this work before you gave it to us to review?"

Although you are giving your personal time to help the author, it is easy for the author to forget this. Even constructive reviews can easily be read as criticism. Ask plenty of questions but be careful that your words and attitude do not imply even a hint of criticism. The proper attitude is "We all make mistakes, and we don't want any mistakes in the final product."

Although all these skills and abilities can be helpful, they are not essential. The critical needs are that you be interested in supporting the team, be concerned about the quality of the team's finished products, and be willing to work at whatever role assignment you are given.

14.3   The Quality/Process Manager's Principal Activities

As quality/process manager, you are responsible for the eight principal activities shown in Table 14.1. They are discussed in the following paragraphs.

Quality/Process Manager Principal Activity 1

Lead the team in producing and tracking the quality plan.   During the planning phase, you lead the team in developing the quality plan, which is discussed in Chapter 5. The principal objective of the quality plan is to have the team members think about quality before they start the development work. Rather than just talk generally about quality, however, they need to agree on specific quality measures. After the team agrees on quality standards and goals, the engineers have an agreed-on reference against which to track their work. If some engineers do not conform to the team's criteria, you can discuss the issue with them. If they do not agree to conform to the agreed goals, raise the issue in the team meeting and ask for clarification. Does the team still want to follow the agreed-on quality goals, or should the goals be changed? If some engineers want to change any of the quality goals, ask them which goals they want to change, why they propose the change, and what data they have to support the change. Be open to any suggestions that are factually supported, but resist changes that result purely from schedule pressure.

Quality/Process Manager Principal Activity 2

Alert the team leader and instructor to quality problems.   The second part of your job is to keep the team leader and instructor informed of quality problems. Although your principal objective is to help the engineers to do quality work, quality problems are a team issue. The objective is not to embarrass the engineers but rather for everyone to learn from the problems and to take steps to ensure that the problems do not recur. Every engineer must strive to produce quality work because any engineer's quality problems will likely affect everyone.

To accomplish this part of your job, look at the data and determine whether the work meets (or is likely to meet) the team's quality objectives. Although this is often a judgment call, it is surprisingly easy to detect poor-quality work when you have precise process data. For example, the engineers may not have spent enough time in reviews, or they did not gather defect data, or they didn't find many defects. All these problems can be detected before the engineers first compile or test their programs. The first step is to raise these issues with the engineers involved and then, if they do not respond promptly, discuss the issue with the team leader and the instructor.

Another part of the quality monitoring responsibility is to handle the reviews of test defects. Every defect found after the unit test phase must be reviewed in the team's weekly meeting; that is, the team should review every such defect to see what went wrong and what needs to be done better in the future. You are responsible for ensuring that each test-phase defect is discussed in a team meeting, that the discussion results are reported in the meeting report, and that the steps described in Chapter 9 are taken.

Quality/Process Manager Principal Activity 3

Lead the team in defining and documenting its processes and in maintaining the process improvement process.   Your third principal activity is to help the team to establish and document its processes. During project planning, you also identify any needed processes and either define them or include the definition work in the development plan. Most processes are fairly easy to define, but if you need information on how to define processes see *A Discipline for Software Engineering,* Chapter 13 [Humphrey 1995].

A key part of process definition is to maintain the process improvement proposal process. You are the focal point for maintaining the team's PIP process, which defines how to capture and document the engineers' process improvement ideas. Ask about PIPs at every weekly meeting and decide which ones to address right away and which ones to defer. Enter all PIPs that require action in the team's issue-tracking system and inform the originator of the actions planned.

Quality/Process Manager Principal Activity 4

Establish and maintain the team's development standards.   Your fourth principal activity is to help the team establish and maintain its standards. Examples of the items that may need standards are

- ☐ Coding
- ☐ Design
- ☐ Documentation
- ☐ Naming
- ☐ Error handling
- ☐ Interfaces
- ☐ Messages
- ☐ Screens
- ☐ Reports
- ☐ Reuse
- ☐ LOC counting

You are responsible for getting these and any other needed standards documented, reviewed, and approved by the team. Make these standards as brief as possible and use existing standards whenever you can. Although the entire team should be involved in developing the standards, you are responsible for maintaining them and for ensuring that they are consistently used. Start thinking about standards during planning and make sure that someone is charged with either obtaining or drafting each needed standard.

Unless you developed the standard yourself, you will lead the team review and approval process for all new standards. If you developed the standard, ask one of the engineers to lead the review for you. It is also your responsibility to check that the team's standards are properly used. Emphasize standards in every planning and design session and in all the product inspections. Also, when appropriate, review standards status in the weekly team meetings.

Quality/Process Manager Principal Activity 5

Review and approve all products before submission to the configuration control board (CCB). This is the quality assurance aspect of the quality/process manager's job. Although your principal objective should be to help the engineers produce quality products, you must also look at the results of what they produce and decide whether they are of high quality. To do this, you must review the engineers' process data and assure yourself that a reasonable effort was made to produce a quality product. In doing so, examine the development time rates and ratios, look at the defect levels, and examine the product itself. You should do this part of your job carefully because you are the only person who will closely examine the detailed data on all of the system's components. If any components are likely to have serious quality problems, you should attempt to determine that before the team wastes a great deal of time in test.

When you approve a product, you are certifying for the team that

□ The necessary process data have been gathered on the product

□ The product was developed with a quality process

□ The data indicate that the product is of suitable quality to be entered in the system baseline

When you are uncertain about any product's quality, discuss your findings with the team leader and, if he or she agrees, review the situation in a team meeting.

Quality/Process Manager Principal Activity 6

Act as the team's inspection moderator. As the quality/process manager, your sixth activity is to act as the moderator for all team inspections. The INS script in Table 14.2 summarizes the inspection process, but if you want more information, read Appendix C and some of the available references [Fagan 1976, Fagan 1986, Gilb 1993, Humphrey 1989]. The inspection process is not complicated. By following the INS script, you should have no trouble in conducting effective inspections. The principal inspection moderator duties are as follows.

□ Work with the author to identify how many and which engineers should be on the inspection team.

□ Ensure that the author is prepared for the initial inspection meeting.

□ In the initial inspection meeting, explain the inspection process, have the author describe the product that is to be inspected, make preparation assignments, and set the inspection meeting time and place.

□ At the beginning of the inspection meeting, make sure that all the reviewing engineers have completed their preparation work and that their preparation time and defect data are recorded on the INS form. If the reviewers are not properly prepared, defer the meeting until they are.

TABLE 14.2 TSPi INSPECTION SCRIPT: SCRIPT INS

Purpose	To help engineers produce quality products
General	• The purpose of inspections is to focus on sophisticated issues and not on finding simple defects or fixing defects. • Even a few simple defects can distract reviewers so that they are more likely to miss sophisticated problems.
Entry Criteria	A completed and reviewed product with available materials

Step	Activities	Description
1	Plan the Inspection	The producer (or developer) • Arranges with the quality/process manager or some other qualified team member to be the inspection moderator • Handles the mechanics of setting up and running the inspection The moderator (usually the quality/process manager) • Reviews the product to ensure it is ready for the inspection • If not, has the producer fix the problems before proceeding • Selects the other inspection members
2	Hold the Inspection Briefing	The moderator describes the inspection process. The producer familiarizes the inspection team with the product. The reviewers select viewpoints or areas for product concentration. • Sample viewpoints are operation, recovery, maintenance, security, installation, size, and performance. In design inspections, the reviewers also ensure that • At least one reviewer will verify each segment of the design • At least one reviewer will use trace table and/or state machine analysis on every design segment The moderator sets the date and time for the inspection meeting.
3	Review the Product	• The reviewers separately make detailed product reviews. • They mark the defects found on the product documentation. • They record their preparation time.
4	Open the Inspection Meeting	The moderator opens the inspection meeting and • If any reviewers are not prepared, reschedules the meeting • Outlines the inspection meeting procedure
5	Conduct a Product Walk-through	The moderator steps through the product sections and • Has the reviewers describe every defect found • Enters the major defect data on the INS form • Notes the engineers who found each major defect • The product owner (producer) enters the major defects in LOGD
6	Estimate the Remaining Defects	• The moderator estimates the defects remaining in the product after the inspection (form INS instructions). • The moderator determines the reviewers' personal yields. • The reviewers note any items to add to their review checklists.
7	Conclude the Inspection Meeting	The inspection team decides • Whether a reinspection is warranted, who should do it, and when • How to verify the defect corrections The moderator and producer complete forms LOGD and INS.
8	Rework the Product and Verify the Fixes	The producer • Makes repairs and updates the product documentation • Holds needed rereviews and/or reinspections • Has the fixes verified as the reviewers recommended in step 7

Exit Criteria	• INS and LOGD forms completed and filed in the project notebook (NOTEBOOK specification in Appendix G) • A fully inspected, high-quality product

☐ Check that the reviewers have spent enough time to find the likely defects. If they have not, defer the inspection meeting until they have done a proper job.

☐ During the inspection meeting, focus on identifying defects and not on fixing them. Without proper guidance, technical teams often waste considerable time debating how to fix the defects. Your job is to limit the defect discussion to the minimum required to fully define each problem and not to fix it.

☐ At the end of the inspection meeting, determine whether the team has found most of the defects. For guidance on how to do this, see the discussion on estimating remaining defects in Appendix C. If a significant number of defects remain, schedule another inspection with different reviewers.

☐ Ensure that all the necessary data are recorded during the meeting and that the major defects are entered in only one LOGD form.

☐ At the end of the meeting, ensure that all inspection data are recorded on the INS form and turned in to the team leader for inclusion in the project notebook.

Quality/Process Manager Principal Activity 7

Act as recorder in all the team meetings.   Your seventh principal duty is to act as recorder during team meetings. It is important that you record all team decisions and all action items. For each action item, get the team to define

☐ What the action is

☐ Who will take the action

☐ When it will be done

Then record this information in the meeting minutes and have the support manager, record the action item in the issue tracking log.

The only exception to your recorder role occurs during inspection meetings, when you are moderator, or in reviews of your personal work. Then you need to ask someone else to act as recorder.

Quality/Process Manager Principal Activity 8

Participate in producing the development cycle report.   As quality/process manager, your final task is to prepare your sections of the cycle report. In doing this task, you work under the leadership of the team leader to produce, review, correct, and submit your assigned portions of this report. In your sections, discuss the work from a quality and process perspective: how accurately and completely the data were gathered, how faithfully the process was followed, and how completely the team members complied with the quality objectives they established. Also, re-

TABLE 14.3 TSPi QUALITY/PROCESS MANAGER PROJECT ACTIVITIES

Phase Week	General	In addition to the engineer's standard tasks, the quality/process manager does the following tasks each week.	References
LAU 2,8,11	Weekly meeting	Participate in the first team meeting.	Chapter 3
STRAT 2,8,11	Development strategy	Participate in developing and reviewing the strategy.	Chapter 4
	Document criteria	Document the selected strategy criteria.	
	Document strategy	Document the selected strategy.	
	Configuration control	Participate in reviewing the configuration control process.	Appendix B
PLAN 3,8,11	Development plan	Participate in making the development plan.	Chapter 5
	Quality plan	Lead the team in making the quality plan.	
REQ 4,9,12	Need statement	Participate in analyzing and clarifying the requirements.	Chapter 6
	Produce SRS	Produce the assigned parts of the SRS.	
	System test plan	Participate in producing the system test plan.	Chapter 9
	SRS inspection	Lead the inspection of the SRS and system test plan.	Appendix C
DES 5,9,12	Design specification	Participate in developing the SDS.	Chapter 7
	Name glossary	Lead the team effort to produce the name glossary.	
	Design standards	Lead the team effort to produce the design standards.	
	Integration plan	Participate in producing the integration test plan.	Chapter 9
	SDS inspection	Lead the inspection of the SDS and integration test plan.	Appendix C
IMP 6,10,13	Planning	Participate in planning the implementation work.	Chapter 8
	Detailed design	Produce and review detailed designs.	
	Unit test plan	Produce and review unit test plans.	Script UT
	DLD inspection	Lead inspections of the detailed designs and unit test plans.	Appendix C
	Test development	Produce unit test materials.	Script UT
	Implementation	Implement and review programs.	Chapter 8
	Compile	Compile programs.	
	Code inspection	Lead the code inspections.	Appendix C
	Unit test	Unit-test programs.	Script UT
	Quality review	Determine whether the components meet quality criteria.	Script UT
TEST 7,10,13	Test development	Participate in the test development tasks.	Chapter 9
	Build	Participate in building the product.	
	Integration	Participate in integrating the product.	
	System test	Participate in system-testing the product.	
	User documentation	Participate in producing the user documentation.	
PM 8,11,15	Cycle report	Participate in reviewing team performance and producing a report on the latest development cycle.	Chapter 10
	Prepare peer reviews	Complete a peer review for the quality/process manager's role and for all the other team roles using form PEER.	
Every Week	Data reporting	Provide agreed weekly data to the planning manager.	Chapter 5
	Quality review	Review the quality of the engineers' work.	Chapter 14
	Weekly meeting	Participate in the weekly team meetings.	Script WEEK

view briefly the quality results and assess how they compared with the team's goals. If the team did not meet its quality objectives, discuss the process data and explain what they indicate about process shortcomings and how they might have led to the problems observed. Finally, comment on how well you and the team followed the TSPi, how you could more faithfully follow the process the next time, and why this would be an improvement. Following this, participate in the team peer reviews.

Quality/Process Manager Principal Activity 9

Act as a development engineer.   As previously noted, every team member is also a development engineer.

14.4   The Quality/Process Manager's Project Activities

The quality/process manager's project activities for a full development cycle are listed in Table 14.3. This table shows where these topics are covered in other parts of this book.

14.5   Summary

All team members must have specific and measurable goals. The TSPi defines goals for the team and for each team member. This chapter describes the goals for the quality/process manager, which are to help the team members record and use their TSPi data, to guide the team in faithfully using the TSPi to produce a quality product, and to perform effectively as the team's inspection moderator and meeting recorder.

A quality/process manager should be interested in and concerned about quality and should have an interest in process and process measurements. It is also helpful to be aware of and to have had experience with inspection and review methods and to be able to conduct constructive reviews.

As quality/process manager, you are responsible for leading the team in producing and tracking its quality plan. You also lead the team in defining and documenting its processes and in helping to establish and maintain the team's standards. In addition, you monitor process and product quality, act as moderator for all the team's inspections, and serve as the recorder in the team meetings. Finally, you work as a development engineer.

The nine principal responsibilities of the quality/process manager are as follows.

1. Lead the team in producing and tracking the quality plan.
2. Alert the team, the team leader, and the instructor to quality problems.
3. Lead the team in defining and documenting its processes and in maintaining the process improvement process.
4. Establish and maintain the team's development standards and the system glossary.
5. Review and approve all products before submission to the CCB.
6. Act as the team's inspection moderator.
7. Act as recorder in all the team's meetings.
8. Participate in producing the development cycle report.
9. Act as a product developer.

14.6 References

[Fagan 1976] Michael Fagan. 1976. "Design and Code Inspections to Reduce Errors in Program Development." *IBM Systems Journal* 15(3).

[Fagan 1986] Michael Fagan. 1986. "Advances in software inspections." *IEEE Transactions on Software Engineering,* SE-12(7), July.

[Gilb] Tom Gilb and Dorothy Graham. 1993. *Software Inspection.* Edited by Susannah Finzi. Reading, MA: Addison-Wesley.

[Humphrey 1989] W.S. Humphrey. 1989. *Managing the Software Process.* Reading, MA: Addison-Wesley.

[Humphrey 1995] W.S. Humphrey. 1995. *A Discipline for Software Engineering.* Reading, MA: Addison-Wesley.

15

The Support Manager Role

This chapter describes the support manager's role. If you have been assigned this role, the chapter gives you helpful pointers on how to perform it most effectively. The topics covered are

- ☐ The support manager's goals
- ☐ Helpful support manager skills and abilities
- ☐ The support manager's principal activities
- ☐ The support manager's weekly activities

The first three sections provide discussion and background on various aspects of the support manager's role. The fourth section lists in one table all the activities you will be responsible for doing in a development cycle. It also provides references to places where these activities are discussed more fully in other chapters. With the TSPi, all engineers fill roles as well as act as development engineers. Thus, as support manager, you participate in the development work along with the other engineers.

15.1   The Support Manager's Goals

With TSPi, all team members have specific and measurable goals defined by the TSPi process. If you want to modify them, you should do the following.

- ☐ Write down the goals that you wish to use.
- ☐ Specify how to measure these new goals.
- ☐ Describe why you have selected these goals instead of the ones provided by the TSPi process.
- ☐ Give a copy of your revised goals to the team and to the instructor.
- ☐ Give a copy of your new goals to the team leader to put in the project notebook.

With the TSPi, every team member has two kinds of goals: everyone has the same goal of being an effective team member, and every team role has its own unique goals. All these goals are described in the following paragraphs.

Common Team Member Goal

Be a cooperative and effective team member.   As support manager, your first priority is to be a cooperative and effective team member. You and all the other team members have the primary goal of working cooperatively with the entire team to produce a high-quality product on the agreed schedule. Above all else, the team's success depends on all team members contributing their personal best efforts, supporting other team members, and working cooperatively to resolve issues and disagreements.

Although the individual roles are important, it is most important to remember that each role represents a single facet of the overall team's assignment. Thus, individual role objectives may occasionally appear to conflict because each role considers the team's activities from only one perspective. To meet the team's overall goals, however, you need to integrate these individual goals into a smoothly functioning whole. You can best do this by giving highest priority to the overall team goal of working cooperatively with the entire team to produce a quality product on the agreed schedule.

The suggested measures for this goal are the following.

- ☐ The PEER form evaluations of the overall team are good (3) or better for team spirit.
- ☐ The PEER form evaluations of the support manager role are good (3) or better for helpfulness and support.

Support Manager Goal 1

The team has suitable tools and methods to support its work.   In helping the team to use proper tools and methods, you identify the team's support needs and lead the effort to get any needed facilities. You are also responsible for helping the team members make effective use of the tools that they already have. The measures of success for this goal are the following.

☐ The team has suitable tools and methods. For example, the engineers have a change management system, an issue-tracking system, a configuration management system, a common development support environment, and the TSPi support system.

☐ You have reviewed the need for tool changes and have arranged to have these changes made.

☐ The team is effectively using the tools that it has.

Support Manager Goal 2

No unauthorized changes are made to baselined products.   To accomplish this goal, you must establish and administer the team's configuration-controlled product baseline. Each product element is put under configuration control after it has been developed, inspected, and corrected, and the configuration control board (CCB) approves its inclusion in the system baseline. The measures for this goal are the following.

☐ All final product elements are configuration-controlled.

☐ All the changes to configuration-controlled products go through the CCB.

☐ When changes are made in the code, they are reflected in the baselined design documentation.

Support Manager Goal 3

All the team's risks and issues are recorded in the issue-tracking system and reported each week.   This topic is discussed more fully in a later section of this chapter. The measure for this goal is

☐ The percentage of all issues and risks that are recorded and tracked in the issue-tracking system.

Support Manager Goal 4

The team meets its reuse goals for the development cycle.   As reuse advocate, you are responsible for the team's reuse strategy. Initially, you work with the quality/process manager to establish the team's reuse standards, review these standards with the team, and get the team's agreement to use these standards. Your job is to ensure that reuse is considered during all planning, design, and implementation work and to maintain the official copies of all the team's reusable parts. You also help the engineers identify reuse opportunities. The measures of success for this goal are as follows.

☐ You have supported the quality/process manager in establishing reuse standards and obtaining team agreement to these standards.

☐ You have established and maintained a list of available reusable parts.

☐ The team's reuse and new-reuse percentages are measured and tracked.

☐ The team achieved some reuse with the first development cycle.

☐ The degree of reuse increased with each development cycle.

Here, reuse is measured as the percentage of total LOC that are taken from the reusable parts library. New reuse is the percentage of new and changed LOC that are developed for this development cycle specifically to be put into the reusable parts library.

15.2   Helpful Support Manager Skills and Abilities

As shown in Table 15.1, the four most helpful characteristics for a support manager are the following.

1. You are interested in tools and methods.

2. You are a competent computer user and feel you could assist the team with its support needs.

3. You have some experience with various support tools and systems.

4. You are generally familiar with the tools that are likely to be used on this project.

Although all these skills and abilities can be helpful, they are not essential. The critical needs are that you be interested in supporting the team, be concerned about the quality of the team's finished products, and be willing to work at whatever role assignment you are given.

TABLE 15.1 TSPi SUPPORT MANAGER ROLE

Objective	The support manager supports the team in determining, obtaining, and managing the tools needed to meet the team's technology and administrative support needs.
Role Characteristics	The characteristics most helpful to support managers are the following. 1. You are interested in tools and methods. 2. You are a competent computer user and feel you could assist the team with its support needs. 3. You have some experience with support tools and systems. 4. You are generally familiar with the tools that are likely to be used on this project.
Goals and Measures	Team member goal: Be a cooperative and effective team member. • Measures: Team PEER ratings for team spirit, overall contribution, and helpfulness and support Goal 1: The team has suitable tools and methods to support its work. • Measure 1.1: The team had a change management system, an issue-tracking system, a configuration management system, a common development environment, and the TSPi support system. • Measure 1.2: The team effectively used the tools that it had. Goal 2: No unauthorized changes are made to baselined products. • Measure 2.1: All final product elements were configuration-controlled. • Measure 2.2: All changes to configuration-controlled products went through the configuration control board (CCB). • Measure 2.3: When changes were made in the code, they were reflected in the baselined design documentation. Goal 3: All the team's risks and issues are recorded in the issue-tracking log (ITL) and reported each week. • Measure 3: The percentage of the risks and issues that were recorded and tracked in the issue tracking system Goal 4: The team meets its reuse goals for the development cycle. • Measure 4.1: The team had a reusable parts list. • Measure 4.2: The reuse and new-reuse percentages were measured and tracked. • Measure 4.3: The team achieved some reuse with the first development cycle. • Measure 4.4: The level of reuse increased with each cycle.

Principal Activities	1. Lead the team in determining its support needs and in obtaining the needed tools and facilities.
	2. Chair the configuration control board and manage the change control system.
	  • Review all changes to controlled products.
	  • Evaluate each change for impact and benefit.
	  • Recommend to the team which changes to make.
	3. Manage the configuration management system.
	  • Maintain a protected master copy of all controlled items.
	  • Make approved changes only to this controlled version.
	  • Maintain master copies of all controlled items and versions.
	4. Maintain the system glossary.
	5. Maintain the team's issue- and risk-tracking system.
	6. Act as the team's reuse advocate.
	7. Participate in producing the development cycle report.
	8. Act as a development engineer.

15.3   The Support Manager's Principal Activities

As support manager, you are responsible for the seven principal activities shown in Table 15.1. They are discussed in the following paragraphs.

Support Manager Principal Activity 1

Lead the team in determining its support needs and in obtaining the needed tools and facilities.   Although you lead the work to identify the team's support needs and obtain and use any needed tools, you should draw on the experiences and capabilities of all the team members. Some engineers have had different experiences, and many of them have useful ideas on tools and support aids. Some team members may know where or how to obtain certain tools or may have pertinent experiences that will help others in learning to use new tools.

Support Manager Principal Activity 2

Chair the configuration control board and manage the change control system.   For this course, you must establish a plan and procedure for managing changes. To manage changes, you will also chair the configuration control board. The other required CCB member is the development manager, but you can include other members if the team as a whole agrees. The change control problem, a suggested change control procedure, and the operations of the CCB are described in Appendix B.

Support Manager Principal Activity 3

Manage the configuration management system.   In managing the configuration management system, you must do the following.

1. Produce the configuration management plan.
2. Have this plan reviewed and approved by the team.
3. Establish a procedure for saving and tracking all baselined product elements and versions.
4. Establish a way for engineers to submit and retrieve product elements from the configuration management support system.
5. Manage the system for handling changes to all baselined product elements.

For more information on how to do this, see Appendix B.

TABLE 15.2 TSPi SUPPORT MANAGER PROJECT ACTIVITIES

Phase Week	General	In addition to the engineer's standard tasks, the quality/process manager does the following tasks each week.	References
LAU 2,8,11	Weekly meeting	Participate in the first team meeting.	Chapter 3
STRAT 2,8,11	Development strategy	Participate in developing and reviewing the strategy.	Chapter 4
	Configuration plan	Define the configuration control process.	Appendix B
	Configuration control	Participate in reviewing the configuration control process.	
PLAN 3,8,11	Development plan	Participate in making the development plan.	Chapter 5
	Quality plan	Participate in making the quality plan.	
REQ 4,9,12	Need statement	Participate in analyzing and clarifying the requirements.	Chapter 6
	Produce SRS	Produce the assigned parts of the SRS.	
	System test plan	Participate in producing the system test plan.	Chapter 9
	SRS inspection	Participate in inspecting the SRS and system test plan.	Appendix C
	SRS baseline	When the SRS is corrected, baseline the SRS.	Appendix B
DES 5,9,12	Design specification	Participate in developing the SDS.	Chapter 7
	Integration plan	Participate in producing the integration test plan.	Chapter 9
	SDS inspection	Participate in inspecting the SDS and the integration test plan.	Appendix C
	SDS baseline	When the SDS is corrected, baseline the SDS.	Appendix B
IMP 6,10,13	Planning	Participate in planning the implementation work.	Chapter 8
	Detailed design	Produce and review detailed designs.	
	Unit test plan	Produce and review unit test plans.	Script UT
	DLD inspection	Participate in inspecting detailed designs and unit test plans.	Appendix C
	Test development	Produce unit test materials.	Script UT
	Implementation	Implement and review programs.	Chapter 8
	Compile	Compile programs.	
	Code inspection	Participate in the code inspections.	Appendix C
	Unit test	Unit-test programs.	Script UT
	Component baseline	When the components are corrected, baseline the components.	Appendix B
TEST 7,10,13	Test development	Participate in the test development tasks.	Chapter 9
	Build	Participate in building the product.	
	Integration	Participate in integrating the product.	
	System test	Participate in system-testing the product.	
	User documentation	Participate in producing the user documentation.	
PM 8,11,15	Cycle report	Participate in reviewing team performance and producing a report on the latest development cycle.	Chapter 10
	Prepare peer reviews	Complete a peer review for the support manager's role and for all the other team roles using form PEER.	
Every week	CCB	Chair the CCB meetings.	Appendix B
	Product baseline	Maintain the product baseline.	
	Manage changes	Manage the change control process.	
	ITL	Maintain the ITL system and report on risk and issue status.	Chapter 15
	Name glossary	Maintain the system name glossary.	
	Data reporting	Provide agreed weekly data to the planning manager.	Chapter 5
	Weekly meeting	Participate in the weekly team meetings.	Script WEEK

from a support perspective: how well the team's work was supported, the effectiveness of the configuration management process in controlling the team's work products, and the level of reuse achieved. In addition, comment on how well you and the team followed the configuration management plan and how well you used reuse principles to improve team productivity. Also discuss how you could better handle these aspects of the work the next time and explain why this would be an improvement. Following this, participate in the team peer reviews.

Support Manager Principal Activity 8

Act as a development engineer.   As previously noted, every team member is also a development engineer.

15.4   The Support Manager's Project Activities

The support manager's project activities for a full development cycle are listed in Table 15.2. This table lists places where these topics are covered in other parts of this book.

15.5   Summary

This chapter describes the support manager's role, goals, helpful skills and abilities, and principal activities. The support manager's principal goals are to ensure that the team has suitable tools and methods to support its work, to make sure that there are no unauthorized changes to baselined products, to record and track all risks and issues, and to help the team meet its reuse goals.

Helpful support manager skills and abilities are as follows.

1. You are interested in tools and methods.
2. You are a competent computer user and feel you could assist the team with its support needs.
3. You have some experience with support tools and systems.
4. You are generally familiar with the tools that are likely to be used on this project.

The eight principal responsibilities of the support manager are as follows.

1. Lead the team in determining its support needs and in obtaining needed tools and facilities.
2. Chair the configuration control board and manage the change control system.
3. Manage the configuration management system.
4. Establish and maintain the system glossary.
5. Handle the team's issue- and risk-tracking.
6. Act as the team's reuse advocate.
7. Participate in producing the development cycle report.
8. Act as a development engineer.

PART FOUR

Using the TSPi

The book's final three chapters discuss many of the issues that you will face in working on software teams. This material is based largely on my personal experiences as an engineer and as a manager. I have worked with many individuals and teams, and in these final chapters I hope to convey some of what I have learned about being effective, both as an individual and as a member of a professional team.

Chapter 16 deals with managing yourself. Until we properly manage ourselves, we cannot manage much else. How do we manage our own capabilities, and how can we take maximum advantage of our personal assets? This chapter addresses self-awareness, self-control, and proactive behavior. It deals with taking charge of your own life and with working constructively in an environment that you do not control. It also discusses personal values and striving for personal excellence.

Chapter 17 discusses the issues of being on a team. Although individual skill and ability are important, few people accomplish very much alone. The essence of most human endeavors is group accomplishment, and the foundation of effective group performance is the relationships among the group's members. The principal issues involved in being on a team concern your responsibilities for the team's performance and your obligations to build and maintain an effective teamwork environment.

Chapter 18 summarizes the key lessons in this book and gives examples of the benefits of effective teamwork. The first three parts of this book deal with processes and methods. This final part summarizes the principles, concepts, and attitudes of working with people in organizations. In Chapter 18, we summarize the four key lessons of this book and discuss their importance to you as you pursue an engineering career.

16

Managing Yourself

Effective self-management is the foundation for almost everything we do. One of the principal questions to think about in managing ourselves is, "Who am I?" When someone asks who you are, what runs through your mind? You might, for example, think about

Your physical being—what is under your skin

Your inner soul, mind, or ego

Your job and what you do

What you have done

What you own

Or you might think more deeply about yourself in relation to the world around you. This leads to considering your dreams and aspirations, your beliefs, your values, and your principles. What are your working ethics, and what are you committed to?

These are large subjects—but subjects you cannot avoid if you are to be effective at what you wish to do. Why this is so will be clearer as we review some of the elements of managing yourself. These elements are

Being responsible

Striving for defined goals

Living by sound principles

16.1   Being Responsible

By being responsible, I am talking about ownership and attitude. Are you responsible for your own behavior? Are you willing to step up to and address issues when you see problems? Behaving this way is rarely easy, as Judy, a lead software engineer, discovered in the following example.

A Failing Project

Some years ago, when I reviewed a small software project, the schedule problem was not yet obvious to anyone except the development team. This was July, and Judy, the team leader, knew that the year-end deadline was impossible. She did not want to tell her manager, however, because she had complained about the schedule at the beginning of the project and had been ignored. So she and the team kept plugging away, hoping for some miracle to save them. There was no miracle, however, and the project was late, management was irate, and Judy and her small team were considered failures.

Judy's project was to modify an accounting program so that it would conform to a new tax law. The work had to be done by the end of the year, because that was when the new law took effect. Judy and two other engineers had been working for several months, and they knew that the planned date was impossible. They also knew, however, that there was no choice, for this was the law. So she blamed Congress and her management for the problem.

Sound familiar? This is a little like blaming your problems on the weather or a bad astrological sign. There was no point in trying to change the law. Judy knew that she could not. The problem was that no one—not Judy, not her manager, not the managers above him—acted responsibly. In the last analysis, however, Judy was the only person who really understood the problem. The other two engineers were totally engrossed in the project details, and the managers kept hoping that things would work out. To behave responsibly, Judy should have convinced her manager that the schedule truly was impossible, at least for the three engineers assigned to the job. Although that would not have been easy to do, it was the only responsible course of action.

Acting Responsibly

Being responsible is a way to look at life. When faced with a problem, we generally have three choices.

1. We can get emotional, cry, wave our arms, or blame other people.
2. We can ignore the problem and keep grinding ahead in the hope that things will somehow work out.

3. We can step up to the challenge, look around for what we can constructively do, and then work to get it done.

Not Giving Up

Being responsible means taking choice 3. We must either control the circumstances of our lives, or these circumstances will control us. To see what I mean, consider another example.

On Friday afternoon, an engineer in this software company's New York City laboratory learned that he had to be in California for an important Monday morning meeting. When he went to the laboratory cashier's office for a travel advance, however, he found that it had closed early, and the cashier was at a finance department meeting. The engineer tried to get the meeting interrupted so that he could get the money, but the finance manager's secretary would not interrupt the meeting.

At this point, the engineer had a choice: Would he be a victim of this situation, or would he act responsibly? He could have just given up and said that he couldn't make it to the Monday meeting, but he saw the problem as a challenge. So he went to his boss and told him the problem. The boss also called the finance manager. Again the secretary refused to interrupt the meeting. The manager also refused to give up, however, so they both went to the laboratory director. The director called the secretary and told her to have the finance manager call him immediately. The finance manager did call, and the problem was quickly resolved.

Although this might seem like a minor problem, the world is full of minor problems, and any one of these problems can delay things, cause inconvenience, or even result in serious problems. Often, no one has been given responsibility for addressing any of these problems. And if no one decides to handle them, they will fester, and some will continue to cause problems, possibly for years.

Facing Facts

It is uniquely human to take charge, to address problems, and to seek to change the world. So what does being responsible involve, and why is it hard? Take Judy's case. When I looked at her project in early July, the three engineers had been working for several months and it was obvious to them that they were not going to finish on time.

Of course, the source of the problem was that Judy's manager had been unreasonable at the very beginning of the project. Rather than have Judy and her two engineers make a plan that they felt was achievable, he demanded an impossible schedule. He also, it turns out, faced the same unreasonable demands from his management. The point is that with an impossible schedule, the project will be late, regardless of the law. The responsible actions for Judy and her managers would have been to understand and address the problem at the beginning, and not just blindly proceed in the hope that things would somehow work out.

In addition to unreasonable management, Judy and her team had another problem: she had only stated an opinion that the schedule was too tight. As long as it was a question of opinions, her manager preferred his opinion to hers. However, if she had made a detailed plan, she might have convinced him of the problem. Then he could have taken action. He might have added staff in an attempt to meet the schedule, or he could have alerted the users to prepare backup procedures. But doing nothing was irresponsible. In the end, everyone lost.

The Risks of Being Responsible

Why is it difficult to act responsibly? Actually, it is not difficult at all; people just think it is. The reason is that most of us are afraid that we won't be listened to, or we are unsure of our responsibilities. When we are unsure, we hang back to see whether someone else will handle the problem. Usually, however, no one else has clear responsibility either, so the problem just festers. In Judy's case, Congress had set the date and her manager had agreed to the project. So he was responsible and not Judy. Although it sounds rational to put blame where it belongs, doing so invariably leads to failed projects.

Acting responsibly can seem risky. In fact, it is the least risky alternative. When a project appears to the engineers to be in trouble, it almost certainly is. When people keep quiet and hope someone else will recognize the problem, the issue gets progressively harder to address. Every day that you wait to act is a day that you can't use to solve the problem. Delay also exposes you to the question of why you delayed telling management. If you can say that you just found out about the problem, that is reasonable. But if you have to admit that you have known for months but lacked the nerve to tell someone, you are more likely to be criticized. So delay is almost always the worst alternative.

Stating the Facts

Speaking up involves exposing yourself to criticism. Responsible actions often involve changing the status quo, and this never looks easy, particularly if you are an engineer and the status quo was established by a senior manager. But when the facts are known and senior managers understand the facts, they are usually reasonable.

Of course, what makes stating the facts risky is the chance that the senior manager will be unreasonable. Because engineers rarely know these managers and because these engineers will rarely be blamed for not personally taking action, it seems much safer to wait and see whether someone else will solve the problem. Although that is always an option, it is irresponsible.

Perhaps the best example of how facts can change an executive's point of view was cited by Covey in his wonderful book, *The Seven Habits of Highly Effective People* [Covey, 1990, page 33].

Two battleships assigned to the training squadron had been at sea on maneuvers in heavy weather for several days. I was serving on the lead battleship and was on watch on the bridge as night fell. The visibility was poor with patchy fog, so the captain remained on the bridge keeping an eye on all activities.

Shortly after dark, the lookout on the wing of the bridge reported, "Light, bearing on the starboard bow."

"Is it steady or moving astern?" the captain called out.

Lookout replied, "Steady, captain," which meant we were on a dangerous collision course with that ship.

The captain then called to the signalman, "Signal that ship: We are on a collision course, advise you change course 20 degrees."

Back came a signal, "Advisable for you to change course 20 degrees."

The captain said, "Send, I'm a captain, change course 20 degrees."

"I'm a seaman second class," came the reply. "You had better change course 20 degrees."

By that time, the captain was furious. He spat out, "Send, I'm a battleship. Change course 20 degrees."

Back came a flashing light, "I'm a lighthouse."

We changed course.

So if you know the facts and can make these facts clear to management, think of yourself as a lighthouse. Then all these executive battleships will have to pay attention.

Facts Are Often Debatable

Of course, facts don't come with labels that say "Believe me." They are often opinions based on estimates and judgments. It is here that TSPi comes in. It shows you how you and your team can make estimates and plans that you believe. And, surprisingly, when you have done a thorough job of planning, you will believe in your own plans. This turns out to be the key to convincing others, even senior managers, that these are the facts.

16.2 Striving for Defined Goals

Goals provide an objective and a focus. They help us to set priorities and to ignore unimportant details. To achieve something important, start by defining precisely what you are trying to accomplish. Vague directions and imprecise goals waste time.

Focusing on the Schedule

Some years ago, when I managed a software group, the marketing people came to me with an urgent need for a project. They sought a major enhancement to our recent product release and had been debating the requirements with the engineers for several weeks. They needed the product by the following November and had been unable to reach agreement. After hearing their story, I concluded that the problem was a lack of urgency. So I told the engineers and the marketers to agree on a plan in two weeks or else I would kill the project. Because both groups wanted to do the job, they skipped the normal marketing and design reviews and quickly agreed on a plan. I then funded the project, and the engineers got right to work.

As November approached, the time came to announce the product's availability. The team drafted the announcement letter and sent it to marketing for review. From this, marketing quickly realized that this product was not what they wanted. In their rush to get started, the engineers had developed what they thought was needed. It turned out, however, that they had misunderstood marketing and had built the wrong product. The entire effort was a waste of time, and the product was scrapped.

The problem here was one of goals. I had thought that the engineers and marketing people were not serious about reaching agreement and had given them an arbitrary date. Rather than take the time to truly understand each other, the two groups then quickly compromised on a vague statement that would get the project funded. Because I had made the date paramount, the focus came off the result. They finished by the date I had given them, but they built the wrong product.

Goals Provide Focus and Priorities

Goals are important for two reasons: they provide a focus for the effort and they establish priorities. Without clear and agreed goals, engineers rarely do good work. With a clear goal, however, you know what is to be done and you have a clear direction for the work.

The goal also sets priorities. The goal is first, and everything else is secondary. Although this helps when the goal is appropriate, it is often a problem when it is not. In my case, I focused the team on a two-week objective. I assumed that they would produce a quality result, but I did not emphasize the paramount importance of producing a viable product.

What Do You Want Me to Do?

Confusion about goals is a common problem in software engineering. In my early days as an engineer, managers often asked me for products on seemingly impossible schedules. One question I wish I had thought to ask was, "Does it have to work?" This would have gotten an annoyed response of "Of course it does," but I could then have asked, "Then can it have defects, and if so, how many?" Although such questions do not make managers very happy, they at least start a discussion of the implicit goal of quality in all the work we do.

When people tell you what they want you to do, they generally have a goal but have not taken the trouble to explain it. Even more often, they intuitively know what they want done but have not explicitly defined it. Only you can know whether you have a clear goal for what you are going to do. Even if your peers and managers think that the goal is clear, if it is not clear to you, you must speak up. Insist on getting your questions resolved. Often, you will find that others had exactly the same questions but were afraid to ask. You can perform a real service by asking your managers to clearly define the goals that they want you to meet. If they can't do this, put together a version of what you think their goals are and check it with them before you start the work. Then make sure that you and they agree.

16.3   Living by Sound Principles

We all live by certain principles: honesty is the best policy, do unto others as you would have them do unto you, and so forth. We have learned these principles from our families, our schools, our friends, and our religions. Although we rarely think about them, these principles affect everything we do and everyone we deal with.

Not Joining the Team

Take the case of Dick. He was a senior engineer with a great deal of experience working on advanced communication systems. When Dick joined the new project, the overall design concept had already been completed and approved by the customer. The team was now working out the details of how the system would work.

Dick attended the next design meeting and had a lot of questions about the design approach. He disagreed with some of the team's earlier decisions and suggested that they follow a different strategy. Because no one agreed to make these changes, Dick went off by himself to work out the details of his alternative design. After several weeks, Dick had completed a fairly detailed description of his ideas, and he came back to present them to the team. Although his approach appeared likely to work, Dick could not explain why the team should scrap the work that had been done and switch to the new design. At this point, Dick and the team reached an impasse: the team would not switch to Dick's design, and Dick refused to work on the team's design. Management then removed Dick from the project.

So even though Dick probably knew more about this kind of system than any other engineer in the company, he had to be removed from the team. Because of his unwillingness to work cooperatively with the other engineers, the design and development was done without him. In fact, Dick soon left the company and ended up working as an independent consultant. His remarkable talents were largely untapped, entirely because he was unwilling to participate cooperatively in developing a system he did not design.

The problem here is one of principle. Although Dick was a competent engineer, he had an image of himself as a super designer. Rather than help complete someone else's design, he concentrated on finding fault with the existing design in an effort to convince the team to adopt his ideas instead. Design debates are usually constructive, but on development projects there is a time for debate and there is a time for getting on with the job. Every engineer must make this transition, and all of us must learn to contribute to projects that others have designed. If we cannot do this, we are unlikely to have a rewarding engineering career.

How to Live by Sound Principles

In living by sound principles, there are three issues to consider:

Your opinion of yourself

Your opinion of others

Your commitment to excellence

16.4   Your Opinion of Yourself

How you think about yourself relates to the question I asked at the beginning of the chapter: "Who are you?" One way to think about yourself is in terms of your values. Do you have confidence in and respect for yourself? Do you accept your talents and abilities? Are you willing to accept and acknowledge your weaknesses and shortcomings?

Each of us is unique, with special talents and abilities, most of which we haven't yet discovered. So honor and respect yourself for your uniqueness, for your known talents, and for those talents that you have yet to develop. When you respect yourself, you can be objective. You can focus on the job and how to do it rather than worry about your future or what other people think about you. Instead of worrying about the next promotion or wondering why your design was not selected, you can devote your energies to the work to be done. This, it turns out, is the true key to success, and even the key to the next promotion. After all, the principal way that management judges your capabilities is by how you perform on a job. So if you objectively concentrate on doing your best at your present job, your future will generally take care of itself.

16.5   Your Opinion of Others

Respect for yourself is essential, but, for working on teams, respect for others is also critical. The case of Dick is a good example. He was preoccupied with his own ideas and felt he was a better designer than the other engineers on the team. He was more concerned with getting his design accepted than with making a contribution. He was so hung up with his image of himself as a designer that he was unable to work as a member of the team. As a result, he ended up being removed from the project.

The key to working on a team is how you see yourself in relation to the people you work with. Do you respect them for what they are? Can you submerge your personal ambitions and contribute humbly as part of the team? Can you help others to make their contributions and objectively consider their ideas along with your own?

The key is to strive for understanding and mutual support; to recognize that you depend on others and that they, too, must rely on you. Although there are many other basic values, these two—respect for yourself and respect for others—are perhaps most fundamental to teamwork. If you can truly believe and live by these values, you will function effectively by yourself and be a valued team member.

16.6   Your Commitment to Excellence

To be a superior engineer, you must care about the quality of the products you produce. It is not easy, however, to consistently strive for excellence. It requires conviction, perseverance, and a high degree of personal commitment. But the results can be highly rewarding.

As you strive for excellence, think of your job as the most important thing that you have to do. Try to do it with distinction. Make it something to be proud of, and resist the temptation to take shortcuts. *Now* is the only time that counts in life. The past is over, and nothing is ever done in the future. You only live *now*. So make what you do *now* something to be proud of.

The key to doing excellent software work is to know the most effective methods and consistently use them. There are lots of known and proven methods, but software engineers rarely use them, at least not consistently. But to build superior systems, every engineer must do superior work. So every time that you are tempted to skip an inspection, rush through a design, or not record a defect, think about your commitment to excellence and remember that you can achieve excellence only by properly handling all the details of the job.

Excellence Starts with You

Although the team can help in your drive for excellence, excellence must start with you. First, focus on what excellence means to you. Do you seek a highly usable product, a beautiful design, a defect-free program, or perhaps all three? Next, decide on the disciplines needed to do such work, and then consistently follow these disciplines when you do the job.

To use disciplines consistently, however, is much easier said than done. The reason is that our lives are full of disciplines we should follow but don't. For example, few people exercise daily even though it is proven beyond a doubt that daily exercise will lengthen our productive lives. Similarly, giving up smoking, eating a healthy diet, drinking in moderation, and the like are examples of personal disciplines that are honored more in the breach than in practice.

Make Discipline a Habit

So what can motivate us to really follow a discipline that we have tried and failed to follow? Several techniques can help. First, force of habit is probably the best way to maintain a discipline. If you can keep forcing yourself to do disciplined work for long enough, pretty soon it will become automatic. Covey defines a habit as "the intersection of knowledge, skill, and desire" [Covey, 1990, page 47]. A habit is something we do essentially automatically, and that is precisely what we want our disciplines to become.

Before habits become natural, however, we must have three things. We require the knowledge of why this habit is important. We need the skill to do it, and we must have a strong desire to do it. Although we can gain knowledge and skill from studying and reading, the key is desire.

Desire is intense and urgent. Desire concerns life's lessons. It involves much more than the intellect. For example, all of us know people who have tried for years to stop smoking but never could. After becoming pregnant, however, when the doctor tells them to stop smoking or they'll injure the baby, miraculously, many women manage to stop smoking. That is desire, and it is not easy to achieve.

Motivating Desire

How can we motivate a desire to consistently strive for excellence in our work? Desire can be achieved in three ways. It can be a personal matter of life or death, as with a smoker or a drug addict. Or, like a policeman or a teacher, management may require these actions. Although this motivation can be effective, it is not professional. Do you want to be treated like a child or a criminal for the rest of your life?

On the other hand, a desire can be something that we truly want to do. It is the only method that we, as professionals, should need. Because this kind of self-motivation is not easy, especially alone, this is where the team can help. When a cohesive team works together with a defined process and explicit goals, the members are motivated to strive for the common goal. When someone does not follow the process, all the team members know it and can exert pressure to conform.

One technique that can help teams to maintain their discipline is to recognize that members will occasionally slip up, particularly at first. The trick is not to treat these lapses as failures but rather to look on them as opportunities to learn. Examine each lapse and understand why and how it happened. Then figure out how either to avoid these conditions in the future or to devise ways to better manage these circumstances when they occur.

The team itself is the best means to motivate and maintain the discipline of its members. Management needs to help the team establish its plans and goals, but the team should monitor and maintain its own behavior. Team pressure can be a strong motivator. And when this pressure is coupled with a personal drive for excellence, it can be very effective.

Improving Yourself

Achieving excellence is a constant struggle, principally because the world is changing. What was once considered excellent no longer is. For example, the history of human life is one of surpassed records. In sports, world records are broken every year. In the 1920s, Johnny Weismuller, an early Tarzan of the movies, held 67 world records in swimming. He also won five Olympic gold medals. Before he died in 1984, he said, "Today, my world records are routinely being beaten by high school girls."

The facts are astounding. Human capabilities increase every year. Although diet, better equipment, and better tools certainly help, the key is the human will to excel. This means that we must continually focus on improving our personal capabilities. In working to improve yourself, however, recognize that talents are not just innate gifts to be discovered. Capabilities are developed. So while you are searching for your talents, remember that people grow and improve and that discovering talents is a matter of finding latent abilities that you can develop.

When people strive to excel, they often find that they can do even better work than they imagined. So strive to improve yourself and to be an even better software engineer than you are today. You will be surprised at how good you can be.

16.7 Summary

Effective self-management is the foundation for almost everything people do. In this chapter, we review the elements of managing yourself: being responsible, striving for defined goals, and living by sound principles.

Being responsible concerns how we handle problems. We can get emotional, we can ignore the problem and hope that things will work out, or we can step up to the challenge. Being responsible means stepping up to the challenge. Although this is generally the least risky alternative, it usually requires that we have a convincing plan for what we propose to do. Then we can generally convince management to agree to what we propose.

The second topic in the chapter concerns goals. Goals provide focus and priorities. Only you can know whether you have a clear goal for what you are doing. If you do not, insist on clarifying the goal. This often means that you must take responsibility for defining these goals and then for checking them with your manager to make sure they are correct. Gaining this clarity is critically important, however, because clear goals often make the difference between project success and failure.

The third topic in the chapter concerns living by sound principles. Here, there are three issues: your opinion of yourself, your opinion of others, and your commitment to excellence. How you think about yourself concerns your values, your self-confidence, and your willingness to accept yourself for what you are. How you think about and treat others is critical for working on teams. We all depend on others, and they must be able to rely on us.

To be a superior engineer, you must also care about the quality of the products you produce. The key is to know what the most effective methods are and to consistently use them. Although the team can help in this, excellence starts with the individual. Achieving excellence is a constant struggle, principally because the world is changing. What was once considered excellent no longer is. This means that we must continually focus on improving our personal capabilities.

16.8 Reference

Stephen R. Covey. 1990. *The Seven Habits of Highly Effective People: Powerful Lessons in Personal Change.* New York: Simon & Schuster.

17

Being on a Team

When you work on a team, the situation is quite different from working alone. Now, in addition to doing your own work, you must mesh your efforts with those of your teammates. Your objectives also change. Instead of trying to be most efficient personally, your focus now is on making the team most efficient. This means that you will not always be able to do the tasks you prefer to do. You should, however, still do your assigned tasks to the best of your ability. This chapter discusses the issues of working on a team and describes how team membership affects your behavior. The chapter starts with a brief discussion of jelled teams and then covers two categories of team-member obligations.

- ☐ Teamwork obligations
- ☐ Team-building obligations

17.1 The Jelled Team

There is something magical about an effective team. It has an ethic, an attitude, and an energy that permeate everything it does. The teammates support one another, they intuitively know when and how to help, and they rally round at just the right time. The members are part of a common effort, and they have a sense of belonging and a feeling of camaraderie. DeMarco calls this a jelled team [DeMarco].

When a team clicks, it seems to perform beyond itself. The members are on a new and different plane, and they can perform feats that even they could not have imagined. It is not that they are especially empowered but rather that they have forgotten themselves. When the team is fully aligned on a clear objective, it finds strengths it never suspected it had. We see this in sports, in marketing, and in engineering. The power of motivated teams is extraordinary.

Membership in such teams is rewarding. People remember the joy of meeting a tough challenge, not so much because of the result but because of the team. The power of the team is in its membership. The goal knits them together, but it is the common bond of team membership that provides the strength.

There is no simple rule or procedure that produces jelled teams. One thing is always required, however, and that is the full commitment of all the team members to their team. They willingly submerge their personal interests and aspirations to those of the team. Without this full commitment, teams do not break records and they often do not even finish the job. To have a rewarding and productive team experience, commit yourself to the team's success and try to get your teammates to commit themselves as well.

17.2 Teamwork Obligations

Effective teamwork results only from the combined efforts of all the team members. All of them must participate and contribute, and all of them must view effective teamwork as the single most important part of their jobs. The elements of effective teamwork are three: communication among team members, making and meeting commitments, and participating in the team's activities.

17.3 Communication Among Team Members

In building a jelled team, communication is critical. Without timely and complete communication, the team members do not know what their teammates are doing, they cannot support one another, and they don't have a sense of progress. Without complete and open communication, no team can work as a unit. This means it can't jell. For teams, the three most important elements of communication are visibility, listening, and negotiation.

Visibility

Visibility is a matter of team style. Is everything open and aboveboard, or are there hidden agendas and private assignments? High-performance teams know what is happening. They can anticipate problems and quickly adjust to changes. They know when someone needs help and can see the effects of their work. On jelled teams, all the members are in constant contact. Everyone knows what is going on, and there is a sense of excitement and daily progress.

On small teams, communication is usually simple and informal. As team size grows beyond about six to eight members, however, or if any team members work in different locations or on incompatible schedules, teams can quickly lose a sense of identity. Without open communication, people get suspicious or discouraged, or they lose enthusiasm and energy.

The team also needs to meet frequently to discuss issues, to resolve problems, and to plan the work. In fact, effective teams make a practice of meeting at least once a week to communicate and support one another. Although frequent team meetings may seem to take too much time and daily contact among the team members may seem unnecessary, they are essential to having a jelled team.

Listening

People think of a good communicator as someone who speaks clearly, uses compelling examples, and commands your attention. This is wrong. The best communicators are great listeners. After they have listened and really understood, then they can communicate in a way that deals directly with your issues and concerns. This kind of communication always starts with listening.

According to Covey, there are five levels of listening [Covey, pages 240, 253].

1. *Ignoring* is not really listening at all.

2. *Pretending* is acting as if we are listening when we are not.

3. *Selective listening* is hearing only selected parts of the conversation.

4. In *attentive listening*, we are paying attention and focusing on the words being said.

5. The fifth level, *empathic listening*, is listening with the intent to understand.

Empathic listening is active, and it is particularly important for software teams. To truly understand complex technical issues, it is essential to focus completely on what the speaker is saying. It is hard enough to communicate a full understanding of a complex issue, but when people don't listen carefully it is almost impossible.

Surprisingly, empathic listening is relatively easy. All you need to do is to periodically play back what is being said. "Oh, what you mean is . . ." Or "In other words, you think that . . ." If it is not what the speaker meant, ask for a restatement and keep rephrasing and playing back until you both agree. That is empathic or active listening.

Although empathic listening may take longer than you think it should, it is far more efficient in the long run. Miscommunication is a major source of both software and team problems, so it is important that you and your teammates learn to be empathic listeners.

Negotiating

The final—and, in many ways, the most important—communication skill is negotiating. A large proportion of all our human interactions concern negotiations. Whether we are making commitments, debating estimates, creating designs, or inspecting programs, we are really resolving differing points of view. That is negotiating. It is not just a matter of luck that some people are better at negotiating than others. Either through experience or training, good negotiators have learned to use an effective negotiating strategy [Fisher, page 13].

Take the example of Tina, the team leader, who was helping the engineers on an industrial team select their roles. Most of the roles were quickly settled, but two engineers wanted the design manager role. Al was an older engineer with a great deal of design background, and Jeanne was a newer engineer with high potential but not much experience. Although Al would most likely be the best design manager, Tina did not want to hurt Jeanne's feelings.

To understand how Tina handled this negotiation, look first at Table 17.1 and then read the following discussion [Fisher, page 13]. Tina's approach followed the guidelines for principled negotiation. First, she avoided positions. Although both Al and Jeanne started by stating opposing positions, Tina did not even discuss these positions. She immediately got them talking about interests. She did this by asking them to explain why they wanted the job.

Al said he had a lot of background with this kind of product and had a number of design ideas. In fact, he had even built a prototype of some of the key functions. Jeanne, however, said she had a lot of knowledge about design methods but was principally interested in learning more about design. She felt that being design manager would give her more design experience.

Then Tina asked the team members for alternative ideas for solving the problem. They made several suggestions. The idea that seemed most attractive was to have Al be the design manager with Jeanne as his alternate. That would allow Jeanne to lead the design work when Al was not there and would involve Jeanne in all the design meetings and discussions.

Next, Tina discussed the criteria for a solution. She was careful to keep personalities out of the debate and to focus on the criteria for the best result. Everyone, including Al and Jeanne, agreed that the choice should be based entirely on the likelihood of getting the highest quality design.

TABLE 17.1 NEGOTIATION STRATEGIES

Element	Soft Negotiation	Hard Negotiation	Principled Negotiation
Participants	Participants are friends.	Participants are adversaries.	Participants are problem solvers.
Goal	Agreement	Victory	A wise outcome reached efficiently and amicably
Approach	Make concessions to cultivate personal relationships.	Demand concessions as a condition of the relationship	Separate the people from the problem.
Trust	Trust others.	Distrust others.	Proceed independent of trust.
Focus	Change your position easily. Make offers.	Dig in to your position. Make threats.	Focus on interests, not positions. Explore interests.
Bottom Line	Disclose your bottom line.	Mislead as to your bottom line.	Avoid having a bottom line.
Options	Accept one-sided losses to reach agreement.	Demand one-sided gains as the price of agreement.	Invent options for mutual gain.
Deciding	Search for the single answer: the one *they* will accept.	Search for the single answer: the one *you* will accept.	Develop multiple options to choose from; decide later.
Criteria	Insist on agreement.	Insist on your position.	Insist on objective criteria.
Will	Try to avoid a contest of will.	Try to win a contest of will.	Try to reach a result based on standards independent of will.
Pressure	Yield to pressure.	Apply pressure.	Reason and be open to reasons; yield to principle, not pressure.

In exploring the options against the criteria, Jeanne wasn't sure how the proposed option would work. She and Al talked about how they would work together, and they both finally agreed on a reasonable approach. At that point, Jeanne agreed that Al was probably a better choice and that she would be willing to be the alternate design manager.

Why Principled Negotiation Works

The reason that principled negotiation is effective is that it avoids the polarization of positions. When the two sides to a negotiation work from opposing positions, they have no way to agree. A win for one is a loss for the other. The only way out of this dilemma is to move from positions to interests. What is each party after, and what do they really want? Note that to find out what they really want, the team must practice empathic or active listening.

The basis for principled negotiation is a recognition that a position is only one way to satisfy an interest. By focusing on interests instead of positions, you free up the debate while obtaining the information needed to arrive at a sound and effective solution.

Take Enough Time

Although these debates can sometimes take a great deal of time, the key is to stay objective and to take as long as is required to arrive at a solution that all parties will accept. When the team realizes that the team leader will keep the meeting in session until the question is settled, even if it takes until late at night, people start to get much more reasonable. Then issues can be settled quickly.

This exhaustion strategy can work well, but only if the leader can stick to the principled negotiation strategy. As long as the team can objectively debate the issues and look for creative solutions, the members will continue to work on the problem. If positions get frozen, however, the meeting will quickly degenerate and people are likely to get angry and storm out. Principled negotiation may take a lot of time, but it is much more effective in the long run.

17.4   Making and Meeting Commitments

The second teamwork obligation is to make and meet commitments. When one person makes a pact with another and both of them expect it to be kept, that is a commitment. The following is a good example [Humphrey 1997, page 14].

> In one case a programming project was threatened by a change in an engineering schedule. The programmers were completing the control program for a special-purpose machine when the engineering manager called to say the first test machine would be delayed by two months. Since they were about to start testing, the programmers were in a panic. The programming manager had been an engineer, however, and he knew what to do. He called the engineering manager and told him the programming schedule was to-

tally dependent on delivery of the test machine, and if it didn't arrive on time, he would call an immediate meeting with the president to tell him the cause of the delay.

In the turmoil that followed, the engineers found they could keep the date for the test machine after all. They had needed an additional machine for the service department and thought they could divert the programming machine to solve the problem. When forced to take responsibility for the delay, they found another answer. Engineering had committed the current schedule to the president and they were proud of always meeting their commitments.

Responsible Commitments

As a team member, you should make responsible commitments and strive to meet them. This is the only way that teams can operate. The members must trust one another to do what they say. Responsibly plan to finish your committed work on the allotted date. Some organizations have a tradition of never missing commitments. When someone has a problem, everyone offers to help. Commitment is an ethic that must be learned. After you see its benefits, however, you will never want to work any other way.

Responsible commitments must be based on a plan to do the work. You make a plan based on what you know of the job and your experience with similar work. Then you examine your other work and compare it to the priority of this job. Only then can you responsibly say when you will complete the job. This is what it takes to make a responsible commitment.

Making Commitments

The motivation to meet a commitment is largely the result of the way it was made. First, the commitment must be freely assumed; that is, in making a commitment you must have had a choice. Second, the commitment is public. You have personally made the commitment, and your credibility is on the line.

Third, to make a responsible commitment you must prepare; that is, you define and estimate the work and conclude you can do it. If several people are involved, all of them must participate in this planning and their views must be carefully considered. It takes time to make everyone familiar with the job and what they are expected to do, but this is the only way to establish a solid commitment foundation.

After you and your instructor or manager or customer or teammates have agreed on the commitment, the final step is performance. When everything goes according to plan, there is no problem; but this is rarely the case. There are always surprises, and in technology there is an unwritten law that all surprises involve more work. With experience, engineers learn to allow for this, but their plans can never be entirely accurate. A final crash effort is thus often needed to meet the agreed-on deadline. With good planning, however, the plans are usually close enough so that the job can be finished with a modest final push.

When the smoke has cleared, the team should reassess the work to understand what went wrong and how to make a better commitment next time. The estimates should be reviewed to see what was overlooked, and the contingencies should be revised to include the new experiences. By comparing actual performance with the estimates, engineers soon learn to make better estimates. This is why the people who will do the work should make their own plans: to learn how to consistently make commitments they can meet.

17.5   Participation in the Team's Activities

After communication and commitment, the third teamwork obligation is participation in the team's activities. Teams provide more than just bodies; they also offer a range of skills and perspectives. Because of its combined knowledge and experience, a team can be a powerful resource, but only if properly used. For example, when the team members meet to solve a problem, produce a design, or make a plan, it is important for everyone to contribute ideas. Although there is no special trick to doing this, the primary need is for the meeting leader or facilitator to ensure that everyone participates. If someone tries to say something and is drowned out, the facilitator should note the fact and call on this member as soon as there is an opportunity to do so.

Caving In

In team problem solving, some members may be so accommodating that they do not defend their own views. If you have a strong opinion and are not convinced that the team has considered it, do not cave in too quickly. Try to understand the facts and ask the team to help you understand why you should change your mind. Keep the discussion on a rational plane and search for a logical reason. Remember that every new idea starts as a minority of one. If you are the one, you have a responsibility to that idea and to the team. Often, if you merely stop and ask the team members to explain their logic, entirely new options show up. The team may take a different and totally unanticipated direction. This is called *synergy*. One idea spawns questions. In answering them, you raise further questions. Each question stimulates more thought, and these thoughts produce better answers. As a team member, part of your job is to stimulate this discovery process.

Supporting the Holdout

I know of no statistics on this subject, but in many juries everyone initially agrees with one position except for a single holdout. In a surprising number of cases, however, when the final verdict is rendered, that one holdout has swung the entire jury to unanimous agreement with the reverse position. Although such holdouts can be powerful, they need support. You may not agree with the holdout's position, but you should make sure that it is explored. You could be the critical ally that this individual needs to persist. Although your support may not swing the decision, it is important that the team fully consider and understand all the team members' viewpoints.

Getting Attention

The experiences of aircraft flight crews illustrate the importance of real participation. Valente [1989] tells the following story:

> Tapes show that the co-pilot on an Air Florida jet that crashed in a snowstorm in Washington, D.C., in 1982 raised questions about the amount of slush on the wings before takeoff. Again during takeoff, he repeatedly warned that something was "not right." Through it all the captain remained silent until the co-pilot called out, "We're going down!" "I know it," were the captain's last words.

The most common type of airliner accident is called "controlled flight into terrain"—in other words, a properly functioning aircraft is flown into the ground. Almost always, the cause is a flight crew teamwork problem. Often, a study of the black box tapes shows that at least one member of the flight crew knew about the problem but failed to get action taken in time.

To have a smoothly functioning team, it is crucial for every team member to contribute what he or she knows. If no one is paying attention, do whatever it takes to get attention. Under these conditions, think of yourself as the co-pilot. Make sure you are heard and understood. Don't give up. Get the team's attention.

Paying Attention

The stories of airline flight crews have two messages. The first is one we have already discussed: speaking up and getting the team's attention. The second message is about paying attention and accepting help. One of the major problems with airline flight crews is the common attitude of "I don't need help; I can do it myself."

This hotshot image of being fully competent and self-sufficient is common to fighter pilots who are used to flying alone. The fighter-pilot ideal is known as having the "right stuff." Unfortunately, this Lone Ranger image is also common in many other professions, including programming. Another story by Valente illustrates the advantages of accepting help [Valente].

> As soon as he heard the aircraft's tail engine explode, Capt. Dennis Fitch, a United DC-10 training pilot aboard as a passenger, sent word to the cockpit that he was available to help. Capt. Alfred C. Haynes, a 33-year United veteran, readily accepted. The airliner, with the hydraulics that allow pilots to control it crippled, was spiraling downward at about 2,400 feet a minute.
>
> Scrunching down on his knees between the crew seats, Capt. Fitch experimented with the throttles. The two pilots found that they could keep the nose of the plane up if they advanced the two remaining engines to full throttle, and that they could steer with great difficulty, by varying the thrust of each engine.

The manufacturer had relayed word to the crew that a DC-10 without hydraulics could not be flown. But, with the help of a third pilot, this crew was able to bring the plane in to a successful crash landing. Of the 296 people on board, 185 survived, including the three pilots.

The point is that being self-sufficient is important in some situations, but trying to be self-sufficient during a crisis can be dangerous. When you are in trouble, ask for and accept help. When someone is offering to help, pay attention. The odds are that you need it even if you don't think you do.

17.6   Team-building Obligations

Just as teamwork requires the participation and active involvement of all team members, so does team-building. In fact, the principal objective of team-building is to get all the team members to actively participate in the team's work. The team-building obligations are as follows.

- ☐ Accepting responsibility for a team role and performing that role to the best of your ability
- ☐ Participating in establishing team goals and plans and striving to meet these goals and to follow the plans
- ☐ Building and maintaining an effective and cooperative team

---

17.7   Accepting and Performing a Team Role

All team members should have defined roles. Although the TSPi roles are formally defined, most teams do not have such definitions. But even informal team roles must fit the team's mission, mesh with the other roles, and match members' personal talents and abilities. Your role could be vague or open-ended, such as figuring out what tests to run or controlling the design standards. Because roles are important to the proper functioning of a team, TSPi defines them.

Why Have Roles?

There are several reasons for assigning roles to all team members. First, most projects include much more than development work. Plans must be developed and tracked, data gathered and stored, changes managed, standards defined, support facilities obtained, and so on. If no one is responsible for these tasks, they will either not get done or they will be handled in a haphazard way. This situation is generally inefficient and frequently results in important tasks being overlooked or done at the wrong time.

The second reason for defining roles is so that the team members will feel responsible for their own working environment. If there are problems, the engineer with the relevant role will quickly understand the problem and fix it. When the team is responsible for its own support, it is more likely to do the job properly.

Third, no one can design, implement, or test full time. When they try to do so, engineers get stale and are more likely to make mistakes. The various tasks required to perform the role responsibilities provide a ready source of tasks that engineers can interweave with their development work. This approach not only accomplishes the important role tasks, but it also provides a useful break from development work. Surprisingly, you will find that by occasionally taking such a break, you will actually get more done and you will make fewer mistakes.

17.8   Establishing and Striving to Meet Team Goals

An effective team can do more together than the members could do by themselves. The goal is superior performance. If you merely wanted more arms and legs, that would be a working group and not a team. Katzenbach has studied many teams, and he notes that any team can be successful as long as it is focused on performance [Katzenbach]. The key, he says, is to have specific, measurable goals. They cannot be just any goals, however; they must be specific. With a clear charter and tough, specific performance goals, teams can work miracles. The key is to make sure that everyone understands and agrees to the goals.

An aggressive goal can be motivating, but it can't be just any goal. It must be something that the team agrees is important, and it must be something the members feel they can accomplish. It is here that planning comes in. While making a plan, the team members are devising a way to meet the goal. Until they have estimated how much work it will take and have decided who will do each part, the goal is only a hope. When they have a plan, however, they have the knowledge and understanding to commit themselves to meeting the goal.

17.9   Building and Maintaining the Team

The third team-building obligation is to build and maintain the team. If your team has not coalesced into a coherent and cooperative group and you think you know why, do something about it. One way to do this is to meet as a team and to ask some questions.

1. Do we have clearly defined goals?

2. Are the goals important to all the team members?

3. Have we made a plan to achieve these goals?

4. Was everyone involved in making that plan?

5. Do we all agree that this is a good plan?

6. Have all team members committed to do their best to meet the plan?

7. Is everyone making an effort to meet the plan?

8. Are all team members following the commitment guidelines outlined earlier, either meeting their commitments or warning in advance of problems and negotiating a new date?

9. Do we all meet at least once a week to review status, plans, and issues?

If the answer to any of these questions is no, that should give you a good idea about the source of the problem. If you can answer yes to all the questions, your team will likely jell, given enough time.

Difficult Team Members

Sometimes, teams don't jell because one or two members refuse to participate or to carry their fair share of the workload. Team members can often be more effective than managers or team leaders in resolving such problems. In fact, disruptive or uncooperative behavior is often intended to impress the rest of the team. Therefore, the team itself may be the only group that can address the problem. Because every member has an obligation to help maintain order, you need to distinguish between disruptive behavior and real concerns. If someone has an unexplored issue and is being squelched, provide support. If the person is being disruptive, think of ways to support the team leader.

This is the principal area where academic teams differ from working teams. On an industrial team, the members are paid to do a job. If someone doesn't perform, he or she could soon be out of a job. When a team member does not show up, consistently fails to meet commitments, or is otherwise uncooperative, the team should be very direct. Explain the problem and define what the member needs to do to improve. Offer to help if that seems appropriate, but make it clear that if there is no immediate improvement, the team will take the problem to management.

This approach is almost always effective. In most cases, with the team's help, you can get initially uncooperative members to perform. When you cannot, go directly to management and explain the problem. Be specific about the problems and suggest an improvement program if you can. Then management will generally talk to the engineer and explain that without improvement, he or she will likely be dismissed. This is almost always effective in changing the team member's behavior.

Academic Team Problems

In team courses, the situation is entirely different. Here, the team members pay for their education and the faculty provides the courses. Although poor performers can be given lower grades, they cannot be fired. As a result, peer pressure is much less likely to be effective for changing the behavior of difficult team members.

The reason is that some people have been doing the minimum that they can get by with all their lives. They have probably learned to ignore badgering by their parents and teachers and are unlikely to change now just from peer pressure. Usually, the only thing that works in these cases is a serious threat, such as being dismissed from a job. Clearly, this will not work with students.

In addressing such problems, student teams should again start by reviewing the problem with the nonperformer and offering to help if needed. Start by discussing the problems and asking whether the student is having trouble. The student might have had a heavy workload that week, been sick, or had a family crisis. If the problem is truly temporary, one such discussion is usually all that is required.

If the problem is not temporary, make it clear that adequate performance is required. If the student does not respond quickly, go to the instructor and ask that the student be removed from the team. Don't worry about being short-handed. Experience shows that just one drone on a team will reduce everyone else's performance. In fact, removing the nonperforming member will usually improve overall team performance.

Getting Help

Another important responsibility of team members is to call for help. It is surprising how often software engineers struggle alone to solve a difficult problem. Generally, these are problems that others have faced and know how to solve. Had they asked for help in time, they could have quickly solved the problem. By the time others learn about the problem, however, it is often too late to recover.

As a team member, remember that *you are not alone*. If you insist on playing the Lone Ranger, sooner or later you will get into a fix that you cannot get out of by yourself. By waiting to ask for help, you may have destroyed the team's ability to meet its goal.

Support

For software, the support that the team gives to its members is critical. In addition to your official team role, you must be a team citizen and give some of your time to helping everyone else. This means that you should participate in inspections, give advice, and contribute to design sessions. Almost everyone can occasionally use advice or assistance, and peer reviews are an essential part of a mature process. When you have the support of your team, you are far more likely to perform at your best.

The essence of support is to help people to be what they can become. One of my earliest memories is of failing first grade. My dad told me that I had not failed; rather, the school had. He moved the family to a different town, where my brothers and I attended a school that gave me special help. I did not find out until much later that I had a learning disability. Although learning to read was one of the most difficult things I ever did, the most important lesson in my life was that my dad believed in me. That allowed me to believe in myself, and from then on I was able to learn.

This is the key to providing effective support: helping your teammates to believe in their own abilities. When they believe in themselves, they are more likely to strive to do superior work. They may doubt their ability to handle some tasks, and they may need help and guidance, but the key thing to remember is that people can do much more than they think they can.

When engineers know that you and your teammates believe in them, they will often perform beyond what you or they thought possible. Goethe once said [Covey, page 301], "Treat a man as he is and he will remain as he is. Treat a man as he can and should be and he will become as he can and should be."

17.10 Summary

This chapter discusses teamwork issues, including some of the ways that academic and working teams differ. The chapter starts with a discussion of the jelled team, and it then covers the teamwork and team-building obligations of team members. Teamwork obligations include communication among team members, making and meeting commitments, and participating in the team's activities. Team-building obligations concern handling team roles, establishing team goals, and maintaining an effective team.

To build and maintain an effective team, all the team members must be fully committed to the team and its goals. Such teams are called jelled teams. There are several tests that help determine whether a team has jelled, and if not, why it hasn't. The responses to these tests identify basic team problems and suggest the sources of these problems. If the team passes all these tests, it will jell, given time.

For industrial teams, peer pressure is usually an effective way to handle troublesome members. Team members are paid to do a job, and they can be dismissed if they do not do so. In team courses, poor performers can be given lower grades but they cannot be fired. When they have discipline problems, student teams should first review the problem with the poor performer. If the student does not respond reasonably quickly, however, the team should go to the instructor and ask that the student be removed from the team.

As a team member, remember that *you are not alone*. Ask for help when you get into trouble. Also, you must be a good team citizen and give some of your time to help everyone else. Because the essence of support is to help people to be what they can become, the most effective way to support teammates is to help them to believe in their own abilities. When engineers know that you and your teammates believe in them, they will often perform beyond what you or they thought possible.

17.11   References

[Covey] Stephen R. Covey. 1989. *The 7 Habits of Highly Effective People: Powerful Lessons in Personal Change.* New York: Simon & Schuster.

[DeMarco] Tom DeMarco and Timothy Lister. 1987. *Peopleware: Productive Projects and Teams.* New York: Dorset House Publishing Co.

[Fisher] Roger Fisher and William Ury. 1981. *Getting to Yes: Negotiating Agreement Without Giving In.* Boston: Houghton Mifflin.

[Humphrey] Watts S. Humphrey. 1997. *Managing Technical People: Innovation, Teamwork, and the Software Process.* Reading, MA: Addison-Wesley.

[Katzenbach] Jon R. Katzenbach. 1992. "The Right Kind of Teamwork." *The Wall Street Journal.* Nov. 9: A10.

[Valente] Judith Valente and Bridget O'Brian. 1989. "Airline Cockpits are No Place to Solo." *The Wall Street Journal.* August 2: B1.

18

Teamwork

In this final chapter, we review the key lessons of this book and discuss how you might apply them to your software work as well as to many other aspects of your life. There are four key lessons from this book. First, most significant software products are produced by teams. Although individual software engineers can often write a great deal of software by themselves, the size of modern software systems is growing so rapidly, and the demand for timely results is increasing so quickly, that there simply is not time for lone individuals to do most jobs. Teams are commonly needed in software development, both to accelerate the schedule and to apply more skills and experience to the job. We can thus expect that teamwork will be an almost universal characteristic of future software work.

The second lesson is that when software teams have proper skills and when all team members work cooperatively and effectively together, they can produce extraordinary results. The capabilities of committed teams are almost unbelievable. Take, for example, two software development groups. One had experienced and competent software engineers who had written many prior programs together, but they did not follow disciplined methods and did not have a defined teamwork process. They produced a product of 22 KLOC and found 196 defects in system test. System testing took many months, and, even after all this testing, the finished product had many remaining defects. The other product was produced by a TSP team [Webb]. These engineers were also competent, but they were also PSP-trained and followed the TSP process. Their product had 25 KLOC, but they found only

10 defects in system test. What is more, system testing took only six days. Furthermore, after system test, the customer found only one defect in acceptance testing, and the product has been trouble-free in several months of subsequent use.

With proper skills and training and through the use of appropriate teamwork methods, these engineers produced a high-quality product. They also did this work faster than they had worked before. In fact, their productivity with TSP was 2.23 times the productivity they had achieved with their immediate prior project.

The third lesson of this book is that effective teamwork requires eight things.

☐ Agreed team goals

☐ Established team-member roles

☐ A supportive environment in which to work

☐ A common teamwork process

☐ A plan for the work

☐ A mutual team commitment to the goals, roles, and plan

☐ Open and free communication among all the team members

☐ The mutual respect and support of all the team members

These eight conditions for effective teamwork are not new nor complex, but they are also not obvious. They do not happen by accident or luck, and they take time to establish. This is why the TSPi has a launch step: to start the team-building process. It is also why the TSPi uses a defined process to produce the team's goals, strategy, and plan. By following the defined TSPi process, you first build a team. Then, after you have built a team, you have the most powerful, creative, and productive capability mankind has yet devised: a motivated and committed team. Then you use this capability to complete the project.

The fourth lesson may not be obvious to a casual reader, but it will be obvious to anyone who has worked on a successful TSPi team. When teams meet the teamwork conditions, they do superior work, they are more productive, and they enjoy their work.

There is now a growing body of TSP and TSPi experience that shows that engineers like working on well-run teams. Following are some quotations from engineers on TSP teams.

"This really feels like a tight team."

"The TSP forces you to design, to think the whole thing out."

"Design time is way up, but code time decreased to compensate."

"Tracking your time is an eye-opener."

"There was really good teamwork on this project, no duplication of effort."

"I'm more productive."

"The TSP gives you incredible insight into project performance."

"It's wonderful to have team members assigned specific roles."

"The team really came together to make the plan."

"I feel included and empowered."

The TSP is a great way to work, but it does more than improve the engineers' morale. It is also helpful to organizations. For example, one company reported that test defects were reduced from an average of 20/KLOC to 1/KLOC. Several years of company data show that the average cost per defect was six engineering hours. This means that the engineers paid for the full cost of PSP and TSP introduction when they wrote the next 1,000 lines of code. This company saved an estimated $5.3 million in just the first two years after PSP and TSP were introduced.

Teamwork is not only a powerful means to an end, but it is also a way to live. As you think about your working life, you will soon realize that you cannot accomplish very much alone. With few exceptions, and in almost any walk of life, significant success involves many people. This involvement may be with coworkers, customers, or suppliers, but it almost certainly will involve cooperative human interaction.

Throughout your life, you will have many occasions to work with other people. As you do, consider the possibilities of teamwork. Could this job be done by a cooperative team? How could you meld this group into a productive team? How could you empower and facilitate this team so that it, too, could produce extraordinary results?

One of the great lessons in life is that ordinary people possess many unique talents and abilities. What is more, many of these talents are unknown, even to those who have them. Assume that all team members have untapped potential, and try to think of ways to capitalize on the talents of the people you work with. Include them as valued team members, help them to find and contribute their unique talents, and you will then find that together you can produce extraordinary results.

One of the greatest rewards in life is to work on an effective team. The achievements of these teams take on a special meaning. Although you may produce extraordinary products, in retrospect, the most memorable rewards in your life will be the joys of these cooperative team achievements.

18.1   Reference

[Webb] Dave Webb and W.S. Humphrey. 1999. "Using the TSP on the TaskView Project." *Crosstalk* 12(2), February.

APPENDIX A

Need Statements for the TSPi Sample Exercises

Purpose

This appendix provides the functional need statements for two sample TSPi course exercises. These exercises are designed to give student teams experience in developing intermediate-sized software products. Although subsets of these exercises can be implemented with a relatively modest amount of code, even experienced students will find these exercises to be challenging and realistic examples of the type of software development work they will encounter as working software engineers. The principal objective of these exercises, however, is not to provide challenging programming problems but rather to provide experience with sound engineering and team practices.

The exercise objectives are to provide relatively small standard examples that student teams can partially complete within a one-semester team course. It would not be realistic to expect a student team to complete all of an exercise's functions in a single course. In fact, teams should be encouraged to proceed cautiously until they have gathered some data on their work and can make realistic plans. Then they can better judge how large a program they could realistically expect to complete.

These exercise programs can and should be developed in several cycles. Teams should make the first cycle a relatively simple working subset of the desired final product. Then they can add functionality in subsequent development cycles until they have implemented the full product functions or until they run out of time. By quickly producing a first working version, teams will find that their work is more efficient because, in the second and subsequent cycles, they will be an experienced team, they will understand the process, and they will be able to apply the lessons they learned in the first cycle.

The Change Counter Functional Need Statement

The change counter is a software tool to count program size. When you modify programs or develop programs in several development cycles, it is important to know how many lines of code (LOC) were added, deleted, or modified between program versions. Without a tool like this, you must count these data manually.

1. TSPi Change Counter Functions

1.1 Compare a modified program with its prior version.

1.2 Identify the added and deleted LOC in the modified program.

1.3 Count the added and deleted LOC in the modified program.

1.4 Count the total LOC in the modified program.

1.5 Attach a line-label reference for each added or deleted line to indicate the change number.

1.6 Provide a change label in a program header comment, indicating the change number, the date the change was made, who made it, why it was made, and the added, deleted, and total program LOC.

1.7 If the program has had several changes, maintain a record of these changes in the change label.

1.8 When a previously modified program is further modified and counted, all the prior modification records must be maintained.

1.9 Produce a new program source file for the modified program version with the change-label and line-label information.

1.10 Initially design the program to work with one selected programming language (for example, Ada, C++, C, Pascal, or Java).

1.11 Make the full-function program capable of counting at least three different languages (for example C++, Java, and Ada).

1.12 On demand, print a program listing, including the change-label and line-label information.

1.13 On demand, print a program listing with the line number of the modified program inserted at the head of each line of code.

1.14 On demand, print a program-change report with the statistics for the modified program and all prior changes.

2. Counting Specifications

2.1 Have the LOC counter count text lines with a coding standard that requires one logical LOC to be placed on a single text line, as in PSP programs 2A and 3A. For further information on LOC counting, see *A Discipline for Software Engineering,* Chapter 4 [Humphrey 95].

2.2 Enhance the program to fully analyze the program syntax and count logical LOC regardless of program format.

2.3 In comparing a program with its prior version, the comparisons are made as in the following example of counting changes in version 4 of a program.

  2.3.1 If a line is contained in both the original version 3 and the later modified version 4, it is an original and unchanged line.

  2.3.2 If a line is in version 4 only and not in version 3, it is an added line.

  2.3.3 If a line is in version 3 only and not in version 4, it is a deleted line.

2.4 Initially count each changed line as an added and a deleted line.

2.5 As an enhancement, analyze the added-deleted line pairs to see which are minor modifications of the same line and which are true additions and deletions. For this purpose, a modification would consist of a change in parameter names or values, or a change in the sign or criteria for a logical comparison.

2.6 When new sections are moved or copied from one part of the program to another, they would show up as deleted from the original location and added in the new location. Attempting to track such reused or copied code segments is beyond the scope of this exercise.

2.7 Attribute all differences between two program versions to the same change number. To separately identify several smaller changes, make separate program runs.

3. Header Labeling Specifications

3.1 In the program header, insert a comment section below the program name with the change-label information.

3.2 Starting with the most recent modification, list the prior program modifications in descending order.

3.3 For a new program, count the entire program and include a change label with version 0 data, including total program LOC.

3.4 For each modification, provide in the change label the date of the change, the name of the programmer making the change, and the reason for the change.

3.5 Also, include in the change label that program's change data: added LOC, deleted LOC, and total resulting program LOC.

3.6 In the change-label reason field, if the change was made to fix a defect, note the defect number and source.

3.7 If the change was a program enhancement, identify the enhancement project in the change-label reason field.

4. Formatting Specification

In identifying each program line, use the following practices.

4.1 Label each added or deleted line with the change number in a comment at the right-hand end of the program line.

4.2 Where the line was deleted, include the deleted line in a comment at the program location from which the line was deleted.

4.3 Where a previously added line is deleted (or a deleted line added), leave the prior line label and append a new one. Thus, when a line was added in modification 2 and deleted in modification 3, it would look like the following:

{*added line that was later deleted* [2]3}

or

{*deleted line that was later added* [2]}

deleted line that was later added {3}

4.4 When including the program line numbers in the listing, insert the number before each line, moving the lines and comments to the right.

4.5 Where a line is too long to fit on the listing page, roll it to one or more subsequent indented lines. Do this without changing the LOC count.

4.6 To preserve program readability, retain the program's original indenting where possible.

4.7 To clearly identify the rolled lines, indent them to the middle of the listing.

4.8 Where the language does not permit comment identifiers within comments, use symbols such as [,], or * to indicate the inner comment.

5. General Specifications

5.1 The change counter should be independent of the operating system on which it is run. That means, for example, that it cannot use the UNIX *diff* function.

5.2 The change counter documentation must describe program installation and operation.

The Program Analyzer Functional Need Statement

The program analyzer is a software tool to help programmers determine the complexity of the programs they have developed. There is evidence, for example, that McCabe complexity, the coupling/strength ratio, and reachability are useful predictors of program quality. Therefore, these parameters may be of value to software developers when they design programs and later when they seek to modify, extend, or improve them. With the aid of these complexity data, development teams can identify components that likely have design problems. They then can fix these problems before test.

1. **Program Analyzer Functions**

    1.1 Analyze an existing program to determine its characteristics.

    1.2 Count the program logical LOC and the LOC of each of its functions, procedures, or routines.

    1.3 Calculate the program's McCabe cyclomatic complexity and that of each of its functions, procedures, or routines [Schneidewind].

    1.4 Calculate the program's data bindings with its external environment and the data bindings of each of its functions, procedures, or routines [Selby].

    1.5 Calculate the strength of the internal data bindings for the program and for each of its functions, procedures, or routines [Selby].

    1.6 Determine the coupling/strength ratio of the overall program and of each of its functions, procedures, or routines [Selby].

    1.7 Calculate the reachability of each of the program's functions, procedures, or routines [Schneidewind].

    1.8 Produce an analysis report that provides these calculated data in summary form.

    1.9 Initially provide these functions for the language being used.

    1.10 Enhance the program to analyze additional programming languages.

2. **Counting Specifications**

    2.1 Have the LOC counter count text lines with a coding standard that requires one logical LOC to be placed on a single text line, as in PSP programs 2A and 3A. For further information on LOC counting, see *A Discipline for Software Engineering,* Chapter 4 [Humphrey 95].

2.2 As an added feature, enhance the program to fully analyze the program syntax and count logical LOC regardless of program format.

3. Analyzer Specifications

3.1 McCabe cyclomatic complexity V is calculated by

$$V = (\text{number of arcs}) - (\text{number of nodes}) + 2$$

A *node* is a logic branch, and an *arc* is a program segment between branches. There is an assumed arc from the program exit back to the program entry point.

3.2 Data binding, or coupling, is determined by counting the number of variables or parameters that a program shares with its external environment. If a program receives four input parameters and two variables and produces outputs for three different variables, its data binding value would be $4 + 2 + 3 = 9$.

3.3 The internal binding strength of a program is determined by counting the binding among all the routines within that program. This internal strength is determined by counting the number of variable or parameter values passed among a program's internal routines or procedures. For example, if a program has a total of 18 internal variables and parameters that are shared among its routines and procedures, its strength would be 18.

3.4 The coupling/strength ratio is the ratio of the numbers calculated in 3.2 and 3.3. In these examples, it would be $9/18 = 0.5$. From a quality perspective, low values (such as 0.5) of this ratio are considered better than high ones (such as 2.3).

3.5 Reachability is calculated for each program node by counting the number of possible logical paths from the program or procedure entry to that node. Where a loop may be cycled several times, only one path is counted. The reachability of a program, function, or routine is calculated by averaging the reachability of all its nodes.

3.6 Although there are many ways to implement these analysis functions, many of the calculations and analyses are potentially language-independent. If you first produce a counter and a structural analyzer that are language-dependent, the remaining analyses can then be done once for all languages.

4. General Specifications

4.1 The program analyzer documentation must describe program installation and operation.

References

[Humphrey 95] W.S. Humphrey. 1995. *A Discipline for Software Engineering.* Reading, MA: Addison-Wesley.

[Schneidewind] N.F. Schneidewind. 1979. "An Experiment in Software Error Data Collection and Analysis." *IEEE Transactions on Software Engineering,* SE-5(3), May.

[Selby] Richard W. Selby and Victor R. Basili. 1991. "Analyzing Error-Prone System Structure." *IEEE Transactions on Software Engineering* 17(2), February.

APPENDIX B

Software Configuration Management

This appendix briefly explains what software configuration management (SCM) is and why it is important to you. It also describes the TSPi configuration control process and provides the required forms and scripts. Although the procedures described do not cover all important aspects of configuration management, they should be adequate for your purposes. They also give you exposure to most of the configuration management issues you are likely to face in industry.

The Software Configuration Management Problem

Software configuration management is the total set of activities used to manage the content of a software product from the beginning to the end of the development process. The purpose of the SCM process is to ensure that the content of the product is known and available at all times, that the product functions are traceable from the requirements through the design to the final implementation, and that all product contents are properly controlled and protected.

For large and complex products, SCM systems can be quite sophisticated. For TSPi, however, the SCM system is concerned largely with controlling changes. Uncontrolled changes can waste a lot of time, corrupt designs, cause fixes to be

321

misapplied, and even result in products being lost. For example, a large system I worked on some years ago had not yet established an SCM system. One engineering group developed a new version of a COBOL compiler and tested it against all the tests that had been used with the prior version. This new and improved compiler had been advertised as being completely compatible with the prior version, so customers were told that they could switch from their old compiler with no conversion problems.

When the new compiler was distributed, however, thousands of customers called in with problems. It turned out that the new compiler had not been tested against all the changes that had been made to fix defects in the earlier compiler. For the next several months, we stopped all new development work and all the engineers spent full time responding to customer problems. This was necessary because there was no record of the changes that had been made to the prior COBOL version.

Another common problem is the need for coordination. When several people cooperate in developing a single program, coordination problems are common. For example, one engineer might update a module with a defect fix while another simultaneously modified a feature in the same module. When each engineer returns his or her version to the system library, one engineer is likely to overwrite and destroy the other engineer's work. The most common way to handle this problem is to require that only one engineer work on a given module at any one time. With larger teams and bigger products, more sophisticated techniques are needed.

In addition to helping retain control of the product, a software configuration management system provides a repository for storing copies of all key product elements. It also provides a historical record of how products have changed. This record permits you to reconstruct any baselined product that has been lost or corrupted.

Software Configuration Management Overview

Typical software configuration management systems have the following elements:

- ☐ The SCM plan
  - ☐ Configuration identification
  - ☐ A configuration control procedure
  - ☐ A configuration control board (CCB)
  - ☐ A configuration change request form (CCR)
- ☐ The system baseline
- ☐ Baseline submissions

- ☐ Backup procedures and facilities
- ☐ Configuration status reports
☐ Facilities you don't need
- ☐ Hardware items
- ☐ Support tools and facilities
- ☐ Processes and procedures
- ☐ Configuration audits

Facilities You Don't Need

Although the final four items in the preceding list are generally needed on larger projects, you don't need them for the TSPi. For hardware, configuration control can be important when the software supports new or modified hardware features. To enhance or maintain programs, their development support tools and facilities also need to be configuration-controlled. Controlling process and procedure changes is also important in large organizations, particularly when automated tool support is involved. Configuration audits are generally needed in large organizations to ensure that the SCM system is adequate and being properly used. Although these four configuration management categories are important, you can ignore them for this course.

The SCM Plan

The support manager produces the SCM plan. Although this plan can be simple, it must include the configuration identification plan for the project, the configuration control procedures, and the configuration control board membership.

The Configuration Identification Plan

The purpose of configuration identification is to ensure that all the products to be controlled are uniquely named, that a point is established when each product will be baselined (or put under configuration control), and that a product owner is identified for every product. The principal items to control are

- ☐ The approved list of configuration items
- ☐ The requirements

☐ The product design

☐ The program source code

☐ Test materials and test results

☐ Product design standards, such as module and system naming standards, interface standards, standard messages and screens, and the reusable program library

The Configuration Control Procedure

To ensure that changes do not conflict, no program should be changed by more than one engineer at any time. This means that when one person is changing a baselined product, that product element should be locked so that no one else can change it. When a product is locked, it means that no changes can be made until it is unlocked and that all people using the product must work with the new version as soon as it is available.

To ensure that design integrity is not compromised, all changes to baselined products must be approved by the product owner and the configuration control board (CCB) before they can be entered into the baseline. The product owner is the engineer who is responsible for maintaining the product's design integrity and for ensuring that all fixes and changes are properly made. This person is usually the engineer who developed the product.

The Configuration Control Board

The principal role of the CCB is to ensure that all baselined products and all changes to these products are properly justified and of suitable quality. The CCB should be chaired by the support manager and should include the development manager. If the team wishes to include further members, it may do so. The CCB should meet whenever changes have been proposed to baselined products. During integration and system test, the board may even have to meet daily, particularly if there are many defects.

The Change Request Form

The entire team should know and agree with the criteria that the CCB will use for making change decisions. Suggested criteria are as follows.

1. All of the necessary information has been submitted with a configuration change request form (CCR). (See Table B.1.)

2. The product owner agrees with the change.

TABLE B.1 TSPi CONFIGURATION CHANGE REQUEST: FORM CCR

Name	_____	Date	_____
Team	_____	Instructor	_____
Part/Level	_____	Cycle	_____

Product Information

Product Name	_____	Product Owner	_____
Product/Change Size	_____	Size Measure	_____
Recent Inspection	_____	Moderator	_____
Backup Address	_____		

Change Information

Reason for Change: _____

_____

_____

Change Benefits: _____

_____

_____

Change Impact: _____

_____

_____

Change Description: (For source code, attach listing; for code changes, include defect
number (if any) and listing of changed and unchanged program
segment)

_____

_____

_____

Status

Approved: ☐   Additional Information: ☐   Disapproved: ☐

Information needed: _____

_____

_____

Approvals

Product Owner	_____	Date:	_____
Quality/Process Manager	_____	Date:	_____
CCB	_____	Date:	_____

3. The quality/process manager attests that the product or product change has been developed with the team's agreed process and that the development data show that it meets the team's quality criteria.

4. The change is consistent with customer or user needs, the product design, and the development strategy.

5. Adequate resources are available to make the change.

The System Baseline

A baseline is defined as a foundation or a basis. In software engineering, we use the term *baseline* to refer to that collection of documents and other materials that officially represent the product at any point in time. Thus, the requirements baseline would contain the inspected, updated, and approved SRS (system requirements specification) together with all the relevant supporting materials and data. Similarly, the product baseline would contain the source code, the system design specification (SDS), and the SRS. You should also include or reference the pertinent test and change records as well as any other relevant materials that relate to the baselined products.

A product is said to be baselined when it is entered into the SCM system. Baselined products should be high-quality and stable. After a product element has been baselined, the baseline becomes the official product version, and no one can change it without CCB authorization. Products generally should be put under configuration control after they have been inspected and all the identified problems corrected. For example,

- □ Baseline the SRS after it has completed the requirements inspection and been updated
- □ Baseline the SDS after the high-level design inspection and after all corrections have been made and checked
- □ Baseline the source code after inspection and unit test and before submission to integration

Baseline Submissions

When an engineer submits an item for inclusion in the product baseline, he or she is responsible for submitting all the required materials. The items to include with the CCR submission are as follows.

- □ Product name. Every major product element must have a unique name, and this name must uniquely identify the element and its version level. When the product element is named in the configuration item list, use that name.

☐ Product owner. This is the person responsible for the product, usually the developer. When in doubt, consult the configuration item list, where all the products are named with their owners.

☐ Date. This is the date when you submit the item for inclusion in the baseline.

☐ Product/change size. For programs or program changes, provide the new and changed, base, added, deleted, and reused LOC. For documents and document changes, provide the number of pages or changed pages. Again, where applicable, use the categories of new and changed, base, added, deleted, and reused. For other product types, use appropriate measures such as detailed design lines of pseudocode, pages of high-level design, and so on.

☐ Inspection status. Here, list the inspections completed for the product. Also describe fix status for the inspection and test defects and attach copies of the INS and LOGTEST forms.

☐ Where backup is stored. In submitting a product for the baseline, the developer (owner) should keep a backup copy in a safe location. List this location and any needed addresses or routings to find and retrieve a copy.

☐ Reason for the change. Briefly summarize the reason for the change. This could be, for example, to correct a system test defect (give the defect number) or to incorporate a specified requirements change.

☐ Change benefits. List here the benefits of the change. This could be, for example, to correct a defect that caused incorrect product results (briefly describe the problem). For a requirements change, briefly give the proposed benefits of the change.

☐ Change impact. Here, list the estimated engineering hours and calendar time required to make the change as well as any other significant impacts.

☐ Change description. Briefly describe the change to be made.

☐ Quality approval. The only approvals required before a product can be submitted to the CCB are from the quality/process manager (suitable product quality and complete process data) and from the product owner.

☐ The product. This is a copy of the actual product to be baselined. For programs, submit a printed program listing and an electronic copy. For other products, submit both printed and electronic copies (where applicable).

The CCB must insist that only quality products and changes be baselined. Experience has shown that when engineers skip or rush through parts of the process to meet a tight schedule, they generally spend more time fixing the resulting problems than it would have taken to do the job correctly in the first place. If everyone agrees with the CCB criteria and if the CCB strictly enforces these criteria, products will be of higher quality and the development process will be more efficient.

Backup Procedures and Facilities

Backup capability is essential for even the smallest system. With TSPi, you may need to keep only backup diskettes, but you must have a backup copy of every version of the baselined system. One useful practice, for example, is to produce a backup copy of the baseline every time you make a change to the baseline. You must, of course, make sure these backups are properly labeled and dated so that you can find and re-create prior versions whenever you need them.

Configuration Status Reports

Configuration status reports are needed to help teams track the status of the product while they are developing it. For example, graphs of LOC growth over time can indicate implementation progress. Similarly, an historical record of the volume of change activity generally indicates how quickly a product is stabilizing during test. Although the TSPi status reports need not be very sophisticated, you should provide weekly reports giving the total volume of product in the baseline and the change activity. The configuration status report (CSR) form in Table B.2 gives suggested content for this weekly report.

Automating the SCM Process

For TSPi, start with a manual SCM process. This is not because automated methods would not be useful, but because, for the typically small size of TSPi projects, the time investment required to set up and learn to use an automated system would probably not be worthwhile. With modest practice, you will find that the SCM process takes little time and effort. Also, even when automated systems are available, setting up and learning to use them invariably takes more time than you expect. After the first development cycle, you will be in a much better position to make an informed decision on automation.

The Software Configuration Management Process

Table B.3 shows the TSPi software configuration management process. The steps in this process are described in the following paragraphs.

TABLE B.2 TSPi CONFIGURATION STATUS REPORT: FORM CSR

Name _____ Date _____

Team _____ Instructor _____

Part/Level _____ Cycle _____

Configuration Change Process: Activity

	Current Week	Cycle to Date
CCRs submitted	_____	_____
CCRs approved	_____	_____
CCRs rejected	_____	_____
CCRs deferred	_____	_____
CCRs outstanding	_____	_____
CCRs reversed	_____	_____

Configuration Change Process: Status

	Current Week	Change from Prior Week
Product volume under SCM control		
Text pages	_____	_____
Design pages	_____	_____
Pseudocode Lines	_____	_____
LOC—total	_____	_____
LOC—new and changed	_____	_____
Test case LOC	_____	_____
Test material pages	_____	_____
Test results pages	_____	_____
Other items	_____	_____
Other items	_____	_____

Comments_____

_____

_____

_____

_____

_____

_____

_____

_____

_____

_____

_____

_____

_____

_____

TABLE B.3 TSPi SOFTWARE CONFIGURATION MANAGEMENT: SCRIPT SCM

Purpose	To manage the content of a software product, ensure that the product contents are known and available, ensure that the product functions are traceable, and ensure that all product contents are controlled and protected
Entry Criteria	The TSPi team has been formed and roles assigned.
General	The configuration management process includes producing the SCM plan, managing the system baseline, managing changes, and reporting SCM status.

Step	Activities	Description
1	Produce the SCM Plan	The team produces the project configuration item list. This includes • The name and type of each approved configuration item • The point in the process when it should be baselined • The item owner and storage location The support manager identifies the members for the configuration control board and defines their procedures. • The support manager and the development manager • Optional additional members The team reviews and approves the CCB and procedures.
2	Manage the System Baseline	To baseline a product, the engineer submits a CCR with • Product name, owner, date, product size, and inspection data • Where the backup copy is stored and how it can be retrieved • Reasons for the change, benefits, impact, and description • The product, in machine- and human-readable form Approval from the quality/process manager means that • Process data are available • The product meets the quality criteria The CCB reviews the submission and approves or disapproves. • If approved, the product is entered in the baseline. • If not approved, the engineer is told the information needed. The support manager retains backups of all baselined items. • All versions of baselined items are retained as backup. • The product owner also retains a copy of the product version. Team members may obtain baselined items at any time unless • The CCB has imposed restrictions on product availability • The product owner has limited the product's availability The development manager ensures that only official baselined product versions are used in designing and building products. • All build, integration testing, and system testing must use unchanged official versions of baselined products. • When possible, all development work should use unchanged official versions of baselined products.
3	Manage Changes	• Engineers submit all proposed changes to baselined items to the CCB with a completed CCR. • Multiple fixes may be submitted at the same time.
4	Report SCM Status	The support manager reports weekly on baseline status (CSR). • CCR status and change activity in the last week and to date • The volume of product by type under configuration control
Exit Criteria		• All products are baselined. • All baseline changes are documented and approved.

Step 1: Produce the SCM plan

For TSPi, the items needed for the SCM plan are the configuration item list, the CCB membership, and the SCM procedures.

The Configuration Item List

The approved list of configuration items is produced and approved as part of the SCM plan. Each item on the configuration item list should contain the following information:

- ☐ The item name and type
- ☐ The point in the process when the item is to be baselined
- ☐ The product owner
- ☐ Storage location

For example, consider the SRS. This is a requirements document, it is to be baselined after the requirements inspection and update, and it is owned by the development manager. That is all you need to put in the CCR plan on this item.

CCB Membership.   The members of the CCB should be identified in the SCM plan.

SCM Procedures.   The team should review and agree with the procedures for submitting baseline items and for handling changes to baselined items.

Step 2: Manage the System Baseline

The general steps required to manage the system baseline are as follows.

1. With the owner's agreement, the development engineer prepares a baseline submission, using the CCR form.
2. The quality/process manager attests to the quality of the product by signing the CCR form.
3. The CCB reviews the submission and either approves or disapproves it.
4. The support manager retains backups of all baselined items.
5. Product owners also retain backups of baselined items.
6. Team members may obtain copies of baselined items on request.
7. The development manager ensures that only official baselined product versions are used to build or deliver products.

Preparing the Baseline Submission.   As described earlier, an official product copy is submitted to the configuration control board along with a supporting configuration change request.

Attesting to the Product's Quality.   The decision to include a product in the baseline is important because it provides the first opportunity to check that products meet the team's quality criteria. The quality/process manager should review each submission and determine that the process data on that product are available, that the process data are entered into the TSPi support system, that these data show that the team process was followed, and that the product's quality is suitable.

When the product does not meet the quality criteria, the quality/process manager should suggest that the developer take remedial action before adding the product to the baseline. If the developer chooses not to take this remedial action, he or she can go to the CCB for a waiver. If a waiver is granted by the CCB, the quality process manager should briefly report

- ☐ What remedial action was proposed
- ☐ Why remedial action was needed
- ☐ The likely consequences of not taking this action

This report should be included in the team's normal WEEK report to the instructor and/or management and a copy put in the project notebook. In any event, the developer must include a completed CCR form with the submission.

Reviewing the Submission.   When it receives a CCR submission, the CCB takes the following steps:

- ☐ Checks to make sure all the required materials have been submitted
- ☐ Reviews the submission and either approves the submission, requests more information, or rejects the submission
- ☐ Marks the CCR accordingly and informs the submitting engineer
- ☐ Files a copy of each approved CCR in the project notebook

In conducting the review, the CCB either follows the criteria described earlier or establishes and documents its own criteria.

Retained Materials.   The materials to retain with configuration-controlled products are all those materials submitted with the CCR form as well as the completed and approved CCR form.

Backup Copies.   Backup copies should be retained for all baselined items. A master backup record should also be retained specifying the product version that is backed up, when it was backed up, and where the backup is kept. The support manager and product owner must both ensure that these backups are secure from failure and are retained in both machine- and human-readable form.

Obtaining Baselined Items.   When team members need copies of controlled products, they request them from the support manager. In general, the latest version should be made available on request. The only exception is that the product owner or the CCB has restricted product availability. This exception generally occurs when the product is currently under active change and the changes are judged to affect the other team members' work.

Official Baselined Product Versions.   Only official product versions that have been taken directly from the baseline repository are to be used to build, integrate, system-test, or distribute products. This policy is particularly important because, without care, different product versions can easily be used in testing or distributing the same product. This not only wastes time but can also result in inadequately tested products and unhappy users. If several different test systems are being run simultaneously, make changes only to the baseline and then redistribute the updated products for continued testing.

   With TSPi, it is likely that you will use only a single test system. Under these conditions, you could accumulate a number of changes and submit them through the CCB. Then return this official updated product version for continued testing. In using this approach, ensure that all fixes are made sequentially so that they do not conflict. As noted next under step 3, document every change as you make it. If you do not record the information immediately, you will likely have trouble reconstructing the materials that the quality/process manager and the CCB will need to approve the change request.

Step 3: Manage Changes

When team members need to change controlled items, they submit a CCR to the CCB for approval. The submitted materials should provide sufficient detail so that the changes could be backed out if needed. This backtracking is often necessary when a fix turns out to be defective or when you're trying to diagnose a particularly difficult defect. The items to include in the change are the same as those required for a product submission.

Step 4: Report SCM Status

The support manager reports SCM status to the team and the instructor every week. The items to be reported are

- ☐ Change activity for this week and the project to date
- ☐ The status of outstanding changes
- ☐ Data on SCM activity and status
- ☐ Report on the CSR form

If you use a standard status report, the status information will be easier to understand. It will also be comparable from week to week, trends will be more obvious, and the report is more likely to be complete and accurate. You can also show the size growth of each product category and trends in change activity. By observing these trends, you can often predict when products will become stabilized.

APPENDIX C

Software Inspections

Reviews and inspections provide the most effective method for improving the quality of the programs you develop. This appendix describes what inspections are, how to conduct inspections, and how a well-designed inspection process can complement your personal reviews. It also describes a method for estimating how many defects are left in a product after the inspection and includes two examples of this estimation method.

What Are Inspections?

In an inspection, two or more engineers review another engineer's product to find its defects and problems. Their objective is not to fix these problems but rather to find them so that the developer can fix them. The time to do an inspection is when an engineer has finished developing a product, has personally reviewed it, and has corrected all the obvious problems. At that point, the engineer usually needs help in finding the remaining defects.

Inspections can be used on almost any kind of software or software-related product. Some examples are program source code, detailed designs, high-level designs, requirements documents, test cases, and user manuals.

How Are Inspections Done?

The inspection process has four phases: the briefing phase, the review phase, the meeting phase, and the repair phase. In the briefing, the inspection team learns about the product and agrees on how to do the inspection. In the review phase, each reviewing engineer personally reviews the product to find defects. In the meeting phase, the entire inspection team goes through the product one section at a time. Their objective is to identify the defects and resolve any questions. Finally, in the repair phase, the developing engineer fixes the identified problems and verifies the corrections.

When to Do Inspections

Start doing inspections as soon as your team starts producing products. The earlier that defects are injected and the longer they remain in the product, the harder they are to find and fix. Thus, the longer you delay inspecting a product, the larger the volume of incorrect work, and the longer it will take to find and fix the problems. So start doing inspections at the beginning of the project and keep doing them until all the product elements have been developed and inspected.

Using a Defined Inspection Process

To be most effective, inspections should follow a defined process. Although inspections are not complicated, they involve a number of steps. A defined process tells you what steps to take and when to take them. It also defines the key inspection measures and provides forms for tracking, measuring, evaluating, and improving your inspections.

What Makes Inspections Effective?

There are four reasons that inspections are effective: they look at the entire program at one time, they use more combined knowledge, they take advantage of different viewpoints, and they improve the odds of finding problems. These points are discussed in the following paragraphs.

Inspecting the Entire Program

The principal reason that inspections are more effective than testing is that in an inspection you see all the cases, combinations, and conditions at once. With testing, however, you can try only one case, with one set of data values, and under one set of conditions. Thus, with an inspection you can look once at a 10-condition case statement and see whether all the cases are correct. You can even see whether any necessary conditions are missing or whether conditions overlap or conflict. With testing, however, you must run at least 10 tests and then you still cannot be sure that you have covered all the potential problems. With an inspection you can look for things that are not there, whereas with testing you test only what is there and test it only incompletely.

Using Combined Knowledge

When several people study a single program, they can focus their combined knowledge on finding the problems. The engineers on an inspection team usually have a broader base of knowledge and experience than the developer alone. Some of the problems that they find will have been known previously by one or more members of the team, and other errors will be discovered during the inspection. Examples of problems that commonly surface in an inspection are interface conflicts, misunderstood dependencies, and naming confusion. Most of these problems are found because the inspection team as a group knows more about these topics than the developer does.

Using Different Viewpoints

Developers can get a kind of myopia; we see what we know should be there and tend to overlook obvious things that conflict with our expectations. Thus, we develop a kind of blindness to our own mistakes.

When you have spent many hours designing a complex program, you know exactly what it is supposed to do. Now is a particularly important time to have other people look at what you have done. Not only will they have different interests, perspectives, and backgrounds, but also they will provide another benefit: as you listen to your explanation of what you were trying to do, problems that you overlooked will often become obvious. When explaining your work, you look at it from a different perspective, and often this is all it takes to help you see previously overlooked problems.

Improving the Odds

When several people review the same material, even if each of them finds only a fraction of the problems their combined reviews often find many more of the problems than any one engineer could find alone. For example, suppose that four people review a program, and each person finds only one-half of the problems. If you also assume that the likelihood of finding each problem is random, the combined yield for the group is around 94%. Why? When each engineer misses half the defects, two engineers will miss only one-quarter of them and three engineers will miss only one in eight. Thus, a four-engineer inspection team in which everyone has a 50% yield would miss only one defect in 16, or 6.25% of the total, giving the team a 93.75% inspection yield.

Of course, defects are not random, and some defects are much more difficult to find than others. But, particularly with hard-to-find problems, it is important to have multiple reviewers. The chance of someone finding the truly difficult problems will then be substantially better.

The Importance of Thorough Testing

Even though inspections are highly effective, you should still do thorough testing. The reason is that inspections are done by people, and people are prone to error. However, thorough reviews and inspections also change the testing process. With the TSP, for example, we have found that when developers have thoroughly reviewed and inspected their programs, their testing is much more effective. In several cases, after the engineers completed reviewing and inspecting their programs, only a few problems were found in final testing and no defects were later found by the product's users.

This seems to imply that when products have very few defects, a few carefully designed tests can find them all. Conversely, it appears that when there are many defects in a product, the defects are much harder to find. Although there is not yet enough evidence to prove this, it is probably safe to assume that test yields will improve as defect densities decline.

Inspect Only Reviewed Products

Just as in testing, it appears that inspection yields also decline with higher defect densities. For effective inspections, therefore, the developers must first personally review their products and remove all the obvious defects. The reason is that simple defects are distracting. When reviewers see trivial problems, they are likely to concentrate on them and are less likely to see the more difficult problems.

Inspection Methods

Although inspections take time, doing effective inspections involves more than just spending enough time: you must also spend that time properly. This is a question of method. Some inspection methods are general and apply to any kind of product, whereas others are specific and are used only with particular product types. This appendix discusses only the general methods. The product-specific topics are addressed in the chapters on requirements, design, and implementation. The general inspection methods are checklists, viewpoints, and product concentration. These methods are discussed in the following paragraphs.

Checklists

The key to having a high yield in the review phase of an inspection is to use a personal checklist that is derived from your personal defect data. The reason that checklists are helpful is that people are repetitive and they tend to make the same kinds of mistakes regularly. Thus, when you know the types of mistakes you have made in the past, you also know what to look for in the future.

To make a checklist, gather data on all the defects that escape a given phase—say, detailed design. Then list the defects that are most prevalent and put them in a convenient order to check during a review. This is all it takes to make a checklist.

One caution, however, is that people change and new problems are always likely in technical work. As you gain experience, work on new applications, use different methods, or try various tools, you will make different mistakes. Thus, it is always important to check products for new or unsuspected problems. Also, keep your checklist up-to-date by periodically reviewing your defect data to add new defect categories or to delete obsolete ones.

Use your personal checklist during the review phase of an inspection. Because many engineers make similar mistakes when doing similar work, you will probably find it most effective to use a checklist that you are familiar with. However, it would be a good idea to ask the developer whether he or she can suggest any specific additional defect types to look for.

Viewpoints

There is a saying that what you see depends on where you stand. When you look at a program from the point of view of a developer, you will see different things than if you looked at it from the user's perspective. Similarly, maintenance engineers, security specialists, library managers, and testers look for—and probably see—different kinds of problems.

When the various reviewers in an inspection adopt different points of view, you are likely to have a much more effective inspection. Select these viewpoints based on the type of product and on the knowledge and background of the inspection team members. You might even consider having someone join the inspection team so that you can take advantage of that person's point of view.

Product Concentration

Another useful inspection method is to have the reviewers concentrate on particular aspects or product areas, thereby reducing the amount of duplicate work the reviewers do. Some review methods take a great deal of time, and if they are done well it would not make sense to have everyone use them on every element of the product. One example is state machine analysis. Although it is important that someone do such an analysis of every state-dependent part of the product, it would be a waste of time for everyone to do it. Thus, if one or two reviewers selected a product area for a state machine analysis, the others could skip that review of the same area. If the product is particularly critical or complex, however, you might have two engineers cover the same area with the same methods. In this way, they are much more likely to find any problems.

Unless the reviewers have consistently done high-yield personal reviews and unless they have previously used the review methods that they will be applying in this inspection, it is not a good idea to have them concentrate on selected product areas and ignore others. If they did, then most parts of the product would have only one reviewer and the inspection would likely miss too many defects.

Inspection Practice

In doing an inspection, have the author print a listing of the product and then conduct the inspection review on this paper copy. When engineers do their reviews on a computer screen, their yields are consistently low. If you don't believe this, do inspections both ways and gather data on the results. You will quickly see the difference.

Inspection Data

Just as in any other human activity, you can improve inspection performance with practice. To make this informed practice, however, you need measures of inspection quality, something that calls for data. The data required to track, evaluate, and improve inspections are measures of review rates, development ratios, and inspection yields. These measures are discussed in the following paragraphs.

Inspection Rates

To produce high-quality products, you must spend an adequate amount of time doing inspections. In the TSPi, inspection rates are measured in terms of product reviewed per hour—that is, LOC per hour and pages per hour. You should gather your own data to see what rates are best for you, but until you have such data use the guidelines given in Chapter 5.

☐ Requirements reviews and inspections: fewer than 2.0 single-spaced text pages/ hour

☐ High-level design reviews and inspections: fewer than 5 design pages/hour

☐ Detailed-design reviews and inspection preparation reviews: fewer than 100 pseudocode lines/hour

☐ Source code reviews and inspection preparation reviews: fewer than 200 LOC/hour

Based on the data we have gathered on the PSP and TSP, these rates are a little high for most people. It is a good idea to view these guidelines as maximum rates.

Development Ratios

Although rates are useful, they do not tell whole story. When a design is very difficult, for example, you need to conduct a very careful review. This is the time to also consider development ratios. For example, suppose a trivial design involves a regular structure with many cases and takes many pages to print. Conversely, a complex design might involve intricate logic but take only a single page. Even though the complex design takes fewer pages, its design would take longer and its inspection time should be correspondingly longer.

The general guideline is to spend about 50% of design time in the design inspection. If a designer spends two hours producing the detailed design, each reviewing engineer should spend about one hour in the review phase of the design inspection. Although this may seem like a lot of time, the key is to spend an adequate amount of time doing the review and to use effective review methods. When in doubt, get your own data and see what rates and ratios you need to get high yields. When you miss a lot of defects, slow down and take more time.

Inspection Yield

Inspection yield measures the percentage of the defects that were in the product at the beginning of the inspection and were found in the inspection. This measure is important because a high-yield process saves time. To see why, consider that software organizations that conduct no reviews or inspections typically spend about 50% of their development schedules in testing. With high-yield inspections, testing times are much less. For example, assume that a software team is doing a project that takes four months (or a full 16-week semester). Without reviews and inspections, the engineers would typically need to spend 6 to 8 weeks testing the product.

When TSP teams use sound review and inspection methods, their testing time is less than 10% of the schedule. One U.S. Air Force project, for example, reported that by using the TSP, integration and system testing was reduced from the normal 22% of the development schedule to only 2.7% [Webb]. Similarly, two undergraduate TSPi teams each had pretest yields of 87% for the first development cycle and 97% for the second. Each team did all its testing in less than one week.

The Inspection Report: Form INS

A copy of the INS inspection form is shown in Table C.1, and its instructions are given in Table C.2. Although some of the material in this form is self-explanatory, the discussion on estimating defects is a bit more complex. The next section of this chapter describes this part of the form and gives two examples of the calculations.

The header of form INS contains the same information as those of all the other TSPi forms. It also includes space to enter the names of the inspection moderator and the product developer or owner.

To complete the inspection summary section, follow the INS form instructions. The data that you need for these entries are produced during the inspection. The way to calculate these values and the way you will use them will be clearer after you have read the next section of this chapter on estimating remaining defects.

In the *Engineer Data* section, enter the defects, the preparation time in minutes, and the product size for each engineer. If you decide to concentrate on specific sections, note the size of the section each engineer personally reviewed. Also, calculate and enter the rate for each engineer's personal inspection review phase. Gather and enter all these data at the beginning of the inspection meeting. If any engineer has not suitably prepared for the inspection meeting, defer the meeting until everyone is ready. Unprepared engineers will either delay the meeting while they try to review the product in the meeting or will not contribute to the inspection. Either way, they will waste the team's time.

Complete the *Defect Data* section of the form during the inspection meeting, again as explained in the following chapter section. Also complete the estimated yield calculation as explained next.

TABLE C.1 TSPi INSPECTION REPORT: FORM INS

Name _____ Date _____
Team _____ Instructor _____
Part/Level _____ Cycle _____
Moderator _____ Owner _____

Engineer Data

Name	Defects[1]		Preparation Data			Est. Yield
	Major	Minor	Size	Time	Rate	
Totals:						

Defect Data

No.	Defect Description	Defects		Engineers (finding major defects)				A	B
		Maj	Min						
Totals									
Unique Defects									

Inspection Summary   **Product Size:** _____   **Size Measure:** _____
Total Defects for A: _____   **Total Defects for B:** _____   **C (# common):** _____
Total Defects (AB/C): _____   **Number Found (A+B–C):** _____   **Number Left:** _____
Meeting Time: _____   **Total Inspection Hours:** _____   **Overall Rate:** _____

[1]Major defects either change the program source code or would ultimately cause a source code change if not fixed in time; all other defects are considered minor.

TABLE C.2 TSPi INSPECTION REPORT INSTRUCTIONS: FORM INS

Purpose	• Use this form to gather and analyze inspection data.
General	• These data *must* be gathered during the inspection because they generally cannot be obtained later. • Record the preparation data at the beginning of the inspection meeting. • Complete the form at the end of the inspection meeting. • It is helpful to have line and page numbers on the printed product text.
Header	Enter your name, the team name, instructor's name, and the date. • the product, level, and development cycle • the names of the moderator and product owner
Engineer Data	For each reviewer, enter the reviewer's name and preparation time as well as • The number of major and minor defects that reviewer found • The LOC, lines, or pages each reviewer inspected (reviewers may concentrate on program sections) • The preparation rate in LOC, pseudocode lines, or pages per hour Enter total preparation time, total major and minor defects, and overall rate. The moderator calculates total and engineer yields at the end of the meeting.
Defect Data: No.	• Enter a number for each defect found in the inspection. • It is generally most convenient to use the document line and page number.
Defect Data: Defect Description	• Describe each defect and check whether it is major (Maj.) or minor (Min.).
Defect Data: Engineers	• In the first row below the *Engineers* heading, enter the initials of each engineer who is participating in the inspection. • For major defects, check the column for each engineer who found that defect during inspection preparation.
Summary	At the end of the inspection, complete the summary data. Product size: • For requirements or high-level design inspections, enter the text pages. • For detailed-design inspections, enter the LOC or pseudocode lines. • For source code, enter the source code LOC. For the defect summary values, see the following explanation. Enter meeting time, total inspection hours, and overall inspection rate.
Summary: Estimate Remaining Defects	• After all defects are entered, count the major defects each engineer found that no other engineer found (the engineer's unique defects). • Identify the engineer who found the most unique defects. • Check each defect that engineer found in column A. • In column B, check all the defects found by the other engineers. • Count the common defects (C for common) between columns A and B. • The estimated total defects in the product is AB/C. • Round fractional results to the nearest integer. • The number found in the inspection is A+B–C. • The number left is the total minus the number found: (AB/C)–(A+B–C). • This defect estimate is reliable only when all the numbers A and B are greater than 4 and A–C and B–C are both greater than 1. • Even with these criteria, the total defect error is likely to be 10% or more. • When one or more engineers' yields are 70% or better, the estimates are generally quite accurate. • If A=B=C, you have likely found all the defects. • If several engineers found the same largest number of unique defects, repeat these calculations, using each of these engineers as A, and use the largest resulting number as the total defect estimate.

Estimating Remaining Defects

After you conduct an inspection, it would be nice to know whether you have found all the defects. If you failed to find a significant percentage of the defects, you might even want to do another inspection or take some other corrective action. You should also look at the inspection checklists and review the inspection rates and ratios to see why the inspection was ineffective. Although there is no way to know precisely how many defects are left in a product after an inspection, there is a way to get a good idea. It is called the capture-recapture method.

Estimating Populations

Statisticians estimate the total size of a population by using the capture-recapture method. This statistical method assumes that the population is homogeneous and randomly distributed. An example of capture-recapture is an effort to determine the number of fish in a lake. To do this, first catch a sample of the population—say, 20 fish—tag them, and then release them. Give these tagged fish time to mix evenly with the rest of the fish population and then catch another group—say, 25 more fish. Finally, see how many fish in this second group are tagged.

Suppose you find that 5 of the second group of 25 fish were already tagged. If this was a representative sample of all the fish in the lake, this would mean that one-fifth (5/25), or 20%, of the total population of fish in the lake were tagged. Because you already know that exactly 20 fish were tagged, this means that the total fish population of the lake is 5*20=100 fish.

Estimating Defects in Programs

Although defects are not the same as fish, we can use the same statistical method for determining the defect population in programs. To do this with inspections, all the engineers track and record all the major defects they find.

For example, suppose one engineer records the defects he or she found in a program and we call these the "tagged" defects. Then we see what proportion of the defects found by a second engineer are tagged. With that data, we estimate the likely number of defects in the product. You also know how many defects the engineers have already found, so you can estimate how many defects are left in the product after the inspection.

The Software Inspection Capture-recapture Method

In explaining how to use the capture-recapture method for inspections, we start with the simplest case of a two-engineer inspection team. The steps in the process are as follows.

1. Count the number of defects the first engineer finds and call this A.
2. Count the number of defects the second engineer finds and call this B.
3. Count the number of these defects they both found and call this C.
4. Estimate the total defects in the product as A∗B/C.
5. Calculate the total number of defects found as A+B–C.
6. The estimated remaining defects are then A∗B/C – (A+B–C).
7. Finally, estimate the yield for the inspection as

$$Yield = \frac{100*(A + B - C)*C}{A*B}$$

A Two-engineer Estimating Example

Suppose that you had two engineers inspect a small program and they got the data shown in Table C.3. Here, engineer A found 7 defects and engineer B found 5. By examining the table, you can see that both engineers found the defects in lines 19, 29, and 31. This means that C, the number of defects that both of the engineers found, is equal to 3. Therefore the total number of defects they both found is 9, or 7+5–3=9. To get this, you add the number each engineer found and subtract the number they both found.

Using these numbers, the estimate for the total defects in the product is A∗B/C = 7∗5/3 = 11.667, or 12. Next, because the engineers found 9 defects, there are 3 defects left in the product, or 12–9=3.

To calculate the inspection yields, divide the number of major defects each engineer found by the estimated total defects in the product. In the Table C.3 example, the total estimate was 12 defects, and engineer A found 7. Thus, A's yield is 100∗7/12 = 58.3%. Similarly, B's yield is 41.7% Because the total inspection found 9 defects, the estimated inspection yield is 100∗9/12 = 75%.

To find the total inspection time, multiply the meeting time by the number of engineers in the meeting, add the preparation time for all the engineers, and divide this number by 60 to get the inspection hours. For this example, there were three engineers in the meeting (the developer plus two reviewers), so total meeting time was 43∗3=129 minutes. The total preparation time for engineers A and B is shown on the inspection form as 153 minutes, so the total inspection time was 282 minutes, or 4.7 hours.

A Three-engineer Estimating Example

For an inspection with three or more engineers, the method is the same except that it has an additional step. As shown in Table C.4, you enter the data as before. Now, however, you must decide which engineer to treat as engineer A. You then combine the data for all the other engineers and treat that combination as engineer B.

TABLE C.3 TWO-ENGINEER INSPECTION REPORT EXAMPLE

Name _____ Date _____
Team _____ Instructor _____
Part/Level _____ Cycle _____
Moderator _____ Owner _____

Engineer Data

Name	Defects[1]		Preparation Data			Est. Yield
	Major	Minor	Size	Time	Rate	
A	7	3	380	85	268	58.3
B	5	4	380	68	335	41.7
Totals:	12	7	760	153	298	75.0

Defect Data

No.	Defect Description	Defects		Engineers (finding major defects)				A	B
		Maj	Min					A	B
1	} =>)	1							1
9	, => ;	1						1	
12	Convert => Converter	1						1	
13	Test not declared	1						1	
19	N := 10000	1						1	1
29	>=	1						1	1
31	Begin	1						1	1
37	Flag := true	1							1
41	Misspelling	1						1	
Totals		9						7	5
Unique Defects								4	2

Inspection Summary	**Product Size:**	380	**Size Measure:** LOC
Total Defects for A: 7	**Total Defects for B:**	5	**C (# common):** 3
Total Defects (AB/C): 12	**Number Found (A+B−C):**	9	**Number Left:** 3
Meeting Time: 43	**Total Inspection Hours:**	4.7	**Overall Rate:** 80.9

[1]Major defects either change the program source code or would ultimately cause a source code change if not fixed in time; all other defects are considered minor.

To do this, look for the engineer who found the most unique defects—that is, find the engineer who found the greatest number of defects that no one else found. Then put that engineer's data in column A. In this example, engineer DB is the only one who found the defect on line 12. Every other defect he found was also found by one or both of the other engineers. The number of his unique defects is thus 1. Similarly, engineer BP is the only one who found the defects on lines 15 and 35, and engineer PA found no unique defects. Because engineer BP found the most unique defects, copy his data into the A column. Next, combine the data for the other two engineers and treat the combination as engineer B. Here, in the B column, put a 1 for every defect that either DB or PA or both of them found.

Now make the estimate exactly as before. As you can see from Table C.4, this gives

$A = 9$

$B = 9$

$C = 7$

So the total estimated defects are $A*B/C = 9*9/7 = 11.57 = 12$, and the number found is $9 + 9 - 7 = 11$. So one defect is left to find.

From this example, you can see that adding one engineer to the inspection team increased the inspection yield from 75% in the example in Table C.3 to 91.7% in the Table C.4 example. The improvement is so great because the added engineer, BP, had a personal yield of more than 70%.

Cautions

As with any statistical method, the capture-recapture approach involves a number of assumptions. First, there must be an equal chance of finding every defect. This would certainly not be the case if the engineers decided to specialize on different product areas or to use different review methods. Similarly, if no one looked for an entire category of defect, none of these defects would be found even though the estimate might show that no defects remained in the product. This would be a little like using worms to catch perch and expecting the estimate of the fish in the lake to include the bass and trout (which you won't likely catch with worms).

The second caution is that the numbers of defects found must be reasonably large. As is true of all statistical methods, the capture-recapture approach deals with probabilities. Thus, accuracy generally requires that the numbers of items involved be reasonably large. Also, the number of unique defects found by engineers A and B must be reasonably large. If this number is 0 or 1, the method will not work, or the estimating error will be quite large.

In small, high-quality programs, the number of defects that you find will probably be small. I have found, however, that if the numbers A and B are both 5 or

TABLE C.4 THREE-ENGINEER INSPECTION REPORT EXAMPLE

Name		Date	
Team		Instructor	
Part/Level		Cycle	
Moderator		Owner	

Engineer Data

Name	Defects[1]		Preparation Data			Est.
	Major	Minor	Size	Time	Rate	Yield
DB	7	3	380	85	268	58.3
BP	9	2	380	97	235	75.0
PA	5	4	380	68	335	41.7
Totals:	21	9	1140	250	274	91.7

Defect Data

No.	Defect Description	Defects		Engineers (finding major defects)					
		Maj	Min	DB	BP	PA		A	B
1	} =>)	1			1	1		1	1
9	, +> ;	1		1	1			1	1
12	Convert => Converter	1			1				1
13	Test not declared	1		1	1			1	1
15	SomeError := 0	1			1			1	
19	N := 10000	1		1	1	1		1	1
29	>=	1		1		1			1
31	Begin	1		1	1			1	1
35	= => :=	1			1			1	
37	Flag := true	1			1	1		1	1
41	Misspelling	1		1	1			1	1
Totals		11		7	9	5		9	9
Unique Defects				1	2	0		2	2

Inspection Summary	**Product Size:**	380	**Size Measure:**	LOC
Total Defects for A: 9	**Total Defects for B:**	9	**C (# common):**	7
Total Defects (AB/C): 12	**Number Found (A+B−C):**	11	**Number Left:**	1
Meeting Time: 43	**Total Inspection Hours:**	7.0	**Overall Rate:**	54.0

[1]Major defects either change the program source code or would ultimately cause a source code change if not fixed in time; all other defects are considered minor.

larger and if A–C and B–C are both greater than or equal to 2, the method should give a reasonable yield estimate. Even then, expect errors of around 10% or a little more. In general, the higher the engineers' yields, the more accurate the estimate is likely to be. Remember, however, that these estimates should never be used as absolutes. They are useful only as general guidelines on the quality of the inspection.

Note, however, that in these calculations you should count only defects that affect program operation. Don't count comments and, if they don't affect the generated code, don't count standards and formatting problems. However, any defect whose fix changes the noncommented source code should be counted.

Some Statistical Refinements

There are more refined statistical methods for making capture-recapture estimates. For example, an unbiased estimate of total defects (T) would be [Chapman]

$$T = \frac{(A + 1)*(B + 1)}{C + 1} - 1$$

For the small numbers of defects likely in TSPi, both the unbiased and the preceding estimating formulas give nearly the same results. Similarly, the variance of the data can be calculated as follows [Wittes]:

$$\sigma^2 = \frac{(A + 1)*(B + 1)*(A - C)*(B - C)}{(C + 1)^2*(C + 2)}$$

The variance value is needed to calculate the 95% prediction interval around T—that is, the range within which the true value of total defects will likely fall 95% of the time. This range is [Wittes]

$$UPI = T + 1.96\sigma$$
$$LPI = T - 1.96\sigma$$

Here, UPI is the upper prediction interval and LPI is the lower prediction interval. Although there are more sophisticated methods, these should be sufficient for most TSPi projects [Chao, Runeson].

The Importance of High Personal Yields

If you make some simplifying assumptions about statistical distributions, you can calculate the likely impact of each engineer's personal yield on a team inspection. The results of these calculations are shown in Figure C.1. Here, the engineers' average personal yield is shown on the x axis and the overall inspection yield is given

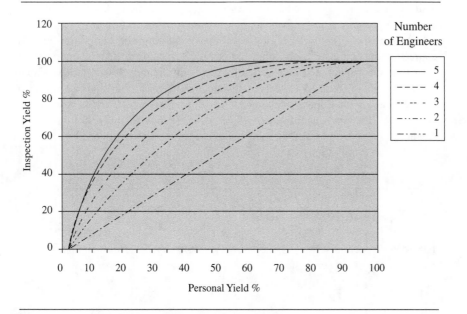

FIGURE C.1 INSPECTION YIELD VERSUS PERSONAL YIELDS FOR VARIOUS NUMBERS OF ENGINEERS

on the y axis. Thus, when each of two engineers has a personal yield of 50%, their combined yield would be 75%. Similarly, three engineers who each had a 50% yield would have a combined inspection yield of 87.5%, and so forth.

As the figure shows, each additional engineer improves the inspection yield, but the marginal benefit decreases with each addition. Also, when personal yields are more than 70%, the difference in inspection yield between three and four engineers is quite small. This means that if you can maintain personal review yields at around 70% or higher, your team can get very high inspection yields with only two reviewers. Conversely, when personal yields fall to less than about 60%, you should add a third reviewer and possibly even a fourth. In general, the lower the engineers' personal yields, the more reviewers are needed.

Scheduling Inspections

When you have only two engineers on an inspection team, it is rather easy to schedule the inspection. The scheduling problem increases proportionately, however, as you add more engineers. One way to reduce scheduling problems is for teams to agree on a specific day of the week to do inspections. During the implementation phase, you might have to pick two or three inspection days.

In scheduling inspections, try not to have any engineer spend more than a couple of hours on inspections in any one day. When engineers spend too much of their time on inspections, they generally have significantly lower yields. About two or three hours appears to be a reasonable upper limit for any one day. It is also a good idea to avoid doing inspections on two consecutive days. The best approach is to gather data on your inspection yields as a function of inspection hours per day and per week. Then you can see where the yield starts to fall off.

The TSPi Inspection Script

The TSPi inspection script (INS) is shown in Table C.5. The following paragraphs describe each of the script steps.

Entry Criteria

Any product can be inspected as long as it has completed a development stage and has been personally reviewed. The necessary inspection materials must be available.

Arrange Inspection

The product developer (called the *producer* in inspection terminology) is responsible for arranging for the inspection. He or she first arranges for a moderator to lead the inspection. This person is usually the quality/process manager, or it could be any other engineer who knows how to lead an inspection. The producer works with the moderator to decide how many other engineers are needed for the inspection and to arrange for their participation. The producer also handles the mechanics of setting up the inspection.

During this initial phase, the moderator looks over the product materials and briefly assesses their completeness, adequacy, and quality. The moderator also checks that the producer used notations and formats that provide enough precision and detail to permit a productive inspection. If the producer has not personally reviewed the product or if the product appears to have quality problems, the moderator asks the producer to correct the problems before proceeding with the inspection. Examples of quality problems would be incomplete defect data, inadequate time spent in reviews, or high levels of compile defects.

TABLE C.5 TSPi INSPECTION SCRIPT: SCRIPT INS

Purpose	To help engineers produce quality products
Entry Criteria	A completed and reviewed product with available materials
General	• The purpose of inspections is to focus on sophisticated issues and not on finding simple defects or fixing defects. • Even a few simple defects can distract reviewers so that they are more likely to miss sophisticated problems.

Step	Activities	Description
1	Plan the Inspection	The producer (or developer) • Arranges with the quality/process manager or some other qualified team member to be the inspection moderator • Handles the mechanics of setting up and running the inspection The moderator (usually the quality/process manager) • Reviews the product to ensure it is ready for the inspection • If not, has the producer fix the problems before proceeding • Selects the other inspection members
2	Hold the Inspection Briefing	The moderator describes the inspection process. The producer familiarizes the inspection team with the product. The reviewers select viewpoints or areas for product concentration. • Sample viewpoints are operation, recovery, maintenance, security, installation, size, and performance. In design inspections, the reviewers also ensure that • At least one reviewer will verify each segment of the design • At least one reviewer will use trace table and/or state machine analysis on every design segment The moderator sets the date and time for the inspection meeting.
3	Review the Product	• The reviewers separately make detailed product reviews. • They mark the defects found on the product documentation. • They record their preparation time.
4	Open the Inspection Meeting	The moderator opens the inspection meeting and • If any reviewers are not prepared, reschedules the meeting • Outlines the inspection meeting procedure
5	Conduct a Product Walk-through	The moderator steps through the product sections and • Has the reviewers describe every defect found • Enters the major defect data on the INS form • Notes the engineers who found each major defect • The owner (producer) enters the major defects in LOGD
6	Estimate the Remaining Defects	• The moderator estimates the defects remaining in the product after the inspection (form INS instructions). • The moderator determines the reviewers' personal yields. • The reviewers note any items to add to their review checklists.
7	Conclude the Inspection Meeting	The inspection team decides • Whether a reinspection is warranted, who should do it, and when • How to verify the defect corrections The moderator and producer complete forms LOGD and INS.
8	Rework the Product and Verify the Fixes	The producer • Makes repairs and updates the product documentation • Holds needed rereviews and/or reinspections • Has the fixes verified as the reviewers recommended in step 7
Exit Criteria		• INS and LOGD forms completed and filed in the project notebook (NOTEBOOK specification in Appendix G) • A fully inspected, high-quality product

Inspection teams should always contain at least the producer and two other engineers. If the moderator will not be a reviewer, a minimum-sized inspection team would require four engineers: the producer, two reviewers, and the moderator.

Hold the Inspection Briefing

In the inspection briefing, the moderator describes the inspection process. The objective here is to familiarize the inspection team with the key aspects of the inspection process. Following this discussion, the producer describes the product and answers the team's questions.

At this point, the reviewers should decide on the viewpoints that each one will take during the inspection. They can also allocate product areas and inspection techniques among the team members. For example, in design inspections at least one engineer should thoroughly analyze every logical element in the product. In the inspection preparation reviews, the engineers should do more than look at the design. Unless engineers use a technique such as a trace table or a state machine analysis, they are unlikely to find the sophisticated design problems. Note, however, that if the engineers decide to specialize in product areas, the capture-recapture method will not work for estimating the remaining defects.

Finally, the moderator sets a date for the inspection meeting. This should be a date when everyone will be available and by which all the team members agree to be fully prepared.

Review the Product

The inspection review phase is the most important part of an inspection. At this time, each engineer carefully reviews the product to find any problems or areas of confusion. It is important that they use sound review methods and that they take the time to do a thorough job. They also need to record the time that they spend and mark every defect on the product materials. The engineers should not record the defects they find on the LOGD form at this time. The reason is that there would then be multiple reports for the defects that were found by several engineers. Wait and enter the major defect data on the INS and LOGD forms during the inspection meeting.

Open the Inspection Meeting

The first step in the inspection meeting is for the moderator to obtain the preparation data from each engineer. If anyone is not adequately prepared, the moderator defers the meeting until a date when everyone promises to be prepared. Conducting an inspection meeting with unprepared reviewers is a waste of time and will not be effective. If the meeting had to be deferred, the moderator should mention this fact in the team's weekly status report and say why.

Conduct a Product Walk-through

During the inspection meeting, the moderator steps through the product one line or product segment at a time. At each line or section, the engineers identify any defects or questions they have identified for that product area. The producer answers questions and decides whether or not an item is a major defect. The moderator then enters the data concerning the major defects in the INS form and marks the line and page number so that the defect can be easily identified. The moderator also enters a brief defect description and makes a check mark beside that defect in the column for each engineer who found that same defect during inspection preparation. The product owner also records every major defect in the LOGD form so that the inspection defects will be included in the SUMP and SUMQ summaries.

Minor defects can be important and should not be ignored. Because correction of such defects has been found to substantially improve program maintainability, it is important to correct them. Thus, the minor defects should be discussed and the producer should correct them. The minor defects are not considered in the defect estimation method, however, because they do not affect program operation and because identifying them involves considerable judgment. Other than counting the minor defects and discussing them with the producer, there is no need to record any other data about minor defects on the INS form.

Estimating the Remaining Defects

After you complete the product review, follow the procedure described in the INS form instructions for calculating the number of defects that are likely to remain in the product after the inspection. Also calculate the inspection yield. The easiest way to estimate the inspection yield is as follows:

Estimated Inspection Yield = 100*(Total defects found)/(Total estimated defects)
$$= 100*(A+B-C)/(A*B/C)$$

Enter this value in the INS form under *Engineer Data,* in the *Est. Yield* column, and in the *Totals* row. In Table C.4, this number is 91.7%. These calculations may look complex, but they take only a few minutes, and after you have done them once or twice they will seem simple.

Next, the moderator determines and enters the yields that the engineers achieved in the inspection preparation review. This is the percentage of the estimated total defects that each engineer personally found. The engineers should also check the defects they personally missed and determine which ones to add to their personal checklists.

Conclude the Inspection Meeting

As the final inspection meeting action, the inspection team decides how the defect corrections are to be verified. The moderator or a reviewer can check the corrections with the producer, or the inspection team can hold a reinspection. Generally, a reinspection will be required if the inspection yield was much less than 85% to 90%. In that case, the team decides who should participate in the reinspection and when it should be done. Even with a high inspection yield, a reinspection should be done if the product required substantial rework, if a large number of defects was found, or if the fix for one or more of the defects was particularly complex or large.

The final inspection meeting action is for the moderator to enter the inspection data in the INS form and put a copy of the INS form in the project notebook. The product owner then records the major defects in LOGD.

Rework the Product and Verify the Fixes

Following the inspection meeting, the producer corrects the identified defects and personally verifies the corrections. Then he or she has these corrections checked in the way that the inspection team specified.

Exit Criteria

At the conclusion of the inspection, you should have a completely inspected product with all the identified defects corrected and the corrections verified. Also, the inspection moderator should have completed the INS form, recorded the defects in LOGD, and filed a copy of the INS form in the project notebook.

References

[Chao] A. Chao. 1987. "Estimating the Population Size for Capture-Recapture Data with Unequal Catchability." *Biometrics* 43:783–791.

[Chapman] D. Chapman. 1951. "Some Properties of the Hypergeometric Distribution with Applications to Zoological Censuses." *University of California Publications in Statistics* 1:131–160.

[Runeson] Per Runeson and Claes Wohlen. 1998. "An Experimental Evaluation of an Experience-Based Capture-Recapture Method in Software Code Inspections." *Empirical Software Engineering* 3:381–406.

[Webb] Dave Webb and W.S. Humphrey. 1999. "Using the TSP on the TaskView Project." *Crosstalk,* February.

[Wittes] J. Wittes. 1972. "On the Bias and Estimated Variance of Chapman's Two-Sample Capture-Recapture Population Estimate." *Biometrics* 28:592–597.

APPENDIX D

The TSPi Scripts

This appendix contains copies of all the TSPi scripts. These scripts are described in the various book chapters and are included here for reference. The following table gives the scripts in this appendix in alphabetical order by abbreviation. It also gives the appendix pages for the scripts and the textbook page where each script is described.

Name	Abbreviation	Chapter Reference	Page
Cycle 1 Design	DES1	133	361
Cycle n Design	DESn	134	362
Development	DEV	11	363
Cycle 1 Implementation	IMP1	152	365
Cycle n Implementation	IMPn	153	366
Inspection	INS	261, 353	367
Cycle 1 Team Launch	LAU1	39	368
Cycle n Team Launch	LAUn	40	369
Cycle 1 Development Plan	PLAN1	75	370
Cycle n Development Plan	PLANn	76	371
Cycle 1 Postmortem	PM1	188	372
Cycle n Postmortem	PMn	189	373
Cycle 1 Requirements Development	REQ1	115	374
Cycle n Requirements Development	REQn	116	375
Software Configuration Management	SCM	330	376
Cycle 1 Development Strategy	STRAT1	55	377
Cycle n Development Strategy	STRATn	56	378
Cycle 1 Integration and System Test	TEST1	178	379
Cycle n Integration and System Test	TESTn	179	380
Unit Test	UT		381
The Weekly Meeting	WEEK	44, 210	382

TSPi CYCLE 1 DESIGN: SCRIPT DES1

Purpose	To guide a team through developing and inspecting the software design specifications for a team development project
Entry Criteria	• A development strategy and plan • A completed and inspected SRS • The students have read textbook Chapter 7.
General	The design process produces the software design specification (SDS), which defines the overall product structure for cycle 1. • Major product components and their interface specifications • The allocation of use cases to components The SDS also specifies • File and message standards, definitions, naming conventions • Design notation and standards

Step	Activities	Description
1	Design Process Review	The instructor describes the design process and its products. • How the design process is performed and a sample SDS • How the design inspection is conducted and reported • Design standards and conventions
2	High-Level Design	The development manager leads the team through • Defining the cycle-1 product structure • Naming the product components • Allocating use cases to these components • Identifying the design tasks to be completed and documented
3	Design Standards	The quality/process manager leads the effort to produce the name glossary and design standards.
4	Design Tasks	The development manager leads the team through • Outlining the SDS document and the work to produce it
5	Task Allocation	The team leader helps allocate the tasks among the team members and • Obtains commitments for when they will complete these tasks
6	The Design Specification	Each team member • Produces and reviews his or her portions of the SDS document • Provides these to the development manager The development manager produces a composite SDS draft.
7	Integration Test Plan	The development manager leads the team in producing and reviewing the integration test plan.
8	Design and Integration Test Plan Inspection	The quality/process manager leads the team through inspecting the SDS draft and integration test plan (see script INS) so that • Every use case is covered and referenced in the design • The design is complete and correct • The integration test plan is adequate • Each problem is recorded and fix responsibility assigned The inspection is documented in form INS, and defects are recorded in LOGD.
9	Design Update	The development manager obtains the updated SDS sections and • Combines them into a final SDS • Verifies traceability to the SRS
10	Update Baseline	The support manager baselines the SDS.

Exit Criteria	• A completed and inspected SDS and integration test plan • The design standards and name glossary • Updated SUMP and SUMQ forms and INS inspection forms • Updated project notebook

TSPi CYCLE n DESIGN: SCRIPT DESn

Purpose	**To guide a team through developing and inspecting the software design specifications for a second or subsequent development cycle**
Entry Criteria	The team has an updated development strategy, plan, and SRS.
General	The subsequent-cycle design process produces an updated SDS that defines • The overall product structure for the second or subsequent cycle • The new or modified product components • The allocation of new use cases to each component • An updated component interface specification For this cycle, the team also updates • File and message standards, definitions, and naming conventions • Design notation and standards

Step	Activities	Description
1	Design Process Review	The instructor describes the cyclic design process. • Things to consider in enhancing a product • Common enhancement problems and pitfalls • Any problems with the prior cycle design process, methods, or standards to be corrected in this cycle
2	High-Level Design	The development manager leads the team through • Defining the second or subsequent cycle structure • Naming for any new product components • Allocating use cases to the new or modified components • Identifying the design tasks to be completed and documented
3	Design Standards	The quality/process manager leads the team in updating the name glossary and design standards.
4	Design Tasks	The development manager leads the team through • Outlining the SDS document and the work to produce it
5	Task Allocation	The team leader helps allocate the tasks among the team members and • Obtains commitments for when they will complete these tasks
6	The Design Specification	Each team member • Produces and reviews his or her portions of the SDS document • Provides these to the development manager The development manager produces an updated SDS draft.
7	Integration Test Plan	The development manager leads the team in producing and reviewing the integration test plan.
8	Design and Integration Test Plan Inspection	The quality/process manager leads the team through inspecting the updated SDS draft and integration test plan (see script INS) so that • Every new use case is covered and referenced in the design • The design changes are complete and correct • The integration test plan is adequate • Each problem is recorded and fix responsibility assigned The inspection is documented in form INS, and defects are recorded in LOGD.
9	Design Update	The development manager obtains the updated SDS sections and • Combines them into a final updated SDS • Updates the product element to use case cross reference • Submits the SDS for change control
10	Update Baseline	The support manager baselines the updated SDS.
Exit Criteria		• A completed and inspected SDS document for this cycle • Updated SUMP and SUMQ forms and INS inspection forms • Updated name glossary and project notebook

TSPi DEVELOPMENT: SCRIPT DEV

Purpose	To guide a team through developing a software product
Entry Criteria	• An instructor guides and supports one or more five-student teams. • The students are all PSP-trained (*Discipline for Software Engineering* or *Introduction to the Personal Software Process*). • The instructor has the needed materials, facilities, and resources to support the teams. • The instructor has described the overall product objectives.
General	The TSPi process is designed to support three team modes. 1. Develop a small- to medium-sized software product in two or three development cycles. 2. Develop a smaller product in a single cycle. 3. Produce a product element, such as a requirements document, a design specification, a test plan, and so on, in part of one cycle. Follow the scripts that apply to your project and mode of operation.

Week	Step	Activities
1	Review	• Course introduction and PSP review. • Read textbook Chapters 1, 2, and Appendix A.
2	LAU1	• Review course objectives and assign student teams and roles. • Read textbook Chapter 3, Appendix B, and one of Chapters 11–15.
	STRAT1	• Produce the conceptual design, establish the development strategy, make size estimates, and assess risk. • Read textbook Chapter 4.
3	PLAN1	• Produce the cycle 1 team and engineer plans. • Read textbook Chapter 5 and Appendix C.
4	REQ1	• Define and inspect the cycle 1 requirements. • Produce the system test plan and support materials. • Read textbook Chapter 6 and the test sections of Chapter 9.
5	DES1	• Produce and inspect the cycle 1 high-level design. • Produce the integration test plan and support materials. • Read textbook Chapter 7.
6	IMP1	• Implement and inspect cycle 1. • Produce the unit test plan and support materials. • Read textbook Chapter 8.
7	TEST1	• Build, integrate, and system test cycle 1. • Produce user documentation for cycle 1. • Read textbook Chapter 9.

THE TSPi DEVELOPMENT: SCRIPT DEV (continued)

Week	Step	Activities
8	PM1	• Conduct a postmortem and write the cycle 1 final report. • Produce role and team evaluations for cycle 1. • Read textbook Chapters 10, 16, 17, and 18.
	LAU2	• Re-form teams and roles for cycle 2. • Read the rest of textbook Chapters 11–15.
	STRAT2, PLAN2	• Produce the strategy and plan for cycle 2. • Assess risks.
9	REQ2	• Update the requirements and system test plan for cycle 2.
	DES2	• Produce and inspect the cycle 2 high-level design. • Update the integration plan for cycle 2.
10	IMP2	• Implement and inspect cycle 2, produce unit test plan.
	TEST2	• Build, integrate, and system test cycle 2. • Produce user documentation for cycle 2.
11	PM2	• Conduct a postmortem and write the cycle 2 final report. • Produce role and team evaluations for cycle 2.
	LAU3	• Re-form teams and roles for cycle 3.
	STRAT3, PLAN3	• Produce the strategy and plans for cycle 3. • Assess risks.
12	REQ3	• Update the requirements and system test plan for cycle 3.
	DES3	• Produce and inspect the high-level design for cycle 3. • Update the integration plan for cycle 3.
13	IMP3	• Implement and inspect cycle 3, produce unit test plans.
	TEST3	• Build, integrate, and system test cycle 3.
14	TEST3	• Produce and review the user manual for the finished product. • Review and update the user manual for usability and accuracy.
15	PM3	• Conduct a postmortem and write the cycle 3 final report. • Produce role and team evaluations for cycle 3. • Review the products produced and the processes used. • Identify the lessons learned and propose process improvements.
Exit Criteria		• Completed product or product element and user documentation. • Completed and updated project notebook. • Documented team evaluations and cycle reports.

TSPi CYCLE 1 IMPLEMENTATION: SCRIPT IMP1

Purpose	To guide a team through implementing and inspecting the software for cycle 1 of a team development project

Entry Criteria	• The team has the development strategy and plan
	  • SRS and SDS specifications and name glossary
	  • Documented coding and other standards
	• The students have read textbook Chapter 8.

General	The implementation process produces a reviewed, inspected, and unit-tested product that must • Completely cover the SDS and SRS functions and use cases • Conform to established coding and design standards • Follow the PSP2.1 or PSP3 process

Step	Activities	Description
1	Implementation Process Overview	The instructor describes the implementation process, including • The importance of a quality implementation • The need for and content of the coding standards • The strategy for handling poor-quality components
2	Implementation Planning	The development manager leads the work to • Define and plan the implementation tasks (SUMP, SUMQ)
3	Task Allocation	The team leader helps allocate the tasks among the team members and • Obtains commitments for when they will complete these tasks
4	Detailed Design	The engineers produce the detailed design. • Do a design review using thorough design review methods. • Complete forms LOGD and LOGT.
5	Unit Test Plan	The engineers produce the unit test plans.
6	Test Development	The engineers follow script UT to develop the unit test cases, test procedures, and test data.
7	Detailed-design Inspection	The quality/process manager leads the team in a DLD inspection of each component (script INS and forms INS and LOGD).
8	Code	The engineers produce the component source code. • Do a code review using a personal checklist. • Compile and fix the code until it compiles without error. • Complete forms LOGD and LOGT.
9	Code Inspection	The quality/process manager leads the team in a code inspection of each component (script INS and forms INS and LOGD).
10	Unit Test	The engineers, following script UT, • Conduct the unit tests and complete forms LOGD and LOGT

11	Component Quality Review	The quality/process manager reviews each component's data to determine if component quality meets established team criteria.
		• If so, the component is accepted for integration testing.
		• If not, the quality/process manager recommends either
		  • That the product be reinspected and reworked
		  • That it be scrapped and redeveloped

12	Component Release	• When the components are satisfactorily implemented and inspected, the engineers release them to the support manager. • The support manager enters the components in the configuration management system.

Exit Criteria	• Completed, inspected, configuration-controlled components • Completed INS forms for the design and code inspections • Unit test plans and support materials • Updated SUMP, SUMQ, SUMS, LOGD, and LOGT forms • Updated project notebook

TSPi CYCLE n IMPLEMENTATION: SCRIPT IMPn

Purpose		**To guide a team through implementing and inspecting the software for a second or subsequent development cycle**
Entry Criteria		The team has updated its development strategy and plan. • SRS and SDS specifications and the name glossary
General		The implementation process produces products that must • Be thoroughly reviewed, inspected, and unit tested • Completely cover the SDS and SRS functions and use cases • Conform to established coding and design standards

Step	Activities	Description
1	Implementation Process Review	The instructor describes the enhancement implementation process. • Things to consider in enhancing a product • Common enhancement problems and pitfalls • Any problems with the prior-cycle implementation process, methods, or standards to be corrected in this cycle
2	Implementation Planning	The development manager leads the work to • Define and plan the implementation tasks (SUMP and SUMQ)
3	Task Allocation	The team leader helps allocate the tasks among the team members and • Obtains commitments for when they will complete these tasks
4	Detailed Design	The engineers produce the detailed design. • Do a design review using thorough design review methods. • Complete forms LOGD and LOGT.
5	Unit Test Plan	The engineers produce the unit test plans.
6	Test Development	The engineers follow script UT to develop the unit test cases, test procedures, and test data.
7	Detailed-Design Inspection	The quality/process manager leads the team in a DLD inspection of each component (script INS and forms INS and LOGD).
8	Coding	The engineers produce the component source code. • Do a code review using a personal checklist. • Compile and fix the code until it compiles without error. • Complete forms LOGD and LOGT.
9	Code Inspection	The quality/process manager leads the team in a code inspection of each component (script INS and forms INS and LOGD).
10	Unit Test	The engineers follow script UT to • Conduct the unit tests and complete forms LOGD, SUMP, and SUMQ

11	Component Quality Review	The quality/process manager reviews the updated component's data to determine if component quality meets established team criteria.
		• If so, the component is accepted for integration testing.
		• If not, the quality/process manager recommends either
		  • That the product be reinspected and reworked
		  • That it be scrapped and redeveloped

12	Component Release	• When the components are satisfactorily implemented and inspected, the engineers release them to the support manager. • The support manager enters the components in the configuration management system.

Exit Criteria		• Completed, inspected, configuration-controlled components • Completed INS forms for the design and code inspections • Unit test plans and support materials • Updated SUMP, SUMQ, SUMS, LOGD, and LOGT forms • Updated project notebook

TSPi INSPECTION SCRIPT: SCRIPT INS

Purpose	To help engineers produce quality products
Entry Criteria	A completed and reviewed product with available materials
General	• The purpose of inspections is to focus on sophisticated issues and not on finding simple defects or fixing defects. • Even a few simple defects can distract reviewers so that they are more likely to miss sophisticated problems.

Step	Activities	Description
1	Plan the Inspection	The producer (or developer) • Arranges with the quality/process manager or some other qualified team member to be the inspection moderator • Handles the mechanics of setting up and running the inspection The moderator (usually the quality/process manager) • Reviews the product to ensure it is ready for the inspection • If not, has the producer fix the problems before proceeding • Selects the other inspection members
2	Hold the Inspection Briefing	The moderator describes the inspection process. The producer familiarizes the inspection team with the product. The reviewers select viewpoints or areas for product concentration. • Sample viewpoints are operation, recovery, maintenance, security, installation, size, and performance. In design inspections, the reviewers also ensure that • At least one reviewer will verify each segment of the design • At least one reviewer will use trace table and/or state machine analysis on every design segment The moderator sets the date and time for the inspection meeting.
3	Review the Product	• The reviewers separately make detailed product reviews. • They mark the defects found on the product documentation. • They record their preparation time.
4	Open the Inspection Meeting	The moderator opens the inspection meeting and • If any reviewers are not prepared, reschedules the meeting • Outlines the inspection meeting procedure
5	Conduct a Product Walk-through	The moderator steps through the product sections and • Has the reviewers describe every defect found • Enters the major defect data on the INS form • Notes the engineers who found each major defect • The owner (producer) enters the major defects in LOGD
6	Estimate the Remaining Defects	• The moderator estimates the defects remaining in the product after the inspection (form INS instructions). • The moderator determines the reviewers' personal yields. • The reviewers note any items to add to their review checklists.
7	Conclude the Inspection Meeting	The inspection team decides • Whether a reinspection is warranted, who should do it, and when • How to verify the defect corrections The moderator and producer complete forms LOGD and INS.
8	Rework the Product and Verify the Fixes	The producer • Makes repairs and updates the product documentation • Holds needed rereviews and/or reinspections • Has the fixes verified as the reviewers recommended in step 7
Exit Criteria		• INS and LOGD forms completed and filed in the project notebook (NOTEBOOK specification in Appendix G) • A fully inspected, high-quality product

TSPi CYCLE 1 TEAM LAUNCH: SCRIPT LAU1

Purpose	To start the teams on the first development cycle
Entry Criteria	• All the students have satisfactorily completed a PSP course. • The students have read textbook Chapters 1, 2, 3, and Appendix A.
General	This launch script starts the team projects. The principal objectives are to describe the course. • Form the teams and assign team roles. • Explain the objectives for the product to be developed. • Establish team meeting and reporting times. Steps 1, 2, and 3 are completed during the first class session. Steps 4 through 8 are completed during the second class session.

Step	Activities	Description
1	Course Overview	The instructor describes the TSPi team course objectives. • What the students are expected to accomplish • How their work will be evaluated and graded • The basic principles of teamwork • The TSPi process
2	Student Information	The instructor explains the criteria for making team assignments. • The information needed to make proper assignments • The team roles, responsibilities, and qualifications The instructor also asks the students to • Complete and return the INFO form before the end of the class • Read textbook Chapter 4 and Appendix B • Read the textbook chapters on the roles that interest them
3	Product Objectives	The instructor describes the product objectives. • The critical product objectives that must be satisfied • The optional and desirable objectives • The criteria for evaluating the finished product
4	Team Assignments	The instructor gives the students their team and role assignments.
5	Team Goals	The instructor describes goal setting. • Why goals are needed and typical team and role goals
6	Team Meetings	The instructor explains the team meeting, its purpose, and conduct. • The meeting purpose, scheduling, and reporting • Weekly data requirements
7	The First Team Meeting	The team leader holds the first meeting of his or her team. • Discusses team members' roles • Discusses and agrees on cycle 1 goals • Establishes a standard time for the weekly team meeting • Agrees on a specific time each week when all team members will provide their weekly data to the planning manager
8	Data Requirements	The planning manager reviews for the team the • Data required from every team member every week • Reports to be generated and provided the team from these data
9	Project Start	The team starts work on the project using the STRAT1 script.

Exit Criteria	• Each student has completed and submitted an INFO form. • The development teams are formed and roles assigned. • The instructor has described the overall product objectives. • The instructor has reviewed and discussed the TSPi and the team's and role goals. • The team has agreed on cycle 1 goals, weekly meeting times, and the weekly data to report.

TSPi CYCLE n TEAM LAUNCH: SCRIPT LAUn

Purpose	To start the teams on the second or subsequent development cycle
Entry Criteria	The student teams have completed a prior TSPi development cycle.
General	This launch script starts the second or subsequent project cycle. The principal objectives are to • Review lessons from the prior cycle. • Re-form the teams if necessary and assign new team roles. • Establish team meeting and reporting times. Steps 1 and 2 are completed during one class session. Steps 3 through 8 are completed during the next class session.

Step	Activities	Description
1	Lessons Learned	The instructor reviews the results of the prior cycle and • Discusses any process problems and their likely causes • Suggests steps the teams should take to minimize the problems with this cycle • Reviews any teamwork concepts that were problems during the prior cycle and explains how to handle them
2	Student Information	The instructor reviews • The reasons for making role changes • The lessons learned about the roles from the prior cycles • Any role performance problems and how to better handle them in the next project cycle The instructor also asks the students to • Complete and return a new INFO form • Include any changes in their personal schedules • Give their current preferences for team membership and roles
3	Team Assignments	The instructor gives the students their team and role assignments. The students read the chapters on their role assignments.
4	Goal Setting	The instructor discusses goal performance and the need to strive for improved performance with each development cycle.
5	Team Meetings	The instructor discusses the team meetings. • Meeting scheduling • Weekly reporting • Weekly data requirements
6	The First Team Meeting	The team leader holds the first meeting of his or her new team. • Discusses the team member roles. • Reviews and updates the team goals. • Establishes a standard time for the weekly team meeting. • Agrees on a specific time each week when all team members will provide weekly data to the planning manager.
7	Data Requirements	The planning manager reviews for the team the • Data required from every team member every week • Reports to be generated and provided the team from these data
8	Project Start	The team starts work on the project using the STRATn script.
Exit Criteria		• Each student has completed and submitted an updated INFO form. • The development teams are formed and roles assigned. • The team has agreed on an updated set of cycle goals, weekly meeting times, and the weekly data to report.

TSPi CYCLE 1 DEVELOPMENT PLAN: SCRIPT PLAN1

Purpose	To guide a team through producing individual and team task, schedule, and quality plans for development cycle 1
Entry Criteria	• The team has a development strategy and conceptual design. • The students have read textbook Chapter 5.
General	The task plan defines the • Time required to perform each process task • Rough order in which the tasks will be performed • Planned value of each task The schedule plan gives • Each engineer's planned time for each project week • The total planned team hours by week • The anticipated completion week for each task • The planned value for each week If the task and schedule plans indicate the project will not be completed on time, readjust the strategy and replan.

Step	Activities	Description
1	Planning Overview	The instructor describes the planning process. • The task and schedule plans and how they are produced • The quality plan and how it is produced
2	Enter the Size Estimates in Form STRAT	Starting with the conceptual design and STRAT form produced in the strategy phase, the planning manager leads the team in • Identifying any other products to be produced and their sizes • Recording the STRAT form and other size data in SUMS
3	Produce the Task Plan	The planning manager leads the team through • Producing a task list with team and engineer time estimates • Entering these data in the TASK form
4	Produce the Schedule Plan	The planning manager obtains the estimated number of hours each team member plans to spend on the project each week and • Enters the weekly hours in the SCHEDULE form • Produces the team TASK and SCHEDULE forms • Reworks the plan if the hours are inadequate
5	Produce the Quality Plan	The quality/process manager leads the team through • Reviewing the team's quality objectives • Estimating the defects injected and defect-removal yields • Generating and assessing trial SUMP and SUMQ plans • Making needed process adjustments to get a satisfactory plan
6	Produce the Individual Engineer Plans	The planning manager helps the engineers make personal plans. • Allocating the tasks among team members • Estimating the time to perform each task • Entering the data in the TASK and SCHEDULE forms • Producing the planned-value schedule and task completion dates
7	Balance Team Workload	The planning manager leads the team through • Identifying workload imbalances • Reallocating tasks to minimize the schedule • Producing balanced engineer plans • Producing the consolidated team plan (TASK, SCHEDULE, SUMP, and SUMQ forms)
Exit Criteria		• Completed team and engineer TASK and SCHEDULE forms • Completed SUMP, SUMQ, and SUMS forms • Updated project notebook

TSPi CYCLE n DEVELOPMENT PLAN: SCRIPT PLANn

Purpose	To guide a team through producing individual and team task, schedule, and quality plans for a second or subsequent cycle
Entry Criteria	• Completed plan and actual data for the prior cycles
General	The subsequent-cycle task plans are based on • The actual tasks and times from prior cycles The schedule plan is based on • The actual hours the team members have spent on prior cycles The quality plan is based on • The team's quality criteria • The original team quality goals If the task and schedule plans indicate the cycle will not be completed on time, adjust the strategy and replan.

Step	Activities	Description
1	Planning Overview	The instructor briefly describes any problems with the prior plans and suggests how to improve the plans for this cycle.
2	Update the Size Estimates	Starting with the updated STRAT form, the planning manager leads the team through updating the product list and the size estimates. • Recording these data in the SUMS form
3	Produce the Updated Task Plan	The planning manager leads the team through • Producing a next-cycle task list with time estimates • Allocating these tasks among team members • Estimating each member's time for these tasks • Entering the data in the TASK form
4	Produce the Updated Schedule Plan	The planning manager obtains the estimated number of hours each team member plans to spend on the project each week and • Enters the weekly hours in the SCHEDULE form • Produces the overall team TASK and SCHEDULE forms • Produces a composite team planned-value schedule • Reworks the plan if the hours are inadequate
5	Produce the Updated Quality Plan	The quality/process manager leads the team through • Comparing the team's quality performance with objectives • Establishing improvement goals for the next development cycle • Estimating the defects injected and defect-removal yields • Generating and assessing trial SUMP and SUMQ plans • Making needed adjustments to get a satisfactory plan
6	Produce the Individual Engineer Plans	The planning manager helps the engineers make personal plans. • Allocating the tasks among team members • Estimating the time to perform each task • Entering the data in the TASK and SCHEDULE forms • Producing the planned-value schedule and task plans
7	Balance Team Workload	The planning manager leads the team through • Reviewing the team and individual plans • Identifying workload imbalances • Reallocating tasks to minimize the schedule • Producing balanced engineer plans • Producing the consolidated team plan (TASK, SCHEDULE, SUMP, and SUMQ forms)
Exit Criteria		• Completed team and engineers' TASK and SCHEDULE forms • Completed SUMP, SUMQ, and SUMS forms • Updated project notebook

TSPi CYCLE-1 POSTMORTEM: SCRIPT PM1

Purpose	• To gather, analyze, and record project data • To evaluate the team's and each role's performance • To identify ways to improve the cycle-2 process • To produce the cycle-1 report
Entry Criteria	• The engineers have completed and tested the product. • They have gathered all the data and completed all the forms. • The students have read textbook Chapter 10, 16, 17, and 18.
General	The cycle-1 report contains an analysis of the project by each role. • Overall team performance: team leader • Plan versus actual performance: planning manager • Overall product design and standards: development manager • Change management and project support: support manager • Process and product quality: quality/process manager The cycle report should • Use process data to support the engineers' statements • Thoughtfully consider the meaning of the results produced • Be short and concise

Step	Activities	Description
1	Postmortem Process Overview	The instructor describes the postmortem process. • The need for complete and accurate process data • The contents of the cycle report • The peer evaluation process and forms
2	Review Process Data	The quality/process manager leads the team in analyzing project data and identifying problem and improvement areas. • Leadership, planning, process, quality, or support • Suggested team actions and responsibilities • Areas for instructor or facility improvement The engineers prepare and submit PIPs on these improvement suggestions.
3	Evaluate Role Performance	The team leader leads the team in evaluating the effectiveness of the team roles, the instructor's actions, and the support facilities. • Where they were effective • Where there is room for improvement
4	Prepare Cycle-1 Report	The team leader leads the team in outlining the cycle-1 report. • Allocating report work to the team members • Obtaining commitments for report section completion • Assembling, reviewing, and correcting the completed report
5	Prepare Role Evaluations	Each engineer completes an evaluation of the team and of each team role using form PEER. • Each role's difficulty and contribution • Percents must total 100% • The effectiveness of each role on a scale of 1 (inadequate) to 5 (superior).
Exit Criteria		• The development cycle has produced a high-quality product with all required documentation. • The completed product is under configuration control. • All process data have been evaluated and PIPs submitted. • The peer evaluations are done and submitted (PEER). • The cycle-1 report has been completed and submitted. • SUMP and SUMQ forms are completed for the system and all its components. • The project notebook has been updated.

TSPi CYCLE n POSTMORTEM: SCRIPT PMn

Purpose		• To gather, analyze, and record data for the latest cycle • To evaluate the team's and each role's performance • To identify ways to improve the subsequent cycle process • To produce the cycle report
Entry Criteria		• The engineers have completed and tested the product. • They have gathered all the data and completed all the forms.
General		The cycle report contains an analysis of the project by each role. • Overall team performance: team leader • Plan versus actual performance: planning manager • Overall product design and standards: development manager • Change management and project support: support manager • Process and product quality: quality/process manager The cycle report should • Use process data to support the engineers' statements • Thoughtfully consider the meaning of the results produced • Be short and concise
Step	**Activities**	**Description**
1	Postmortem Process Review	The instructor describes any problems with the prior-cycle postmortem process that should be corrected for this cycle.
2	Review Process Data	The quality/process manager leads the team in • Analyzing project data and identifying problem areas • Assessing the effectiveness of prior-cycle PIPs and actions Where improvement is needed, identify • Leadership, planning, process, quality, or support items • Suggested team actions and responsibilities • Areas for instructor or facility improvement Prepare and submit PIPs on these improvement suggestions.
3	Evaluate Role Performance	The team leader leads the team in evaluating the effectiveness of team roles, the instructor's actions, and the support facilities. • Where they were effective • Where there is room for improvement
4	Prepare Cycle n Report	The team leader leads the team in outlining the cycle n report. • Allocating report work to the team members • Obtaining commitments for report section completion • Assembling, reviewing, and correcting the completed report
5	Prepare Role Evaluations	Each engineer completes an evaluation of the team and of each team role using form PEER. • Each role's difficulty and contribution • Percents must total 100% • The effectiveness of each role on a scale of 1 (inadequate) to 5 (superior).
Exit Criteria		• The development cycle has produced a high-quality product with all required documentation. • The completed product is under configuration control. • All process data have been evaluated and PIPs submitted. • The peer evaluations are done and submitted (form PEER). • The cycle-n report has been completed and submitted. • SUMP and SUMQ forms are completed for the system and all its components. • The project notebook has been updated.

TSPi CYCLE 1 REQUIREMENTS DEVELOPMENT: SCRIPT REQ1

Purpose	To guide a team through developing and inspecting the requirements for cycle 1 of a team development project
Entry Criteria	• The team has a development strategy and plan. • The students have read Chapter 6, the test sections of Chapter 9, and the need statement.
General	The requirements development process produces the Software Requirements Specification (SRS), which defines • the functions the product is to perform • use-case descriptions for each normal and abnormal function The team should be cautious about expanding the requirements. • Without experience with similar applications, seemingly simple functions can take substantially more work than expected. • It is generally wise to add functions in small increments. • If more time remains, add further increments.

Step	Activities	Description
1	Requirements Process Overview	The instructor describes the requirements process and its products. • How the requirements process is performed • How the requirements inspection is conducted and reported
2	Need Statement Review	The development manager leads the team in reviewing the product need statement and formulating questions for the instructor about • The functions to be performed by the various product versions • How these functions are to be used
3	Need Statement Clarification	The development manager provides consolidated questions to the instructor, who discusses the answers with the team.
4	Requirements Tasks	The development manager leads the team through • Outlining the SRS document and the work to produce it
5	Task Allocation	The team leader helps allocate the tasks among the team members and • Obtains commitments for when they will complete these tasks
6	Requirements Documentation	Each team member • Produces and reviews his or her portions of the SRS document • Provides these to the development manager The development manager produces the SRS draft.
7	System Test Plan	The development manager leads the team in producing and reviewing the system test plan (see Chapter 9 on system test).
8	Requirements and System Test Plan Inspection	The quality/process manager leads the team through • Inspecting the SRS draft and system test plan (see script INS) • Identifying questions and problems • Defining who will resolve each question and problem and when • Documenting the inspection in form INS
9	Requirements Update	The development manager obtains the updated SRS sections and • Combines them into a final SRS • Verifies traceability to the need statement or other sources
10	User SRS Review	• The development manager provides a copy of the final SRS to the instructor (user) for approval. • After approval, the team fixes any identified problems.
11	Requirements Baseline	• The support manager baselines the SRS.

Exit Criteria	• A completed and inspected SRS document and system test plan • A completed INS form for the requirements inspection • Time, defect, and size data entered in the TSPi support system • Updated project notebook

TSPi CYCLE n REQUIREMENTS DEVELOPMENT: SCRIPT REQn

Purpose	To guide a team through updating and inspecting the requirements for a second or subsequent development cycle
Entry Criteria	• The team has an updated development strategy and plan.
General	Update the software requirements specification to reflect • Requirements problems with the prior cycles • Previously specified SRS functions that were not developed • Previously unspecified SRS functions that are now required The team should be cautious about expanding the requirements. • Without experience with similar applications, seemingly simple functions can take substantially more work than expected. • It is generally wise to add functions in small increments. • If more time remains, add further increments. The updated SRS defines the new product functions, including added use-case descriptions for each normal and abnormal user action.

Step	Activities	Description
1	Requirements Update Considerations	The instructor describes any problems with the prior requirements process that should be corrected for this cycle.
2	Need Statement Review	The development manager leads the team in reexamining the product need statement and formulating any new questions about • The functions to be performed by this product version • How these functions are to be used
3	Need Statement Clarification	The development manager provides consolidated questions to the instructor, who discusses the answers with the team.
4	Update Tasks	The development manager leads the team through • Identifying the requirements changes to be made • Updating the component functional allocations
5	Task Allocation	The team leader helps allocate the tasks among the team members and • Obtains commitments for when they will complete these tasks
6	Update Documentation	• Each team member updates and reviews his or her SRS sections and provides them to the development manager. • The development manager produces the updated SRS.
7	System Test Plan	The development manager leads the team in updating and reviewing the system test plan.
8	Update Inspection	The quality/process manager leads the team through • Inspecting the SRS draft and system test plan (see script INS) • Identifying questions and problems • Defining who will resolve each question and problem and when • Documenting the inspection in form INS
9	Requirements Update	The development manager • Combines these sections into the final updated SRS • Verifies traceability to the need statement or other sources
10	User SRS Review	• The development manager provides a copy of the final SRS to the instructor for approval. • After approval, the team fixes any identified problems.
11	Update Baseline	• The support manager baselines the updated SRS.

Exit Criteria	• An updated and inspected SRS document and system test plan • A completed INS form for the requirements inspection • Time, defect, and size data entered in the TSPi support system • Updated project notebook

Purpose	To manage the content of a software product, ensure that the product contents are known and available, ensure that the product functions are traceable, and ensure that all product contents are controlled and protected
Entry Criteria	The TSPi team has been formed and roles assigned.
General	The configuration management process has four elements. • Producing the SCM plan • Managing the system baseline • Managing changes • Reporting SCM status

Step	Activities	Description
1	Produce the SCM Plan	The team produces the project configuration item list. This includes • The name and type of each approved configuration item • The point in the process when it should be baselined • The item owner and storage location The support manager identifies the members for the configuration control board and defines their procedures. • The support manager and the development manager • Optional additional members The team reviews and approves the CCB and procedures.
2	Manage the System Baseline	To baseline a product, the engineers submits a CCR with • Product name, owner, date, product size, and inspection data • Where the backup copy is stored and how it can be retrieved • Reasons for the change, benefits, impact, and description • The product, in machine- and human-readable form Approval from the quality/process manager means that • Process data are available • The product meets the quality criteria The CCB reviews the submission and approves or disapproves. • If approved, the product is entered in the baseline. • If not approved, the engineer is told the information needed. The support manager retains backups of all baselined items. • All versions of baselined items are retained as backup. • The product owner also retains a copy of the product version. Team members may obtain baselined items at any time unless • The CCB has imposed restrictions on product availability • The product owner has limited the product's availability The development manager ensures that only official baselined product versions are used in designing and building products. • All build, integration testing, and system testing must use unchanged official versions of baselined products. • When possible, all development work should use unchanged official versions of baselined products.
3	Manage Changes	• Engineers submit all proposed changes to baselined items to the CCB with a completed CCR. • Multiple fixes may be submitted at the same time.
4	Report SCM Status	The support manager reports weekly on baseline status (CSR). • CCR status and change activity in the last week and to date • The volume of product by type under configuration control
Exit Criteria		• All products are baselined. • All baseline changes are documented and approved.

TSPi CYCLE 1 DEVELOPMENT STRATEGY: SCRIPT STRAT1

Purpose	To guide a team through producing a TSPi development strategy and preliminary size and time estimates
Entry Criteria	• The students have read textbook Chapter 4. • The instructor has reviewed and discussed the TSPi process. • The instructor has described the overall product objectives. • Development teams have been formed and roles assigned. • The teams have agreed on goals for their work.
General	The development strategy specifies the order in which product functions are defined, designed, implemented, and tested. • The way the product will be enhanced in future cycles • How to divide the development work among the team members The development strategy is produced at the beginning of the process to guide size estimating and resource planning. • If the development strategy changes during planning, requirements, or development, it must be updated. The preliminary size and time estimates • Cover the planned work for each development cycle • Provide the basis for allocating work among team members

Step	Activities	Description
1	Strategy Overview	The instructor describes the development strategy. • What the strategy is, how it is produced, and how it is used • Criteria for an effective strategy • The need for and ways to produce the size and time estimates
2	Establish Strategy Criteria	• The development manager leads discussion of strategy criteria. • The meeting reporter (quality/process manager) documents these criteria and provides copies to the team members and instructor.
3	Produce the Conceptual Design	The development manager leads the team in producing the conceptual design for the overall product.
4	Select the Development Strategy	The development manager leads the team through producing the development strategy. This involves • Proposing and evaluating alternative strategies • Allocating product functions to each development cycle • Defining how to subdivide and later integrate the product
5	Produce the Preliminary Estimate	The planning manager leads the team through producing the preliminary size and time estimates, which must include • Size and time estimates for all the current-cycle products • Rough estimates for the products of subsequent cycles
6	Assess Risks	Identify and assess project risks and enter them in ITL.
7	Document the Strategy	The meeting reporter documents the selected strategy (STRAT).
8	Produce the Configuration Management Plan	The support manager produces the configuration management plan. • Identifies the configuration control board and its procedures • Specifies any needed support tools and facilities • Reviews the procedures with the team for their agreement
Exit Criteria		• A completed and documented development strategy • Completed and documented size and time estimates for all product elements to be produced during the next cycle • Completed and documented estimates for the products to be produced in subsequent development cycles • Documented configuration management procedure • Risks and issues entered in the ITL log • Conceptual design and completed STRAT form • Updated project notebook

Purpose	To guide a team through updating the strategy, size estimates, and time estimates for a second or subsequent development cycle
Entry Criteria	• The prior development cycles have been completed and evaluated. • Team membership is adjusted if needed and roles reassigned. • The engineers have read the textbook chapters on their roles.
General	The degree to which the development strategy should be changed depends on the results of the prior cycles. • If the strategy was followed and it worked, don't change it. • If the team did not follow the strategy, adjust it. Note: if the strategy worked, the team should avoid changing it. • Every job is a learning experience. • It is usually a mistake to change course in the middle of a project unless you discover major errors or mistakes. The estimate should be updated to reflect the prior-cycle results. • Measure the first cycle products and use the data in the update.

Step	Activities	Description
1	Strategy Review	The instructor describes why the strategy should be updated. • When changes are appropriate and why to avoid them • The technical and business symptoms of strategy problems • The logic for determining the next-cycle size and size range The instructor also describes any problems with the prior strategy process that should be corrected for this development cycle.
2	Update the Development Strategy	The development manager leads the team through updating the development strategy. • Review results of prior cycles and make needed changes. • Define how to subdivide and later integrate the cycle products. If no strategy changes are needed, the team should skip STRATn steps 3 and 5.
3	Produce the Updated Size and Time Estimates	The planning manager leads the team through producing the updated size and time estimates. These cover • Size and time estimates for all the next-cycle products • Rough sizes for the products of any subsequent cycles Note that these estimates should generally be updated while the development strategy is being revised.
4	Assess Risks	Review, update, and assess project risks and enter in ITL.
5	Document the Strategy	The meeting reporter documents the selected strategy (STRAT).
6	Review and Update the Configuration Management Plan	The support manager leads the team in reviewing the configuration management plan and identifying needed modifications to • The configuration control board or change control procedures • The support tools and facilities
Exit Criteria		• A documented update to the development strategy • Updated and documented size and time estimates for all product elements to be produced during the next development cycle • Completed and documented estimates for the products to be produced in any subsequent development cycles • Updated configuration management procedure • Updated risks and issues entered in the ITL log • Updated conceptual design and STRAT form • Updated project notebook

TSPi CYCLE-1 INTEGRATION AND SYSTEM TEST: SCRIPT TEST1

Purpose	To guide a team through integrating and testing the product components into a working cycle-1 system
Entry Criteria	The team has a development strategy and plan. • Completed and inspected SRS and SDS specifications • Implemented, inspected, and unit-tested components under configuration control The students have read textbook Chapter 9.
General	When defects are found in build, integration, or system test, the quality/process manager determines whether testing should continue. Every defect found in integration or system testing is recorded in the defect log (LOGD) and reviewed by the entire team to determine • Where similar defects might remain in the product • How and when to find and fix these defects • The process changes to prevent similar defects in the future

Step	Activities	Description
1	Test Process Overview	The instructor describes the integration and system test process. • The need for quality components before testing • The need for and content of the testing standards • The strategy for handling poor-quality components
2	Test Development	The development manager or alternate leads test development. The team leader helps allocate the test development and testing tasks among the team members. The test team members perform their test development tasks. • Define any required build processes and procedures. • Develop the integration test procedures and facilities. • Develop the system test procedures and facilities. • Measure the size and running time for each test. • Review the test materials and correct errors.
3	Build	The team builds the product and checks it for completeness. • Verify that all needed parts are on hand. • Build the product and provide it to integration test. • Record all defects in the defect log (LOGD).
4	Integration	The development manager or alternate leads the integration tasks. • Check completeness and integration-test the product. • Record all test activities in the test log (LOGTEST). • Record all defects in the defect log (LOGD).
5	System Test	The development manager or alternate leads the system test tasks. • Test the product for normal and stress conditions. • Test the product for installation, conversion, and recovery. • Record all test activities in the test log (form LOGTEST). • Record all defects in the defect log (LOGD).
6	Documentation	The development manager or alternate leads the team in • Producing the user-documentation outline and tasks • Allocating these tasks to the documentation team • Reviewing the outline with the test team for completeness • Drafting the first-cycle user documentation • Reviewing, correcting, and producing the user documentation
Exit Criteria		• An integrated and tested cycle-1 product • Completed LOGD and LOGTEST forms for all the tests • Completed and reviewed user documentation • Time, size, and defect data entered in the TSPi support system

TSPi CYCLE n INTEGRATION AND SYSTEM TEST: SCRIPT TESTn

Purpose	To guide a team through integrating and testing the product components into a working cycle-2 or subsequent cycle system
Entry Criteria	The team has a development strategy and plan. • Completed and inspected SRS and SDS specifications • Implemented, inspected, and unit-tested components and prior product versions under configuration control
General	When defects are found in build, integration, or system test, the quality/ process manager determines whether testing should continue. Every defect found in integration or system testing is recorded in the defect log (LOGD) and reviewed by the entire team to determine • Where similar defects might remain in the product • How and when to find and fix these defects • The process changes to prevent similar defects in the future

Step	Activities	Description
1	Test Process Review	The instructor describes problems with the prior-cycle integration and test process to be corrected in this cycle. • The reasons for regression testing • How to do regression testing
2	Test Development	The development manager or alternate leads test development. The team leader helps allocate the test development and testing tasks among the team members. The test team members perform their test development tasks. • Define any required build processes and procedures. • Develop the integration test procedures and facilities. • Develop the system test procedures and facilities. • Measure the size and running time for each test. • Review the test materials and correct errors.
3	Build	The team builds the product and checks it for completeness. • Verify that all needed parts are on hand. • Build the product and provide it to integration test. • Record all defects in the defect log (LOGD).
4	Integration	The development manager or alternate leads the integration tasks. • Check completeness and integration-test the product. • Record all test activities in the test log (LOGTEST). • Records all defects in the defect log (LOGD).
5	System Test	The development manager or alternate leads the system test tasks. • Test the product for normal and stress conditions. • Test the product for installation, conversion, and recovery. • Regression-test the system. • Record all test activities in the test log (LOGTEST). • Record all defects in the defect log (LOGD).
6	Documentation	The development manager or alternate leads the team in • Updating the user-documentation outline and tasks • Allocating these tasks to the documentation team • Reviewing the outline with the test team for completeness • Drafting the subsequent-cycle user documentation • Reviewing, correcting, and producing the user documentation

Exit Criteria	• An integrated and tested cycle-2 or subsequent system • Completed LOGD and LOGTEST forms for all tests • Updated and reviewed user documentation • Time, size, and defect data entered in the TSPi support system

TSPi UNIT TEST AND TEST DEVELOPMENT: SCRIPT UT

Purpose	To lead engineers through unit testing their components
General	• Although all defects should already have been found, thorough unit testing ensures that few if any defects remain. • Care is warranted because defects missed in unit test can take as much as 5 to 40 hours each to find in later testing. • When unit test defects are fewer than 5 per KLOC, components generally have no defects found in subsequent testing or use. • Careful unit testing can generally find all the defects in properly developed programs. • It is important to carefully review and retest every test fix. • Errors are much more likely with test fixes than new code.
Entry Criteria	• The component has been developed, reviewed, compiled, and inspected.

Step	Activities	Description
1	Unit Test Plan	• Develop a test plan to cover all script steps with a minimum of test duplication.
2	Unit Test Development	• Develop the required test cases and test data. • Review the test materials to ensure they are not defective. • In test, test case defects are generally harder to find than product defects.
3	Unit Test	• Run the defined tests and fix all defects that are found.
4	Scenario Tests	• Test all the use-case scenarios.
5	Logic Tests	• Test every logic branch path. • Test every condition of every case statement. • Verify the proper stepping and termination of every loop. • Check for pointer allocate, free, null, and stepping problems.
6	Interface Tests	Check the proper behavior of every interface. Test that • There are proper returns for all input cases • The types match • Interface error conditions are handled as specified and so on.
7	Error Tests	Test all program error conditions for • Improper values or types • Overflow and underflow • Integer, long integer, real number problems, and so on.
8	Variable Tests	Check every variable and parameter value • At nominal, maximum, and minimum values • Above the upper specified value • Below the minimum specified value • For proper operation with 0, no input, incorrect data type, and so on
9	Device Tests	Check for proper device operation. • Printers, displays, inputs, sensors, and so on • Normal and incorrect operation: no paper, jam, power off, and so on
10	Other Tests	Check other important product specifications. • Buffer size, limits, and overflow • Throughput performance and response time • Data rates and limits • Dates and date calculations • Security, compatibility, conversion, installation, recovery
Exit Criteria		• A completed unit test with all defects fixed • Unit test data entered in forms LOGD, LOGT, and LOGTEST

TSPi WEEKLY MEETING: SCRIPT WEEK

Purpose	To guide the team in conducting the weekly status meeting
Entry Criteria	• All team members are present. • All the team members have provided updated TASK, SCHEDULE, and WEEK forms to the planning manager. • The planning manager has produced the composite weekly team status report from the team members' data (form WEEK). • The team leader has issued a meeting agenda.
General	In advance of the meeting, the team leader has • Asked team members for meeting agenda topics • Prepared and distributed the meeting agenda The team leader leads the weekly meeting. • The quality/process manager records the meeting topics. • Each team member generally reports his or her role work and development work at the same time. After the meeting, the team leader • Issues and distributes the meeting report • Puts a report copy in the project notebook

Step	Activities	Description
1	Agenda Review	The team leader opens the meeting and • Reviews the agenda and asks for additions or changes • Checks that all team members are fully prepared and defers the meeting if any are not
2	Role Reports	Starting with the development manager, the engineers report • Any overall role issues or concerns • Status on any role-related tasks or activities • Status on any issue or risk items that the engineer is tracking The development manager reports on development status. • Items designed, reviewed, inspected, implemented, and tested The planning manager reports on planning status. • Team hours and earned-value status against the plan The quality/process manager reviews data on • Each inspection and every integration and system test defect • The percentage of engineers following the process • Any suspected quality problems The support manager reports the status of the SCM and ITL systems. • Items submitted this week, changes made, system inventory
3	Engineer Reports	Each engineer reports his or her development status. • The hours worked this week and cycle compared to the plan • The earned value gained this week and cycle versus the plan • Times for the tasks accomplished this week and the plan times • The tasks to be accomplished in the next week • The hours to be worked in the next week • Any problem areas or topics of general team interest
4	Meeting Close	The team leader leads the discussion of any remaining topics and • Checks that all committed tasks have been reported • Verifies that all risks and issues have been reviewed • Ensures that next week's tasks have been identified and assigned • Discusses the items to include in the team's weekly report
Exit Criteria		• The meeting report completed and filed in the project notebook • Updated team and engineer TASK, SCHEDULE, WEEK, and CSR forms in the project notebook • Updated copy of the ITL log in the project notebook

APPENDIX E

Role Scripts

This appendix contains the scripts that describe each of the five TSPi team roles. These scripts were described in the five chapters on the roles, and they are included here for ready reference. The following table lists the scripts in this appendix, the pages on which they appear, and the chapters in which they are described. The scripts are listed in alphabetical order.

Name	Reference	Page
Development Manager Role	222	384
Development Manager Project Activities	231	385
Planning Manager Role	239	386
Planning Manager Project Activities	247	387
Quality/Process Manager Role	256	388
Quality/Process Manager Project Activities	263	389
Support Manager Role	271	390
Support Manager Project Activities	275	391
Team Leader Role	205	392
Team Leader's Project Activities	215	393

TSPi DEVELOPMENT MANAGER ROLE

Objective	The development manager leads and guides the team in defining, designing, developing, and testing the product.
Role Characteristics	The characteristics most helpful to development managers are the following. 1. You like to build things. 2. You want to be a software engineer and would like the experience of leading a design and development project. 3. You are a competent designer and feel you could lead a development team. 4. You are generally familiar with design methods. 5. You are willing to listen to other people's design ideas and can objectively and logically compare the qualities of their design ideas with yours.
Goals and Measures	Team member goal: Be a cooperative and effective team member. • Measures: Team peer ratings for team spirit, overall contribution, and helpfulness and support Goal 1: Produce a superior product. • Measure 1.1: The team produced a useful and fully documented product that met the basic requirements of the need statement. • Measure 1.2: The requirements are traceable from the need statement to the SRS, to the SDS, and to the final implementation. • Measure 1.3: The product design is fully documented and meets the team's design standards. • Measure 1.4: The implementation faithfully represents the design. • Measure 1.5: The product met all quality criteria. • Measure 1.6: The product met its functional and operational objectives. Goal 2: Fully utilize the team members' skills and abilities. • Measure 2.1: peer evaluations of how well the development manager role was performed • Measure 2.2: peer evaluations of the development manager's helpfulness and support • Measure 2.3: peer evaluations of product quality
Principal Activities	1. Lead the team in producing the development strategy. 2. Lead the team in producing the preliminary size and time estimates for the products to be produced. 3. Lead the development of the requirements specification (SRS). 4. Lead the team in producing the high-level design. 5. Lead the team in producing the design specification (SDS). 6. Lead the team in implementing the product. 7. Lead the team in developing the build, integration, and system test plans. 8. Lead the team in developing the test materials and running the tests. 9. Lead the team in producing the product's user documentation. 10. Participate in producing the development cycle report. 11. Act as a development engineer.

TSPi DEVELOPMENT MANAGER PROJECT ACTIVITIES

Phase Week	General	In addition to the engineer's standard tasks, the development manager does the following tasks each week.	References
LAU 2,8,11	Project launch	Participate in the first team meeting.	Chapter 3
STRAT 2,8,11	Strategy criteria	Lead the team in establishing strategy criteria.	Chapter 4
	Development strategy	Lead the team in developing and reviewing the strategy.	
	Preliminary estimates	Lead the work to make preliminary size and time estimates.	
	Risk assessment	Lead the team in identifying and assessing project risks.	
	Configuration control	Participate in reviewing the configuration control process.	Appendix B
PLAN 3,8,11	Development plan	Participate in making the development plan.	Chapter 5
	Quality plan	Participate in making the quality plan.	
REQ 4,9,12	Need statement	Lead the team in clarifying the need statement.	Chapter 6
	Questions	Clarify the need statement with the instructor.	
	Outline SRS	Lead the team through outlining the SRS.	
	Produce SRS	Lead the team in producing the SRS.	
	System test plan	Lead the team in producing the system test plan.	Chapter 9
	SRS inspection	Participate in inspecting the SRS and system test plan.	Appendix C
	Final SRS	Obtain updates and produce the final SRS.	Chapter 6
	SRS approval	Obtain SRS approval from the instructor.	
DES 5,9,12	HLD	Lead the team in producing the high-level design.	Chapter 7
	Produce SDS	Lead the team in producing the SDS.	
	Integration plan	Lead the team in producing the integration test plan.	Chapter 9
	SDS inspection	Participate in inspecting the SDS and integration test plan.	Appendix C
	Final SDS	Obtain updates and produce the final SDS.	Chapter 7
IMP 6,10,13	Planning	Lead the planning for the implementation work.	Chapter 8
	Detailed design	Produce and review detailed designs.	
	Unit test plan	Produce and review unit test plans.	Script UT
	DLD inspection	Participate in inspecting detailed designs and unit test plans.	Appendix C
	Test development	Produce unit test materials.	Script UT
	Implementation	Implement and review programs.	Chapter 8
	Compile	Compile programs.	
	Code inspection	Participate in inspecting programs.	Appendix C
	Unit test	Unit-test programs.	Script UT
TEST 7,10,13	Test development	Lead the test development work.	Chapter 9
	Build	Lead the work to build the product.	
	Integration	Lead the integration testing work.	
	System test	Lead the system testing of the product.	
	User documentation	Lead the development and review of the documentation.	
PM 8,11,15	Cycle report	Participate in reviewing team performance and producing a report on the latest development cycle.	Chapter 10
	Prepare peer reviews	Complete a peer review for the development manager's role and for all the other team roles using form PEER.	
Every Week	Data reporting	Provide agreed weekly data to the planning manager.	Chapter 5
	Weekly meeting	Participate in the weekly team meetings.	Script WEEK
	CCB	Participate as a member of the configuration control board.	Appendix B
	Build control	Ensure that only baselined products are used in build, integration, and system test of the product.	

TSPi PLANNING MANAGER ROLE

Objective	The planning manager supports and guides the team members in planning and tracking their work.
Role Characteristics	The characteristics most helpful to planning managers are the following. 1. You have a logical mind and feel most comfortable when following a plan for doing your work. 2. Although you may not always be able to produce a plan, you tend to plan your work when given the opportunity. 3. You are interested in process data. 4. You are willing to press people to track and measure their work.
Goals and Measures	Team member goal: Be a cooperative and effective team member. • Measures: Team PEER ratings for team spirit, overall contribution, and helpfulness and support Goal 1: Produce a complete, precise, and accurate plan for the team and for every team member. • Measure 1.1: The team's plan covered all the tasks in the development cycle. • Measure 1.2: The plan was fully documented in TASK and SCHEDULE templates. • Measure 1.3: The average task hours were less than 5, and no individual engineer's tasks were more than about 10 hours. • Measure 1.4: The weekly hours and total plan hours accurately represented the actual cycle results. Goal 2: Accurately report team status every week. • Measure 2.1: You provided complete and accurate weekly team status reports. • Measure 2.2: The team members updated their personal TASK, SCHEDULE, and WEEK forms and provided them to you on time. • Measure 2.3: If one or more team members did not report all their data on time, you sought help from the team leader and the instructor.

Principal Activities	1. Lead the team in producing the task plan for the next development cycle.
	  • Define the products to be produced and their estimated sizes.
	  • Specify the tasks and task hours needed to produce the products.
	  • Document the tasks in the TASK form.
	2. Lead the team in producing the schedule for the next development cycle.
	  • Determine the weekly hours that each engineer will spend on the project.
	  • Enter the individual and team hours on the SCHEDULE template.
	  • Produce the team SCHEDULE form.
	3. Lead the team in producing the balanced team plan.
	  • Obtain detailed plans from each engineer.
	  • Identify workload imbalances among team members.
	  • Lead the team in adjusting workload to achieve balance.
	  • Generate the consolidated team plan.
	  • Obtain detailed personal plans from each engineer.
	4. Track the team's progress against the plan.
	  • Get the team members' weekly data.
	  • Produce a weekly team earned-value and time chart of team status.
	  • Generate the weekly status report.
	  • Produce a weekly analysis of the team's actual performance against plan.
	  • Report personal and consolidated team status to the instructor.
	5. Participate in producing the development cycle report.
	6. Act as a development engineer.

TSPi PLANNING MANAGER PROJECT ACTIVITIES

Phase Week	General	In addition to the engineer's standard tasks, the planning manager does the following tasks each week.	References
LAU 2,8,11	Weekly meeting	Participate in the first team meeting.	Chapter 3
	Weekly data	Obtain agreement on the data to be provided every week.	
STRAT 2,8,11	Development strategy	Participate in developing and reviewing the strategy.	Chapter 4
	Configuration control	Participate in reviewing the configuration control process.	Appendix B
PLAN 3,8,11	Products and sizes	Lead the work to identify the project's products and sizes.	Chapter 5
	Task list	Lead the team effort to produce the task list.	
	Task hours	Lead the team in estimating the task hours.	
	Weekly hours	Obtain engineers' estimates for their weekly hours.	
	Team plan	Produce the preliminary team plan.	
	Quality plan	Participate in making the quality plan.	
	Individual plans	Help each engineer make a personal plan.	
	Balance the plan	Lead the team in balancing team workload.	
	Final plan	Produce final team and individual engineer plans.	
REQ 4,9,12	Need statement	Participate in analyzing and clarifying the requirements.	Chapter 6
	Produce SRS	Produce the assigned parts of the SRS.	
	System test plan	Participate in producing the system test plan.	Chapter 9
	SRS inspection	Participate in inspecting the SRS and system test plan.	Appendix C
DES 5,9,12	Design specification	Participate in developing the SDS.	Chapter 7
	Integration plan	Participate in producing the integration test plan.	Chapter 9
	SDS inspection	Participate in inspecting the SDS and integration test plan.	Appendix C
IMP 6,10,13	Planning	Participate in planning the implementation work.	Chapter 8
	Detailed design	Produce and review detailed designs.	
	Unit test plan	Produce and review unit test plans.	Script UT
	DLD inspection	Participate in inspecting detailed designs and unit test plans.	Appendix C
	Test development	Produce unit test materials.	Script UT
	Implementation	Implement and review programs.	Chapter 8
	Compile	Compile programs.	
	Code inspection	Participate in inspecting programs.	Appendix C
	Unit test	Unit-test programs.	Script UT
TEST 7,10,13	Test development	Participate in the test development tasks.	Chapter 9
	Build	Participate in building the product.	
	Integration	Participate in integrating the product.	
	System test	Participate in system-testing the product.	
	User documentation	Participate in producing the user documentation.	
PM 8,11,15	Cycle report	Participate in reviewing team performance and producing a report on the latest development cycle.	Chapter 10
	Prepare peer reviews	Complete a peer review for the planning manager's role and for all the other team roles using form PEER.	
Every Week	Data	Obtain the engineers' weekly data.	Chapter 5
	Weekly report	Generate the team's WEEK report.	
	Weekly analysis	Generate a brief analysis of team performance versus plan.	
	Weekly meeting	Participate in the weekly team meetings.	Script WEEK

TSPi QUALITY/PROCESS MANAGER ROLE

Objective	The Quality/Process Manager supports the team in defining the process needs, in making the quality plan, and in tracking process and product quality.
Role Characteristics	The characteristics most helpful to quality/process managers are the following.
	1. You are concerned about software quality.
	2. You are interested in process and process measurements.
	3. You have some experience with or awareness of inspection and review methods.
	4. You are willing and able to constructively review and comment on other people's work without antagonizing them.
Goals and Measures	Team member goal: Be a cooperative and effective team member.
	• Measures: Team PEER ratings for team spirit, overall contribution, and helpfulness and support
	Goal 1: All team members accurately report and properly use TSPi data.
	• Measure 1: The extent to which the team faithfully gathered and used all the required TSPi data
	Goal 2: The team faithfully follows the TSPi and produces a quality product.
	• Measure 2.1: How well the team followed the TSPi
	• Measure 2.2: How well the team's quality performance conformed to the quality plan
	• Measure 2.3: The degree to which you kept the team leader and instructor informed of quality problems
	• Measure 2.4: The degree to which you accomplished this goal without antagonizing the team or any team members
	Goal 3: All team inspections are properly moderated and reported.
	• Measure 3.1: All inspections were conducted according to the INS script and the team's quality standards.
	• Measure 3.2: INS forms are completed for all team inspections and all major defects reported on the owners' LOGD forms.
	Goal 4: All team meetings are accurately reported and the reports put in the project notebook.
	• Measure 4: The percentage of the team meetings with reports filed in the project notebook
Principal Activities	1. Lead the team in producing and tracking the quality plan.
	2. Alert the team, the team leader, and the instructor to quality problems.
	3. Lead the team in defining and documenting its processes and in maintaining the process improvement process.
	4. Establish and maintain the team's development standards.
	5. Review and approve all products before submission to the CCB.
	6. Act as the team's inspection moderator.
	7. Act as recorder in all the team's meetings.
	8. Participate in producing the development cycle report.
	⸱ Act as a development engineer.

TSPi QUALITY/PROCESS MANAGER PROJECT ACTIVITIES

Phase Week	General	In addition to the engineer's standard tasks, the quality/process manager does the following tasks each week.	References
LAU 2,8,11	Weekly meeting	Participate in the first team meeting.	Chapter 3
STRAT 2,8,11	Development strategy	Participate in developing and reviewing the strategy.	Chapter 4
	Document criteria	Document the selected strategy criteria.	
	Document strategy	Document the selected strategy.	
	Configuration control	Participate in reviewing the configuration control process.	Appendix B
PLAN 3,8,11	Development plan	Participate in making the development plan.	Chapter 5
	Quality plan	Lead the team in making the quality plan.	
REQ 4,9,12	Need statement	Participate in analyzing and clarifying the requirements.	Chapter 6
	Produce SRS	Produce the assigned parts of the SRS.	
	System test plan	Participate in producing the system test plan.	Chapter 9
	SRS inspection	Lead the inspection of the SRS and system test plan.	Appendix C
DES 5,9,12	Design specification	Participate in developing the SDS.	Chapter 7
	Name glossary	Lead the team effort to produce the name glossary.	
	Design standards	Lead the team effort to produce the design standards.	
	Integration plan	Participate in producing the integration test plan.	Chapter 9
	SDS inspection	Lead the inspection of the SDS and integration test plan.	Appendix C
IMP 6,10,13	Planning	Participate in planning the implementation work.	Chapter 8
	Detailed design	Produce and review detailed designs.	
	Unit test plan	Produce and review unit test plans.	Script UT
	DLD inspection	Lead inspections of the detailed designs and unit test plans.	Appendix C
	Test development	Produce unit test materials.	Script UT
	Implementation	Implement and review programs.	Chapter 8
	Compile	Compile programs.	
	Code inspection	Lead the code inspections.	Appendix C
	Unit test	Unit-test programs.	Script UT
	Quality review	Determine whether the components meet quality criteria.	Script UT
TEST 7,10,13	Test development	Participate in the test development tasks.	Chapter 9
	Build	Participate in building the product.	
	Integration	Participate in integrating the product.	
	System test	Participate in system-testing the product.	
	User documentation	Participate in producing the user documentation.	
PM 8,11,15	Cycle report	Participate in reviewing team performance and producing a report on the latest development cycle.	Chapter 10
	Prepare peer reviews	Complete a peer review for the quality/process manager's role and for all the other team roles using form PEER.	
Every Week	Data reporting	Provide agreed weekly data to the planning manager.	Chapter 5
	Quality review	Review the quality of the engineers' work.	Chapter 14
	Weekly meeting	Participate in the weekly team meetings.	Script WEEK

TSPi SUPPORT MANAGER ROLE

Objective	The support manager supports the team in determining, obtaining, and managing the tools needed to meet the team's technology and administrative support needs.
Role Characteristics	The characteristics most helpful to support managers are the following. 1. You are interested in tools and methods. 2. You are a competent computer user and feel you could assist the team with its support needs. 3. You have some experience with support tools and systems. 4. You are generally familiar with the tools that are likely to be used on this project.
Goals and Measures	Team member goal: Be a cooperative and effective team member. • Measures: Team PEER ratings for team spirit, overall contribution, and helpfulness and support Goal 1: The team has suitable tools and methods to support its work. • Measure 1.1: The team had a change management system, an issue-tracking system, a configuration management system, a common development environment, and the TSPi support system. • Measure 1.2: The team effectively used the tools that it had. Goal 2: No unauthorized changes are made to baselined products. • Measure 2.1: All final product elements were configuration-controlled. • Measure 2.2: All changes to configuration-controlled products went through the configuration control board (CCB). • Measure 2.3: When changes were made in the code, they were reflected in the baselined design documentation. Goal 3: All the team's risks and issues are recorded in the issue-tracking log (ITL) and reported each week. • Measure 3: The percentage of the risks and issues that were recorded and tracked in the issue tracking system Goal 4: The team meets its reuse goals for the development cycle. • Measure 4.1: The team had a reusable parts list. • Measure 4.2: The reuse and new-reuse percentages were measured and tracked. • Measure 4.3: The team achieved some reuse with the first development cycle. • Measure 4.4: The level of reuse increased with each cycle.
Principal Activities	1. Lead the team in determining its support needs and in obtaining the needed tools and facilities. 2. Chair the configuration control board and manage the change control system. • Review all changes to controlled products. • Evaluate each change for impact and benefit. • Recommend to the team which changes to make. 3. Manage the configuration management system. • Maintain a protected master copy of all controlled items. • Make approved changes only to this controlled version. • Maintain master copies of all controlled items and versions. 4. Maintain the system glossary. 5. Maintain the team's issue and risk-tracking system. 6. Act as the team's reuse advocate. 7. Participate in producing the development cycle report. 8. Act as a development engineer.

TSPi SUPPORT MANAGER PROJECT ACTIVITIES

Phase Week	General	In addition to the engineer's standard tasks, the support manager does the following tasks each week.	References
LAU 2,8,11	Weekly meeting	Participate in the first team meeting.	Chapter 3
STRAT 2,8,11	Development strategy	Participate in developing and reviewing the strategy.	Chapter 4
	Configuration plan	Define the configuration control process.	Appendix B
	Configuration control	Participate in reviewing the configuration control process.	
PLAN 3,8,11	Development plan	Participate in making the development plan.	Chapter 5
	Quality plan	Participate in making the quality plan.	
REQ 4,9,12	Need statement	Participate in analyzing and clarifying the requirements.	Chapter 6
	Produce SRS	Produce the assigned parts of the SRS.	
	System test plan	Participate in producing the system test plan.	Chapter 9
	SRS inspection	Participate in inspecting the SRS and system test plan.	Appendix C
	SRS baseline	When the SRS is corrected, baseline the SRS.	Appendix B
DES 5,9,12	Design specification	Participate in developing the SDS.	Chapter 7
	Integration plan	Participate in producing the integration test plan.	Chapter 9
	SDS inspection	Participate in inspecting the SDS and integration test plan.	Appendix C
	SDS baseline	When the SDS is corrected, baseline the SDS.	Appendix B
IMP 6,10,13	Planning	Participate in planning the implementation work.	Chapter 8
	Detailed design	Produce and review detailed designs.	
	Unit test plan	Produce and review unit test plans.	Script UT
	DLD inspection	Participate in inspecting detailed designs and unit test plans.	Appendix C
	Test development	Produce unit test materials.	Script UT
	Implementation	Implement and review programs.	Chapter 8
	Compile	Compile programs.	
	Code inspection	Participate in the code inspections.	Appendix C
	Unit test	Unit-test programs.	Script UT
	Component baseline	When the components are corrected, baseline the components.	Appendix B
TEST 7,10,13	Test development	Participate in the test development tasks.	Chapter 9
	Build	Participate in building the product.	
	Integration	Participate in integrating the product.	
	System test	Participate in system-testing the product.	
	User documentation	Participate in producing the user documentation.	
PM 8,11,15	Cycle report	Participate in reviewing team performance and producing a report on the latest development cycle.	Chapter 10
	Prepare peer reviews	Complete a peer review for the support manager's role and for all the other team roles using form PEER.	
Every week	CCB	Chair the CCB meetings.	Appendix B
	Product baseline	Maintain the product baseline.	
	Manage changes	Manage the change control process.	
	ITL	Maintain the ITL system and report on risk and issue status.	Chapter 15
	Name glossary	Maintain the system name glossary.	
	Data reporting	Provide agreed weekly data to the planning manager.	Chapter 5
	Weekly meeting	Participate in the weekly team meetings.	Script WEEK

TSPi TEAM LEADER ROLE

Objective	The team leader leads the team and ensures that engineers report their process data and complete their work as planned.
Role Characteristics	The characteristics most helpful to team leaders are the following. 1. You enjoy being leader and naturally assume a leadership role. 2. You are able to identify the key issues and objectively make decisions. 3. You do not mind occasionally taking unpopular actions and are willing to press people to accomplish difficult tasks. 4. You respect your teammates, are willing to listen to their views, and want to help them perform to the best of their abilities.
Goals and Measures	Team member goal: Be a cooperative and effective team member. • Measures: Team PEER ratings for team spirit, overall contribution, and helpfulness and support Goal 1: Build and maintain an effective team. • Measure 1.1: project performance against cost, schedule, quality goals • Measure 1.2: PEER evaluations of overall team effectiveness • Measure 1.3: PEER evaluations of the team leader's overall contribution • Measure 1.4: team members' PEER ratings of how well the team leader's role was performed Goal 2: Motivate all team members to work aggressively on the project. • Measure 2.1: All team members worked their committed hours. • Measure 2.2: The team members met their earned-value commitments. • Measure 2.3: The team members followed the TSPi process, recorded all data, and completed all required forms. Goal 3: Resolve all the issues team members bring to you. • Measure 3: the team members' PEER ratings of the team leader's role for helpfulness and support. Goal 4: Keep the instructor fully informed about the team's progress. • Measure 4.1: accurate and complete weekly status reports • Measure 4.2: the instructor's timely awareness of project status Goal 5: Perform effectively as the team's meeting facilitator. • Measure 5: the team's PEER evaluation of the project as a rewarding experience

Principal Activities	1. Motivate the team members to perform their tasks.
	2. Every week, either before or at the start of the first weekly class or laboratory session, run the weekly team meeting to
	  • Track all committed tasks to see that they have been completed
	  • Check that all team members have submitted the required data
	  • Check that all required forms have been completed on the work accomplished to date
	  • Check on the status of project risks and issues
	  • Identify the tasks to be accomplished in the next week and by whom
	3. Every week, report team status to the instructor.
	  • Show the project notebook with the team weekly data.
	  • Seek guidance from the instructor on engineers who consistently fail to complete tasks or submit data on time.
	  • Obtain guidance from the instructor to pass along to the team.
	4. Help the team in allocating tasks and resolving issues.
	5. Act as facilitator and timekeeper for all team meetings.
	6. Maintain the project notebook.
	7. Lead the team in producing the development cycle report.
	8. Act as a development engineer.

TSPi TEAM LEADER'S PROJECT ACTIVITIES

Phase Week	General	In addition to the engineer's standard tasks, the team leader does the following tasks each week.	References
LAU 2, 8, 11	Project launch	Hold the first team meeting. • Review the required weekly data and reports	Chapter 3
STRAT 2, 8, 11	Development strategy	Participate in developing and reviewing the strategy.	Chapter 4
	Configuration control	Participate in reviewing the configuration control process.	Appendix B
PLAN 3, 8, 11	Development plan	Participate in making the development plan.	Chapter 5
	Quality plan	Participate in making the quality plan.	
REQ 4, 9, 12	Need statement	Participate in analyzing and clarifying the requirements.	Chapter 6
	Produce SRS	Produce the assigned parts of the SRS.	
	System test plan	Participate in producing the system test plan.	Chapter 9
	SRS inspection	Participate in inspecting the SRS and system test plan.	Appendix C
DES 5, 9, 12	Design specification	Participate in developing the SDS.	Chapter 7
	Integration plan	Participate in producing the integration test plan.	Chapter 9
	SDS inspection	Participate in inspecting the SDS and integration test plan.	Appendix C
IMP 6, 10, 13	Planning	Participate in planning the implementation work.	Chapter 8
	Detailed design	Produce and review detailed designs.	
	Unit test plan	Produce and review unit test plans.	Script UT
	DLD inspection	Participate in inspecting detailed designs and unit test plans.	Appendix C
	Test development	Produce unit test materials.	Script UT
	Implementation	Implement and review programs.	Chapter 8
	Compile	Compile programs.	
	Code inspection	Participate in inspecting programs.	Appendix C
	Unit test	Unit-test programs.	Script UT
TEST 7, 10, 13	Test development	Participate in the test development tasks.	Chapter 9
	Build	Participate in building the product.	
	Integration	Participate in integrating the product.	
	System test	Participate in system testing the product.	
	User documentation	Participate in producing the user documentation.	
PM 8, 11, 15	Plan cycle report	Lead the team in planning and producing a report on its work in the latest development cycle. • Allocate report work to the team members. • Obtain completion commitments for this work. • Assemble the completed report.	Chapter 10
	Cycle report	Lead the team in reviewing team performance and producing a report on the latest development cycle.	
	Prepare peer reviews	Complete a peer review for the team leader's role and for all other team roles using form PEER.	
Every week	Data reporting	Provide agreed weekly data to the planning manager.	Chapter 5
	Weekly meeting	Lead the team weekly meeting. • Track committed tasks. • Check on completeness of team member data. • Check on completeness of forms. • Check on the status of project risks and issues. • Identify the tasks for the next week and who will do them.	Script WEEK
	Instructor reports	Every week, report team status to the instructor.	Chapter 11
	Tasks and issues	Help the team in allocating tasks and resolving issues.	
	Project notebook	Maintain a complete record of the team activities in the project notebook.	Appendix G

APPENDIX F

TSPi Forms
and Instructions

This appendix contains copies of all the TSPi forms together with instructions that describe how to complete each form. The following table lists the forms in the alphabetical order of their abbreviations, the pages where the form appears in the appendix, and references to where the form is discussed in this text. Many of these forms are described in this text, but additional information can also be obtained from my earlier textbook, *A Discipline for Software Engineering,* Addison-Wesley, 1995.

Form	Abbreviation	Reference	Page
Configuration Change Request	CCR	325	397
Configuration Status Report	CSR	329	399
Student Information Sheet	INFO	41	401
Inspection Report	INS	343	403
Issue Tracking Log	ITL		405
Defect Recording Log	LOGD		407
Time Recording Log	LOGT		409
Test Log	LOGTEST	172	411
Team and Peer Evaluation	PEER	194	413
Process Improvement Proposal	PIP	186	415
Schedule Planning Template	SCHEDULE	84	417
Strategy Form	STRAT	58, 136	419
Defects Injected Summary	SUMDI		421
Defects Removed Summary	SUMDR		423
Plan Summary	SUMP	92	425
Quality Plan	SUMQ	88	428
Size Summary	SUMS	79	432
Development Time Summary	SUMT		434
Task Summary	SUMTASK		436
Task Planning Template	TASK	82	438
Weekly Status Report	WEEK	45	441

TSPi CONFIGURATION CHANGE REQUEST: FORM CCR

Name _____   Date _____
Team _____   Instructor _____
Part/Level _____   Cycle _____

Product Information

Product Name _____   Product Owner _____
Product/Change Size _____   Size Measure _____
Recent Inspection _____   Moderator _____
Backup Address _____

Change Information

Reason for Change: _____
_____
_____
_____

Change Benefits: _____
_____
_____
_____

Change Impact: _____
_____
_____
_____

Change Description: (For source code, attach listing; for code changes, include defect
number (if any) and listing of changed and unchanged program
segment)

_____
_____
_____

Status

Approved: ☐   Additional Information: ☐   Disapproved: ☐
Information needed: _____
_____
_____

Approvals

Product Owner _____   Date: _____
Quality/Process Manager _____   Date: _____
CCB _____   Date: _____

TSPi CONFIGURATION CHANGE REQUEST INSTRUCTIONS: FORM CCR

Purpose	• This form is used when submitting an item to the configuration control board (CCB) for inclusion in the product baseline.
General	• The item could be a product to be baselined or a change to a baselined product. • All new products are reviewed and approved by the CCB before inclusion in the product baseline. • All changes to baselined products must be submitted in advance to the CCB for approval. • A copy of the product or change must be provided with the CCR.
Header	• Enter your name, date, team name, and instructor's name. • Name the part or assembly and its level. • Enter the cycle number.
Product Information	Enter the following information on the product or change. • the product name or identifying number • the product owner, usually the developer • the estimated or actual size of the product or change • the size measure used: new and changed pages or LOC If the product has been inspected, provide • the type of inspection and when it was done • the name of the inspection moderator • a copy of the INS form Describe where a backup copy of the product or change is retained. Also give the file address.
Change Information	For changes, give the reason to make the change. Example reasons: • To fix defect #xyz • To update the design for an approved code change • To change the SRS in response to an approved customer request Describe the estimated change benefits. Example benefits: • Enables function abc to work correctly • Improves performance by qr% Estimate the change impact. • The engineering hours required to make the change • The calendar time estimated to make the change • Any other impacts such as other changes affected Change description. Here, give a description of the change. • 13 LOC changed • 3 lines changed in the SRS and 11 lines changed in the SDS
Approvals	• These spaces are completed by the parties indicated when they approve the submission.

TSPi CONFIGURATION STATUS REPORT: FORM CSR

Name _____	Date _____
Team _____	Instructor _____
Part/Level _____	Cycle _____

Configuration Change Process: Activity

	Current Week	Cycle to Date
CCRs submitted	_____	_____
CCRs approved	_____	_____
CCRs rejected	_____	_____
CCRs deferred	_____	_____
CCRs outstanding	_____	_____
CCRs reversed	_____	_____

Configuration Change Process: Status

	Current Week	Change from Prior Week
Product volume under SCM control		
Text pages	_____	_____
Design pages	_____	_____
Pseudocode Lines	_____	_____
LOC—total	_____	_____
LOC—new and changed	_____	_____
Test case LOC	_____	_____
Test material pages	_____	_____
Test results pages	_____	_____
Other items	_____	_____
Other items	_____	_____

Comments_____
_____
_____
_____
_____
_____
_____
_____
_____
_____
_____
_____
_____
_____

TSPi CONFIGURATION STATUS REPORT INSTRUCTIONS: FORM CSR

Purpose	• This form is used to provide weekly status information on the software configuration management (SCM) system.
General	• By regularly recording these measures, teams can judge the rate at which the product is stabilizing. • For example, in test, a historical record of the change activity can be used to project when the product will complete test.
Header	• Enter your name, date, team name, and instructor's name. • Name the part or assembly and its level. • Enter the cycle number.
Configuration Change Process Activity	Enter the indicated data for the current week and the development cycle to date. • The number of CCRs submitted to the CCB for approval • The number of CCRs approved by the CCB • The number of CCRs that the CCB has rejected (note that rejected CCRs are not to be resubmitted) • The number of CCRs deferred (deferral is typically to obtain additional information) • The number of CCRs outstanding (submitted and not yet approved, rejected, or deferred) • The number of CCRs reversed (a reversed CCR is a change that was made and later found to be mistaken or based on incorrect information)
Configuration Change Process Status	Give the current volume of product under configuration control. • Give the status as of the current week. • Also give the change in each measure from the prior week. For example: • A total of 43 text pages (SDS) were submitted this week. • The total text pages under configuration control are 67.
Comments	Note any significant events or issues that came up during the week.

TSPi STUDENT INFORMATION SHEET: FORM INFO

Name _____   Instructor _____

Date _____   Number of College Credits _____

Major _____   Expected Graduation Date _____

Briefly describe your relevant experience and interests:

_____
_____
_____

Briefly describe your work on other team projects:

_____
_____
_____

Briefly describe any leadership or management positions you have held (at work or in clubs/organizations):

_____
_____
_____
_____

State your team preferences, if any:

_____

List your class schedule and other times when you have scheduled activities such as work, ROTC, clubs, sports teams, etc.							
Time	Mon.	Tue.	Wed.	Thu.	Fri.	Sat.	Sun.
800–900							
915–1015							
1030–1130							
1145–1245							
1300–1400							
1415–1515							
1530–1630							
1645–1745							

Rank from 1 (least) to 5 (most) your preferences for serving in the following team roles:					
Team Leader	1	2	3	4	5
Development Manager	1	2	3	4	5
Planning Manager	1	2	3	4	5
Quality/Process Manager	1	2	3	4	5
Support Manager	1	2	3	4	5

TSPi STUDENT INFORMATION SHEET INSTRUCTIONS: FORM INFO

Purpose	Use this form to describe your interests and experiences.
General	• Complete this form and give it to the instructor during the first laboratory period of the TSPi course. • The instructor will use it to make team and role assignments. • The schedule information is needed so that teams can be formed that are able to meet during selected times of the week. • For questions about the roles, see the role descriptions in Appendix E and in Part III. • Use additional pages if necessary.
Header	Enter • Your name, the instructor's name, and the date • The number of credits you expect from this course • Your major field of study • Your expected graduation date
Relevant Experience and Interests	• List any experience and interests you feel would be helpful to the instructor in making team and role assignments. • Examples would be language fluency, PSP experience, database design and development, and so on.
Other Team Projects	• List any team experience you feel would be helpful to the instructor in making team and role assignments. • Examples would include the type of project, roles performed, the tools or methods used, and so on.
Leadership or Management	• List any leadership or management experiences you feel would be helpful to the instructor in making team and role assignments. • Examples would include a club business manager, work as a teaching assistant, time spent in office work, and so on.
Team Preferences	• If you have preferences regarding working with particular groups, state them. • You need not make any statement.
Schedule	• List the times you have commitments for classes or other activities. • If the times do not precisely line up with those given, mark the rough periods and note below the precise times.
Role Preferences	• Rank your team role preferences from 1 (least desired) to 5 (most desired). • Note that you can list several as 1s or 5s if you feel they are all equally desirable or undesirable.

TSPi INSPECTION REPORT: FORM INS

Name	_____	Date	_____
Team	_____	Instructor	_____
Part/Level	_____	Cycle	_____
Moderator	_____	Owner	_____

Engineer Data

Name	Defects[1]		Preparation Data			Est. Yield
	Major	Minor	Size	Time	Rate	
Totals:						

Defect Data

No.	Defect Description	Defects		Engineers (finding major defects)				A	B
		Maj	Min						
Totals									
Unique Defects									

Inspection Summary	**Product Size:** _____	**Size Measure:** _____	
Total Defects for A: _____	**Total Defects for B:** _____	**C (# common):** _____	
Total Defects (AB/C): _____	**Number Found (A+B–C):** _____	**Number Left:** _____	
Meeting Time: _____	**Total Inspection Hours:** _____	**Overall Rate:** _____	

[1]Major defects either change the program source code or would ultimately cause a source code change if not fixed in time; all other defects are considered minor.

TSPi INSPECTION REPORT INSTRUCTIONS: FORM INS

Purpose	• Use this form to gather and analyze inspection data.
General	• These data *must* be gathered during the inspection because they generally cannot be obtained later. • Record the preparation data at the beginning of the inspection meeting. • Complete the form at the end of the inspection meeting. • It is helpful to have line and page numbers on the printed product text.
Header	Enter your name, the team name, instructor's name, and the date. • the product, level, and development cycle • the names of the moderator and product owner
Engineer Data	For each reviewer, enter the reviewer's name and preparation time as well as • The number of major and minor defects that reviewer found • The LOC, lines, or pages each reviewer inspected (reviewers may concentrate on program sections) • The preparation rate in LOC, pseudocode lines, or pages per hour Enter total preparation time, total major and minor defects, and overall rate. The moderator calculates total and engineer yields at the end of the meeting.
Defect Data: No.	• Enter a number for each defect found in the inspection. • It is generally most convenient to use the document line and page number.
Defect Data: **Defect Description**	• Describe each defect and check whether it is major (Maj.) or minor (Min.).
Defect Data: **Engineers**	• In the first row below the *Engineers* heading, enter the initials of each engineer who is participating in the inspection. • For major defects, check the column for each engineer who found that defect during inspection preparation.
Summary	At the end of the inspection, complete the summary data. Product size: • For requirements or high-level design inspections, enter the text pages. • For detailed-design inspections, enter the LOC or pseudocode lines. • For source code, enter the source code LOC. For the defect summary values, see the following explanation. Enter meeting time, total inspection hours, and overall inspection rate.
Summary: Estimate **Remaining Defects**	• After all defects are entered, count the major defects each engineer found that no other engineer found (the engineer's unique defects). • Identify the engineer who found the most unique defects. • Check each defect that engineer found in column A. • In column B, check all the defects found by the other engineers. • Count the common defects (C for common) between columns A and B. • The estimated total defects in the product is AB/C. • Round fractional results to the nearest integer. • The number found in the inspection is A+B−C. • The number left is the total minus the number found: (AB/C)−(A+B−C). • This defect estimate is reliable only when all the numbers A and B are greater than 4 and A−C and B−C are both greater than 1. • Even with these criteria, the total defect error is likely to be 10% or more. • When one or more engineers' yields are 70% or better, the estimates are generally quite accurate. • If A=B=C, you have likely found all the defects. • If several engineers found the same largest number of unique defects, repeat these calculations, using each of these engineers as A, and use the largest resulting number as the total defect estimate.

TSPi ISSUE TRACKING LOG: FORM ITL

Name _____ Date _____

Team _____ Instructor _____

Part/Level _____ Cycle _____

Date	Risk/Issue	Number	Priority	Owner	FU Date	Resolved
[ ]	[ ]	[ ]	[ ]	[ ]	[ ]	[ ]

Description: _____

_____

Date	Risk/Issue	Number	Priority	Owner	FU Date	Resolved
[ ]	[ ]	[ ]	[ ]	[ ]	[ ]	[ ]

Description: _____

_____

Date	Risk/Issue	Number	Priority	Owner	FU Date	Resolved
[ ]	[ ]	[ ]	[ ]	[ ]	[ ]	[ ]

Description: _____

_____

Date	Risk/Issue	Number	Priority	Owner	FU Date	Resolved
[ ]	[ ]	[ ]	[ ]	[ ]	[ ]	[ ]

Description: _____

_____

Date	Risk/Issue	Number	Priority	Owner	FU Date	Resolved
[ ]	[ ]	[ ]	[ ]	[ ]	[ ]	[ ]

Description: _____

_____

Date	Risk/Issue	Number	Priority	Owner	FU Date	Resolved
[ ]	[ ]	[ ]	[ ]	[ ]	[ ]	[ ]

Description: _____

_____

Date	Risk/Issue	Number	Priority	Owner	FU Date	Resolved
[ ]	[ ]	[ ]	[ ]	[ ]	[ ]	[ ]

Description: _____

_____

Date	Risk/Issue	Number	Priority	Owner	FU Date	Resolved
[ ]	[ ]	[ ]	[ ]	[ ]	[ ]	[ ]

Description: _____

_____

Date	Risk/Issue	Number	Priority	Owner	FU Date	Resolved
[ ]	[ ]	[ ]	[ ]	[ ]	[ ]	[ ]

Description: _____

_____

TSPi ISSUE TRACKING LOG INSTRUCTIONS: FORM ITL

Purpose	• Use this form to record and track project risks and issues.
Responsibilities	• The support manager maintains the issue-tracking log. • In each team meeting, the support manager provides status data on the risks and issues. • Examples are the number of issues or risks with past-due follow-up dates, number with current dates, and so on. • The team decides who should address each risk or issue and when.
General	• Issues are certainties; without action, they will likely cause problems. • Risks are things that may or may not happen. • Record a risk or issue in each segment of the form. • Use additional copies of the form as needed. • If the number of risks or issues becomes too large, use a database system to track them.
Header	• Enter your name, date, team name, and instructor's name. • Name the part or assembly and its level. • Enter the cycle number.
Date	• Enter the date the risk or issue was entered in the ITL system.
Risk/Issue	• Enter an *R* for a risk or an *I* for an issue.
Number	• Assign a control number to each risk and issue.
Priority	• For risks, enter the risk evaluation. • Use H, M, or L for high, medium, or low evaluations. • Evaluate the risk in terms of likelihood and schedule impact. • A priority of HM would be a risk with a high likelihood of occurring and a medium schedule impact on the project.
Owner	• Name the engineer who is tracking the risk or issue.
Follow-up Date	• Note the date when the risk or issue should be resolved.
Date Resolved	• Record the date the risk or issue was resolved.
Description	Describe the risk or issue as clearly as possible. For example: • A change to be made or interface to be checked • A requirements question to answer • A possible delay in obtaining a support tool Describe the risk or issue completely enough to permit you or someone else to later take the needed action.

Defect Types			
10	Documentation	60	Checking
20	Syntax	70	Data
30	Build, Package	80	Function
40	Assignment	90	System
50	Interface	100	Environment

TSPi DEFECT RECORDING LOG: FORM LOGD

Name _____   Date _____

Team _____   Instructor _____

Assembly _____   Cycle _____

Date	Number	Type	Inject	Remove	Fix Time	Fix Defect
[ ]	[ ]	[ ]	[ ]	[ ]	[ ]	[ ]

Description: _____
_____

Date	Number	Type	Inject	Remove	Fix Time	Fix Defect
[ ]	[ ]	[ ]	[ ]	[ ]	[ ]	[ ]

Description: _____
_____

Date	Number	Type	Inject	Remove	Fix Time	Fix Defect
[ ]	[ ]	[ ]	[ ]	[ ]	[ ]	[ ]

Description: _____
_____

Date	Number	Type	Inject	Remove	Fix Time	Fix Defect
[ ]	[ ]	[ ]	[ ]	[ ]	[ ]	[ ]

Description: _____
_____

Date	Number	Type	Inject	Remove	Fix Time	Fix Defect
[ ]	[ ]	[ ]	[ ]	[ ]	[ ]	[ ]

Description: _____
_____

Date	Number	Type	Inject	Remove	Fix Time	Fix Defect
[ ]	[ ]	[ ]	[ ]	[ ]	[ ]	[ ]

Description: _____
_____

Date	Number	Type	Inject	Remove	Fix Time	Fix Defect
[ ]	[ ]	[ ]	[ ]	[ ]	[ ]	[ ]

Description: _____
_____

Date	Number	Type	Inject	Remove	Fix Time	Fix Defect
[ ]	[ ]	[ ]	[ ]	[ ]	[ ]	[ ]

Description: _____
_____

Date	Number	Type	Inject	Remove	Fix Time	Fix Defect
[ ]	[ ]	[ ]	[ ]	[ ]	[ ]	[ ]

Description: _____
_____

TSPi DEFECT RECORDING LOG INSTRUCTIONS: FORM LOGD

Purpose	Use this form to hold data on the defects you find and correct.
General	• Keep a separate log for each program component. • Record each defect separately and completely. • If you need additional space, use another copy of the form.
Header	• Enter your name, date, team name, and instructor's name. • Name the assembly. • Enter the cycle number.
Date	• Enter the date you found the defect.
Number	• Enter the defect number. • For each program component (or module), use a sequential number starting with 1 (or 001 and so on).
Type	• Enter the defect type from the defect type list summarized in the top right corner of the form. • See Appendix G for the defect type specification. • Use your best judgment in selecting which type applies.
Inject	• Enter the phase when this defect was injected. • Use your best judgment.
Remove	• Enter the phase during which you fixed the defect. • This is generally the phase when you found the defect.
Fix Time	• Enter the time you took to fix the defect. • This time can be determined by stopwatch or by judgment.
Fix Defect	• If you or someone else injected this defect while fixing another defect, record the number of the improperly fixed defect. • If you cannot identify the defect number, enter an X in the Fix Defect box.
Description	• Write a succinct description of the defect that is clear enough to later remind you about the error and help you to remember why you made it. • If the defect was injected in a prior cycle, give the cycle number and put an * by the phase injected (such as code* or design*).

TSPi TIME RECORDING LOG: FORM LOGT

Name _____   Date _____
Team _____   Instructor _____
Assembly _____   Cycle _____

Date	Start	Stop	Interruption Time	Delta Time	Phase/ Task	Assembly	Comment

TSPi TIME RECORDING LOG INSTRUCTIONS: FORM LOGT

Purpose	Use this form to record the time spent on each project task
General	• Either keep one log and note the task and product element for each entry or keep separate logs for each major task. • Record all the time you spend on the project. • Record the time in minutes. • Be as accurate as possible. • If you need additional space, use another copy of the form. • If you forget to record the starting, stopping, or interruption time for a task, promptly enter your best estimate.
Header	• Enter your name, date, team name, and instructor's name. • Name the assembly. • Enter the cycle number.
Date	• Enter the date when you made the entry. • For example, 10/18/99
Start	• Enter the time when you start working on a task. • For example, 8:20
Stop	• Enter the time when you stop working on that task. • For example, 10:56
Interruption Time	• Record any interruption time that was not spent on the task and the reason for the interruption. • If you have several interruptions, enter their total time. • For example, 37—took a break
Delta Time	• Enter the clock time you actually spent working on the task, less the interruption time. • For example, from 8:20 to 10:56 less 37 minutes is 119 minutes.
Phase/Task	• Enter the name or other designation of the phase or task you worked on. • For example, planning, code, test, and so on
Assembly	• If the task was for a unique product, enter the name of the product.
Comments	• Enter any other pertinent comments that might later remind you of any unusual circumstances regarding this activity. • For example, had a requirements question and needed help.

TSPi TEST LOG: FORM LOGTEST

Name	_____	Date	_____
Team	_____	Instructor	_____
Part/Level	_____	Cycle	_____

Date	Test/ Phase	Product	Start	Stop	Interruption Time	Delta Time	Problems	Comments

TSPi TEST LOG INSTRUCTIONS: FORM LOGTEST

Purpose	• The test log contains a summary of the tests run and the results obtained. • With the test log data, you can readily determine which tests were run and which found the most defects. • You can also determine the test run time and the defects found per testing hour. • Data from this log can help you select the most efficient strategy for regression-testing modified programs.
General	• Use this log to track unit, integration, and system testing. • A test run is an uninterrupted run of the test. • When a test must be stopped, either to fix the program being tested or to change the test materials, that test run is concluded. • When the test is resumed after the change, record this as a new test run.
Header	• Enter your name, date, team name, and instructor's name. • Name the part or assembly and its level. • Enter the cycle number.
Date	Enter the date each test was run.
Test/Phase	• Uniquely identify each test and phase. • Use the same name or number as in the test plan.
Product	Name the product being tested.
Start	• Enter the time when the test was started.
Stop	• Enter the time when the test was stopped, either because it finished successfully or was aborted for any program or test-related reason
Interruption Time	• If the test was temporarily suspended for a reason not connected with the program, that is interruption time. • For example, the tester took a break.
Delta Time	• The time between starting and stopping the test, less interruption time.
Problems	• The number of test problem reports • If one or more problems is determined to be a defect, note that under comments.
Comments	Briefly note the test results. For example: • The test finished successfully. • The test was completed, but the result was incorrect. • The test failed with 3 problems, 1 defect. • Where possible, give additional information on test results, test configuration, or anything else that would permit reproducing the test results.

TSPi TEAM AND PEER EVALUATION: FORM PEER

Name _____ Team _____ Instructor _____

Date _____ Cycle No. _____ Week No. _____

For each role, evaluate the work required and the relative difficulty in % during this cycle.		
Role	**Work Required**	**Role Difficulty**
Team Leader		
Development Manager		
Planning Manager		
Quality/Process Manager		
Support Manager		
Total Contribution (100%)		

Rate the overall team against each criterion. Circle one number from 1 (inadequate) to 5 (superior).

Team spirit	1	2	3	4	5
Overall effectiveness	1	2	3	4	5
Rewarding experience	1	2	3	4	5
Team productivity	1	2	3	4	5
Process quality	1	2	3	4	5
Product quality	1	2	3	4	5

Rate role for overall contribution. Circle one number from 1 (inadequate) to 5 (superior).

Team Leader	1	2	3	4	5
Development Manager	1	2	3	4	5
Planning Manager	1	2	3	4	5
Quality/Process Manager	1	2	3	4	5
Support Manager	1	2	3	4	5

Rate each role for helpfulness and support. Circle one number from 1 (inadequate) to 5 (superior).

Team Leader	1	2	3	4	5
Development Manager	1	2	3	4	5
Planning Manager	1	2	3	4	5
Quality/Process Manager	1	2	3	4	5
Support Manager	1	2	3	4	5

Rate each role for how well it was performed. Circle one number from 1 (inadequate) to 5 (superior).

Team Leader	1	2	3	4	5
Development Manager	1	2	3	4	5
Planning Manager	1	2	3	4	5
Quality/Process Manager	1	2	3	4	5
Support Manager	1	2	3	4	5

TSPi TEAM AND PEER EVALUATION INSTRUCTIONS: FORM PEER

Purpose	• This form holds the team and peer evaluations.
General	• The teams complete PEER forms in each cycle postmortem. • Complete every entry. • Rate your own performance as well as that of the others. • On the back of the form or on separate sheets, add any other comments or suggestions you wish to make.
Header	• Enter your name and the instructor's name. • Enter the team name, cycle number, date, and week number.
Role Work Required and Difficulty	For each role • Estimate the relative amount of work you feel was required by each role during this development cycle. • Also rank the roles in terms of overall difficulty. In making these rankings • Provide percent estimates that total 100%. • For example, if you feel all roles were relatively equal on some measure, list 20, 20, 20, 20, and 20. • If some roles involved more work or difficulty, you might list 20, 30, 15, 20, and 15.
Overall Team Evaluation	On a scale of 1 (inadequate) to 5 (superior) rate the team on • Team spirit • Overall effectiveness • Whether this project was a rewarding experience for you • Productivity • Process and product quality
Role Overall Contribution	• Rate each role for the contribution you feel the engineer in that role made to the project during this development cycle. • Circle the applicable number, with 1 being the lowest overall contribution and 5 the highest. • The ratings need not be relative. That is, all could be 5's, all 1's, or any combination.
Role Overall Helpfulness and Support	• Rate each role for how helpful the engineer in that role was to you during this project development cycle. • Circle the applicable number, with 1 being the least helpful and 5 the most. • The ratings need not be relative. That is, all could be 5's, all 1's, or any combination.
Overall Role Performance	• Rate each role for how well you feel it was performed. • This rating should be based on how well you feel the role's defined tasks and responsibilities were handled. • Circle the applicable number, with 1 being the poorest overall performance and 5 the best. • The ratings need not be relative. That is, all could be 5's, all 1's, or any combination.

TSPi PROCESS IMPROVEMENT PROPOSAL: FORM PIP

Name _____   Date _____
Team _____   Instructor _____
Part/Level _____   Cycle _____
Process _____   Phase _____

PIP Number _____   Priority _____

Problem Description
Briefly describe the problem encountered and its impact.

_____
_____
_____
_____
_____
_____
_____
_____
_____
_____

Proposal Description
Describe suggested changes as completely as possible, including affected forms, scripts, and so on.

_____
_____
_____
_____
_____
_____
_____
_____
_____
_____

Submit completed PIP to the quality/process manager and keep a copy.

Do not write below this line

PIP Control # _____   Organization _____
Received _____   Acknowledged _____
Updated _____   Closed _____
Changes _____
_____
_____

TSPi PROCESS IMPROVEMENT PROPOSAL INSTRUCTIONS: FORM PIP

Purpose	• To record process problems and improvement ideas • To provide an orderly record of your process improvement ideas for use in later improvement
General	Use the PIP form to • Record process improvement ideas as they occur to you • Establish priorities for your improvement plans • Describe lessons learned and unusual conditions Keep PIP forms on hand while using the TSPi. • Record process problems even without proposed solutions. • Submit the PIPs for use in process improvement.
Header	• Enter your name, date, team, and instructor's name. • Name the part or assembly and its level. • Enter the cycle number. • Enter the process and process phase where appropriate.
PIP Number	• Use for your own identification purposes.
Priority	• Indicate if PIP priority is urgent, normal, or routine. • Under problem description give the reason for the priority.
Problem Description	Describe the problem as clearly as possible: • The difficulty encountered • The impact on the product, the process, and you Include related problems if relevant.
Proposal Description	• Describe your proposed process improvement as explicitly as possible. • Where possible, reference the specific process elements affected and the words or entries to be changed. • Where several problems are listed, indicate the problem(s) each proposal relates to.
Submit Completed PIP	After you have completed the PIP • Keep a copy • Submit a copy to the quality/process manager
Quality/Process Manager	Use the space at the bottom of the PIP form to track PIP status. Review all PIPs and • Acknowledge receipt • Group duplicates and related PIPs • Identify high-priority PIPs Submit PIP copies to the instructor.

TSPi SCHEDULE PLANNING TEMPLATE: FORM SCHEDULE

Name _____   Date _____

Team _____   Instructor _____

Part/Level _____   Cycle _____

Week No.	Date	Plan			Actual			
		Direct Hours	Cumulative Hours	Cumulative Planned Value	Team Hours	Cumulative Hours	Week Earned Value	Cumulative Earned Value

TSPi SCHEDULE PLANNING TEMPLATE INSTRUCTIONS: FORM SCHEDULE

Purpose	• To record estimated and actual hours expended by week • To show the cumulative planned value by week • To track earned value versus planned value as tasks are completed
General	• Expand this template or use multiple pages as needed. • Complete in conjunction with the TASK form. • Where possible, use the TSPi support tool for planning. • If you use the TSPi support tool, it will complete all the calculations for the TASK and SCHEDULE forms. • If not, you will have to do the calculations yourself.
Header	• Enter your name, date, team name, and instructor's name. • Name the part or assembly and its level. • Enter the cycle number.
Week No.	From the cycle start, enter a week number, starting with 1.
Date	• Enter the calendar date for each week. • Pick a standard day in the week—for example, Monday.
Plan: Direct Hours	• Enter the number of hours you plan to work each week. • Consider nonwork time such as vacations, holidays, and so on. • Consider other committed activities such as classes, meetings, and other projects.
Plan: Cumulative Hours	• Enter the cumulative planned hours through each week.
Plan: Cumulative Planned Value	For each week, take the plan cumulative hours from the SCHEDULE form and • On the TASK form, find the task with nearest equal or lower plan cumulative hours and note its cumulative PV • Enter this cumulative PV in the SCHEDULE form for that week • If the cumulative value for the prior week still applies, enter it again
Actual	During development, enter the actual hours, cumulative hours, and cumulative earned value for each week. • To determine status against plan, compare the cumulative planned value with the actual cumulative earned value. • Also compare cumulative planned hours with cumulative actual hours. • If you are behind schedule and actual hours are less than the plan, you are not spending enough time. • If you are behind schedule and actual hours are equal to or greater than the plan, the problem is poor planning.

TSPi STRATEGY FORM: FORM STRAT

Name		Date	
Team		Instructor	
Part/Level		Cycle	

Reference	Functions	Cycle LOC			Cycle Hours		
		1	**2**	**3**	**1**	**2**	**3**
Totals							

TSPi STRATEGY FORM INSTRUCTIONS: FORM STRAT

Purpose	• This form is used to record strategic decisions. • It is used during strategy development to allocate product functions to cycles. • It is also used during high-level design to allocate SRS functions to components.
General	• This form suggests a way to record strategic decisions. • Use it or any other format that contains the same data.
Header	• Enter your name, date, team name, and instructor's name. • Name the part or assembly and its level. • Enter the cycle number.
Reference	• Use this column to list the need statement or SRS paragraph or sentence number for every function.
Functions	• In this column, list all the functions to be included in the product in all cycles.
Cycle LOC	• Use these columns for the estimated LOC for each function. • Enter the LOC estimated for each function under the number of the cycle that will include that function. • If you plan to implement a function partially in two or even three of the cycles, enter the estimated new and changed LOC for each cycle. • If one function is included in another function's LOC, mark it with an X.
Cycle Hours	• Use these columns for the estimated time required to develop each function. • Enter the time estimated for each function under the number of the cycle in which you plan to include that function. • If you plan to implement a function partially in two or even three of the cycles, enter the estimated development time for each cycle. • If one function is included in another function's hours, mark it with an X.

TSPi DEFECTS INJECTED SUMMARY: FORM SUMDI

Plan _____ Assembly _____ Actual _____

Name _____ Date _____

Team _____ Instructor _____

Part/Level _____ Cycle _____

Phase	Strategy and Planning	Requirements	System Test Plan	Requirements Inspection	High-level Design	Integration Test Plan	HLD Inspection	Detailed Design	Detailed Design Review	Test Development	Detailed Design Inspection	Code	Code Review	Compile	Code Inspection	Unit Test	Build and Integration	System Test
Parts																		
Total																		

TSPi DEFECTS INJECTED SUMMARY INSTRUCTIONS: FORM SUMDI

Purpose	This form summarizes the data for defects injected in the parts of an assembly.
General	• Note: The number of rows in this form is variable, depending on the number of parts in the assembly.
When Using the TSPi Tool	• If you are using the TSPi tool, these data are automatically obtained from the part defect logs and SUMP forms and rolled up to the next level SUMP form.
When Not Using the TSPi Tool	If you are not using the TSPi tool, use a copy of this form to summarize the defect data for the parts of each assembly. • Obtain defect data from the part defect logs or SUMP forms. • Enter the totals from the SUMDI form in the SUMP form for the high-level assembly.
Header	• Enter your name, date, team name, and instructor's name. • Name the part or assembly and its level. • Enter the cycle number.
Plan/Assembly/ Actual	Check whether this form is for plan, assembly, or actual data. • Plan: In system-level planning, use SUMDI to summarize the estimated defects to be injected in each assembly's parts. • Assembly: Use a separate SUMDI form to summarize the estimated defect data for the parts of each assembly. • Actual: Use a separate SUMDI form to summarize the actual defect data for the parts of each assembly.
Phase	• The phases of the development process are listed across the top of the form.
Parts	• List the name or number of each module, component, product, or subsystem in the left column.
Columns	• Under each phase heading, enter, for each part, the number of defects injected in that phase.
Total	• At the bottom of the form, enter the totals of the defects injected in all the parts in that phase.

TSPi DEFECTS REMOVED SUMMARY: FORM SUMDR

Plan _____ **Assembly** _____ **Actual** _____

Name _____   Date _____
Team _____   Instructor _____
Part/Level _____   Cycle _____

Phase		Parts	Total
Strategy and Planning			
Requirements			
System Test Plan			
Requirements Inspection			
High-level Design			
Integration Test Plan			
HLD Inspection			
Detailed Design			
Detailed Design Review			
Test Development			
Detailed Design Inspection			
Code			
Code Review			
Compile			
Code Inspection			
Unit Test			
Build and Integration			
System Test			

TSPi DEFECTS REMOVED SUMMARY INSTRUCTIONS: FORM SUMDR

Purpose	This form summarizes the data for defects removed from the parts of an assembly.
General	• Note: the number of rows in this form is variable, depending on the number of parts in the assembly.
When Using the TSPi Tool	• If you are using the TSPi tool, these data are automatically obtained from the part defect logs and SUMP forms and rolled up to the next level SUMP form.
When Not Using the TSPi Tool	If you are not using the TSPi tool, use a copy of this form to summarize the defect data for the parts of each assembly. • Obtain defect data from the part defect logs or SUMP forms. • Enter the totals from the SUMDR form in the SUMP form for the high-level assembly.
Header	• Enter your name, date, team name, and instructor's name. • Name the part or assembly and its level. • Enter the cycle number.
Plan/Assembly/ Actual	Check whether this form is for plan, assembly, or actual data. • Plan: In system-level planning, use SUMDR to summarize the estimated defects to be removed from each assembly's parts. • Assembly: Use a separate SUMDR form to summarize the estimated defect data for the parts of each assembly. • Actual: Use a separate SUMDR form to summarize the actual defect data for the parts of each assembly.
Phase	• The phases of the development process are listed across the top of the form.
Parts	• List the name or number of each module, component, product, or subsystem in the left column.
Columns	• Under each phase heading, enter, for each part, the number of defects removed in that phase.
Total	• At the bottom of the form, enter the totals of the defects removed in all the parts in that phase.

TSPi PLAN SUMMARY: FORM SUMP

Name	_____	Date	_____
Team	_____	Instructor	_____
Part/Level	_____	Cycle	_____

Product Size	Plan	Actual
Requirements pages (SRS)	_____	_____
Other text pages	_____	_____
High-level design pages (SDS)	_____	_____
Detailed design lines	_____	_____
Base LOC (B) (measured)	_____	_____
Deleted LOC (D)		
	(Estimated)	(Counted)
Modified LOC (M)	_____	_____
	(Estimated)	(Counted)
Added LOC (A)	_____	_____
	(N–M)	(T–B+D–R)
Reused LOC (R)	_____	_____
	(Estimated)	(Counted)
Total New and Changed LOC (N)	_____	_____
	(Estimated)	(A+M)
Total LOC (T)	_____	_____
	(N+B–M–D+R)	(Measured)
Total New Reuse LOC	_____	_____
Estimated Object LOC (E)	_____	
Upper Prediction Interval (70%)	_____	
Lower Prediction Interval (70%)	_____	

Time in Phase (hours)	Plan	Actual	Actual %
Management and miscellaneous	_____	_____	_____
Launch	_____	_____	_____
Strategy and planning	_____	_____	_____
Requirements	_____	_____	_____
System test plan	_____	_____	_____
Requirements inspection	_____	_____	_____
High-level design	_____	_____	_____
Integration test plan	_____	_____	_____
High-level design inspection	_____	_____	_____
Implementation planning	_____	_____	_____
Detailed design	_____	_____	_____
Detailed design review	_____	_____	_____
Test development	_____	_____	_____
Detailed design inspection	_____	_____	_____
Code	_____	_____	_____
Code review	_____	_____	_____
Compile	_____	_____	_____
Code inspection	_____	_____	_____
Unit test	_____	_____	_____
Build and integration	_____	_____	_____
System test	_____	_____	_____
Documentation	_____	_____	_____

(continued)

TSPi PLAN SUMMARY: FORM SUMP (continued)

Name _____   Date _____

Team _____   Instructor _____

Part/Level _____   Cycle _____

Time in Phase (hours)	Plan	Actual	Actual %
Postmortem			
Total			
Total Time UPI (70%)			
Total Time LPI (70%)			
Defects Injected	**Plan**	**Actual**	**Actual %**
Strategy and planning			
Requirements			
System test plan			
Requirements inspection			
High-level design			
Integration test plan			
High-level design inspection			
Detailed design			
Detailed design review			
Test development			
Detailed design inspection			
Code			
Code review			
Compile			
Code inspection			
Unit test			
Build and integration			
System test			
Total Development			
Defects Removed	**Plan**	**Actual**	**Actual %**
Strategy and planning			
Requirements			
System test plan			
Requirements inspection			
High-level design			
Integration test plan			
High-level design inspection			
Detailed design			
Detailed design review			
Test development			
Detailed design inspection			
Code			
Code review			
Compile			
Code inspection			
Unit test			
Build and integration			
System test			
Total Development			

TSPi PLAN SUMMARY INSTRUCTIONS: FORM SUMP

Purpose	• This form holds plan and actual data for program assemblies.
General	• An assembly could be a system with multiple products, a product with multiple components, or a component with multiple modules. • A part could be an object, module, component, or product. • Note: the lowest-level assemblies or modules typically have no system-level data, such as requirements, high-level design, or system test.
Using the TSPi Tool	When using the TSPi tool, the plan values are automatically generated. • The time and size data are computed from the TASK and SUMS forms. • The defect values are automatically generated during the quality planning process (SUMQ). The actual values are also automatically generated by the TSPi tool. • Time and size values come from the LOGT, TASK, and SUMS forms. • Defect data come from the LOGD forms. When not using the TSPi tool, follow the instructions below.
Header	• Enter your name, date, team name, and instructor's name. • Name the assembly and its level. • Enter the cycle number.
Columns	• Plan: This column holds the part or assembly plan data. • Actual: For assemblies, this column holds the sum of the actual data for the parts of the assembly (at the lowest level, the modules).
Product Size	• For text and designs, enter only the new and changed size data. • For program parts or assemblies, enter all the indicated LOC data. • Obtain the data from the SUMS form.
Time in Phase	• Enter estimated and actual time by phase. • At the lowest level obtain these data from the TASK forms. • For higher-level assemblies, obtain the part-level time data from the totals on the SUMT form and the assembly-level data from the assembly-level TASK form. • For example, HLD time would come from the assembly TASK form and total module unit test time would come from the SUMT form. • Actual %: Enter the percent of the actual development time by phase.
Defects Injected	• Enter estimated and actual defects injected by phase. • Enter the defect estimates while producing the quality plan. • For modules, obtain actual data from the LOGD forms for those modules. • For assemblies, get module-level defect data from the totals of the SUMDI form and assembly-level data from the assembly LOGD form. • For example, HLD defects would come from the assembly LODG form and the total module coding defects would come from the SUMDI form. • Actual %: Enter the percent of the actual defects injected by phase.
Defects Removed	• Enter estimated and actual defects removed by phase. • Enter the defect estimates while producing the quality plan. • For modules, obtain actual data from the LOGD forms for those modules. • For assemblies, obtain module-level defect data from the totals of the SUMDR form and assembly-level data from the assembly LOGD form. • For example, HLD review defects would come from the assembly LOGD form and the total module code review defects would come from the SUMDR form. • Actual %: Enter the percent of the actual defects removed by phase.

TSPi QUALITY PLAN: FORM SUMQ

Name	_____	Date _____
Team	_____	Instructor _____
Part/Level	_____	Cycle _____

Summary Rates	Plan	Actual
LOC/hour		
% Reuse (% of total LOC)	_____	_____
% New Reuse (% of N&C LOC)	_____	_____
Percent Defect-free (PDF)		
In compile	_____	_____
In unit test	_____	_____
In build and integration	_____	_____
In system test	_____	_____
Defect/page		
Requirements inspection	_____	_____
HLD inspection	_____	_____
Defects/KLOC		
DLD review	_____	_____
DLD inspection	_____	_____
Code review	_____	_____
Compile	_____	_____
Code inspection	_____	_____
Unit test	_____	_____
Build and integration	_____	_____
System test	_____	_____
Total development	_____	_____
Defect Ratios		
Code review/Compile	_____	_____
DLD review/Unit test	_____	_____
Development time ratios (%)		
Requirements inspection/Requirements	_____	_____
HLD inspection/HLD	_____	_____
DLD/code	_____	_____
DLD review/DLD	_____	_____
Code review/code	_____	_____
A/FR	_____	_____
Review rates		
DLD lines/hour	_____	_____
Code LOC/hour	_____	_____
Inspection rates		
Requirement pages/hour	_____	_____
HLD pages/hour	_____	_____
DLD lines/hour	_____	_____
Code LOC/hour	_____	_____

TSPi QUALITY PLAN: FORM SUMQ (continued)

Name _____   Date _____

Team _____   Instructor _____

Part/Level _____   Cycle _____

	Plan	Actual
Defect-injection Rates (Defects/Hr.)		
Requirements	_____	_____
HLD	_____	_____
DLD	_____	_____
Code	_____	_____
Compile	_____	_____
Unit test	_____	_____
Build and integration	_____	_____
System test	_____	_____
Defect-removal Rates (Defects/Hr.)		
Requirements inspection	_____	_____
HLD inspection	_____	_____
DLD review	_____	_____
DLD inspection	_____	_____
Code review	_____	_____
Compile	_____	_____
Code inspection	_____	_____
Unit test	_____	_____
Build and integration	_____	_____
System test	_____	_____
Phase Yields		
Requirements inspection	_____	_____
HLD inspection	_____	_____
DLD review	_____	_____
Test development	_____	_____
DLD inspection	_____	_____
Code review	_____	_____
Compile	_____	_____
Code inspection	_____	_____
Unit test	_____	_____
Build and integration	_____	_____
System test	_____	_____
Process Yields		
% before compile	_____	_____
% before unit test	_____	_____
% before build and integration	_____	_____
% before system test	_____	_____
% before system delivery	_____	_____

TSPi QUALITY PLAN INSTRUCTIONS: FORM SUMQ

Purpose	This form holds plan and actual quality data for parts or assemblies.
General	• Where possible, establish goals based on your own historical data. • Where data are not available, use the QUAL standard for guidance (see Appendix G). • Before making the quality plan, you must have a partially completed SUMP form with size and development time data by process phase.
Make the Quality Plan	To make the quality plan, do the following: • Estimate the defects injected in each phase (use plan data and the QUAL standard for defects injected per hour times hours spent by phase). • Estimate the yield for each defect-removal phase (QUAL standard). • The defects removed in each phase are estimated as the number of defects at phase entry, times the estimated yield for that phase, divided by 100. • Examine the defects/KLOC values for reasonableness. • If the defects/KLOC values are not reasonable, adjust phase times, defect injection rates, or yields (use QUAL standard for guidance). • When the numbers appear reasonable, the quality plan is complete.
Record Actual Quality Data	To complete the quality plan with actual values, enter the following data. • Record development time in the time log and summarize in SUMP. • Record the defects found in the defect log and summarize in SUMP. • Enter the size of each product produced and summarize in SUMP. With the completed SUMP data, complete the SUMQ form with the TSPi tool or as described below and in Chapter 5.
TSPi Tool	• If you use the TSPi tool, it will complete all the SUMQ calculations. • Without the tool, you will have to make the SUMQ calculations as you complete each step described above. • At part completion, make the quality calculations by following the instructions below and in Chapter 5.
Header	• Enter your name, date, team name, and instructor's name. • Name the part or assembly and its level. • Enter the cycle number.
Summary Rates	• LOC/hour: new and changed LOC divided by total development hours. • % Reuse: The percentage of total LOC that was reused. • % New reuse: The percentage of new and changed LOC that were inserted in the reuse library.
Percent Defect-free (PDF)	• PDF refers to the percentage of a program's components that had no defects in a development or test phase. • Thus, if 3 of a program's 10 components had no defects in compile, that program would have a PDF of 30% in compile. • Base the plan PDF values on the QUAL standard.
Defects/Page and Defects/KLOC	• Set the defect/page and defect/KLOC plan values during planning. • Defects/page are calculated as (no. of defects)/(no. of pages). • Defects/KLOC are calculated as 1000*(no. of defects)/(N&C LOC).

TSPi QUALITY PLAN INSTRUCTIONS: FORM SUMQ (continued)

Defect Ratios	• These are the ratios of the number of defects found in various phases. • Thus, the (code review)/compile ratio is the ratio of the defects found in code review to those found in compile. • These ratios can also be calculated from the defects/KLOC values. • When the denominator phase values are 0, enter **inf.**
Development Time Ratios (%)	• These are the ratios of the times spent in each development phase. • Thus, the DLD/code ratio is the ratio of the time spent in detailed design to the time spent in coding a program. • Calculate the planned and actual ratios from the SUMP data. • When the denominator phase values are 0, enter **inf.**
A/FR	• A/FR is calculated as the ratio of appraisal to failure time. • Appraisal time is the time spent reviewing and inspecting programs. • Failure time is the time spent compiling and testing programs. • To calculate A/FR, divide the total detailed-design review, code review, and inspection times by total compile and unit test times. • Use the sum of personal review and total team inspection times. • When the denominator phase values are 0, enter **inf.**
Review or Inspection Rates	• Calculate the review and inspection rates by dividing the size of the reviewed product by the total review or inspection time in hours. • Make this calculation for each review and inspection. • In planning, use the QUAL standard for guidance (Appendix G). • When the denominator phase values are 0, enter **inf.**
Defect Injection and Removal Rates	• The defect rates are calculated in defects injected per hour. • Thus, for coding, if you spent 2 hours coding a 100-LOC module and injected 12 defects, you would have injected 6 defects/hour. • Similarly, if you spent 1 hour reviewing this module and found 4 defects, you would have removed 4 defects/hour. • Based on the QUAL standard, establish standard team rates.
Phase Yield	• Phase yield refers to the percentage of the defects in the product that were removed in that phase. • Thus, in reviewing a 100-LOC module, if the review found 4 and you later determine that there were 6 defects in the module, the phase yield would be 100*4/6=66.7%. • In planning, use historical data to estimate the yield values needed for each defect-removal phase. • After each phase, calculate the estimated yield values.
Process Yield	• Process yield refers to the percentage of the defects injected into a product that were removed before a given phase. • Thus, for a 100-LOC module, if you later determine that a total of 8 defects were injected into a module before compile and 5 were removed before compile, the yield before compile would be 100*5/8=62.5%. • In planning, use the QUAL standard or your own data to estimate the yield values for each defect-removal phase.

TSPi SIZE SUMMARY: FORM SUMS

Plan _____ **Assembly** _____ **Actual** _____

Name	_____		Date	_____
Team	_____		Instructor	_____
Part/Level	_____		Cycle	_____

Product or Part Names and/or Numbers	Size Measure	Base	Deleted	Modified	Added	Reused	New and Changed	Total	Total New Reuse
Totals									

TSPi SIZE SUMMARY INSTRUCTIONS: FORM SUMS

Purpose	• This form summarizes the data for product size. • At the lowest level, it summarizes all the part size data. • At higher levels, it summarizes the size data for an assembly and its parts.
General	• Use this form to hold size data for the parts of an assembly. • If you are using the TSPi tool, these data are automatically rolled up to the next-level SUMP form. • If you are not using the TSPi tool, enter the totals from this form in the appropriate places in the assembly-level SUMP form. • Note: the number of rows in this form is variable, depending on the number of products and parts.
Header	• Enter your name, date, team name, and instructor's name. • Name the part or assembly and its level. • Enter the cycle number.
Plan/Assembly/ Actual	Check whether this form is for plan, assembly, or actual data. • Plan: In system-level planning, use SUMS to hold the estimated sizes of the system and all its parts. • Assembly: Use a separate SUMS form for the estimated size data for the parts of each assembly. • Actual: Use a SUMS form for the actual size data for the parts of each assembly.
Product and Part Names	• List the name or other identification of each product or part. • It is also a good idea to number the product components, particularly if there will be very many of them. • Include system-level products such as SRS and HLD.
Size Measure	• Enter the size measures used for each product item listed.
Program Size	• For each product, enter the actual or estimated program base, deleted, added, modified, reused, and new and changed LOC.
Totals	• Enter the totals for each size category and column.

TSPi DEVELOPMENT TIME SUMMARY: FORM SUMT

Plan _____ Assembly _____ Actual _____

Name _____ Date _____
Team _____ Instructor _____
Part/Level _____ Cycle _____

Phase
Strategy and Planning
Requirements
System Test Plan
Requirements Inspection
High-level Design
Integration Test Plan
HLD Inspection
Detailed Design
Detailed Design Review
Test Development
Detailed Design Inspection
Code
Code Review
Compile
Code Inspection
Unit Test
Build and Integration
System Test
Postmortem

Parts

Total

TSPi DEVELOPMENT TIME SUMMARY INSTRUCTIONS: FORM SUMT

Purpose	This form summarizes the data for the development time spent in each phase for the parts of an assembly.
General	• Note: the number of rows in this form is variable, depending on the number of parts in the assembly.
When Using the TSPi Tool	• If you are using the TSPi tool, these data are automatically obtained from the part time logs and SUMP forms and rolled up to the next level SUMP form.
When Not Using the TSPi Tool	If you are not using the TSPi tool, use a copy of this form to summarize the time data for the parts of each assembly. • Obtain time data from the part time logs or SUMP forms. • Enter the totals from the SUMT form in the SUMP form for the high-level assembly.
Header	• Enter your name, date, team name, and instructor's name. • Name the part or assembly and its level. • Enter the cycle number.
Plan/Assembly/ Actual	Check whether this form is for plan, assembly, or actual data. • Plan: In system-level planning, use SUMT to summarize the estimated times for each phase of each assembly's parts. • Assembly: Use a separate SUMT form to summarize the estimated time data for the parts of each assembly. • Actual: Use a separate SUMT form to summarize the actual time data for the parts of each assembly.
Phase	• The phases of the development process are listed across the top of the form.
Parts	• List the name or number of each module, component, product, or subsystem part in the left column.
Columns	• Under each phase heading, enter, for each part, the plan or actual time for that development phase.
Total	• At the bottom of the form, enter the total development time for all parts in that phase.

TSPi TASK SUMMARY: FORM SUMTASK

Name _____   Date _____

Team _____   Instructor _____

Part/Level _____   Cycle _____

Products of the task _____

Task users/customers _____

Overall requirements/message _____

Specifications/constraints _____

Product Elements	Size Unit	Plan Units	Plan Rate	Plan Time	Actual Units	Actual Time	Actual Rate
_____	___	___	___	___	___	___	___
_____	___	___	___	___	___	___	___
_____	___	___	___	___	___	___	___
_____	___	___	___	___	___	___	___
_____	___	___	___	___	___	___	___
Total				___		___	

Time in Phase	Plan	Actual	%	Base Times
Planning	_____	_____	_____	_____
Research	_____	_____	_____	_____
Outline/high-level design	_____	_____	_____	_____
Peer review and correct	_____	_____	_____	_____
Draft/detailed-level design	_____	_____	_____	_____
Design review	_____	_____	_____	_____
Peer review and correct	_____	_____	_____	_____
Implementation/Rewrite	_____	_____	_____	_____
Review	_____	_____	_____	_____
Peer review and correct	_____	_____	_____	_____
Test/trial use	_____	_____	_____	_____
Postmortem	_____	_____	_____	_____
Total time (minutes)	_____	_____	_____	_____
Total time (hours)	_____	_____	_____	_____

TSPi TASK PLAN SUMMARY INSTRUCTIONS: FORM SUMTASK

Purpose	• To facilitate planning and tracking task activities. • Use this form for tasks that take more than about 10 hours. • This form is for those general tasks that are large enough to warrant detailed project plan summaries.
Header	• Enter your name, date, team name, and instructor's name. • Name the part or assembly and its level. • Enter the cycle number.
Product of the Task	• Describe the product to be produced by this task: test scripts, requirements documents, database designs, and so on.
Task Users/ Customers	• Note who will use or be the customer for this product. • For example, if it is a process the team will use, list **team.**
Overall Requirements/ Message	• Briefly list the product requirements. • If the product is a document, give a brief outline of the principal topics or document sections. • For a process, list its principal steps and elements.
Specifications/ Constraints	• Summarize any special task or product constraints. • For example, prerequisites, page limits, number of slides, and so on.
Product Elements	• List the various product elements to be produced. • Give the size unit for each element type. • Estimate the development rate in minutes per unit. • Estimate the new and changed units per element type and the time. • Record the actual units, time, and rate when done.
Time in Phase	• Record the planned and actual times for the task phases. • Where some phases are not appropriate or differ from those in the form, make appropriate changes.
% and Base Times	• When your personal plan contains tasks of more than 10 hours, use % and Base Times columns to divide tasks into smaller steps.
Percent (%)	• The percent of time you now plan for each task phase.
Base Times	• Using the phase % values, allocate the original total estimated task time among the phases. • Because the base times add up to the original estimate, using these values will preserve the original earned-value plan.
Example	Suppose, during the launch, you planned a task to take 30 hours and did not divide it into smaller time steps. • You now estimate the task to take 50 hours. • Your current phase estimates in hours are planning: 2, research: 10, design: 9, implementation: 8, review: 6, peer review: 8, trial: 6, and postmortem: 1. • These percents are, respectively, 4, 20, 18, 16, 12, 16, 12, 2. • In Base Times, enter 1.2 for planning (4*30/100), 6 for research (20*30/100), and so on. • To preserve your earned-value plan, enter new rows for these tasks and times and set the original 30-hour estimate to 0.

TSPi TASK PLANNING TEMPLATE: FORM TASK

Name _____   Date _____

Team _____   Instructor _____

Part/Level _____   Cycle _____

Task			Plan Hours							Plan Size/Value					Actual		
Phase	Part	Task Name	# Engineers	Team Leader	Development Manager	Planning Manager	Quality/Process Manager	Support Manager	Total Team Hours	Cumulative Hours	Size Units	Size	Week No.	Planned Value	Cumulative PV	Hours	Cumulative Hours	Week No.

TSPi TASK PLANNING TEMPLATE INSTRUCTIONS: FORM TASK

Purpose	• To estimate the development time for each project task • To compute the planned value for each project task • To estimate the planned completion date for each task • To provide a basis for tracking schedule progress even when the tasks are not completed in the planned order
General	• Expand this form or use multiple pages as needed. • Include every significant task. • Use task names and numbers that support the activity and are consistent with the project and product structure. • Where possible, use the TSPi tool for planning.
Produce the Task Plan	Use the TSPi tool to produce the task plan. • Start with the list of tasks given by the TSPi process. • If you feel additional tasks are needed, insert them. • Estimate the sizes of the products involved with each task (use data from form SUMS where appropriate). • Estimate the engineering hours for each task. • Enter these data as described in the rest of this instruction. If you do not have the TSPi tool, you must make the calculations yourself, as described below and in Chapter 5.
Update the Task Plan	To update the task plan during and after development • Enter the task times from the TSPi time logs (LOGT) • Record the week number when you finish a task • The TSPi tool will complete the calculations for you If you do not have the TSPi tool, you must make the calculations yourself, as described below and in Chapter 5.
Header	• Enter your name, date, team name, and instructor's name. • Name the part or assembly and its level. • Enter the cycle number.
Phase	Enter the TSPi process phase in which the task will be done. • For example, requirements, code inspection, compile, and so on.
Part	Enter the name of the part with which the task is associated. • For a requirements inspection, the part would be SRS. • For coding, the part would be the program or module.
Task Name	Enter a task number and name. • List the tasks in the order in which you expect to complete them. Select tasks that have explicit completion criteria. • For example, planning completed, program compiled and all defects corrected, testing completed and all test cases run, and so on.
# Engineers	Enter the number of engineers who will participate in this task.
Plan Hours	Enter the planned hours for each task. • Enter the hours planned for each engineer. • Enter the total hours for all engineers on the team.

(continued)

TSPi TASK PLANNING TEMPLATE INSTRUCTIONS: FORM TASK (continued)

Plan: Cumulative Hours	• Enter the cumulative sum of the plan hours down through each task.
Size Units	Enter the size unit. • For a program, the size unit is typically LOC. • For the SRS, the size unit is typically pages.
Size	Enter the size of the product involved in that task.
Week No.	• For each cumulative hours entry, find the plan cumulative hours entry on the SCHEDULE form that equals or just exceeds it. • Enter the week number from the row of the SCHEDULE form as the plan date on the TASK form. • If several weeks on the SCHEDULE form have the same cumulative value, enter the earliest date. • Pick the plan date as the Monday of the week during which completion for that task is planned.
Planned Value	• Total the planned hours for all the tasks. • For each task, calculate the percent its planned hours are of the total planned hours. • Enter this percent as the planned value for that task. • The total planned value should equal 100.
Cumulative Planned Value	• Enter the cumulative sum of the planned values down through each task. • Complete the SCHEDULE form down through plan: cumulative hours before proceeding. • Then complete the SCHEDULE and TASK forms together.
Actual Hours	As each task is completed, enter the total actual hours expended by the team on that task.
Cumulative Hours	As each task is completed, total the hours for all completed tasks to date.
Week No.	Enter the week number when the task was completed.
Earned Value	When a task is completed, enter the following data in your personal form WEEK for that week: • The task name and its planned and actual hours • The task earned value (from the planned value column for that task in form TASK) • The planned week number for the task Also enter the earned value for all tasks completed in the week on form SCHEDULE.

TSPi WEEKLY STATUS REPORT: FORM WEEK

Name _____   Team _____   Instructor _____
Date _____   Cycle No. _____   Week No. _____

Weekly Data	Planned	Actual
Project hours for this week	_____	_____
Project hours this cycle to date	_____	_____
Earned value for this week	_____	_____
Earned value this cycle to date	_____	_____
Total hours for the tasks completed this phase to date	_____	_____

Team Member Weekly Data	Hours Planned	Hours Actual	Planned Value	Earned Value
Team Leader	_____	_____	_____	_____
Development Manager	_____	_____	_____	_____
Planning Manager	_____	_____	_____	_____
Quality/Process Manager	_____	_____	_____	_____
Support Manager	_____	_____	_____	_____
	_____	_____	_____	_____
Totals	_____	_____	_____	

Development Tasks Completed	Hours Planned	Hours Actual	Earned Value	Planned Week
	_____	_____	_____	_____
	_____	_____	_____	_____
	_____	_____	_____	_____
	_____	_____	_____	_____
	_____	_____	_____	_____
	_____	_____	_____	_____
Totals	_____	_____	_____	

Issue/Risk Tracking
Issue/Risk Name   Status
_____   _____
_____   _____
_____   _____
_____   _____

Other Significant Items
_____
_____
_____
_____
_____

TSPi WEEKLY STATUS REPORT INSTRUCTIONS: FORM WEEK

Purpose	Use this form to prepare the weekly status reports.
General	• Each team member completes this form every week showing work accomplished last week and plans for the next week. • Every week, the planning manager prepares a copy of form WEEK with a composite summary of the team's status and week's accomplishments. • Attach additional sheets if needed.
Header	• Enter your name and the instructor's name. • Enter the team name, cycle number, date, and week number.
Weekly Data	• Enter the total hours actually spent on the project this week and the hours planned for the week. • Also enter the actual and planned cumulative hours spent during this development cycle. • Enter the planned value and the actual earned value for the week. • Enter the cumulative planned value and cumulative earned value for the development cycle to date. • Enter the total planned and actual hours for the tasks completed on this development cycle to date.
Team Member Weekly Data	For each team member report • Enter the total actual and planned time for each engineer. • Enter the engineer's planned and earned value for the week. • Enter the engineer's total planned and actual hours worked.
Team Weekly Data	For the composite team report • Enter the total actual and planned time for the team. • Enter the team's planned and earned value for the week. • Enter the team's total planned and actual hours worked.
Development Tasks Completed	For the tasks completed this week • Enter the name of each task. • Enter the total actual and planned time for that task. • Enter the week number when it was planned. • Enter the earned value for the task.
Issue/Risk Tracking	• For the risks and issues tracked, summarize the status and any important changes this week.
Other Significant Items	• List any significant accomplishments or events during the week. • Role examples include coding standard completed, change control procedure approved, and so forth. • Development examples include designing, coding, inspecting, or testing the various product elements.

APPENDIX G

The TSPi Standards and Specifications

This appendix contains copies of all the TSPi standards. These standards are described in the various book chapters and are included here for reference. The standards are listed in alphabetical order by their abbreviations. Also given here are the appendix pages for the standards and the textbook pages where each standard is described.

Name	Abbreviation	Chapter Reference	Page
Defect types	DEFECT	126	444
Project notebook	NOTEBOOK	47, 213	445
Quality criteria	QUAL	86	446

THE PSP DEFECT TYPE STANDARD

Type Number	Type Name	Description
10	Documentation	Comments, messages
20	Syntax	Spelling, punctuation, typos, instruction formats
30	Build, package	Change management, library, version control
40	Assignment	Declaration, duplicate names, scope, limits
50	Interface	Procedure calls and references, I/O, user formats
60	Checking	Error messages, inadequate checks
70	Data	Structure, content
80	Function	Logic, pointers, loops, recursion, computation, function defects
90	System	Configuration, timing, memory
100	Environment	Design, compile, test, or other support system problems

TSPi PROJECT NOTEBOOK: SPECIFICATION NOTEBOOK

Purpose	To describe the contents of the project notebook
General	• The project notebook holds the complete project record. • It includes copies of all important project documents. • The notebook contains the official project record. • The project notebook is given to the instructor at the end of each development cycle and at the end of the course. • The team leader maintains the project notebook.
Notebook Format	The notebook should be in an appropriate format. • Small project notebooks may be in a three-ring binder. • Larger notebooks may be in file folders and multiple three-ring binders.
Notebook Sections	The standard notebook sections are as follows. • Outline • Summary • Project cycle reports • Task and schedule plans and actuals • Process documents • System and component plan and actual data • Test plans and data • Inspection reports and defect logs • Working notes and documents These sections are further explained elsewhere in this table.
Outline	• An outline of the notebook contents
Summary	• The project name, dates, team members, and role assignments • The SUMP and SUMQ forms with plan and actual system data • Team TASK and SCHEDULE forms with plan and actual data
Project and Cycle Reports	• Final reports for each development cycle • During the project, this file can be used as a repository for documents to include later in the final report.
Task and Schedule Plans and Actuals	Include all plan and actual resource and schedule data. • A summary of task and schedule performance versus plan • Engineer TASK, SCHEDULE, LOGD, and LOGT forms
Process Documents	• If changed, the defined processes used and all PIPs • The change control procedure and any related documents • The configuration management process • The issue and risk tracking process
Component Data	• The SUMP and SUMQ forms for every product component
Test Plans and Data	• The build, integration, and system test plans • Test logs and test data (LOGTEST) • Test defect review records
Inspection Reports	• All inspection reports (INS) and defect logs (LOGD)
Reports	• The engineers' and team's WEEK report forms
Working Documents	• System requirements specification (SRS) • The development strategy • System design specification (SDS) with SRS traceability • All design documents (design templates, etc.) • Other important documents (CCR, CSR, SUMTASK, etc.)

TSPi QUALITY CRITERIA: STANDARD QUAL

Measure	Goal	Comments
Percent Defect Free (PDF)		
Compile	> 10%	
Unit Test	> 50%	
Integration Test	> 70%	
System Test	> 90%	
Defects/KLOC		
Total defects injected	75–150	If not PSP trained, use 100–200
Compile	< 10	All defects flagged by compiler
Unit Test	< 5	Only major defects
Build and integration	< 0.5	Only major defects
System Test	< 0.2	Only major defects
Defect Ratios		
DLD review defects/unit test defects	> 2.0	Only major defects
Code review defects/compile defects	> 2.0	Only major defects
Development Time Ratios		
Requirements inspection/requirements time	> 0.25	Include elicitation time
HLD inspection/HLD time	> 0.5	Design work only, not studies
DLD/coding time	> 1.00	
DLD review/DLD time	> 0.5	
Code review/code time	> 0.5	
Review and Inspection Rates		
Requirements pages/hour	< 2	Single-spaced text pages
HLD pages/hour	< 5	Formatted design logic
DLD text lines/hour	< 100	Pseudocode lines equal about 3 LOC each
Code LOC/hour	< 200	Logical LOC

Defect Injection Rates		
Requirements defects/hour	0.25	Only major defects
HLD defects/hour	0.25	Only major defects
DLD defects/hour	2.0	Only design defects
Code defects/hour	4.0	Only major defects
Compile defects/hour	0.3	All defects flagged by the compiler
Unit test defects/hour	0.2	Only major defects
Defect Removal Rates		
Requirements inspection defects/hour	0.5	Only major defects
HLD inspection defects/hour	0.5	Only major defects
DLD review defects/hour	2.0	Only design defects
DLD inspection defects/hour	0.5	Only design defects
Code review defects/hour	6.0	Only major defects
Code inspection defects/hour	1.0	Only major defects
Phase Yields		
Requirements inspections	~ 70%	Not counting editorial comments
Design reviews and inspections	~ 70%	Using state analysis, trace tables
Code reviews and inspections	~ 70%	Using personal checklists
Compile	~ 50%	90+ % of syntax defects
Unit test at 5 or fewer defects/KLOC	~ 90%	For high defects/KLOC: 50–75%
Build, integration, system test at < 1.0 defects/KLOC	~ 80%	For high defects/KLOC: 30–65%
Process Yields		
Before compile	> 75%	Assuming sound design methods
Before unit test	> 85%	Assuming logic checks in reviews
Before build and integration	> 97.5%	For small products, 1 defect max.
Before system test	> 99%	For small products, 1 defect max.

INDEX

Supplements for
Introduction to the Team Software Process

The following supplements are freely available via the Internet to adopters and purchasers of this book at

http://www.awl.com/cseng/titles/0-201-47719-x/

1. **TSPi Support Tool.** This computer-based tool, created by James W. Over at the Software Engineering Institute, is designed to help teams plan, track, and report on both individual and team work. The tool also combines data to provide overall team results, automatically completes all needed forms, and generates project summary reports. **System requirements:** To use the tool, each team member must have access to Windows 95 or Windows NT 4.0 or later and Excel 97 or later. Users will need at least 4MB of hard drive free space to install and run the support tool.

2. **TSPi Support Tool Instructions.** The instructions describe how to use the TSPi tool.

3. **Instructor's Guide.** The Guide explains how to work with a team to perform the activities discussed in *Introduction to the Team Software Process*. Designed principally for instructors using the text in a software project team course, the ten-chapter Guide also helps team leaders to support working engineers with the process described in the book.

   If preferred, instructors may request a printed, hardcopy version of the Instructor's Guide. To contact your local Addison-Wesley representative, send email to TSPi @awl.com.

   Instructor's Guide Contents: Chapter 1: Introduction; Chapter 2: General Suggestions; Chapter 3: Specific Course Suggestions; Chapter 4: Course Overview; Chapter 5: Team Selection; Chapter 6: A PSP Refresher; Chapter 7: The Weekly Team-Leader Meeting; Chapter 8: The Process Phases; Chapter 9: Checking Forms and Data; Chapter 10: Later Development Phases; Chapter 11: Grading Team Courses; Chapter 12: Handling People Problems; Chapter 13: The Rewards of Teaching Teams; Appendix A: PSP Familiarization Exercises; Appendix B: PSP Familiarization Exercise Answers.

4. **The TSPi Forms.** This supplement contains electronic copies of all the TSPi forms. **System requirements:** Windows 95 and Microsoft Office 97.

   Note: The TSPi forms are copyright © 2000 by Addison Wesley Longman. Contents may be downloaded for individual use, and for instructors to duplicate and distribute in class.

Trademark Acknowledgments

Personal Software Process (PSP) and Team Software Process (TSP) are service marks of Carnegie Mellon University.

Capability Maturity Model and CMM are registered marks with the U.S. Patent and Trademark offices.

Credits

Page 16: From an article by Tom DeMarco, "Looking for Lost Keys," in *IEEE Software,* April, 1988. Copyright © 1988 IEEE.

Page 20: From *Peopleware: Productive Projects and Teams, 2nd edition.,* p. 123, by Tom DeMarco and Timothy Lister. Copyright © 1999, 1987 by Tom De-Marco and Timothy Lister. Reprinted by permission of Dorset House Publishing, 353 W. 12th St., New York, N.Y. 10014 (www.dorsethouse.com). All rights reserved.

Page 285: Reprinted with the permission of Simon & Schuster, Inc., from *The Seven Habits of Highly Effective People,* by Stephen R. Covey. Copyright © 1989 by Stephen R. Covey.

Page 297: Adapted from *Getting to Yes*, 2nd ed., by Roger Fisher, William Ury, and Bruce Patton. Copyright © 1981, 1991 by Roger Fisher and William Ury. Reprinted by permission of Houghton Mifflin Co. All rights reserved.

Page 301: From an article entitled "Airline Cockpits Are No Place to Solo," by Judith Valente and Bridget O'Brian, in *The Wall Street Journal,* August 2, 1989, page B1. Republished by permission of Dow Jones, Inc. Copyright © 1989 Dow Jones and Company, Inc. All rights reserved worldwide.

The SEI Series in Software Engineering

Introduction to the Team Software Process℠
by Watts S. Humphrey
0-201-47719-X • 2000 • Hardcover • 496 pages

Watts Humphrey provides software engineers with precisely the teamwork training and practice they need. While presenting a quick and comprehensive perspective of what team software development is all about, the book provides practitioners and students in any projects-based software engineering environment with a practical and realistic teamworking experience. The Team Software Process (TSP) is built on and requires knowledge of the author's influential Personal Software Process (PSP), which details how programmers can (and should) manage time and achieve quality in their own work. The TSP shows how to apply similar engineering discipline to the full range of team software tasks, leading ultimately to greater productivity.

Introduction to the Personal Software Process℠
by Watts S. Humphrey
0-201-54809-7 • 1997 • Paperback • 304 pages

This workbook provides a hands-on introduction to the basic discipline of software engineering. Designed as a programming course supplement to integrate the PSP into a university curriculum, the book may also be adapted for use by industrial groups or for self-improvement. By applying the book's exercises, you can learn to manage your time effectively and to monitor the quality of your work.

A Discipline for Software Engineering
by Watts S. Humphrey
0-201-54610-8 • 1995 • Hardcover • 816 pages

This book scales down successful methods developed by the author to a personal level for managers and organizations to evaluate and improve their software capabilities. The author's concern here is to help individual software practitioners develop the skills and habits they need to plan, track, and analyze large and complex projects and to develop high-quality products.

Managing the Software Process
by Watts S. Humphrey
0-201-18095-2 • 1989 • Hardcover • 512 pages

This landmark book introduces the author's methods, now commonly practiced in industry, for improving software development and maintenance processes. Emphasizing the basic principles and priorities of the software process, the book's sections are organized in a natural way to guide organizations through needed improvement activities.

The SEI Series in Software Engineering

Managing Technical People
Innovation, Teamwork, and the Software Process
by Watts S. Humphrey
0-201-54597-7 • 1997 • Paperback • 352 pages

This insightful book—drawing on the author's extensive experience as a senior manager of software development at IBM—describes proven techniques for managing technical professionals. The author shows specifically how to identify, motivate, and organize innovative people, while tying leadership practices to improvements in the software process.

The Capability Maturity Model
Guidelines for Improving the Software Process
by Carnegie Mellon University/Software Engineering Institute
0-201-54664-7 • 1995 • Hardcover • 464 pages

This book provides a description and technical overview of the Capability Maturity Model (CMM), with guidelines for improving software process management. The CMM provides software professionals in government and industry with the ability to identify, adopt, and use sound management and technical practices for delivering quality software on time and within budget.

Managing Risk
Methods for Software Systems Development
by Elaine M. Hall
0-201-25592-8 • 1998 • Hardcover • 400 pages

Written for busy professionals charged with delivering high-quality products on time and within budget, this book is a comprehensive guide that describes a success formula for managing software risk. The book is divided into five parts that describe a risk management road map designed to take you from crisis to control of your software project.

Software Architecture in Practice
by Len Bass, Paul Clements, and Rick Kazman
0-201-19930-0 • 1998 • Hardcover • 480 pages

This book introduces the concepts and practice of software architecture—what a system is designed to do and how its components are meant to interact with each other. It covers not only essential technical topics for specifying and validating a system, but also emphasizes the importance of the business context in which large systems are designed. Enhancing both technical and organizational discussions, key points are illuminated by substantial case studies undertaken by the authors and the Software Engineering Institute.

The SEI Series in Software Engineering

Cleanroom Software Engineering
Technology and Process
by Stacy Prowell, Carmen J. Trammell, Richard C. Linger,
and Jesse H. Poore
0-201-85480-5 • 1999 • Hardcover • 400 pages

Written by the creators and preeminent practitioners of cleanroom
software engineering, this book provides an introduction and in-depth
description of topic. Following an explanation of Cleanroom theory and
basic practice, the authors draw on their extensive experience in industry
to elaborate in detail on the Cleanroom development and certification
process and show how this process is compatible with the Software
Engineering Institute's Capability Maturity Model (CMM).

Software Design Methods for Concurrent
and Real-Time Systems
by Hassan Gomaa
0-201-52577-1 • 1993 • Hardcover • 464 pages

This book provides a basic understanding of concepts and issues in
concurrent system design, while surveying and comparing a range of
applicable design methods. The book explores two object-oriented
design methods for the effective design of concurrent and real-time
systems and describes a practical approach for applying real-time
scheduling theory to analyze the performance of real-time designs.

Developing Software for the User Interface
by Len Bass and Joelle Coutaz
0-201-51046-4 • 1991 • Hardcover • 272 pages

The authors of this book explain the concepts behind the development
of user interfaces both from the end user's perspective and from the
developer's perspective. The book provides a categorization of the
levels of abstraction of various tools and systems.

Measuring the Software Process
Statistical Process Control for Software Process Improvement
by William A. Florac and Anita D. Carleton
0-201-60444-2 • 1999 • Hardcover • 352 pages

With this book as your guide, you will learn how to use measurements
to manage and improve software processes within your organization.
The authors explain specifically how quality characteristics of software
products and processes can be quantified, plotted, and analyzed, so that
the performance of software development activities can be predicted,
controlled, and guided to achieve both business and technical goals.

Other Titles of Interest from Addison-Wesley

The Mythical Man-Month, Anniversary Edition
Essays on Software Engineering
by Frederick P. Brooks, Jr.
0-201-83595-9 • 1995 • Paperback • 336 pages

Fred Brooks blends software engineering facts with thought-provoking opinions to offer insight for anyone managing complex projects. Twenty years after the publication of this influential and timeless classic, the author has revisited his original ideas and added new thoughts and advice, both for readers already familiar with his work and for readers discovering it for the first time.

CMM Implementation Guide
Choreographing Software Process Improvement
by Kim Caputo
0-201-37938-4 • 1998 • Hardcover • 336 pages

This book provides detailed instruction on how to put the SEI's Capability Maturity Model (CMM) into practice, and thereby, on how to raise an organization to the next higher level. Drawing on her own first-hand experience leading software process improvement groups in a large corporation, Caputo provides invaluable advice and information for anyone charged specifically with implementing the CMM.

Software for Use
A Practical Guide to the Models and Methods of Usage-Centered Design
by Larry L. Constantine and Lucy A. D. Lockwood
0-201-92478-1 • 1999 • Hardcover • 608 pages

The authors focus on models and methods that help you deliver software that allows users to accomplish tasks with greater ease and efficiency. Aided by concrete techniques, experience-tested examples, and practical tools, the book guides you through a systematic software development process called usage-centered design that weaves together two major threads in software-development: Use Cases and essential modeling. The book illustrates those techniques that have to work and have proved to be of greatest practical value.

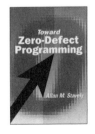

Toward Zero-Defect Programming
by Allan Stavely
0-201-38595-3 • 1999 • Paperback • 256 pages

The book describes current software-engineering methods for writing (nearly) bug-free programs. In a precise presentation, it shows how to apply these methods in three key areas of software development: specification which forces the programmer to program more clearly; verification which uncovers additional defects as a team process; and testing which compensates for human fallibility.

TSPi Glossary

Term	Definition or Formula	Reference
Peer review	See *inspection*.	335
Percent defect-free (PDF)	The percent of a system's parts that have no defects in a specified defect-removal phase.	98
Phase	A process typically has several steps or phases, each one generally described by one or more scripts.	10
Phase yield	The percentage of the defects in a product that are removed during a specified phase. Compile phase yield refers to the percentage of the defects in the product at compile entry or injected during compile that are removed during compile. See also *yield*.	106
PIP	The process improvement proposal, a TSPi form.	186
Planned value (PV)	The percentage of the total job that is represented by a single task.	67
Prediction interval	The limits within which an estimate is likely to fall. Typical prediction intervals include a percentage, say 95%, of the items being estimated.	350
Process yield	The percentage of the defects injected before a phase that are removed before that phase. Yield before compile refers to the percentage of the defects injected before compile that are removed before compile. See also *yield*.	106
Product owner	The engineer responsible for maintaining product design integrity and recording and tracking its defects, typically the developer.	324
Project notebook	The official record of all the team's estimates, work products, reports, plans, and forms.	213, 214
Quality plan	The planned and actual quality performance of every part and assembly in the system.	97
Rates, inspection and review	One measure of the quality of a review or an inspection. Typically, rates are measured in LOC or pages per hour.	102
Recorder	The person who documents meeting results, principally the decisions and planned actions.	262
Regression test	When programs are modified, functions that were previously tested may no longer work. Regression testing checks for such problems.	182
Reuse	The use of unmodified previously developed program elements in a new program. Typically, reused program elements are taken from a reuse library that is designed specifically for reuse.	54
Review	In the PSP and TSPi, reviews are done by engineers to find defects in their personally produced products.	131
Risk	A problem that may or may not occur.	53
Role	A defined area of responsibility for a team member.	302
Script	A listing of the actions required to accomplish a specific process or portion of a process.	10
SCM	See *configuration management*.	321
SDS	See *software design specification*.	135